BIBLE
SYNOPSIS

DR. MARK
MILLER

TRUSTED
BOOKS
A DIVISION OF DEEP RIVER BOOKS

This book is dedicated to all who are seeking the Word. If this book makes just one person a believer, then it was all worthwhile!

FOREWORD

The Bible was written through divine Inspiration. *Bible Synopsis* was written for a worldly audience in order to help understand The Word. This project started as a small Bible study and became a syllabus of sorts for a Sunday school class. I eventually developed an accompanying PowerPoint presentation that allowed our class to walk through the Bible in a year. We were all rewarded at the end of that year with a richer understanding of the Bible, and a better appreciation for what it represents. I believe that the best way to apply this magnificent book to your daily life is to first gain a fundamental understanding of the stories that it tells. In this second edition, I have attempted to correct grammar and typographical mistakes, but I am sure that I may have missed some, and apologize. This book is a result of the efforts of many, and I am blessed to have been given the opportunity to summarize the Greatest Book ever written. I am sure that I may have over-simplified many important passages and lessons, but am confident that this book will leave you with a solid foundation for your own study. God Bless you all!

ISBN-13: 978-1-63269-185-9
Library of Congress Catalog Card Number: 2004195518

TABLE OF CONTENTS

OLD TESTAMENT

Pentateuch

History

FIGURES

Overview of the Bible

Introduction

There are sixty-six books in the Bible, each written through divine inspiration from God Himself. Prophets, priests, leaders, and kings wrote the thirty-nine books in the Old Testament. Apostles wrote the twenty-seven books in the New Testament. The Old Testament covers the period from the beginning of man until about 400 years before Christ. The New Testament begins shortly before the birth of Christ, focuses on the period of Christ's time on earth and a hundred or so years after, and continues into the future.

General Organization

The Old Testament is organized as follows:

Law	Five books (Genesis, Exodus, Leviticus, Numbers, Deuteronomy) These five books are referred to as the *Pentateuch*.
History	Twelve books (Joshua, Judges, Ruth, 1 & 2 Samuel, 1 & 2 Kings, 1 & 2 Chronicles, Ezra, Nehemiah, Esther). These books overlap each other, and many cover a similar time period.
Wisdom/Poetry	Five books (Job, Psalms, Proverbs, Ecclesiastes, Song of Songs [Solomon]).

Major Prophets   Five books (Isaiah, Jeremiah, Lamentations, Ezekiel, Daniel).
Minor Prophets   Twelve books (Hosea, Joel, Amos, Obadiah, Jonah, Micah, Nahum, Habakkuk, Zephaniah, Haggai, Zechariah, Malachi).

The New Testament is organized as follows:

Gospel   Four books (Matthew, Mark, Luke, John).
Acts   One book that chronicles Peter and Paul's exploits and the early church.
Paul's letters   Thirteen books (Romans, 1 & 2 Corinthians, Galatians, Ephesians, Philippians, Colossians, 1 & 2 Thessalonians, 1 & 2 Timothy, Titus, Philemon).
Others' letters   Eight books (Hebrews, James, 1 & 2 Peter, 1-3 John, Jude).
Revelation   One book of prophecy.

INDIVIDUAL BOOKS OF THE BIBLE—THEMES

OLD TESTAMENT

Genesis	Creation, Rebellion of Man, Abraham and Descendants as Chosen Ones.
Exodus	Escape from Slavery in Egypt, Moses and Laws.
Leviticus	Laws Focusing on Holiness and Worship.
Numbers	Forty-year Desert Wanderings with Two Censuses.
Deuteronomy	Moses Farewell Speeches—a reminder of their history and a plea to be good.
Joshua	Entry and Conquest of the Promised Land (Canaan)—Joshua's leadership.
Judges	God Establishes Leaders/Judges—an attempt to keep the Israelites in line.
Ruth	Two Widows' Stories of Love and Loyalty.
1 Samuel	The Transition Between Leadership by Judges and Kings—Samuel appoints the first king, Saul, who tries to prevent David from becoming the second king.
2 Samuel	Life of David—succeeds as king but fails as a husband.
1 Kings	David's Son Solomon Becomes King and Builds the Temple. A civil war follows his death. A series of bad kings follows. The prophet Elijah confronts the evil King Ahab.
2 Kings	Records the History of the Divided Kingdoms—bad kings rule the northern kingdom (Israel), but there are several good kings who occasionally rule

	the southern kingdom (Judah). Israel is conquered first. Judah lasts several hundred years longer, but is eventually conquered by Babylon.
1 Chronicles	Genealogy and the Life of David (Similar to 2 Samuel).
2 Chronicles	History of the Rulers of Judah—focus on the good kings (Similar to 1 and 2 Kings).
Ezra	Return to Israel after Babylonian Captivity.
Nehemiah	Rebuilding of the Wall around Jerusalem and Religious Revival.
Esther	Captive Jews in Persia are Saved by their Queen.
Job	Suffering and Testing of a Devout Man.
Psalms	Prayers and Hymns Worshiping God.
Proverbs	Instructions for Living a Wise and Rewarding Life.
Ecclesiastes	Life without God is Full of Despair.
Song of Songs	Solomon's Tale of God's Love.
Isaiah	Chronicle of the Failure of the Israelites—points to a future Messiah.
Jeremiah	Unsuccessful Warning to Judah—return to God before the Babylonians conquer.
Lamentations	Poems of Sorrow for the Fallen City of Jerusalem.
Ezekiel	Prophet to the Jews in Babylonian Captivity.
Daniel	Babylonian Captive who Faced Adversity to Become a Leader.
Hosea	Preached a Message of Unfaithfulness to God.
Joel	Foretold God's Judgment on Judah.
Amos	Advocate of the Poor during a Period of Prosperity in Israel.
Obadiah	Warned Edom, Israel's Neighbor.
Jonah	Punished for Reluctance to go to Nineveh—he successfully preached to Israel's enemies.
Micah	Detailed the Corruption of the Israelites—promised forgiveness and restoration to God's people.
Nahum	Foretold of the Destruction of Nineveh.
Habakkuk	Discusses Suffering and Justice with God.
Zephaniah	Tells of the Coming of the Day of the LORD.
Haggai	Established Priorities for the Rebuilding of Jerusalem—Temple before homes.
Zechariah	Encourages Temple Rebuilding—its importance for the coming of the Messiah.
Malachi	Sought to Draw People Back to God.

New Testament

Matthew	Gospel Written for a Jewish Audience—Jesus' authority and power.
Mark	Gospel Written for Roman Readers—emphasizes action and chronicles Jesus' work on earth.
Luke	Doctor's Gospel—focused on human interest including the needy and poor.
John	Reflective Gospel Account—includes seven signs that Jesus is the Son of God.
Acts	Account of Jesus' Followers after His Ascension—focus is on Peter and Paul; Paul's transition from a persecutor to devout servant and minister.
Romans	Letter to a Sophisticated Readership—describes theology.
1 Corinthians	Chronicles Problems in the Church at Corinth.
2 Corinthians	Paul Defends Himself against False Accusations.
Galatians	Describes Christ's Delivery of Freedom—not bondage through law.
Ephesians	Encouraging Account of the Advantages of Being a Christian.
Philippians	Friendly Letter of Joy.
Colossians	Faith in Christ is Complete.
1 Thessalonians	History of the Early Church—Paul's advice.
2 Thessalonians	Answers Questions—the Second Coming and other topics.
1 Timothy	
2 Timothy	
Titus	Instructions Regarding How to Minister in Crete.
Philemon	Paul Instructs Philemon—forgive the slave and accept him as a Christian brother.
Hebrews	Old Testament Interpretation in Light of Christ.
James	How to Act Like a Christian.
1 Peter	Comfort and Encouragement for Persecuted Christians.
2 Peter	Highlights Problems with the Church—warns against false teachers.
1 John	Basic Truths about Christian Life.
2 John	Warnings about False Teachers.
3 John	Hospitality towards True Teachers.
Jude	Dealing with Heretics.
Revelation	Prophecy of the Second Coming—the new heaven and earth.

Old Testament Chronology

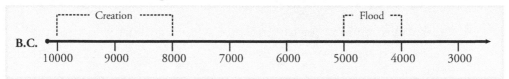

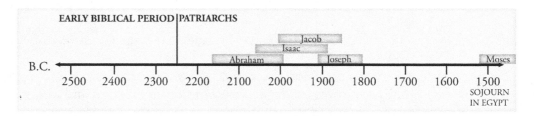

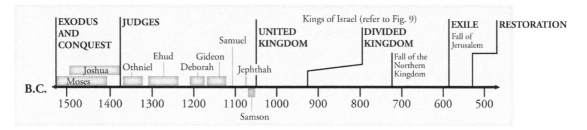

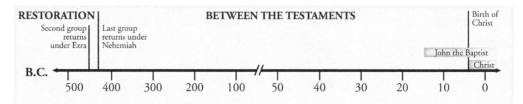

New Testament Chronology

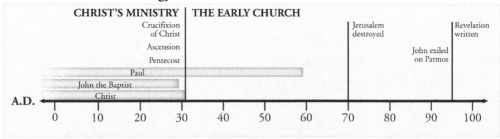

Figure 1: Bible Chronology

OLD TESTAMENT

Pentateuch

GENESIS

GENESIS 1

Verse 1: *In the beginning God created the heavens and the earth.*

God created:

Day 1: Day and night
Day 2: Water and sky
Day 3: Land and vegetation
Day 4: Sun, moon, and stars
Day 5: Creatures of the sea and birds
Day 6: Livestock, wild animals, and man to rule over them

GENESIS 2

Verse 4a: *This is the account of the heavens and the earth when they were created.*

God rested on the seventh day and made it holy. God then created the Garden of Eden including the tree of life and the tree of knowledge of good and evil. Eden also had a river with four headwaters:

1. Pishon which winds through Havilah, rich in minerals
2. Gihon which winds through Cush
3. Tigris which runs along the east side of Asshur
4. Euphrates

God instructed the first man (Adam) to eat from any tree in the garden with the exception of the tree of knowledge of good and evil, which would cause man to "surely die." Adam named all of the animals and birds but did not find a suitable helper. Therefore, God created woman (Eve) from one of his ribs. God noted that men and women would unite in marriage and become one flesh.

GENESIS 3

Verse 22: *And the* LORD *God said, "The man has now become like one of us, knowing good and evil. He must not be allowed to reach out his hand and take also from the tree of life and eat, and live forever."*

A crafty serpent convinced Eve to eat from the forbidden tree, then she gave some to Adam. After eating the forbidden fruit, they were no longer unashamed and realized they were naked. They covered themselves with fig leaves. God discovered them and immediately recognized what had happened. He cursed the serpent, and subjected man to future pain, turmoil, and a limited lifespan on earth. He also banished Adam and Eve from the Garden of Eden, leaving the tree of life guarded by cherubim (angels) and a flaming sword.

GENESIS 4

Verse 7: *If you do what is right, will you not be accepted? But if you do not do what is right, sin is crouching at your door; it desires to have you, but you must master it.*

Eve gave birth to Cain and later Abel. Cain was a farmer and Abel a shepherd. God looked favorably upon an offering by Abel, but not upon Cain's. Cain became angry, and despite God's counseling to do what is right, Cain killed his brother Abel. When questioned by God, Cain replied, "Am I my brother's keeper?" God condemned Cain to be a restless wanderer for his sin. The LORD marked him so that he would not be killed (or his life would be avenged seven times), and Cain went to live in Nod, east of Eden. Cain and his wife had a son named Enoch. Several generations later, one of his offspring, Lamech (not Noah's father) killed a man and said that if Cain were avenged seven times, he would be avenged seventy-seven times. Adam and Eve's third son, Seth, later had a son named Enosh.

GENESIS 5

Verse 1: *This is the written account of Adam's line. When God created man, he made him in the likeness of God.*

Adam lived 930 years. Seth, who fathered Enosh as well as other children, lived 912 years. The lineage from Seth proceeded as follows:

Enosh	905 years
Kenan	910 years
Mahalalel	895 years
Jared	962 years
Enoch	365 years *then God took him away*
Methuselah	969 years
Lamech	777 years
Noah	950 years
Shem, Ham, and Japheth	

GENESIS 6

Verse 9b: *Noah was a righteous man, blameless among the people of his time, and he walked with God.*

God recognized that the population was increasing and limited man's life span to 120 years. He also knew that man had become wicked and evil, and planned to wipe man and beast from the face of the earth. However, Noah, a righteous man, found favor with the LORD, and was spared. God instructed Noah to build an ark from cypress wood and gave him detailed instructions to follow. God spared Noah, his wife, his sons (Shem, Ham, and Japheth), and their wives, as well as two of every creature of the earth by providing for them on the ark.

GENESIS 7

Verse 5: *Noah did all that the LORD commanded him.*

God instructed 600-year-old Noah to take seven pairs of all clean animals and birds and one pair of all unclean animals into the ark with his family. Seven days later, rain fell on the earth for the first time and continued for forty days and nights. The water rose to a level twenty feet above the highest mountain. All creatures on the earth (except the inhabitants of the ark) perished.

GENESIS 8

Verse 22: *As long as the earth endures, seedtime and harvest, cold and heat, summer and winter, day and night will never cease.*

One hundred and fifty days later, the water receded. The ark came to rest on Mount Ararat. After forty more days, Noah sent out a raven, then a dove, but neither found dry land. Seven days later, Noah sent the dove out again and it returned with an olive leaf. In seven more days, Noah sent out the dove a third time but it did not return. As per God's instructions, Noah released all the animals from the ark. He then built an altar to the Lord and offered a sacrifice. God promised that He would never again destroy the earth.

GENESIS 9

Verse 16: *Whenever the rainbow appears in the clouds, I will see it and remember the everlasting covenant between God and all living creatures of every kind on the earth.*

God encouraged Noah and his sons to multiply and offered them all other creatures for food (but only after the blood was removed). He also instructed them not to kill another man. God made a covenant with Noah and his children and promised He would never again flood the earth and offered a rainbow as a symbol of this. Noah drank too much wine and fell asleep naked. Ham (Noah's son and father of Canaan) noted this and attempted to embarrass Noah by telling his two brothers Shem and Japheth. The two brothers did not look at their naked father but instead placed a cover over him. When Noah awoke and discovered what happened, he cursed Ham by proclaiming that his son Canaan would be a slave (to his uncles) and praised Shem and Japheth.

GENESIS 10

Verse 32: *These are the clans of Noah's sons, according to their lines of descent, within their nations. From these the nations spread out over the earth after the flood.*

Each of Noah's sons had several sons who in turn had sons. They spread out through the inhabited portions of the earth.

Japheth: Gomer, Magog, Madai, Javan, Tubal, Meshech, and Tiras
Gomer: Ashkenaz, Riphath, and Togarmah.
Javan: Elishah, Tarshish, Kittim, Rodanim

Ham: Cush, Mizraim, Put, and Canaan
Cush: Seba, Havilah, Sabtah, Raamah, and Sabteca
Raamah: Sheba and Dedan
Nimrod (a mighty hunter) was also of this lineage.
Mizraim: Ludites, Anamites, Lehabites, Naphtuhites, Pathrusites,
        Casluhites (Philistines) and Caphtorites.
Canaan: Sidon, Hittites, Jebusites, Amorites, Girgashites, Hivites,
Zemarites, and Hamathites.

Shem: Elam, Asshur, Arphaxad, Lud, and Aram.
Aram: Uz, Hul, Gether, and Meshech
Arphaxad: Shelah
Shelah: Eber
Eber: Peleg, Joktan
Joktan: Almodad, Sheleph, Hazarmaveth, Jerah,
        Hadoram, Uzal, Diklah, Obal, Abimael, Sheba,
        Ophir, Havilah, and Jobab.

GENESIS 11

Verse 9: *That is why it was called Babel—because there the LORD confused the language of the whole world. From there the LORD scattered them over the face of the whole earth.*

In the plains of Shinar (Babylonia), the people began to build the tower of Babel. The LORD was concerned that because they all spoke the same language, the people could work together too easily (not always for good). He therefore gave them different languages and scattered the people all over the earth. Peleg (descendant of Shem) was the father of Reu, and the lineage then followed with Serug, Nahor, and Terah. Terah, in turn, fathered Abram, Nahor, and Haran (Lot's father). Abram married Sarai, and Nahor married Milcah (Haran's daughter). Terah took Abram, Sarai, and Lot and settled in Haran.

GENESIS 12

Verse 3: *I will bless those who bless you, and whoever curses you I will curse; and all peoples on earth will be blessed through you.*

The LORD spoke to Abram and instructed him to leave his home. He took Sarai and Lot and headed to the land of Canaan. God again spoke to Abram and promised the land they were passing through to his offspring. After building an altar, Abram continued his travels. Due to a famine, Abram was forced to go into Egypt. While there, he was afraid that he would be killed because of his beautiful wife, Sarai, so he instructed her to tell the Egyptians that she was his sister. She was taken into the Pharaoh's household. Pharaoh treated Abram well, but the LORD inflicted punishment on Pharaoh. When he found out the truth about Sarai, Pharaoh released Abram and her with all their accumulated wealth and possessions.

GENESIS 13

Verse 17: *Go, walk through the length and breadth of the land, for I am giving it to you.*

The land could not support the flocks of both Abram and Lot, so Abram gave Lot first choice of the land and they separated. Lot and half of the livestock headed to Jordan and Abram and the other livestock stayed in Canaan. The LORD again promised all of the territory they were in to Abram and his offspring. Sodom, which was in Jordan, was wicked and full of sinners.

GENESIS 14

Verses 19b, 20a: *Blessed be Abram by God Most High, Creator of heaven and earth. And blessed be God Most High, who delivered your enemies into your hand.*

A war between the kings of Shinar (Babylonia), Ellasar, Elam and Goiim and the kings of Sodom, Gomorrah, Admah, Zeboiim and Bela erupted in the valley of Siddim (the Salt Sea).

Sodom and Gomorrah were seized, and Lot—who was living in Sodom—was kidnapped. When Abram learned that Lot had been captured, he gathered his 318 men and rescued Lot and his possessions from King Kedorlaomer of Elam and his allies. The king of Sodom came out to meet Abram. Then Melchizedek, the ruler of Salem and priest of God Most High, blessed Abram, and Abram gave a tithe of everything to Melchizedek. The king of Sodom was grateful to Abram, and offered him praise as well as all of the goods from the defeat. Abram refused this, however, noting that he had promised God not to take anything from Sodom.

GENESIS 15

Verse 6: *Abram believed the LORD, and he credited it to him as righteousness.*

God appeared to Abram and promised that his heirs would be as numerous as the stars in heaven, and inherit all the land between Egypt and the Euphrates River. Abram was skeptical because he and his wife were old, but God persuaded him. God also forecast that Abram's descendants would first be enslaved and mistreated for 400 years before they received the land and its possessions.

GENESIS 16

Verse 15: *So Hagar bore Abram a son, and Abram gave the name Ishmael to the son she had borne.*

Sarai, Abram's wife, convinced Abram to have children with her servant Hagar, because Sarai was barren. When Hagar became pregnant, she had a fight with Sarai and ran away. The angel of the LORD pursued her and told her to return to Sarai. He also assured her that she would prosper, and told her to name her son Ishmael. The angel also prophesied that Ishmael would live a life of turmoil and conflict.

GENESIS 17

Verse 7: *I will establish my covenant as an everlasting covenant between me and you and your descendants after you for the generations to come, to be your God and the God of your descendants after you.*

God renewed His covenant with Abram, changed his name to Abraham, and told him that he would be the father of many nations. He stipulated that all of Abraham's descendants should be circumcised as a sign of the covenant. God also stated that Abraham's wife would henceforth be named Sarah, and she would bear a son. At first Abraham did not believe that this was possible, but the LORD assured him that she would indeed have a son, and he was to be named Isaac. Abraham then had all of the males in his household circumcised, based on God's instructions.

GENESIS 18

Verse 19: *For I have chosen him, so that he will direct his children and his household after him to keep the way of the LORD by doing what is right and just, so that the LORD will bring about for Abraham what he has promised him.*

The LORD appeared to Abraham with two angels disguised as men. Abraham showed them hospitality and the LORD renewed His promise that Sarah would have a child in one year. Sarah laughed (although she later denied it) and God asked her "Is anything too hard for the LORD?" The LORD then announced to Abraham that He was going to check on Sodom and Gomorrah because He had heard the outcry of their sin. Abraham pleaded with Him to save the city if there were as few as fifty righteous people in Sodom. After He agreed, Abraham proceeded to beg God to lower this number to 45, 40, 30, 20, and finally 10. God agreed to spare the city if He found ten righteous people.

GENESIS 19

Verse 29: *So when God destroyed the cities of the plain, he remembered Abraham, and he brought Lot out of the catastrophe that overthrew the cities where Lot had lived.*

The two angels arrived in Sodom and reluctantly agreed to stay with Lot, at his insistence. The men of Sodom surrounded Lot's house, and asked that the two angels come out so that they could have sex with them. Lot offered his daughters instead, but the men insisted and stormed the house. The angels blinded the men so that they could not find the door, and instructed Lot to gather his family and leave the city. At the urging of the angels, Lot left with his wife and two daughters. Their fiancés thought it was a joke and did not leave. The angels instructed Lot and his family to flee and not look back, then God destroyed Sodom and Gomorrah with burning sulfur. Lot's wife did look back however, and was turned into a pillar of salt. Lot and his two daughters moved to a cave in the mountains. The daughters were concerned that they would not have children to preserve the family line, so they got their father drunk on wine and they both slept with him. Lot was not aware of either encounter, and both daughters became pregnant. The older daughter had a son named Moab (father of the Moabites) and the younger daughter had a son named Ben-Ammi (father of the Ammonites).

GENESIS 20

Verse 7: *Now return the man's wife, for he is a prophet, and he will pray for you and you will live.*

Abraham moved to Gerar, where he again claimed that Sarah was his sister. Abimelech, the king of Gerar, sent for Sarah, but God intervened before the king touched her. When Abimelech asked Abraham why he said Sarah was his sister, Abraham explained that he was afraid he would be killed. He also noted that Sarah was actually his half sister because they shared the same father. King Abimelech gave Abraham livestock, slaves, and money and allowed him to live anywhere he wanted in his kingdom. The LORD then looked favorably upon Abimelech's household.

GENESIS 21

Verse 1: *Now the LORD was gracious to Sarah as he had said, and the LORD did for Sarah what he had promised.*

Isaac was born and Abraham (now 100) circumcised his son when he was eight days old. Sarah laughed and suggested that anyone who heard that she and Abraham had a son at their late age would also laugh. Abraham hosted a feast when Isaac was weaned. Ishmael, Hagar and Abraham's son, mocked Isaac, and Sarah asked Abraham to send Hagar and Ishmael away. Abraham was distressed, but God told him that Ishmael was also destined to be a leader of a nation. God helped Hagar and Ishmael in the Desert of Paran. Abraham and Abimelech made a treaty at Beersheba where Abraham lived.

GENESIS 22

Verse 14: *So Abraham called that place The LORD Will Provide. And to this day it is said, "On the mountain of the LORD it will be provided."*

God tested Abraham by asking him to make a burnt offering of his son Isaac. Abraham obeyed the LORD, who intervened at the last moment to save Isaac and a ram was sacrificed in his place. The LORD blessed Abraham for his faithfulness and his willingness to sacrifice his only son. God renewed His covenant with Abraham. Nahor, Abraham's brother, and his wife Milcah had eight sons: Uz, Buz, Kemuel (Aram's father), Kesed, Hazo, Pildash, Jidlaph, and Bethuel (Rebekah's father).

GENESIS 23

Verse 20: *So the field and the cave in it were deeded to Abraham by the Hittites as a burial site.*

Sarah died at the age of 127 in the town of Hebron in Canaan. Abraham asked Ephron the Hittite for permission to bury her in their country. Ephron offered Abraham his field and cave, but Abraham insisted on paying for it, and they agreed to a price (400 shekels of silver). Abraham then buried Sarah in the cave at Hebron.

GENESIS 24

Verse 15: *Before he had finished praying, Rebekah came out with her jar on her shoulder. She was the daughter of Bethuel son of Milcah, who was the wife of Abraham's brother Nahor.*

Abraham asked his chief servant to return to his homeland and find a wife for Isaac. He went to the town where Nahor (Abraham's brother) lived and with God's help found Rebekah (Nahor's granddaughter) at the spring. The servant gave gifts to Rebekah and her family and brought Rebekah back to Canaan. Isaac and Rebekah were then married.

GENESIS 25

Verse 23: *The LORD said to her, "Two nations are in your womb, and two peoples from within you will be separated; one people will be stronger than the other, and the older will serve the younger."*

Abraham married another woman, Keturah, and they had six sons: Zimran, Jokshan (father of Sheba and Dedan), Medan, Midian (father of Ephah, Epher, Hanoch, Abida, and Eldaah), Ishbak, and Shuah. Abraham lived 175 years then died, and left all his possessions to Isaac. Isaac (who lived near Beer Lahai Roi) and Ishmael buried their father in the cave of Machpelah with his wife Sarah. Ishmael lived 137 years and had twelve sons who settled near the Egyptian border and became rulers of hostile tribes. Like Sarah, Rebekah was barren. Isaac prayed to the Lord for her and she became pregnant with twins who jostled with each other in her womb. When she asked the Lord why this was occurring, she was told that her sons would become leaders of two nations and the older would serve the younger. She bore two sons, Esau (who would lead the Edomites) and Jacob (who would lead the Israelites). Esau (favored by Isaac) was a hunter and Jacob (favored by Rebekah) was more of a homebody. Jacob tricked Esau into trading his birthright to him for a meal that he had prepared.

GENESIS 26

Verse 24: *That night the Lord appeared to him and said, "I am the God of your father Abraham. Do not be afraid, for I am with you; I will bless you and will increase the number of your descendants for the sake of my servant Abraham."*

There was a famine in the land, so Isaac moved to the Valley of Gerar, a territory belonging to the Philistines. The Lord appeared to him there and told him not to go on to Egypt. He also renewed the covenant He made with Abraham. Isaac had introduced Rebekah as his sister, but when Abimelech, the Philistine king learned that she was his wife, he made her off limits. Isaac planted crops and prospered. The Philistines became jealous and filled all of Abraham's old wells in the Valley of Gerar with dirt. Abimelech told Isaac to move away, so he moved into the valley and reopened all of the wells. There were some quarrels with the Philistines regarding the ownership of some of the wells, but Isaac was blessed by the Lord and he built an altar to Him in the land. Abimelech and his staff made a treaty with Isaac, because they could tell that the Lord was with him. When he was forty, Esau married two Hittite women, Judith and Basemath, who were a constant source of grief to Isaac and Rebekah.

GENESIS 27

Verse 36: *Esau said, "Isn't he rightly named Jacob? He has deceived me these two times: He took my birthright, and now he's taken my blessing!" Then he asked, "Haven't you reserved any blessing for me?"*

Isaac, who was blind in his old age, instructed Esau to hunt for some wild game and prepare it for him. After eating, Isaac would give him his blessing. Rebekah overheard this and instructed Jacob to bring her choice young goats from the flock so she could prepare a meal for Isaac. Together, they tricked Isaac into giving Jacob the blessing intended for Esau. Esau returned and learned what had occurred and asked for his father's blessing as well, but Isaac was unable to bless him. Esau was angry that Jacob had now received his birthright and his father's blessing, and he plotted to kill his brother. Rebekah learned of this and instructed Jacob to flee to her brother Laban's home in Paddan Aram in Haran.

GENESIS 28

Verse 15: *I am with you and will watch over you wherever you go, and I will bring you back to this land. I will not leave you until I have done what I have promised you.*

Isaac blessed Jacob and instructed him to proceed on his journey and to marry one of Laban's daughters. Esau learned that his parents were unhappy with his wives, so he married Ishmael's daughter Mahalath as well. Jacob stopped at Bethel for the night and had a dream in which he saw a stairway to heaven. God stood at the top of the stairway and spoke to Jacob, renewing the covenant that He had made with his grandfather, Abraham. Jacob awoke the next morning, praised God, and placed a pillar where he had laid his head, to honor Him.

GENESIS 29

Verse 31: *When the LORD saw that Leah was not loved, he opened her womb, but Rachel was barren.*

Jacob arrived in Paddan Aram and met some shepherds at a well. He met and fell in love with Laban's younger daughter Rachel. Jacob asked for Rachel's hand in marriage in exchange for seven years of work. After seven years, Laban had a wedding feast and tricked Jacob into marrying and sleeping with his older daughter Leah instead of Rachel. Jacob confronted Laban who explained that it was customary for the older daughter to marry first. He agreed that Jacob could also have Rachel as a wife if he agreed to serve him for another seven years. Rachel was barren, but Leah bore Jacob four children, Reuben, Simeon, Levi, and Judah.

GENESIS 30

Verse 22: *Then God remembered Rachel, he listened to her and opened her womb.*

Rachel became jealous of Leah and had her servant, Bilhah, marry Jacob. Bilhah bore two sons, Dan and Naphtali. Leah saw that she was not having any more children, so she gave her servant, Zilpah, to marry Jacob. Zilpah bore two sons, Gad and Asher. Rachel agreed to allow

Leah to sleep with Jacob one evening in exchange for some mandrake plants that Reuben had harvested. This resulted in Leah's fifth son, Issachar. Later, she had a sixth son with Jacob, Zebulun, and a daughter, Dinah. Finally, the LORD answered Rachel's prayers, and she had a son, Joseph. Rachel thanked the LORD and asked Him for another child.

JACOB'S CHILDREN

Leah	**Bilhah**	**Zilpah**	**Rachel**
(1) Reuben	(5) Dan	(7) Gad	(11) Joseph
(2) Simeon	(6) Naphtali	(8) Asher	[(12) Benjamin {later}]
(3) Levi			
(4) Judah			
(9) Issachar			
(10) Zebulun			
(D) Dinah			

Jacob and Laban prospered, and their flocks increased greatly. When Jacob asked Laban for permission to return to his home, Laban agreed to allow Jacob to have all the spotted and dark livestock as payment for his service. Laban attempted to deceive Jacob by removing all spotted and dark animals, but with God's help, these animals multiplied from the remaining herds. Jacob allowed the healthy animals to mate in the shade, which further increased the size and strength of his flocks.

GENESIS 31

Verse 49b: *May the LORD keep watch between you and me when we are away from each other.*

Laban and his sons became envious of Jacob, and the LORD instructed him to return to Canaan. He gathered his family and belongings and left with his livestock without telling Laban. Unbeknownst to Jacob, Rachel also took her father's idols with her. Laban learned that Jacob fled and pursued him. After seven days, Laban caught up with Jacob in Gilead, but was instructed by God in a dream not to confront Jacob. Laban asked Jacob why he did not allow him to give an appropriate send-off and questioned why he had taken his idols. Jacob replied that he was concerned that Laban would not allow him to take his daughters (Jacob's wives) with him, and gave permission for Laban to take anyone who had stolen his idols. Laban commenced his search of all the tents, but Rachel had hidden the objects in her saddle and informed her father that she could not dismount because she was having her period. When his search turned up nothing, Jacob confronted Laban and asked what crime he had committed. Laban and Jacob made a covenant, set up a pillar, and agreed to stay on their respective sides of the pillar in the future. Then Laban returned home.

GENESIS 32

Verse 30: *So Jacob called the place Peniel, saying, "It is because I saw God face to face, and yet my life was spared."*

Jacob went on his way and was greeted by angels in Mahanaim. He sent messengers ahead of him to tell his brother Esau that he was returning in peace. Esau instructed the messengers to tell Jacob that he was coming to meet him with four hundred men. Afraid, Jacob divided his men and flocks in hopes that at least half would get away if attacked, and then prayed to the LORD. He prepared a gift of several hundred livestock for his brother and sent them out to meet Esau. That night Jacob sent his entire family to the other side of the Jabbok River and was left alone. He wrestled with a man (God) all night at Peniel and was touched in the hip, causing him to limp. The man also changed Jacob's name to Israel, which means, "struggles with God." In the morning, God blessed Jacob and allowed him to continue.

GENESIS 33

Verse 4: *But Esau ran to meet Jacob and embraced him; he threw his arms around his neck and kissed him. And they wept.*

Esau arrived and, much to Jacob's surprise, met his brother with open arms. Esau accepted his brother's gifts only after Jacob insisted and welcomed Jacob back. He offered to escort him back home, but Jacob replied that he wanted to move slowly for the benefit of the children and the livestock. Jacob bought land in Canaan and made an altar that he named "El Elohe Israel".

GENESIS 34

Verse 14: *They said to them, "We can't do such a thing; we can't give our sister to a man who is not circumcised. That would be a disgrace to us."*

Shechem, the son of Hamor the Hivite, the ruler of the area, raped Dinah (Leah and Jacob's daughter). Shechem asked his father to help secure Dinah's hand in marriage. Jacob and his sons learned that Dinah had been raped but did not confront Shechem or Hamor. Instead, they agreed to the marriage providing all the men in the city were circumcised. Three days later, when all the men were still in pain, Jacob's sons Simeon and Levi sought revenge, killed all the men, and plundered the city. Jacob chastised his sons for their action and was concerned about a possible counter-attack by the Canaanites and Perizzites. The brothers attempted to justify their actions, asking if they should allow their sister to be treated like a prostitute.

GENESIS 35

Verse 10: *God said to him, "Your name is Jacob, but you will no longer be called Jacob; your name will be Israel." So he named him Israel.*

God instructed Jacob to return to Bethel and build an altar. Jacob instructed his family to get rid of all their idols, purify themselves, and go with him to Bethel. Upon his return, God blessed Jacob, and gave him the name Israel again, renewing the covenant He had made with Abraham and Isaac. Jacob then made an altar at Bethel. During their travels, Rachel bore Jacob another son, Benjamin. Rachel died during childbirth and was buried in Bethlehem. Jacob erected a pillar there. Later, Reuben dishonored his father by sleeping with his concubine Bilhah. Jacob came home to his father Isaac in Hebron. Isaac passed away at the age of 180 years, and Esau and Jacob buried him. Jacob remained in Canaan.

GENESIS 36

Verse 9: *This is the account of Esau the father of the Edomites in the hill country of Seir.*

Esau's descendants were many. He moved to Edom, because the land could not support all the livestock of the brothers. He became the father of the Edomites. Rulers of Edom included: Bela, Jobab, Husham, Hadad, Samlah, Shaul, Baal-Hanan, and Hadan (Hadar).

GENESIS 37

Verse 3: *Now Israel loved Joseph more than any of his other sons, because he had been born to him in his old age; and he made a richly ornamented robe for him..*

Joseph (Jacob's eleventh son and Rachel's first) was favored by Jacob (Israel) over the others. Jacob gave him a richly ornamented robe. Joseph had two dreams. In one, his sheaf of grain rose and the other sheaves bowed down to it. In the other, the sun and moon and eleven stars bowed down to him. His brothers (especially the sons of Bilhah and Zilpah) were jealous and conspired against Joseph. Joseph was sent by Jacob to find his brothers who were shepherding the sheep in the valley of Hebron. Some of the brothers wanted to kill Joseph when he arrived, but Reuben suggested that they just kidnap him and put him into an empty cistern (where he could rescue him later). Judah convinced his brothers to sell him to traveling merchants as a slave instead. When Reuben returned, he discovered what had happened and was distraught. The brothers decided to make it look like Joseph was killed, and so they returned to their father with Joseph's robe stained with blood from a goat they had slaughtered. Jacob (Israel), upon learning of Joseph's death, was inconsolable. In the meantime, Joseph was sold as a slave to Potiphar, one of Pharaoh's officials in Egypt.

GENESIS 38

Verse 26: *Judah recognized them and said, "She is more righteous than I, since I wouldn't give her to my son Shelah." And he did not sleep with her again.*

Judah, Jacob's fourth son, married the daughter of Shua, a Canaanite, and had three sons, Er, Onan, and Shelah. Er, who later married Tamar, was wicked, so the LORD put him to death. Judah instructed Onan to honor his brother by fathering children with Tamar, but he avoided this by spilling his semen on the ground. Because of this, the LORD also put him to death. Judah delayed giving Shelah to Tamar. Judah's wife died, and he was later tricked into sleeping with Tamar, believing her to be a prostitute. Judah gave Tamar his seal and cord as collateral for later payment to the prostitute. When he discovered what had occurred he recognized his guilt for not giving up his son Shelah as he had promised Tamar. Tamar was pregnant with Judah's twins. When they were born, one baby, Zerah, put his hand out first, and the midwife tied a scarlet ribbon on his wrist to identify him as the first-born. Zerah drew back his hand and the other twin, Perez, was actually born first.

GENESIS 39

Verse 2: *The LORD was with Joseph and he prospered, and he lived in the house of his Egyptian master.*

Joseph, who was favored by the LORD, prospered in the Egyptian household of Potiphar, and was put in charge of the house and field. Potiphar's wife invited Joseph to sleep with her but he refused. She persisted, and on one occasion grabbed his cloak. Joseph ran away, leaving his cloak. Potiphar's wife claimed that he had tried to sleep with her and left his cloak beside her. Upon hearing this story, Potiphar imprisoned Joseph. With the LORD's help, Joseph was later put in charge of the prison.

GENESIS 40

Verse 14: *But when all goes well with you, remember me and show me kindness; mention me to Pharaoh and get me out of this prison.*

The king's cupbearer and baker were later imprisoned, under Joseph's care. They both had a dream. The cupbearer dreamed that he saw a grape vine with three branches and he took the grapes from the vine and squeezed them into the Pharaoh's cup. Joseph explained that the dream meant that he would be released in three days and restored to his former position. He asked the cupbearer to remember him when the dream was fulfilled. The baker dreamed that he had three baskets of bread on his head, but birds were eating from the top basket. Joseph interpreted the dream, explaining that in three days the baker would be executed and left for the birds. Both dreams were fulfilled, but the cupbearer did not remember Joseph.

GENESIS 41

Verse 39: *Then Pharaoh said to Joseph, "Since God has made all this known to you, there is no one so discerning and wise as you."*

Two years later, Pharaoh had a dream in which seven fattened cows were eaten by seven ugly and gaunt cows on the banks of the Nile. He had a second dream in which seven healthy heads of grain on a single stalk were swallowed by seven thin and scorched heads of grain. Pharaoh could not find anyone to interpret his dreams. Finally, the cupbearer told Pharaoh of Joseph's previous dream interpretations. Joseph was sent for, and with God's help, interpreted the dreams. He explained that both dreams meant that seven years of abundance would be followed by seven years of famine. Joseph suggested that Pharaoh appoint commissioners to store food during the first seven years for the next seven years, Joseph was put in charge of this effort. He was richly ordained and was given Asenath to be his wife. Joseph went about his duties, successfully storing abundant quantities of food during the first seven years. Joseph and

Asenath had two sons, Manasseh and Ephraim. When the famine began, Joseph proceeded to sell food to Egypt and all surrounding countries.

GENESIS 42

Verse 21: *They said to one another, "Surely we are being punished because of our brother. We saw how distressed he was when he pleaded with us for his life, but we would not listen; that's why this distress has come upon us."*

Jacob learned that there was grain in Egypt, so he sent ten of his remaining eleven sons (Benjamin stayed behind) to Egypt to buy grain. They approached Joseph, who pretended not to recognize them. He accused them of being spies and told them he would hold them until one of them returned with their youngest brother. After three days, Joseph sent all of the brothers but one, Simeon, back to Canaan with bags full of grain with instructions to return with Benjamin. En route, they discovered that Joseph had also given back their money that they had spent for the grain. They arrived home, they told Jacob what had happened. Reuben offered to return, but Jacob feared for Benjamin's life and did not allow it.

GENESIS 43

Verse 14: *And may God Almighty grant you mercy before the man so that he will let your other brother and Benjamin come back with you. As for me, if I am bereaved, I am bereaved.*

When the grain ran out, Jacob instructed his sons to return to Egypt. After some discussion, Judah guaranteed Benjamin's safety to Jacob. Jacob instructed his sons to return with gifts and twice the original amount of silver, believing that the return of the silver on the first visit was a mistake. When they arrived in Egypt, Joseph invited them for a feast. The brothers were frightened, but Joseph's steward told them not to worry and returned Simeon to them. They assembled at Joseph's house and presented gifts to Joseph. When Joseph saw Benjamin, he left to weep privately. When he returned, the feast commenced.

GENESIS 44

Verse 16: *"What can we say to my lord?" Judah replied. "What can we say? How can we prove our innocence? God has uncovered your servants' guilt. We are now my lord's slaves—we ourselves and the one who was found to have the cup."*

Joseph instructed his steward to fill all their sacks with grain, return all their silver in their sacks, and to put his own silver cup in Benjamin's sack. After bowing to Joseph, the brothers left, but before they had gone very far, Joseph sent his steward after them to accuse them of stealing silver including Joseph's own silver cup. The brothers denied these charges and agreed that whoever had the silver cup would be Joseph's slave. When the silver was discovered, Joseph offered to let all of them go except for Benjamin. Judah pleaded with Joseph, asking that he be allowed to be a slave rather than Benjamin.

GENESIS 45

Verse 7: *But God sent me ahead of you to preserve for you a remnant on earth and to save your lives by a great deliverance.*

Joseph asked to be alone with his brothers and revealed his identity. He explained that it was God—not them—who had sent him to Egypt. He told them to get their father and their household and return to Egypt so that he could provide for them during the five remaining years of the famine. Pharaoh heard about this and encouraged Joseph to bring his family to live in the best part of Egypt. Pharaoh also gave them carts and ample provisions for their journey. The brothers returned to Canaan and convinced their initially skeptical father to return to Egypt with them.

GENESIS 46

Verse 3: *"I am God, the God of your father," he said. "Do not be afraid to go down to Egypt, for I will make you into a great nation there."*

Jacob (Israel) went to Beersheba and offered sacrifices to God. The LORD spoke to him in a dream and encouraged him to go the Egypt with his sons. The lineage of Jacob's sons is as follows:

Jacob (With Leah):	thirty-three sons and daughters, including Reuben, Simeon, Levi, Judah, Issachar, Zebulun and Dinah
Reuben:	Hanoch, Pallu, Hezron, Carmi
Simeon:	Jemuel, Jamin, Ohad, Jakin, Zohar, Shaul
Levi:	Gershon, Kohath, and Merari
Judah:	Er, Onan, Shelah, Perez, and Zerah (Er and Onan died in Canaan)

Perez:	Hezron, Hamul
Issachar:	Tola, Puah, Jashub, Shimron
Zebulun:	Sered, Elon, Jahleel
Jacob (With Bilhah):	seven sons and daughters including Dan and Naphtali
Dan:	Hushim
Naphtali:	Jahziel, Guni, Jezer, Shillem
Jacob (With Zilpah):	sixteen sons and daughters including Gad and Asher
Gad:	Zephon, Haggi, Shuni, Ezbon, Eri, Arodi, Areli
Asher:	Imnah, Ishvah, Ishvi, Beriah, (Serah)
Beriah:	Heber and Malkiel.
Jacob (With Rachel):	fourteen offspring including Joseph, Benjamin
Joseph:	Manasseh, Ephraim
Benjamin:	Bela, Beker, Ashbel, Gera, Naaman, Ehi, Rosh, Muppim, Huppim, Ard

More than seventy people made the journey to Egypt. Joseph traveled by chariot to meet his father at Goshen. Joseph welcomed his father and they made plans to settle in Goshen.

GENESIS 47

Verse 27: *Now the Israelites settled in Egypt in the region of Goshen. They acquired property there and were fruitful and increased greatly in number.*

Joseph and his five brothers met with Pharaoh who gave them permission to live and be shepherds in Goshen. Jacob also met Pharaoh, who asked how old he was. Jacob responded that he was 130, then blessed Pharaoh. The famine continued, and the people ran out of money to buy food. Joseph asked for livestock in exchange for food. The following year, the people offered their land and their freedom to Joseph for food. Joseph gave all the land, except that of the priests to the Pharaoh. He then gave the people seed for the fields and made them promise to turn over one fifth of the crop to Pharaoh. The Israelites prospered in Egypt. Jacob, who was now 147, asked Joseph to promise him that he would bury him in his homeland when he died.

GENESIS 48

Verse 5: *Now then, your two sons born to you in Egypt before I came to you here will be reckoned as mine; Ephraim and Manasseh will be mine, just as Reuben and Simeon are mine.*

Joseph brought his two sons, Manasseh and Ephraim, to Jacob's deathbed. Jacob passed on the covenant promises to his two grandsons. He blessed the two boys, giving the greater blessing to the younger son. Joseph pointed this out to his aging father, believing that it was his poor vision that caused the oversight. Jacob insisted that the younger son would become greater than the older one and put Ephraim ahead of Manasseh. Jacob promised his land to Joseph, also younger than most of his brothers.

GENESIS 49

Verse 28: *All these are the twelve tribes of Israel, and this is what their father said to them when he blessed them, giving each the blessing appropriate to him.*

Jacob called for all of his sons so that he could tell them about their futures. He told his oldest son Reuben that he will not excel because of his prior indiscretion with Jacob's concubine. He cursed the anger of his next two sons, Simeon and Levi. He praised Judah, noting that he would be a leader. He forecast that Issachar would be a laborer and Zebulun a shipping merchant. He indicated that Dan would be a serpent, and Naphtali a free spirit. He promised Gad would be attacked, while Asher would prosper. He noted that Joseph would receive all of the LORD's blessings. Finally, he concluded that Benjamin would be a ravenous wolf. In this way, Jacob described the future of the tribes of Israel. Jacob asked to be buried with his father Isaac and grandfather Abraham in the cave in Canaan, and then passed away.

GENESIS 50

Verse 20: *You intended to harm me, but God intended it for good to accomplish what is now being done, the saving of many lives.*

Joseph grieved for his father and then had him embalmed. He received permission from Pharaoh to bury his father. A large burial party proceeded to Canaan, stopping at Atad, near the Jordan, to mourn for Jacob for a week. They buried him and returned to Egypt. Upon his return, Joseph reassured his brothers that he held no grudges. Joseph later died in Egypt at the age of 110, but made his brothers promise him that when God called them out of Egypt that they would bury him in his homeland.

EXODUS

EXODUS 1

Verses 12-13: *But the more they were oppressed, the more they multiplied and spread; so the Egyptians came to dread the Israelites and worked them ruthlessly.*

A new king came into power in Egypt and no longer recognized the commitments of the former Pharaoh towards Joseph. The Israelites were enslaved, but despite being oppressed with hard labor, they continued to multiply. The king instructed the Hebrew midwives to kill all the male children when they were delivered, but the women feared God and did not obey the Egyptian king. When he realized his request was not being carried out, he questioned the midwives who told him that Hebrew women often deliver without their help. The Pharaoh then instructed his people to throw all baby boys into the Nile.

EXODUS 2

Verse 10: *When the child grew older, she took him to Pharaoh's daughter and he became her son. She named him Moses, saying, "I drew him out of the water."*

A Levite family had a son and hid him for three months. When the mother was concerned that she could not hide him any longer, she placed him in a waterproofed basket in the Nile. The Pharaoh's daughter discovered the baby, felt sorry for him, and took the newborn in. The boy's own mother was hired to nurse the child, who was named Moses. After he had grown, Moses observed an Egyptian beating one of his own people, and he killed the Egyptian. When Moses realized that he was discovered, he fled to Midian. When he arrived there, he sat down at a well and soon rescued the daughters of a priest (Jethro) from other shepherds. Later, he was invited to stay with the family. Soon afterwards, the priest gave Moses his daughter, Zipporah, in marriage. Together, they had a son that Moses named Gershom. But God had not forgotten the Israelites; He heard the cry of His enslaved people in Egypt and was concerned about them.

EXODUS 3

Verse 5: "Do not come any closer," God said. "Take off your sandals, for the place where you are standing is holy ground."

While tending Jethro's sheep at Horeb, God appeared to Moses in a burning bush. God identified Himself as the God of his forefathers, and Moses hid his face. The LORD told Moses that He was sending him to Pharaoh to bring the Israelites out of Egypt. Moses was reluctant, but God told him to tell the people "I AM WHO I AM" had sent him. He told Moses to tell them that the God of their fathers—Abraham, Isaac, and Jacob, had sent Moses to deliver them to the land of milk and honey. God instructed Moses to meet with the elders and ask Pharaoh to allow them to take a three-day journey into the desert to worship and make sacrifices to God. He told Moses that the Egyptians would eventually let them go, with bounty from the Egyptians to carry with them.

EXODUS 4

Verses 11, 12: The LORD said to him, "Who gave man his mouth? Who makes him deaf or mute? Who gives him sight or makes him blind? Is it not I, the LORD? Now go; I will help you speak and will teach you what to say."

Moses was still skeptical, and the LORD gave him some signs to display in front of the Egyptians and Israelites. He empowered Moses with a staff that turned into a snake, and the ability to change his hand from normal to leprous and then back to normal again by placing it in his cloak. He also enabled him to change water from the Nile into blood. Moses was still doubtful, this time of his own speaking abilities, so God allowed his brother Aaron to accompany him, and assured him that He would help both of them speak. With Reuel's (Jethro) blessings, Moses returned to Egypt with his wife and sons. The LORD further instructed Moses that He would harden Pharaoh's heart. When they asked him to let God's firstborn son (Israel) go, he would refuse; therefore God would kill his firstborn son. On the way to Egypt, God almost killed Moses for not obeying the covenant promise to have his son circumcised, but Zipporah quickly interceded by circumcising their son. The LORD sent Aaron to meet Moses, and Moses told him all that the LORD had instructed him. They met with the Israelite elders and convinced them that the LORD planned to deliver them from Egypt; and they all bowed and worshiped God.

EXODUS 5

Verse 2: *Pharaoh said, "Who is the LORD, that I should obey him and let Israel go? I do not know the LORD and I will not let Israel go."*

Moses and Aaron met Pharaoh and asked him to allow their people to travel to the desert to worship God, but Pharaoh refused. Instead, he added an extra burden to the enslaved Israelites, forcing them to make bricks without any straw. They had to rummage for stubble to use in the bricks, but their quota remained the same. When they did not meet the quota, the Israelite foremen were beaten. Their pleas to Pharaoh were ignored, and this created resentment toward Moses and Aaron amongst the Israelites.

EXODUS 6

Verses 2, 3: *God also said to Moses, "I am the LORD. I appeared to Abraham, to Isaac and to Jacob as God Almighty, but by my name the LORD I did not make myself known to them."*

The LORD reiterated His covenant to Moses and promised that He would free His people from Egyptian rule. Moses shared this with the Israelites, but they remained discouraged. The LORD instructed Moses to tell Pharaoh to let His people go, but Moses was also discouraged. The LORD encouraged Moses and Aaron to go to Pharaoh. The Israelite clans included the following sons at this time:

Jacob (With Bilhah):	seven sons and daughters including Dan and Naphtali
Jacob (With Leah):	thirty-three sons and daughters, including Reuben, Simeon,
Reuben:	Hanoch, Pallu, Hezron, Carmi
Simeon:	Jemuel, Jamin, Ohad, Jakin, Zohar, Shaul
Levi (who lived 137 years):	Gershon, Kohath, Merari

Gershon:	Libni and Shimei
Kohath (who lived 133 years):	Amram, Izhar, Hebron, Uzziel
	Amram (who lived 137 years): Aaron and Moses
Aaron:	Nadab, Abihu, Eleazar, Ithamar
Eleazar:	Phinehas
Izhar:	Korah, Nepheg, Zicri
Korah:	Assir, Elkanah, Abiasaph
Uzziel:	Mishael, Elzaphan, Sithri
Merari:	Mahli, Mushi

EXODUS 7

Verse 1: *Then the LORD said to Moses, "See, I have made you like God to Pharaoh, and your brother Aaron will be your prophet."*

Moses, now eighty-eight years old, was still doubtful of his ability to speak to Pharaoh, and the LORD instructed him to speak through Aaron (eighty-three years old). God indicated that Pharaoh's heart would be hardened, and that Moses would have to show him several miracles to convince him of the power of the LORD and to allow the Israelites to leave. They went to Pharaoh and Aaron turned his staff into a snake. Pharaoh's sorcerers also turned their staffs into snakes, but Aaron's snake swallowed up all of the others. Pharaoh did not respond. Based on the LORD's instructions, Moses and Aaron returned to Pharaoh and again asked for freedom, and threatened to turn all of the water in Egypt to blood. Pharaoh did not listen, so they fulfilled their promise. Pharaoh's magicians were able to do the same thing, so he ignored the brothers. The people were forced to dig along the sides of the river to obtain water.

EXODUS 8

Verse 1: *Then the LORD said to Moses, "Go to Pharaoh and say to him, 'This is what the LORD says; Let my people go, so that they may worship me.'"*

Once again, the LORD instructed Moses to return to Pharaoh and ask permission to worship God, or else he would release a plague of frogs. He carried this out, but so did Pharaoh's magicians. Pharaoh summoned Moses and Aaron and promised to allow the Israelites go to make sacrifices if they would rid Egypt of the frogs. With God's help, the frogs were removed, and at the time that Pharaoh had proposed, but Pharaoh did not honor his promise. Two more plagues followed—gnats and flies—but this time Pharaoh's magicians could not duplicate the feat and the insects did not affect Goshen, where the Israelites lived. Pharaoh again summoned Moses and Aaron and offered to let them sacrifice right there, but Moses insisted that they be allowed to take their three-day journey. Pharaoh agreed to let them go, but not far, if they would rid the land of the flies. Moses prayed to the LORD, and the flies left, but again Pharaoh did not honor his promise.

EXODUS 9

Verse 23: *I will make a distinction between my people and your people. This miraculous sign will occur tomorrow.*

God instructed Moses to return to Pharaoh and threaten him with a plague on all the livestock (except those belonging to Israel) if he did not allow them to go and sacrifice to the LORD. The plague came about, but Pharaoh's heart was hardened again. Following God's instructions, Moses next carried out the plague of boils in which soot caused festering boils. The plague of hail killed all the Egyptians who did not seek cover. Pharaoh called for Moses and Aaron again, admitted that he had sinned, and asked for the hail to stop. Again, he promised to let the Israelites go, and again Pharaoh failed to keep his promise.

EXODUS 10

Verse 26: *Our livestock too must go with us; not a hoof is to be left behind. We have to use some of them in worshiping the LORD our God, and until we get there we will not know what we are to use to worship the LORD.*

Based on God's instructions, Moses and Aaron confronted Pharaoh and promised a plague of locusts if they were not allowed to go and sacrifice to the LORD. The Pharaoh reluctantly agreed to let only the men leave. This was not acceptable, so the LORD instructed Moses to stretch out his staff to initiate the plague. Pharaoh pleaded with Moses and Aaron and the plague was halted, but not before all trees and plants in Egypt were devoured. A plague of darkness followed, and after three days Pharaoh agreed to allow all the Israelites to go for the sacrifice, but stated they had to leave their livestock. Moses insisted that they needed the livestock for the sacrifice, but Pharaoh did not agree and demanded that Moses leave and never enter his presence again, or he would die.

Exodus 11

Verse 9: *The LORD had said to Moses, "Pharaoh will refuse to listen to you—so that my wonders may be multiplied in Egypt."*

The LORD instructed Moses to have the Israelites ask their Egyptian neighbors (whom the LORD made favorably disposed) for gold and clothing. He then said all of the Egyptian firstborn sons would die at midnight, but the Hebrew children would live.

Exodus 12

Verse 42: *Because the LORD kept vigil that night to bring them out of Egypt, on this night all the Israelites are to keep vigil to honor the LORD for the generations to come.*

God instructed each family to take a lamb, slaughter it at twilight, and mark their doorframes with the blood from the lamb before they roasted the carcass to eat. He gave them further instructions for the first of the LORD's Passover Festivals. On the appointed evening, all of the Egyptian firstborn sons would die, but the angel of death would pass over the marked doorframes. The LORD instructed that the Passover celebration would begin and end with a day of no work except for the preparation of food. The feast would last seven days during which only bread without yeast could be eaten. The Israelites prepared for the first Passover, just as the LORD had instructed. The Passover occurred just as the LORD had promised, and finally Pharaoh agreed to let the Israelites go. The Israelites left Egypt, where they had been for 430 years, with 600,000 men amongst them. En route, God gave Moses and Aaron further instructions for the Passover Festival.

SUMMARY OF THE PLAGUES

1. Blood
2. Frogs
3. Gnats
4. Flies
5. Livestock
6. Boils
7. Hail
8. Locusts
9. Darkness
10. Firstborn

EXODUS 13

Verse 8: *On that day tell your son, "I do this because of what the LORD did for me when I came out of Egypt."*

Moses instructed the people about the importance of celebrating the Passover in future generations. He also indicated that the LORD requested the consecration of the firstborn men and animals. Redemption of the firstborn would be a tribute to the first Passover. Fulfilling a promise, Moses brought the bones of Joseph with them. The LORD used a pillar of cloud during the day and a pillar of fire at night for the Israelites to follow.

EXODUS 14

Verse 14: *The LORD will fight for you; you need only to be still.*

God instructed Moses to have the Israelites camp near the bank of the Red Sea because He had one more lesson to teach the Egyptians. After Pharaoh realized he had lost his entire workforce, he assembled his army to pursue the Israelites. As the Egyptians approached, the Israelites were terrified, and questioned Moses why he did not leave them as slaves in Egypt. Moses told them to believe in the LORD. God instructed Moses to raise his staff, and He parted the Red Sea. The Egyptians pursued them, became confused, and were drowned when the waters were released. When the people saw this, they again trusted Moses and the LORD.

EXODUS 15

Verse 26: *He said, "If you listen carefully to the voice of the LORD your God and do what is right in his eyes, if you pay attention to his commands and keep all his decrees, I will not bring on you any of the diseases I brought on the Egyptians, for I am the LORD, who heals you."*

Moses and the Israelites sang a song of praise to the LORD. The song praised Him for rescuing them from Egypt and forecast His might in their pursuit of the Promised Land. Moses then led the people into the Desert of Shur. They did not find water for three days, and when they did, it was bitter. The Israelites grumbled to Moses, who prayed to the LORD for help. God instructed Moses to throw a piece of wood into the water to make it potable. The LORD promised them that if they did as He commanded them, He would help them. They proceeded to an oasis in Elim.

EXODUS 16

Verse 18: *And when they measured it by the omer, he who gathered much did not have too much, and he who gathered little did not have too little. Each one gathered as much as he needed.*

They moved on through the Desert of Sin, where they grumbled to Moses and Aaron because they had no food. The LORD instructed Moses that He would rain down bread (manna) each morning and the people should gather only as much as they needed each day. On the sixth day, they were instructed to gather twice as much. The LORD appeared in a cloud and promised to provide meat for them in the evening. That evening, quail came and covered the camp. The next morning, dew surrounded the camp, and it became manna. Some of the Israelites did not follow instructions, and those who attempted to save the bread found that it was full of maggots. This angered Moses. On the sixth day, they gathered twice as much, in order to save a portion (that did not spoil) for the Sabbath. Some of the Israelites attempted to gather manna on the seventh day, but there was none. This angered the LORD, who asked Moses why His instructions were not being followed. Per God's instructions, they saved a sample of the manna in order to show future generations.

EXODUS 17

Verse 15: *Moses built an altar and called it The LORD is my Banner.*

The Israelites set out from the Desert of Sin, complaining to Moses frequently. Moses cried out to the LORD in frustration for help. God instructed him to walk ahead with several elders and strike a rock to produce water. After this incident, the Amalekites came and attacked the Israelites. Moses sent Joshua and some men out to fight them, while he, Aaron, and Hur went to the top of the hill. As long as Moses held up his hands, the Israelites won, but when he let his hands down, they lost. When Moses finally tired, Aaron and Hur held up Moses' hands for him, and Joshua and his army were victorious. They praised the LORD and built an altar.

EXODUS 18

Verse 23: *If you do this and God so commands, you will be able to stand the strain, and all these people will go home satisfied.*

Jethro, Moses' father-in-law, brought Zipporah and Moses' two sons (Gershom and Eliezer), to the desert to see Moses. Jethro praised the LORD after Moses had shared all of what had occurred. The next day, Moses served as a judge for the people for the entire day. When Jethro saw the burden Moses was under, he suggested that Moses appoint capable judges to help him resolve minor disputes amongst the people and only personally judge difficult cases. He agreed and instituted this plan, and Jethro then returned to his own country.

EXODUS 19

Verse 8: *The people all responded together, "We will do everything the LORD has said." So Moses brought their answer back to the LORD.*

They came to the Desert of Sinai on the first day of the third month following their exodus from Egypt. The LORD called to Moses from the mountain and instructed him to seek a commitment from the people to obey His commands in order for Him to fulfill the covenant. Moses told the people what God had said and they agreed. Per His instructions, the LORD appeared and called Moses to the top of Mount Sinai.

EXODUS 20

Verse 2: *I am the LORD your God, who brought you out of Egypt, out of the land of slavery.*

God then spoke, giving the people the Ten Commandments:

1. There is only one God and there should be no other gods before Him
2. Do not worship idols
3. Do not misuse the name of the LORD
4. Remember the Sabbath day as a day of rest
5. Honor your father and mother
6. Do not commit murder
7. Do not commit adultery
8. Do not steal
9. Do not give false testimony against your neighbor
10. Do not covet your neighbor's house or wife.

When the people saw the smoke and thunder, they were afraid. Moses reassured the people that God had come to test them and keep them from sinning. The LORD instructed Moses to tell the Israelites not to make any idols and to make an altar to sacrifice to the LORD.

Exodus 21

Verse 1: *These are the laws you are to set before them....*

God then added several other laws. One of these allowed slaves to go free after six years. Another defined penalties for certain crimes, including death for intentional murder, killing or cursing their parents, and kidnapping. Other penalties were laid out including the concept of "an eye for an eye, a tooth for a tooth."

Exodus 22

Verses 22, 23: *Do not take advantage of a widow or an orphan. If you do and they cry out to me, I will certainly hear their cry.*

Other laws and penalties were laid out for protection of property, many of which required double payback for theft. Additional laws were described regarding social responsibility. Death was the punishment for sorcery, bestiality, and sacrifice to other gods. God also instructed them not to eat the meat of an animal torn by wild beasts.

Exodus 23

Verse 23: *My angel will go ahead of you and bring you into the land of the Amorites, Hittites, Perizzites, Canaanites, Hivites and Jebusites, and I will wipe them out.*

Several other laws were outlined concerning justice and mercy. Several other Sabbath laws were also made. Three festivals were planned for each year: Passover, Harvest, and Ingathering. God then sent an angel to guard the Israelites during their journey. The LORD assured them that He would help them in their conquests in the Promised Land. He told them to destroy all of the idols they came across and to worship only God. He noted that He would drive out their enemies one at a time.

Exodus 24

Verse 17: *To the Israelites the glory of the LORD looked like a consuming fire on top of the mountain.*

Moses was given further instructions from the LORD. He built an altar with twelve pillars, representing the twelve tribes. The people promised to obey the LORD. He instructed Moses

to come up the mountain for further instructions and return with the Commandments written on tablets of stone. He went up Mount Sinai, and the glory of the Lord, in the form of a
cloud, settled on the mountain. Moses stayed and listened to the Lord on the mountain for
forty days and forty nights.

Exodus 25

Verse 22: *There, above the cover between the two cherubim that are over the ark of the Testimony,
I will meet with you and give you all my commands for the Israelites.*

First, the Lord instructed Moses to tell His people to bring Him offerings of fine wood,
precious metals, and fine linen in order to build a sanctuary or tabernacle for God. He then gave
Moses exact specifications for each element of the tabernacle. The Lord described the details of
the Ark, a large chest that was to be carried with poles. The Ark was to be overlaid with gold,
with gold rings and two gold cherubim on top of it. He next described exact requirements for
a table and a lampstand. The table was also to have gold rings and poles for carrying and was
to include dishes and pitchers made of gold. The Lord provided detailed instructions for each
of seven lampstands to be made of pure gold, each with numerous cups resembling almond
flowers.

Exodus 26

Verse 30: *Set up the tabernacle according to the plan shown you on the mountain.*

The tabernacle was to be a large tent with elaborate curtains of fine linen and was detailed
by the Lord. Gold rings and bronze clasps were described. Wood frames were planned for the
tabernacle. Details for corners, crossbars, and partitioned areas were described. A sequestered
area for the Ark (the Most Holy Place) was planned to separate it from the Holy Place.

Exodus 27

Verse 21: *In the Tent of Meeting, outside the curtain that is in front of the Testimony, Aaron and his
sons are to keep the lamps burning before the Lord from evening till morning. This is to be a lasting
ordinance among the Israelites for the generations to come.*

The Lord described a portable altar for burnt offerings that was to be overlaid with bronze.
Bronze utensils were also to be made. A large courtyard with specific dimensions and framed

by curtains was also to be constructed. Olive oil was to be used to keep the lamps continually burning.

EXODUS 28

Verse 41: *After you put these clothes on your brother Aaron and his sons, anoint and ordain them. Consecrate them so they may serve me as priests.*

The LORD directed that Moses' brother, Aaron, be the high priest, and that Aaron's sons, Nadab, Abihu, Eleazar, and Ithamar would also be priests. The LORD instructed Moses to have priestly garments made for Aaron and his sons. These included an ephod, a breastpiece, a robe, a woven tunic, a turban, and a sash. He then detailed the specifics of each garment. Two onyx stones on the ephod (the vestment that was to be made of gold) were to have the twelve tribes of Israel engraved on them. The breastpiece included twelve precious stones, one for each tribe, mounted into it. Gold rings in the breastpiece were designed to be tied to similar rings on the ephod. The Urim and the Thummim (Alpha and Omega; sacred lots) were also to be in the breastpiece. The robe was to include bells around the hem so that the priest could be heard (presumably by the LORD) before he enters the Holy Place. The turban was to include a gold plate with the message HOLY TO THE LORD. The tunic and sash were also described. Very specific instructions were given, and the LORD made it clear that if His instructions or protocol for worship were not followed, then the men would die.

EXODUS 29

Verse 35: *Do for Aaron and his sons everything I have commanded you, taking seven days to ordain them.*

The LORD then detailed specific instructions for the consecration of the priests involving the sacrifice of bulls and rams without defects. Sprinkling of blood, anointing with oil, and burnt offerings were all described. The LORD also provided for a portion of the offering to be used by the priests for their own consumption. God instructed that Aaron's position would be handed down to each generation based on the birthright of each son. The priests' portion was to be consumed each day and could not be shared with others. If there were any leftovers, they were to be burned. The consecration ceremony was to take seven days with sacrifices for atonement to be offered each day. The LORD assured Moses that He would dwell among the Israelites and that they would know that He is the LORD their God.

EXODUS 30

Verse 15: *The rich are not to give more than a half shekel and the poor are not to give less when you make the offering to the LORD to atone for your lives.*

A portable altar of incense was detailed, and incense was to be burned every morning and evening. God instructed Moses to take a census of the Israelites and to ask each one for a half shekel as a ransom for their lives. This atonement money was to be used for the service of the Tent of Meeting. A bronze basin was to be placed between the Tent of Meeting and the altar to allow the priests to wash their hands and feet. Anointing oil was to be used for anointing the Tent of Meeting, the Ark of the Testimony, the other items in the tabernacle, and the priests. The preparation of the incense was also detailed.

EXODUS 31

Verse 17: *It will be a sign between me and the Israelites forever, for in six days the LORD made the heavens and the earth, and on the seventh day he abstained from work and rested.*

Bezalel, from the tribe of Judah, and Oholiab, from the tribe of Dan, were selected and given special skills to construct the Tent of Meeting and all of its contents. The LORD told Moses that the Israelites must obey His Sabbaths. Work on the Sabbath was forbidden. When the LORD had finished all of His instructions, He gave Moses the two tablets of the Testimony written by God's own hand.

EXODUS 32

Verse 35: *And the LORD struck the people with a plague because of what they did with the calf Aaron had made.*

The people became restless during the extended time that Moses was gone, and they convinced Aaron to make them gods to worship. Aaron collected gold jewelry from the people and created an idol shaped like a calf. They made sacrifices to this idol and indulged in revelry. The LORD saw this and shared His angry feelings with Moses. Moses convinced God not to bring disaster on the people as He had threatened. Moses then returned from the top of the mountain, saw for himself what was occurring, and in anger broke the two tablets the LORD had given him. He destroyed the calf and shared his disappointment with Aaron. He called for all that were with the LORD to come to him, and all of the Levites did so. Based on the LORD's directions, Moses had the Levites kill all of the Israelites who were wicked. They did as they were instructed, killing about three thousand of their family, friends, and neighbors. The next day Moses met with the people and told them what a great sin they had committed. He then returned up the mountain to ask the LORD to forgive their sins. The LORD told Moses to return and lead His people out of the place, promising to punish the people for their sins.

EXODUS 33

Verse 16: *How will anyone know that you are pleased with me and with your people unless you go with us? What else will distinguish me and your people from all the other people on the face of the earth?*

The LORD told Moses to journey towards the Promised Land, but that He would not be with them. Moses spoke to the LORD at the tent of meeting outside the camp. The pillar of cloud covered the entrance to the tent. After Moses pleaded with the LORD to be with them on their journey, the LORD agreed to go with them, but neither Moses (nor anyone else) could see His face.

EXODUS 34

Verse 6: *And he passed in front of Moses, proclaiming, "The LORD, the LORD, the compassionate and gracious God, slow to anger, abounding in love and faithfulness…."*

The LORD told Moses to chisel out two new tablets so that He could replace the two that were broken. The LORD met Moses on the mountain and proclaimed Himself as LORD, promising to be gracious and loving, but not to let the guilty go unpunished. He declared that they would be punished to the third and fourth generation. Moses found favor in the LORD's eyes, and He renewed His covenant promises to him regarding the Promised Land. He instructed Moses to be careful not to make treaties but to drive out the enemies before him. He reminded him not to worship other gods and not to marry those from other nations who did not believe in God. He instructed Moses to celebrate the Passover, to redeem the firstborn, to obey the Sabbath, to give the LORD the firstfruits, and listed several other directions. In this way, a second set of tablets was written over the course of an additional forty days and nights. Moses then returned from the mountain, his face radiant from speaking with the LORD. He shared what he was told with Aaron and others and veiled his face until he spoke to the LORD again.

EXODUS 35

Verse 29: *All the Israelite men and women who were willing brought to the LORD freewill offerings for all the work the LORD through Moses had commanded them to do.*

Moses outlined the Sabbath regulations to the people, then asked for an offering of materials to build the tabernacle. The people gladly brought even more than was asked. Those that were able busied themselves in preparation to build the project.

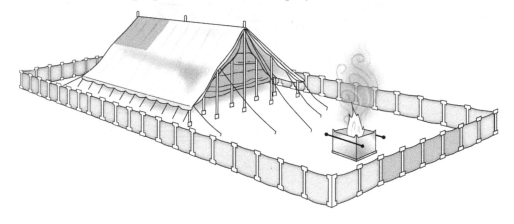

Figure 2: Tabernacle

EXODUS 36

Verse 6: *Then Moses gave an order and they sent this word throughout the camp: "No man or woman is to make anything else as an offering for the sanctuary." And so the people were restrained from bringing more....*

Work began on the sanctuary. Moses had to stop any more offerings because they already had more than enough. The tabernacle was constructed exactly as specified.

EXODUS 37

Verse 9: *The cherubim had their wings spread upward, overshadowing the cover with them. The cherubim faced each other, looking toward the cover.*

Bezalel and Oholiab constructed the Ark, table, lampstand and altar of incense exactly as it was described.

Figure 3: Ark of the covenant

EXODUS 38

Verse 21: *These are the amounts of the materials used for the tabernacle, the tabernacle of the Testimony, which were recorded at Moses command by the Levites under the direction of Ithamar son of Aaron, the priest.*

The altar of burnt offering, the basin for washing, and the courtyard, were also completed to exact specifications. A total of twenty-nine talents and 730 shekels of gold and one hundred talents and 1,775 shekels of silver (some collected during the census) were used in the construction of the tabernacle. Additionally, seventy talents and 2,400 shekels of bronze were used.

EXODUS 39

Verse 32: *So all the work on the tabernacle, the Tent of Meeting, was completed. The Israelites did everything just as the LORD commanded Moses.*

The priestly garments were also made exactly as the LORD had commanded. When they were completed, Moses inspected the tabernacle and blessed the people for following the LORD's instructions.

EXODUS 40

Verse 21: *Then he brought the ark into the tabernacle and hung the shielding curtain and shielded the ark of the Testimony, as the LORD commanded him.*

The LORD instructed Moses to set up the tabernacle and consecrate the priests. He placed the Testimony (two tablets) into the Ark and finished all the work that the LORD had commanded. Upon completion, the glory of the LORD filled the tabernacle and a cloud covered the Tent of Meeting. The cloud became a symbol to the Israelites. When it was present, they stayed in place; when it lifted, they set out on their journey. Everyone could see the cloud during the day, and it became a fire at night.

Chapter 3

LEVITICUS

LEVITICUS 1

Verse 3: If the offering is a burnt offering from the herd, he is to offer a male without defect. He must present it at the entrance to the Tent of Meeting so that it will be acceptable to the LORD.

God gave Moses detailed instructions regarding worship and offerings. The LORD described specific requirements for each of several types of offerings. Most of these involved presentations to the priests (Aaron's sons) at the entrance to the Tent of Meeting (Tabernacle). The burnt offering consisted of sacrificing a bull or ram (or a pigeon or dove for those who could not afford a large animal). This offering was intended to be a voluntary act of worship, an expression of devotion to God, or atonement for non-specific sins.

LEVITICUS 2

Verse 13: Season all your grain offerings with salt. Do not leave the salt of the covenant of your God out of your grain offerings; add salt to all your offerings.

The grain offering involved fine flour, bread baked without yeast, olive oil, and salt. It often accompanied a burnt offering and a fellowship offering, and was offered in recognition of God's goodness and providence.

LEVITICUS 3

Verse 5: *Then Aaron's sons are to burn it on the altar on top of the burnt offering that is on the burning wood, as an offering made by fire, an aroma pleasing to the LORD.*

A fellowship offering was described for fellowship, thanksgiving, and peace. It was to consist of any animal without defect and a variety of breads. The priests were to sprinkle the blood from the animal on the altar and burn all of the fat surrounding the organs. This offering included a communal meal.

LEVITICUS 4

Verse 23: *When he is made aware of the sin he committed, he must bring as his offering a male goat without defect.*

A sin offering consisted of different animals, based on the position of the offender. A priest was to offer a young bull, a leader was to offer a male goat, and others were to offer a female goat or lamb. This was a mandatory atonement for sin. The blood from the animal that was sacrificed was sprinkled in front of the curtain of the sanctuary, as well as other specific locations. The leftover portions of the animal (head, legs, and hide) were to be taken outside the camp and burned on the ash heap. A special sin offering was proposed if all of the Israelite community sinned. In this offering, a young bull was selected and the elders were to lay hands on the animal, sprinkle the blood, and burn the fat, as described for other offerings.

LEVITICUS 5

Verse 10: *The priest shall then offer the other as a burnt offering in the prescribed way and make atonement for him for the sin he has committed, and he will be forgiven.*

Other instructions were given regarding testimony in a public charge, the touching of ceremonially unclean objects, and thoughtless oaths. All of these sins required a sin offering of a female lamb or goat, birds for the poor, or a small amount of flour for the very poor. A guilt offering was to be made for unintentional sin requiring restitution, and a ram without defect was needed for this offering.

LEVITICUS 6

Verse 13: *The fire must be kept burning on the altar continuously; it must not go out.*

Sins that involved deceit or theft required a guilt offering and restitution for the cost of the offense, plus an additional 20% fine. The LORD also described further details regarding each offering. Priestly duties included maintaining a continual fire, removal of ashes and clothing, and transporting them out of camp. The priestly portion of the offerings was also described. Priestly grain offerings were entirely for the LORD.

LEVITICUS 7

Verse 29: *Say to the Israelites: "Anyone who brings a fellowship offering to the LORD is to bring part of it as his sacrifice to the LORD."*

Meat from fellowship offerings given in thanksgiving was required to be eaten by the priests on the same day. Offerings resulting from a vow, however, could be eaten the next day. Ceremonially unclean meat required burning. Eating fat and blood was forbidden. The breast and right thigh of sacrificed animals were the priestly share.

LEVITICUS 8

Verse 23: *Moses slaughtered the ram and took some of its blood and put it on the lobe of Aaron's right ear, on the thumb of his right hand and on the big toe of his right foot.*

The ordination of Aaron and his sons included a bull for a sin offering, two rams, and anointing oil. After ceremonial cleansing, Moses presented his brother and his brother's sons with all of the required priestly garments, and anointed them as God had commanded. Moses slaughtered the bull and consecrated the altar as he was instructed. The bull was prepared and burned on the altar, as were the rams, after Moses anointed the priests and consecrated their garments with oil and blood. As instructed, Aaron and his sons stayed at the tabernacle for the full seven days of the ordination.

LEVITICUS 9

Verse 4: *Fire came out from the presence of the LORD and consumed the burnt offering and the fat portions on the altar. And when all the people saw it, they shouted for joy and fell facedown.*

On the eighth day, the priests conducted a sin offering and a burnt offering for themselves, and a sin offering, a burnt offering, and fellowship offering for the community. Then Aaron blessed the people and met with Moses. The glory of the LORD appeared to the people and fire consumed the offerings as the people shouted for joy.

LEVITICUS 10

Verse 3: *Moses then said to Aaron, "This is what the LORD spoke of when he said: 'Among those who approach me I will show myself holy; in the sight of all the people I will be honored.'" Aaron remained silent.*

Aaron's two oldest sons, Nadab and Abihu, violated certain specific instructions given by the LORD, were engulfed by flames, and died. Moses instructed other priests to carry their bodies outside of camp. He told Aaron and his other sons not to mourn for Nadab and Abihu, but to carry on with their duties. He further instructed Aaron and the other priests not to drink wine when they went to the tabernacle and reminded them of the requirements for consuming the priestly portions of the offerings. Moses questioned why they had not eaten their share of a sacrifice, but when he realized that it was an act of sincerity and not negligence or rebellion, Moses was satisfied.

LEVITICUS 11

Verse 33: *If one of them falls into a clay pot, everything in it will be unclean, and you must break the pot.*

The LORD instructed Moses and Aaron that the Israelites could only eat animals with a split hoof that chew the cud. Camels, rabbits, pigs, and other animals were therefore excluded from their diet. Fins and scales were required for any marine life to be considered clean. Most birds, insects, weasels, rats, lizards, and snakes were also off limits. Even touching these animals was considered unclean. Washing and other methods of purification were required.

LEVITICUS 12

Verse 7: *These are the regulations for the woman who gives birth to a boy or a girl.*

Instructions for purification after childbirth were similar to those following the monthly period. Boys were to be circumcised when they were eight days old. Women were considered to be unclean for seven days following the birth of a son and fourteen days following the birth of a daughter. Women required an additional 33 days to be purified from their bleeding if they had a boy and 66 days if they bore a girl. A burnt offering and a sin offering were required at the end of the time periods.

LEVITICUS 13

Verse 45: *The person with such an infectious disease must wear torn clothes, let his hair be unkempt, cover the lower part of his face and cry out, "Unclean! Unclean!"*

Anyone with a suspected infectious skin disease was required to be examined by the priest who would determine if the person was clean or unclean. A period of isolation was required if there was any question. Ceremonially unclean people were required to live outside the camp. Any clothing with mildew was to be isolated, and if the mildew spread, the clothing was to be destroyed. If it did not spread after seven days, it could be cleaned and isolated for another seven days. If the mildew did not reappear it could be reclaimed, but otherwise it was destroyed.

LEVITICUS 14

Verse 14: *The priest is to take some of the blood of the guilt offering and put it on the lobe of the right ear of the one to be cleansed, on the thumb of his right hand and on the big toe of his right foot.*

If skin infections were resolved, the priest could perform a ritual cleansing of the person and allow him to return to camp. Bathing, shaving, and several offerings were required. Mildew in a house was to be treated similarly to that of clothing and required removal of walls or perhaps even the destruction of the entire dwelling.

LEVITICUS 15

Verse 31: *You must keep the Israelites separate from things that make them unclean, so they will not die in their uncleanness for defiling my dwelling place, which is among them.*

Bodily discharges were considered unclean. Anyone who made contact with either the person with the discharge, or any object the person touched, would also be unclean. After being cleansed from the discharge for seven days, a sin offering and a burnt offering of two doves was required. Similarly, females were considered unclean during their periods.

LEVITICUS 16

Verse 34: *This is to be a lasting ordinance for you: Atonement is to be made once a year for all the sins of the Israelites. And it was done as the LORD commanded Moses.*

The LORD described to Moses the requirements for the annual Day of Atonement. Aaron was to wash, put on his garments, sacrifice a burnt offering, enter the Most Holy Place and place incense, and consecrate it with blood from the bull. A burnt offering was then made using one of two goats, decided by lots. The goat not chosen (the scapegoat) was released after Aaron laid hands on it. This was followed by a burnt offering of a ram for himself and another for the people. Other than on the Day of Atonement (the tenth day of the seventh month), the Most Holy Place was not to be entered.

LEVITICUS 17

Verse 11: *For the life of a creature is in the blood, and I have given it to you to make atonement for yourselves on the altar; it is the blood that makes atonement for one's life.*

The LORD told Moses that anyone who sacrificed animals anywhere other than the tabernacle was to be banished. Idol worship was forbidden, as was eating blood. Blood was to be drained from any animal that was killed prior to eating it because, as the LORD explained, the life of a creature is in the blood.

LEVITICUS 18

Verse 28: *And if you defile the land, it will vomit you out as it vomited out the nations that were before you.*

The LORD instructed Moses to speak to the Israelites regarding His laws and regulations. Sexual relations with close relatives were forbidden. This included mothers, father's other wives, sisters, grandchildren, stepsiblings, aunts, in-laws, and others. Relationships with the mother or daughter of someone a person already had a sexual relationship with were also forbidden. Sexual relationships with a neighbor's spouse, homosexual relationships, bestiality, and child sacrifice were also outlawed. The LORD emphasized anyone who committed any of these transgressions was to be driven out of the Promised Land. He further warned the people not to defile the land, or they would be exiled.

LEVITICUS 19

Verse 2: *Speak to the entire assembly of Israel and say to them: "Be holy because I, the LORD your God, am holy."*

The LORD then told Moses to speak to the entire assembly of Israel regarding being holy. He outlined various other laws including respect for parents, observing the Sabbath, forbidding idolatry, and reviewed several other laws that He had previously given. Several commands regarded treating each other fairly, loving your brother, and respecting the elderly. Other laws forbid mating different kinds of animals or planting two kinds of seed in the same field.

LEVITICUS 20

Verse 26: *You are to be holy to me because I, the LORD, am holy, and I have set you apart from the nations to be my own.*

Sacrifice of children to the pagan god Molech was punishable by death. Also punishable by death was the cursing of parents, adultery, sexual relations with close relatives, bestiality and homosexuality. Lesser punishments were outlined for other sins. Once again, the LORD indicated to Moses that the Israelites needed to follow His decrees, and, in turn, He would deliver the Promised Land to them.

LEVITICUS 21

Verse 6: *They must be holy to their God and must not profane the name of their God. Because they present the offerings made to the LORD by fire, the food of their God, they are to be holy.*

Additional rules were given regarding priests not making themselves ceremonially unclean. Priests were to be holy, and were to be held to higher standards, including marrying only virgins. Likewise, priests descended from Aaron who have a defect (i.e. one who is lame, blind, disfigured, etc.) cannot come near to the LORD to offer a sacrifice.

LEVITICUS 22

Verse 32: *Do not profane my holy name. I must be acknowledged as holy by the Israelites. I am the LORD, who makes you holy....*

The offerings were to be treated with respect. The priests were to be clean in all areas, and all animals used as offerings had to be without defect. Animals were not to be sacrificed until they were at least eight days old. An animal and its offspring were not to be sacrificed on the same day.

LEVITICUS 23

Verse 4: *These are the LORD's appointed feasts, the sacred assemblies you are to proclaim at their appointed times....*

The LORD reminded Moses of His appointed celebrations:
The Sabbath—A day of rest and sacred assembly.
The Passover and Unleavened Bread—Seven days starting from the evening of the fourteenth day of the first month. This celebrated Israel's deliverance from Egypt.
Firstfruits—From the first grains in the Promised Land. Offerings should include a one-year-old lamb, a grain offering, and a drink offering.

Feast of Weeks (Pentecost)—Seven weeks after Firstfruits, celebration of harvest. Bread, seven one-year-old male lambs, one young bull and two rams were to be offered. This was to be followed by a sin offering and a fellowship offering.

Feast of Trumpets (Rosh Hashanah)—First day of the seventh month. An assembly and burnt offering was planned for the LORD's favor.

Day of Atonement (Yom Kippur)—Tenth day of the seventh month. A day of rest and self-denial. On this day, the high priest entered the Most Holy Place.

Feast of Tabernacles—Week-long celebration and offerings beginning the fifteenth day of the seventh month. People were to live in small booths during this festival, celebrating their temporary dwellings after leaving Egypt.

LEVITICUS 24

Verse 22: *You are to have the same law for the alien and the native-born. I am the LORD your God.*

The Israelites were to bring olive oil to keep the lamps at the tabernacle burning. Twelve rows of holy bread were to be set out each Sabbath. Any blasphemy that occurred in the camp at that time was to be punished by death, as was murder. The statement of an eye for an eye, a tooth for a tooth was made signifying that the penalty should match the crime. Therefore, the blasphemer was taken outside the camp and stoned.

LEVITICUS 25

Verse 24: *Throughout the country that you hold as a possession, you must provide for the redemption of the land.*

The LORD told Moses that the seventh year after they enter the Promised Land would be a Sabbath year. This was to be a year of fallow and rest. He indicated that He would provide abundance during the sixth year to provide for this observance. Every fifty years was to be a Year of Jubilee, a year to cancel debts, help the poor, and stabilize society. Other laws outlined by God included a right of redemption for up to one year after a house is sold and the importance of helping one's countrymen. Individuals who become poor could be redeemed by their family and not ruled over ruthlessly.

LEVITICUS 26

Verse 13: *I am the LORD your God, who brought you out of Egypt so that you would no longer be slaves to the Egyptians; I broke the bars of your yoke and enabled you to walk with heads held high.*

The LORD reiterated that idols should not be worshiped as well as the importance of observing the Sabbath. God promised that if they obeyed His decrees that He would provide for them in abundance. Disobedience, however, would be severely punished. God promised defeat and punishment seven times over if they did not follow His decrees. He continued to promise punishment seven times for each failure to follow Him. Devastation was clearly delineated as the outcome for such transgressions.

LEVITICUS 27

Verse 28: *But nothing that a man owns and devotes to the LORD—whether man or animal or family land—may be sold or redeemed; everything so devoted is most holy to the LORD.*

The LORD set a value on amounts of money to be given when dedicating individuals to the LORD. He also indicated that offerings should not be changed. Other items for redemption could be done with an equal value offering plus 20%. Firstborn could not be dedicated, because they already belonged to the LORD. He also provided for a tithe (10%) of everything from the land to go to the LORD.

Chapter 4

NUMBERS

NUMBERS 1

Verse 18b: *The people indicated their ancestry by their clans and families, and the men twenty years old or more were listed by name, one by one....*

The LORD spoke to Moses in the Sinai Desert on the first day of the second month following the exodus from Egypt. He commanded that a census be taken of all men twenty years old who could serve in the army. He instructed that a representative from each of the twelve tribes assist Moses and Aaron in the census. The following were the representatives and the number of men in each tribe:

Reuben:	Elizur	46,500
Simeon:	Shelumiel	59,300
Judah:	Nahshon	74,600
Issachar:	Nethanel	54,400
Zebulun:	Eliab	57,400
Ephraim:	Elishama	40,500
Manasseh:	Gamaliel	32,200
Benjamin:	Abidan	35,400
Dan:	Ahiezer	62,700
Asher:	Pagiel	41,500
Gad:	Eliasaph	45,650
Naphtali:	Ahira	53,400

The total number of Israelite men was 603,550. The Levites were not counted because they were assigned as priests and were in charge of the tabernacle. When the Israelites moved, the tabernacle would be placed in the middle of their camp.

NUMBERS 2

Verse 2: *The Israelites are to camp around the Tent of Meeting some distance from it, each man under his standard with the banners of his family.*

The precise arrangement of the tribes around the tabernacle was specified. The Israelites were to be arranged into four groups of three, each with a lead tribe. The first group, led by Judah, also included Issachar and Zebulun. They were to camp on the east side and were first in marching order. Reuben was to be the leader of the group that also included Simeon and Gad. They camped to the south and marched second. Ephraim was to lead the next group, which also included Manasseh and Benjamin. They were to camp to the west and march third. Finally, Dan was the leader of the group that also included Asher and Naphtali. They camped to the North and marched last.

NUMBERS 3

Verse 13b: *When I struck down all the firstborn in Egypt, I set apart for myself every firstborn in Israel, whether man or animal. They are to be mine. I am the LORD.*

Moses and Aaron represented the Levites. Aaron had four sons: Nadab, Abihu, Eleazar, and Ithamar. Nadab and Abihu had been killed previously because they did not follow the LORD's instructions. The LORD commanded that He wished to take the Levites as His own instead of the first male of every Israelite, as He previously directed. The following was the Levite lineage, beginning with the three original sons of Levi:

Gershon:	Libni and Shimei
Kohath:	Amram, Izhar, Hebron, and Uzziel
Merari:	Mahli and Mushi.

There were 7,500 Gershonites and they were instructed to camp on the west, behind the tabernacle. Lael was their leader, and they were charged with the care of the tabernacle, including the curtains. There were 8,600 Kohathites, and they were to camp on the south side of the tabernacle. Their leader was Elizaphan, and they were responsible for the ark, table, lampstands and other articles of the sanctuary. Eleazar (Aaron's son) was appointed to oversee the care of the sanctuary. There were 6,200 Merarites, and they were to camp on the north side of the tabernacle. Their leader was Zuriel, and they were responsible for all the framing of the tabernacle. Moses and Aaron were to camp on the east side of the tabernacle, in front of the Tent of Meeting and toward the sunrise. They were responsible for the care of the sanctuary. There were 22,000 Levites. The LORD instructed Moses to count all of the firstborn males of all of Israel; there were 22,273. Therefore, based upon His previous decree, He redeemed 22,000 of the firstborn, and asked for five shekels for each of the remaining 273. Per God's instructions, 1365 shekels were collected and given to Aaron and his sons.

NUMBERS 4

Verse 49: At the LORD's command through Moses, each was assigned his work and told what to carry. Thus they were counted, as the LORD commanded Moses.

The LORD told Moses to take a census of the Kohathites from the age of 30 to 50. They were given instructions on how to cover the most holy items when the camp moves. Aaron and his sons were to cover the items (with cloths and sealskins) and only then could the Kohathites move them. Aaron's son, Eleazar, was in charge of the oil for the lamps, the incense, and the entire tabernacle. Additional instructions were given. Failure to obey any of these instructions was punishable by death. Next, the LORD told Moses to take a census of the Gershonites from the age of 30 to 50. They were to carry the curtains and ropes, under the direction of Ithamar, Aaron's son. Finally, the LORD told Moses to take a census of the Merarites from the age of 30 to 50. They were responsible for carrying all of the framing, pegs, and posts, and were also under the direction of Ithamar. The final census totals (age 30 to 50) were as follows:

Kohathites	2,750
Gershonites	2,630
Merarites	3,200

NUMBERS 5

Verse 6: Say to the Israelites: "When a man or woman wrongs another in any way and so is unfaithful to the LORD, that person is guilty...."

The LORD gave instructions to Moses to deal with infectious diseases by sending those individuals outside the camp. He also stated that when one person wrongs another, he must confess his guilt and pay full restitution plus 20% to the person who was wronged, or to the priests, along with a ram for an offering. The LORD then described a test for an unfaithful wife. The wife is to be taken to a priest and instructed to drink bitter water. If the woman was unfaithful, the water would cause her thigh to waste away and her abdomen to swell causing her to lose her childbearing capacity. If she was faithful, the water would not affect her.

NUMBERS 6

Verses 24-26: *The LORD bless you and keep you; the LORD make his face shine upon you and be gracious to you; the LORD turn his face toward you and give you peace.*

The LORD told Moses that if anyone wished to devote himself to God (a Nazirite), he must avoid alcohol, not shave, not touch the dead, and be consecrated only to the LORD. If he is ever in the presence of a dead body, he must make atonement and offer a guilt offering. A special ceremony with numerous offerings is conducted during the dedication of a Nazirite. The LORD also told Moses a blessing that he was to pass onto Aaron and his sons, so that they could bless the people (the Aaronic benediction).

NUMBERS 7

Verse 89: *When Moses entered the Tent of Meeting to speak with the LORD, he heard the voice speaking to him from between the two cherubim above the atonement cover on the ark of the Testimony. And he spoke with him.*

Moses finished setting up the tabernacle and anointed it. People presented offerings and the LORD instructed Moses to use them for the Tent of Meeting. The altar was finished, anointed, and offerings were brought for it. The leaders of each tribe, beginning with Judah and ending with Naphtali, brought offerings of silver, gold, grain, and animals. Moses entered the Tent of Meeting and spoke with the LORD.

NUMBERS 8

Verse 19: *Of all the Israelites, I have given the Levites as gifts to Aaron and his sons to do the work at the Tent of Meeting on behalf of the Israelites and to make atonement for them so that no plague will strike the Israelites when they go near the sanctuary.*

Based on instructions from the LORD through Moses, Aaron set up the seven lamps. Next, the Levites were set apart and made ceremonially clean. Then a grain offering and a sin offering were given. The Israelites assembled, a wave offering was offered to the Lord, and hands were laid on the Levites. Other offerings were made, then Levites commenced their work at the Tent of Meeting. The Lord indicated that He had taken the Levites in lieu of the firstborn. The Levites were to be priests from age 25 to 50.

Numbers 9

Verse 23: *At the Lord's command they encamped, and at the Lord's command they set out. They obeyed the Lord's order, in accordance with his command through Moses.*

The Lord instructed Moses to have the people celebrate the Passover. They did so in the Sinai Desert, in accordance with their customs. When some of the Israelites who were unclean asked if they could still celebrate the Passover, Moses consulted with the Lord and was told that they (and anyone away on a journey) could celebrate the festival on the same day the following month. However, if someone is clean and not on a journey and does not celebrate the Passover, he will pay the consequences of his sin. Aliens who wish to celebrate the Passover must obey the same rules and regulations. The Tent of the Testimony was set up and a cloud covered it, which was the Lord's presence. At night, the cloud looked like fire. The cloud instructed the Israelites when to move; when it lifted they set out, when it settled they encamped. Sometimes they stayed in camp a long time, and other times for only a day. They obeyed the Lord's command through the cloud.

Numbers 10

Verse 35: *Whenever the ark set out, Moses said, "Rise up, O Lord! May your enemies be scattered; may your foes flee before you."*

The Lord instructed Moses to make two trumpets. When both were sounded, the Israelites were to assemble at the entrance to the Tent of Meeting. When one sounded, the leaders were to meet. Other trumpet signals were made for orderly setting out, for battle, and for festivals. Aaron's sons were given the responsibility of sounding the trumpets. The Israelites left the Sinai and moved to the Desert of Paran. They left in order, beginning with Judah and ending with the tribe of Dan as the rear guard. Moses asked Hobab, the son of his father-in-law, who was a Midianite, to travel with them, promising to share the good things of the Lord with him. The Ark traveled with them, and Moses gave tribute to the Lord whenever it set out and came to rest.

NUMBERS 11

Verses 5,6: *We remember the fish we ate in Egypt at no cost—all the cucumbers, melons, leeks, onions and garlic. But now we have lost our appetite; we never see anything but this manna!*

The people complained about hardships, and the LORD became angry. Fire burned and consumed the outskirts of the camp. Moses prayed to the LORD, and the fire stopped. The non-Israelites who were with them complained about not having anything but manna to eat. The Israelites also began to complain again, and Moses was troubled and asked the LORD for help. The LORD instructed him to bring Him seventy leaders to share the burden with Moses. He then told him to tell the people to consecrate themselves in preparation to eat meat the following day. The LORD said that He would provide enough meat for everyone for an entire month, until they were sick of it. He was angry with the complaining people. Moses asked how He could provide enough meat for all of the Israelites for an entire month. The LORD reminded Moses that He could do anything—Is the LORD's arm too short? When the elders assembled, the LORD briefly gave them the gift of prophecy and made them leaders. Eldad and Medad, who did not attend the meeting, also prophesied in camp. Then a wind blew in quail from the sea and the people consumed it. The LORD was angered and brought on a severe plague, killing many of them.

NUMBERS 12

Verse 2: *"Has the LORD spoken only through Moses?" they asked. "Hasn't he also spoken through us?" And the LORD heard this.*

Moses' siblings, Miriam and Aaron, became jealous of him and began talking against him. The LORD instructed the three to come to the Tent of Meeting and spoke to them. He asked Miriam and Aaron why they dared talk badly of Moses when the LORD had chosen him to be a prophet. The LORD was angered, and gave Miriam leprosy. Moses pleaded with the LORD to restore her. He agreed, if she would leave the camp for seven days in disgrace. The people then moved on to the Desert of Paran.

NUMBERS 13

Verse 18: *See what the land is like and whether the people who live there are strong or weak, few or many.*

The LORD instructed Moses to send one leader from each tribe to explore Canaan, which He would give over to them. The group included Joshua from Ephraim and Caleb from Judah. They did as they were instructed and returned at the end of forty days with grapes and figs. They reported that the land did indeed flow with milk and honey. However, they said that the people were powerful and had strong fortifications. Caleb and Joshua spoke up and stated that they could overtake them. The others were afraid and said that the people were too powerful.

Numbers 14

Verse 33: *Your children will be shepherds here for forty years, suffering for your unfaithfulness, until the last of your bodies lies in the desert.*

That night, the people grumbled that they should never have left Egypt and questioned why God would bring them to this place to be defeated. They wanted to select a leader to take them back to Egypt. Moses, Aaron, Caleb, and Joshua tore their clothes and pleaded with the people, saying that the LORD was with them and they could conquer the land. The LORD appeared and was angered. Moses pleaded with Him to have mercy and not to slaughter them because word would get back to Egypt that He had not fulfilled His prophecy. The LORD agreed but assured them that no one who had grumbled would ever see the Promised Land. He then spoke to Moses and Aaron and stated them that no one twenty years or older, except Caleb and Joshua, would ever see the Promised Land. He told them that they would suffer in the desert for forty years—one for each day that they explored the land. The other ten men who explored the land and suggested that they could not conquer it were struck by a plague and died. When the people learned of their plight, they attempted to go to Canaan on their own, but because the LORD was not with them they were defeated.

Numbers 15

Verse 30: *But anyone who sins defiantly, whether native-born or alien, blasphemes the LORD, and that person must be cut off from his people.*

The LORD again spoke to Moses and outlined specific instructions for offerings to be given in the Promised Land. A man was gathering wood on the Sabbath was stoned to death as punishment as the LORD had instructed. The LORD told them to put tassels on the ends of their garments to remind them to follow the Law.

NUMBERS 16

Verse 3: *They came as a group to oppose Moses and Aaron and said to them, "You have gone too far! The whole community is holy, every one of them, and the LORD is with them. Why then do you set yourselves above the LORD's assembly?"*

Korah, a Levite, and Dathan and Abiram, both Reubenites, assembled many of the leaders and challenged Moses and Aaron. Moses was particularly upset with Korah, because of his responsibilities as a leader of the priests. Moses summoned Dathan and Abiram to reason with them, but they refused to come. Moses became very angry, and asked the LORD not to accept any offering from them. The LORD told all of the rebels to assemble at the Tent of Meeting the next morning. When they did so, the LORD told Moses and Aaron to stand aside so that He could punish the assemblage. Moses pleaded with the LORD not to punish them all for the sins of Korah, Dathan, and Abiram. Moses told the people that their circumstances were commanded by the LORD, and that if those three died of natural causes, then he was not speaking the truth. If however, the earth swallowed them and everything they owned, then it was from the LORD. An earthquake occurred and the three men and their families were buried alive. Fire consumed all of the remaining rebels. The following day, the people grumbled and blamed Moses and Aaron. Immediately a plague killed almost 15,000 people and stopped only after Moses and Aaron made atonement for them.

NUMBERS 17

Verse 5: *The staff belonging to the man I choose will sprout, and I will rid myself of this constant grumbling against you by the Israelites.*

The LORD instructed Moses to collect a staff from each tribe. He did so, including Aaron's staff, which represented the tribe of Levi. They were placed in front of the Tent of Meeting. The next day, Aaron's staff budded, flowered, and produced an almond. This demonstrated the LORD's divine intervention. When the people saw this, they were afraid that they would die for challenging Aaron's authority.

NUMBERS 18

Verse 1: *The LORD said to Aaron, "You, your sons and your father's family are to bear the responsibility for offenses against the sanctuary, and you and your sons alone are to bear the responsibility for offenses against the priesthood."*

The LORD instructed Aaron on the importance of his priestly duties to keep the Israelites from wandering again. He reminded him that the priests could keep a portion of the offerings. The priests and their households must be ceremoniously clean to accept them. He told them that the firstborn of some animals must be redeemed at a price but others must be given as offerings. Only the Levites could be near the Tent of Meeting. The Levites would not receive an inheritance in the Promise Land, but would serve the LORD and receive a portion of the offerings. One tenth of what they receive should be tithed to the LORD, giving Him the best portion.

NUMBERS 19

Verse 20: *But if a person who is unclean does not purify himself, he must be cut off from the community, because he has defiled the sanctuary of the LORD. The water of cleansing has not been sprinkled on him, and he is unclean.*

The LORD gave instruction to Moses and Aaron regarding preparation of the water of cleansing. A red heifer without blemish was to be burned outside camp. The ashes would be gathered for the water which was used for purification of sins. Instructions were given for cleansing after being near someone dead.

NUMBERS 20

Verse 8: *Speak to that rock before their eyes and it will pour out its water. You will bring water out of the rock for the community so they and their livestock can drink.*

The Israelites arrived at Kadesh where Miriam died. The people grumbled because there was no food or water. The LORD instructed Moses and Aaron to assemble the people. Moses was instructed to command a rock to bring forth water. Instead, Moses struck the rock twice with his staff and water came forth. The LORD told Moses and Aaron that because he did not do as he was told he would not lead the people into the Promised Land. Moses sent a messenger to the king of Edom asking for passage through his land. The king refused and sent an army to keep them from passing. Therefore, they turned away. They traveled to Mount Hor where

Aaron died. Aaron's son Eleazar was given Aaron's garments and Israel mourned for thirty days.

NUMBERS 21

Verse 35: *So they struck him down, together with his sons and his whole army, leaving them no survivors. And they took possession of his land.*

The Canaanite king of Arad attacked the Israelites. The Israelites prayed to the LORD and the Canaanites were given over to them. As they traveled around Edom, the people grumbled again. The LORD sent venomous snakes amongst them, killing many of them. The people pleaded with Moses to pray for them. He did pray, and was instructed to make a bronze snake and put it on a pole. When anyone was bitten, they could look to the pole and live. The Israelites traveled on to Oboth, to the Zered Valley and then to Arnon, on the border of Moab. They continued on to Beer, where they were given water from a spring, then on to the Valley of Moab. They sent messengers to the king of the Amorites asking for passage, but again they were refused. The Amorites sent an army, and Israel defeated them, then settled into this land. With the LORD's help, they also defeated Og, king of Bashan, and took possession his land.

NUMBERS 22

Verses 2,3: *Now Balak son of Zippor saw all that Israel had done to the Amorites, and Moab was terrified because there were so many people. Indeed, Moab was filled with dread because of the Israelites.*

The Moabites were afraid of Israel. Their king, Balak, sent a message to the pagan prophet Balaam asking him to put a curse on the Israelites. Balaam consulted God, who told him not to curse them. Balak sent other messengers to Balaam and the LORD told him to go with them but to do only as He commanded. The LORD sent an angel to oppose him. When his donkey saw the angel with his sword drawn, it veered off the road and he beat the animal. The angel again appeared and the donkey veered off the path, crushing Balaam's foot against a wall. Again, he beat the animal. Once more, the angel appeared in front of the donkey in a narrow portion of the path. The donkey lay down and he beat her again. The LORD spoke through the donkey and asked why he beat her three times. Balaam told the donkey that she had made him a fool, but then the angel appeared to him as well, and he fell to the ground. The angel instructed him to continue on but to follow the instructions of the LORD. Balak met Balaam and asked why he resisted coming to him. He told him that he could only relay what the LORD told him.

NUMBERS 23

Verse 20: *I have received a command to bless; he has blessed, and I cannot change it.*

Balaam instructed that seven altars be built. The LORD gave him an oracle regarding the success of the Israelites. Balak was unhappy with Balaam, but Balaam told him that he had to relay what the LORD told him. They moved on and built seven more altars. He described a second oracle that Israel was to be blessed and they will conquer their enemies as if a lion devours his prey. Again, Balak was upset, but they moved on and built seven more altars.

NUMBERS 24

Verse 13: *Even if Balak gave me his palace filled with silver and gold, I could not do anything of my own accord, good or bad, to go beyond the command of the LORD—and I must say only what the LORD says.*

Balaam was given a third oracle, again describing the success of Israel over her enemies. Balak was very angry when he heard this and sent Balaam back home. Before leaving, Balaam uttered a fourth oracle describing a star that will come out of Israel and crush Moab. He shared several final oracles regarding other victories for Israel yet to come, then returned home.

NUMBERS 25

Verse 11: *Phinehas son of Eleazar, the son of Aaron, the priest, has turned my anger away from the Israelites; for he was as zealous as I am for my honor among them, so that in my zeal I did not put an end to them.*

While in Shittim, the Israelites practiced sexual immorality and worshiped pagan gods. This angered the LORD who told Moses to punish the leaders. A plague against the Israelites killed 24,000 and only ended when Aaron's grandson, Phinehas, punished an Israelite who seduced a Midianite woman in front of the assemblage by running a spear through both the man and the woman. God rewarded Phinehas for his action and told Moses to treat the Midianites as enemies.

NUMBERS 26

Verse 65: *For the* LORD *had told those Israelites they would surely die in the desert, and not one of them was left except Caleb son of Jephunneh and Joshua son of Nun.*

The LORD commanded Moses and the head priest Eleazar (Aaron's son) to take another census of all men twenty years old or older. The following is a comparison of the numbers in each tribe between the first and second census:

Tribe	First Census	Second Census
Reuben	46,500	43,730
Simeon	59,300	22,200
Gad	45,650	40,500
Judah	74,600	76,500
Issachar	54,400	64,300
Zebulun	57,400	60,500
Ephraim	40,500	32,500
Manasseh	32,200	52,700
Benjamin	35,400	45,600
Dan	62,700	64,400
Asher	41,500	53,400
Naphtali	53,400	45,400
Total	**603,550**	**601,730**

The LORD instructed Moses that each tribe's inheritance would be proportional to their numbers. There were 23,000 Levite males who were at least a month old. As priests, they would not receive an inheritance. Caleb and Joshua were the only two Israelites who were counted in both censuses.

NUMBERS 27

Verses 16,17: *May the Lord, the God of the spirits of all mankind, appoint a man over this community to go out and come in before them, one who will lead them out and bring them in, so the Lord's people will not be like sheep without a shepherd.*

Zelophehad's daughters asked Moses for an inheritance because their father had died and there were no sons in the family. Moses consulted the Lord, and a decree was made to allow for an inheritance in circumstances such as theirs. The Lord then told Moses to go up to the mountain and survey the land. Before he went, he appointed Joshua as the leader before Eleazar the priest and the entire assembly.

NUMBERS 28

Verse 2: *Give this command to the Israelites and say to them: "See that you present to me at the appointed time the food for my offerings made by fire, as an aroma pleasing to me."*

The Lord told Moses to give instructions to the Israelites regarding offerings. Specific instructions were given for daily offerings, Sabbath offerings, monthly offerings, Passover, and Feast of Weeks.

NUMBERS 29

Verse 39: *In addition to what you vow and your freewill offering prepare these for the Lord at your appointed feasts: your burnt offerings, grain offerings, drink offerings and fellowship offerings.*

Additional instructions were given for the Feast of Trumpets, Day of Atonement, and Feast of Tabernacles.

NUMBERS 30

Verse 16: *These are the regulations of the Lord gave Moses concerning relationships between a man and his wife, and between a father and his young daughter still living in his house.*

Moses then instructed the Israelites of the importance of keeping vows. If a young woman makes a vow and her father or husband forbids her, then the vow can be released. The husband may be responsible if he does not take action on the wife's vows.

NUMBERS 31

Verse 2: *Take vengeance on the Midianites for the Israelites. After that, you will be gathered to your people.*

The LORD instructed Moses to take vengeance on the Midianites. He sent a thousand men from each tribe into battle, along with Phinehas the priest. They easily conquered Midian and killed every man including the five kings and Balaam. They saved the women, and this angered Moses. Moses told them to kill all the boys and to also kill any woman who had slept with a man. He gave instructions for purification of anyone who killed the enemy. The spoils were also cleaned and divided, including a tribute for the LORD.

NUMBERS 32

Verse 18: *We will not return to our homes until every Israelite has received his inheritance.*

The Gadites and Reubenites asked Moses if they could inherit the land that they had just conquered rather than crossing the Jordan. Moses reminded them that their ancestors were punished for not following the LORD's instruction regarding conquering the Promised Land. They agreed to fight with their brothers until all of the land was conquered and then return. Moses agreed, but told them that if they did not fight until the end, then they will have sinned against the LORD. Moses gave the Gadites, Reubenites, and the half-tribe of Manasseh the land of the Amorites and Bashan.

NUMBERS 33

Verses 55,56: *But if you do not drive out the inhabitants of the land, those you allow to remain will become barbs in your eyes and thorns in your sides. They will give you trouble in the land where you will live. And then I will do to you what I plan to do to them.*

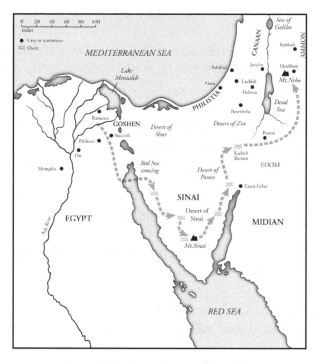

Figure 4: Exodus and Desert Wanderings

The stages of Israel's journey, from Egypt and throughout the various deserts were chronicled. Moses reminded the people to drive out all of the inhabitants of the land, or these people would become a thorn in the Israelites' sides.

Numbers 34

Verse 18: *And appoint one leader from each tribe to help assign the land.*

The LORD specified the boundaries for Canaan. He then told Moses to divide the land by lot and named the men who would be assigned the land for each tribe.

Numbers 35

Verse 25: *The assembly must protect the one accused of murder from the avenger of blood and send him back to the city of refuge to which he fled. He must stay there until the death of the high priest, who was anointed with the holy oil.*

The LORD specified towns for the Levites to live in. He also set aside six of the Levite towns as cities of refuge. Someone who killed another person unintentionally could flee to a city of refuge. There the person would receive a fair trial and atonement could be made for the land.

Numbers 36

Verse 7: *No inheritance in Israel is to pass from tribe to tribe, for every Israelite shall keep the tribal land inherited from his forefathers.*

The brothers of Zelophehad, whose daughters inherited his portion of land, questioned what would happen to the daughters' inheritance if they were to marry a man from a different tribe. The LORD, through Moses, decreed that the Israelite women who have inherited land should marry only within their own tribe.

Chapter 5

DEUTERONOMY

DEUTERONOMY 1

Verse 21: *See, the LORD your God has given you the land. Go up and take possession of it as the LORD, the God of your fathers, told you. Do no be afraid; do not be discouraged.*

Moses spoke to the Israelites in the desert of Moab, east of the Jordan. He reminded the Israelites that the LORD had told them to break camp and proceed to the hill country of the Amorites and into Canaan and Lebanon as far as the Euphrates River. Moses appointed judges over the people and had sent twelve scouts into the land of the Amorites. However, the people grumbled and this angered God. Therefore, only Caleb and Joshua from the first generation of Israelites enter the Promised Land. Moses recalled that when the Israelites tried to enter on their own that they were beaten down.

DEUTERONOMY 2

Verse 30: *But Sihon king of Heshbon refused to let us pass through. For the LORD your God had made his spirit stubborn and his heart obstinate in order to give him into your hands, as he has now done.*

Moses continued to remind the Israelites of their travels. They had traveled around the hill country of Seir until the LORD told them to pass through the land. He instructed them not to provoke the people, who were descendants of Esau, as they passed through the country. He then instructed them to pass through the land of the Ammonites, again telling them not to provoke the people, who were descendants of Lot. They were then told to pass through the land of the Amorites, but Sihon, king of Heshbon would not let them. The two nations met in battle, the Israelites were victorious, and the LORD gave them the plunder.

DEUTERONOMY 3

Verse 2: *The LORD said to me, "Do not be afraid of him, for I have handed him over to you with his whole army and his land. Do to him what you did to Sihon king of the Amorites, who reigned in Heshbon."*

Moses recalled how the Israelites next encountered Og, king of Bashan, who also tried to resist them. They conquered all sixty of Bashan's cities and again kept the livestock and plunder. They divided the conquered land east of the Jordan amongst the Reubenites, the Gadites, and the half tribe of Manasseh. These tribes agreed to help their brothers conquer all of the Promised Land before they returned to their own land, which would be inhabited by their women and children until their return. Moses recalled that Joshua was charged with leading the people across the Jordan and he commissioned and encouraged him.

DEUTERONOMY 4

Verse 34: *Has any god ever tried to take for himself one nation out of another nation, by testings, by miraculous signs and wonders, by war, by a mighty hand and an outstretched arm, or by great and awesome deeds, like all the things the LORD your God did for you in Egypt before your very eyes?*

Moses pleaded with the people to listen to the laws and decrees that he was about to give them, reminding them of the cost of their disobedience when they worshiped Baal of Peor. He told them to follow the Law and to teach their children to follow it as well. He reminded them to be obedient, as they were when the LORD appeared to them when Moses was given the Ten Commandments. He told them not to worship idols or the heavens because the LORD is a jealous God. Moses reminded the people of how wonderful and powerful the LORD is, and the importance of keeping their covenant with Him. He instructed them that the three cities of refuge established so far included Bezer for the Reubenites, Ramoth for the Gadites, and Golan for the Manassites.

DEUTERONOMY 5

Verse 29: *Oh, that their hearts would be inclined to fear me and keep all my commands always, so that it might go well with them and their children forever!*

Moses instructed the people about the Ten Commandments, rreminding them that The LORD spoke to them out of the fire when they were delivered. He went through each of them:

1. There is only one God with no other gods before Him
2. No idolatry
3. Do not misuse the name of the LORD
4. Observe the Sabbath
5. Honor your father and mother
6. Do not murder
7. Do not commit adultery
8. Do not steal
9. Do not give false testimony against your neighbor
10. Do not covet your neighbor's wife or possessions

Moses told the people to obey these commands and walk in the way of the LORD.

DEUTERONOMY 6

Verse 4: *Hear, O Israel: The LORD our God, the LORD is one.*

Moses pleaded with the people to obey the Law after they crossed the Jordan. He told them to love the LORD with all of their hearts, all their souls, and all of their strength. He asked them to impress the commandments on their children and to constantly remind themselves as well. He warned them not to forget who brought them out of slavery into the Promised Land. He admonished them to serve only the LORD and not to test Him. He reminded the Israelites that if the LORD is with them they could not be defeated. Moses pleaded with them, telling them that if they obey the Law as the LORD commanded He would be their righteousness.

DEUTERONOMY 7

Verse 9: *Know therefore that the LORD your God is God; he is the faithful God, keeping his covenant of love to a thousand generations of those who love him and keep his commands.*

Moses instructed them to completely drive out their enemies (the Hittites, Girgashites, Amorites, Canaanites, Perizzites, Hivites, and Jebusites) and not make treaties or show mercy. He told them not to intermarry because this would keep them from following the one true God. Moses told them to destroy all idols that they came across. He reminded them of the covenant, and that God is faithful and loving to those who keep His commands. He warned them that the LORD would also destroy those who do not. He told them to believe in the LORD and not be afraid, and that they would overcome enemies much larger and stronger than they were.

DEUTERONOMY 8

Verse 3: *He humbled you causing you to hunger and then feeding you with manna, which neither you nor your fathers had known, to teach you that man does not live on bread alone but on every word that comes from the mouth of the LORD.*

Moses told the people to obey every command, reminding them that God had led them through the desert for forty years. He detailed the bounties of the land that they were about to enter and told them to praise the LORD for what He had given them. He reminded the Israelites that all glory and credit belonged to the LORD, not to them. He warned them that if they forget the LORD, they would be destroyed.

DEUTERONOMY 9

Verse 6: *Understand, then, that it is not because of your righteousness that the LORD your God is giving you this good land to possess, for you are a stiff-necked people.*

Moses told the people that they were about to go up against enemies who were bigger and taller than they were, but that the LORD would be with them and He would destroy all of their enemies. The LORD would do so not because of their righteousness, but because of the wickedness of their enemies. Moses admonished the Israelites for their rebelliousness in the desert. He reminded them of the golden calf they made and worshiped when Moses was receiving the two stone tablets of the covenant. He also told them how they had angered the LORD on other occasions as well. He recalled how he had saved the people because he pleaded with the LORD to spare them.

DEUTERONOMY 10

Verse 21: *He is your praise; he is your God, who performed for you those great and awesome wonders you saw with your own eyes.*

Moses reminded the people about the second set of tablets and the Ark. He explained how the Levites came to be priests and were put in charge of the Ark of the Covenant. He told them that the LORD only asks that they fear Him, walk in His ways, and serve Him with all of their hearts, and all of their souls. Moses pleaded with the people to circumcise their hearts and not be so stubborn. He encouraged them to worship the mighty God.

DEUTERONOMY 11

Verse 18: *Fix these words of mine in your hearts and minds; tie them as symbols on your hands and bind them on your foreheads.*

Moses told the Israelites to love and obey their God and encourage their children to do the same. He reminded them of their escape from Egypt and the LORD's power. He encouraged them to observe the commands of God after they cross the Jordan. He promised that if they obeyed the LORD, they would have rain and prosper. He warned them not to bow down to idols or they would be punished. He encouraged them to drive out the LORD's enemies in the land before them. He told the Israelites that if they obeyed, they would be blessed. If not, they would be cursed.

DEUTERONOMY 12

Verse 7: *There, in the presence of the LORD your God, you and your family shall eat and shall rejoice in everything you have put your hand to, because the LORD your God has blessed you.*

Moses told the Israelites to destroy all pagan altars and to worship the LORD at a place He would establish. He told them that they should not eat the blood of animals, or tithe grain or wine or the firstborn of their livestock. The Levites would be their priests and make sacrifices to the LORD at the place established for His Tabernacle. Moses warned them again not to follow the religion of their enemies.

DEUTERONOMY 13

Verse 4: *It is the LORD your God you must follow, and him you must revere. Keep his commands and obey him; serve him and hold fast to him.*

Moses instructed them to put false prophets to death. He warned them again not to worship pagan gods under any circumstances. He told them to put anyone who follows these gods to death, even if they were close relatives. He also instructed them to completely burn any town that is proven to house people that worship false gods.

DEUTERONOMY 14

Verse 23: *Eat the tithe of your grain, new wine and oil, and the firstborn of your herds and flocks in the presence of the LORD your God at the place he will choose as a dwelling for his Name, so that you may learn to revere the LORD your God always.*

Moses reminded the people about clean and unclean food. Camels, rabbits, pigs, and other such animals that chew the cud, but did not have divided hoofs were forbidden. Fish without fins or scales were also forbidden. Eagles, vultures, falcons, ravens, owls, storks, and insects were also not allowed. He told them of the importance of tithing and taking care of the Levites.

DEUTERONOMY 15

Verse 11: *There will always be poor people in the land. Therefore I command you to be openhanded toward your brothers and toward the poor and needy in your land.*

Moses told the people about the tradition of canceling debts every seven years. Foreign debts were not affected. He told them that they would prosper and not owe debts to other nations. He instructed them to be generous to the poor. He also told them that they must free fellow Hebrew slaves every seven years, unless the slaves wished to remain. He also told them to set aside firstborn male animals to consecrate to the LORD.

DEUTERONOMY 16

Verse 14: *Be joyful at your Feast—you, your sons and daughters, your menservants and maidservants, and the Levites, the aliens, the fatherless and the widows who live in your towns.*

Moses explained the rules for the celebration of Passover, including the sacrifice of an animal and eating only unleavened bread for seven days. The celebration was to take place only in the city of the LORD's choosing, on the evening of the anniversary of their departure from Egypt (early spring). Moses also gave instructions for the Feast of Weeks (now known as Pentecost—seven weeks after the beginning of harvesting—late summer) commemorating their freedom. Next, he described the Feast of Tabernacles (early fall) celebrating harvest. All men were obliged to give gifts to the LORD for each of these celebrations. Moses then instructed the people to appoint fair and honest judges in every town. He also admonished them about worshiping other gods.

DEUTERONOMY 17

Verse 16: *The king, moreover, must not acquire great numbers of horses for himself or make the people return to Egypt to get more of them, for the LORD has told you, "You are not to go back that way again."*

Moses then told the people not to sacrifice animals with flaws to the LORD. He also told them that if on the testimony of two or three witnesses, a person is found guilty of worshiping other gods, he would be stoned to death outside the city gate. Moses gave the courts of law and the priests the authority to make decisions. He then gave guidance regarding the selection of a future king. The king must come from one of their tribes, be modest, not married to many wives, fair, and must follow the Law.

DEUTERONOMY 18

Verse 15: *The LORD your God will raise up for you a prophet like me from among your own brothers. You must listen to him.*

The Levites would not have an inheritance in the Promised Land because God himself was their inheritance. They were to live off their portion of sacrifices and gifts to the LORD. Moses pleaded with the people not to adopt the detestable practices of the nations that they would conquer including the sacrifice of children, sorcery or witchcraft. He told them not to listen to sorcery, but instead to follow instructions from prophets that God will provide. False prophets, however, were to be put to death.

DEUTERONOMY 19

Verse 13: *Show him no pity. You must purge from Israel the guilty of shedding innocent blood, so that it may go well with you.*

Moses gave instructions for three cities of refuge to be designated in the land. Anyone who killed another man by accident must go to the city of refuge to escape retribution. Anyone who murdered another man, however, would be returned to his home for punishment. At least two witnesses were required to convict a man. The penalty for false testimony is the same as for the crime. Life for life, eye for eye, tooth for tooth....

DEUTERONOMY 20

Verse 1: *When you go to war against your enemies and see horses and chariots and an army greater than yours, do not be afraid of them, because the LORD your God, who brought you up out of Egypt, will be with you.*

Moses gave detailed battle orders. Prior to battle, the priests would address the army. Then, soldiers would be excused if they had reasonable exemptions. When attacking a city outside of the Promised Land, they were to first allow them to surrender and be their slaves. If the people refused, then the Israelites must lay siege to the city. They could spare the women and children and take plunder. When attacking a city, the city itself was part of their inheritance, however, every living thing must be destroyed so the Israelites would not learn the detestable practices of the people. He also instructed them to save the fruit trees but to use other trees as part of the siege.

DEUTERONOMY 21

Verses 22,23: *If a man guilty of a capital offense is put to death and his body is hung on a tree, you must not leave his body on the tree overnight. Be sure to bury him that same day, because anyone who is hung on a tree is under God's curse. You must not desecrate the land the LORD your God is giving you as an inheritance.*

Moses described how to atone for an unsolved murder by sacrificing a heifer and "washing their hands" of innocent blood. He also explained that captured women (other than from the land of their inheritance) can be taken for their wives, but only after the women had shaved their heads and cleansed themselves for a month. He then gave instructions for the rights of a firstborn (double the inheritance) regardless of their mother. A rebellious son was to be brought before the elders and stoned to death. Anyone hanged for capital offenses must not remain hanged overnight.

DEUTERONOMY 22

Verse 22: *If a man is found sleeping with another man's wife, both the man who slept with her and the woman must die. You must purge the evil from Israel.*

Other laws were discussed including instructions for returning lost items, not wearing clothes of the opposite sex, taking eggs but not the mother bird, sanctifying a home, and other miscellaneous things. Other instructions regarding marital relations and punishment for extramarital affairs were also detailed.

DEUTERONOMY 23

Verse 14: *For the LORD your God moves about in your camp to protect you and to deliver your enemies to you. Your camp must be holy, so that he will not see among you anything indecent and turn away from you.*

Those excluded from entering the assembly of the LORD included eunuchs, descendants of forbidden marriages, Ammonites or Moabites, Edomites and third-generation Egyptians. Instructions for camp hygiene and various other laws were also detailed. These included allowing a slave to seek refuge with a family, forbidding prostitution, not charging a fellow Israelite interest, being cautious when making vows to the LORD, and respecting their neighbor's possessions.

DEUTERONOMY 24

Verse 19: *When you are harvesting in your field and you overlook a sheaf, do not go back to get it. Leave it for the alien, the fatherless and the widow, so that the LORD your God may bless you in all the work of your hands.*

Rules regarding divorce, including forbidding remarriages following an interval marriage to another, were detailed. Men were excluded from going to war for one year following their marriages. Other instructions, including not taking millstones for security on a debt, rules against kidnapping, instructions for leprosy, and rules for loans and payments were given. Moses also instructed that fathers would not be put to death for the sins of their children and vice versa. He also told the people to save the leftovers from their crops for the needy to harvest.

DEUTERONOMY 25

Verse 19: *When the LORD your God gives you rest from all the enemies around you in the land he is giving you to possess as an inheritance, you shall blot out the memory of Amalek from under heaven. Do not forget!*

Moses instructed that no man would receive more than forty lashes for punishment. He explained that a brother was to father a son for his brother's widow if his brother dies prematurely. He also told them to be honest in trade and not to show any mercy to the Amalekites.

DEUTERONOMY 26

Verse 18: *And the LORD has declared this day that you are his people, his treasured possession as he promised, and that you are to keep all his commands.*

Moses then described how they should worship the LORD with the firstfruits of their inherited land. He pleaded with the Israelites to follow the LORD's commands so that the LORD could bless them.

DEUTERONOMY 27

Verse 9: *Then Moses and the priests, who are Levites, said to all Israel, "Be silent, O Israel, and listen! You have now become the people of the LORD your God."*

Moses gave directions for the construction of an altar on Mount Ebal once they had crossed the Jordan River. He told them to make sacrifices to the LORD there, then the twelve tribes were to divide in half, with specific tribes going to Mount Gerizim and Mount Ebal. One half would pronounce blessings upon the people, the other half would pronounce cursings concerning anyone who worships idols, dishonors his parents, cheats his neighbor, leads the blind astray, withholds justice, commits adultery or sodomy, murders, accept bribes, or does not follow the Law. Then the people were to agree by saying "Amen."

DEUTERONOMY 28

Verse 14: *Do not turn aside from any of the commands I give you today, to the right or to the left, following other gods and serving them.*

Moses then detailed the bountiful blessings for those who followed the Law. Next, he described the horrible curses that would befall those who did not. He warned that their enemies would destroy them and put a yoke on their necks. He detailed the misery and plagues that would occur and warned them that they would be scattered among the nations.

DEUTERONOMY 29

Verse 29: *The secret things belong to the LORD our God, but the things revealed belong to us and to our children forever, that we may follow all the words of this law.*

Moses assembled all the Israelites and reminded them of their journey. He described their exodus from Egypt, their desert wanderings, and their victory over Heshbon and Bashan. He exhorted them to follow the terms of the covenant—to follow the LORD. He pleaded with them not to worship idols and described the disaster that would occur if they did not keep their part of the covenant.

DEUTERONOMY 30

Verse 14: *No, the word is very near you; it is in your mouth and in your heart so you may obey it.*

Moses explained that if they followed the LORD with all of their hearts and souls they would abound in prosperity. If they did not, they would be destroyed. Moses told them to choose life—for the LORD is life, and He would fulfill His covenant with them.

DEUTERONOMY 31

Verse 13: *Their children, who do not know this law, must hear it and learn to fear the LORD your God as long as you live in the land you are crossing the Jordan to possess.*

Moses told them that he was 120 years old and that he would not lead them into the Promised Land: Joshua would. He told them to be strong and courageous, because the LORD would be with them. Moses wrote down the law and placed it in the Ark of the Covenant. He instructed them to have the priests read it every seven years, the year for canceling debts, during the Feast of Tabernacles. Later, the LORD told Moses that the day of his death was near. He instructed Moses to bring Joshua into the Tent of Meeting. Once there, the LORD appeared in a pillar of cloud. The LORD told them that the Israelites would rebel. He instructed Moses to write down a song that would remind them of their covenant promise that they would not honor. He instructed Joshua to be strong and courageous. Moses assembled the elders and warned them of their fate.

DEUTERONOMY 32

Verse 47: *They are not just idle words for you—they are your life. By them you will live long in the land you are crossing the Jordan to possess.*

Moses then recited the words of the song that the LORD had given him. The song heralded the greatness of God—the Rock—and admonished the Israelites for their corruption. It described how the LORD kept His portion of the covenant, but that the people would not keep theirs. It described the calamities that would occur because of their unfaithfulness. Moses then prepared to go to Mount Nebo that overlooked the Promised Land as the LORD instructed him, where he would die. He would not enter the Promised Land because he was not faithful at the waters of Meribah Kadesh.

DEUTERONOMY 33

Verse 29: *Blessed are you, O Israel! Who is like you, a people saved by the LORD? He is your shield and helper and your glorious sword. Your enemies will cower before you, and you will trample down their high places.*

Moses blessed the Israelites one final time. He addressed each tribe, blessing them and honoring them.

DEUTERONOMY 34

Verse 12: *For no one has ever shown the mighty power or performed the awesome deeds that Moses did in the sight of all Israel.*

Moses climbed Mount Nebo where the LORD showed him the Promised Land. Moses died there. The Israelites grieved for thirty days. Then Joshua was filled with the spirit of wisdom and became their new leader. No Old Testament prophet was superior to Moses.

History

JOSHUA

JOSHUA 1

Verse 8: Do not let this Book of the Law depart from your mouth; meditate on it day and night, so that you may be careful to do everything written in it. Then you will be prosperous and successful.

After Moses death, the LORD instructed Joshua to prepare the people to cross over the Jordan and into the Promised Land. He renewed His covenant and encouraged Joshua to be strong and courageous. He also told him to lead the people and obey His Laws. Joshua rallied the people and prepared for the journey, which he planned to begin three days from that point. He instructed the people that they must all participate in the conquest of the land, and only then return to settle in their own territory. The people were in full support of Joshua.

JOSHUA 2

Verse 11: When we heard of it, our hearts melted and everyone's courage failed because of you, for the LORD your God is God in heaven above and on the earth below.

Joshua sent two spies ahead across the Jordan. They stayed with Rahab, a prostitute who lived in Jericho. Their presence was discovered, and the king of Jericho sent out a search party for them. Rahab lied about their location and hid the spies. She warned the two men about the king's discovery and asked for mercy upon her family when the Israelites conquered the land. They gladly agreed, and Rahab assisted them in their escape. The spies instructed Rahab to tie a scarlet cord in the window of her house to identify her household. They also told to keep her entire family in the house and not to tell anyone else of their agreement or it would be void. The spies told Joshua of their experience and that the people of Jordan were afraid of the Israelites' impending entry into the land.

JOSHUA 3

Verse 5: *Joshua told the people, "Consecrate yourselves, for tomorrow the LORD will do amazing things among you."*

Joshua gave instructions that the people would follow in procession behind the Ark of the Covenant. The LORD encouraged Joshua and temporarily halted the waters of the Jordan for the crossing of the Ark and all of the people of Israel.

JOSHUA 4

Verse 21: *He said to the Israelites, "In the future when your descendants ask their fathers, 'What do these stones mean?' tell them, 'Israel crossed the Jordan on dry ground.'"*

After the entire nation crossed the Jordan, Joshua sent twelve men to build an altar to the LORD with twelve stones taken from the middle of the river. Finally, the Ark, which was held in the middle of the river during the crossing, was carried to the other bank. At that point, the waters returned. The people traveled to the outskirts of Jericho and set up an altar at Gilgal where they camped.

JOSHUA 5

Verse 12: *The manna stopped the day after they ate this food from the land; there was no longer any manna for the Israelites, but that year they ate of the produce of Canaan.*

The Amorite and Canaanite kings heard about the miraculous crossing and were afraid. Per the LORD's instruction, Joshua had all the men circumcised. They then rested and celebrated the Passover, and the manna stopped. An angel of the LORD appeared to Joshua with a drawn sword, instructing him to take Jericho.

JOSHUA 6

Verse 25: *But Joshua spared Rahab the prostitute, with her family and all who belonged to her, because she hid the men Joshua had sent as spies to Jericho—and she lives among the Israelites to this day.*

The Israelites prepared to conquer Jericho, and the city was shut up because the people of Jericho were afraid of them. The LORD told Joshua to march around the city with all of his men, the Ark, and trumpeters for six days. On the seventh day, they were to march around Jericho seven times, and, following the blasts of the trumpets, all of the people were told to shout, and the city walls would collapse. Joshua instructed the Israelites to destroy all living things in Jericho and to turn all valuable possessions in for the LORD's treasury. The people followed their orders, and all the events the LORD had promised occurred. The two spies sought out Rahab and her family and put them in a safe place as they had promised. They burned the city and pronounced a curse against anyone who attempted to rebuild it.

JOSHUA 7

Verse 19: *Then Joshua said to Achan, "My son, give glory to the LORD, the God of Israel, and give him the praise. Tell me what you have done; do not hide it from me."*

Achan (Zimri's grandson from the tribe of Judah) did not obey Joshua's instructions and kept some of the bounty that was supposed to be turned over to the LORD. This angered the LORD, but Joshua was not aware that the event occurred. In the meantime, Joshua sent spies to check out Ai. The spies returned and suggested to Joshua that not all of Israel's resources would be required to fight, because they did not appear to be a formidable foe. Joshua sent three thousand men, and they were routed with thirty-six Israelites killed. Joshua and the elders were grieved by this occurrence and appealed to God. The LORD spoke to Joshua and commanded him to stand up. He told him of Achan's transgression and instructed him to assemble the people the next morning. When confronted, Achan confessed. They recovered the silver and gold that he had stolen. His entire family and he were stoned and burned based on God's instructions. They buried him in the valley of Achor (trouble).

JOSHUA 8

Verse 35: There was not a word of all that Moses had commanded that Joshua did not read to the whole assembly of Israel, including the women and children, and the aliens who lived among them.

The LORD instructed Joshua to attack Ai again. This time the LORD gave them permission to keep the plunder for themselves. They set an ambush against Ai and during their retreat from the attack; the ambush surprised the men of Ai. They captured the city and took no prisoners except the king. The Israelites killed twelve thousand men and women, hanged the king, and burned the city. Joshua then built an altar to the LORD on Mount Ebal and made offerings. He then copied the Law of Moses onto stones and read it to the people of Israel.

JOSHUA 9

Verse 14: The men of Israel sampled their provisions but did not inquire of the LORD. Then Joshua made a treaty of peace with them to let them live, and the leaders of the assembly ratified it by oath.

All of the surrounding kings heard of these events and allied against Israel. Seeing what Israel had done to all the other tribes in the land, the Gibeonites tricked Israel into signing a treaty with them, because they feared for their lives. They claimed that they lived far away when in fact they were neighbors. Joshua kept his promise by not attacking them, but told them that they would be cursed and may only become woodcutters and water carriers for Israel.

JOSHUA 10

Verse 14: There has never been a day like it before or since, a day when the LORD listened to a man. Surely the LORD was fighting for Israel!

Adoni-Zedek, king of Jerusalem, heard about these occurrences and, with the help of the kings of Hebron, Jarmuth, Lachish and Eglon, attacked Gibeon. The Gibeonites sent word to Joshua who was in camp at Gilgal. Joshua, with the LORD's help, assembled his troops and marched to Gibeon where he caught the enemies by surprise. The Israelites pursued them and the LORD rained down hail blocking their retreat, killing many of the enemy in the process. Joshua asked the LORD to have the sun stop in the middle of the sky for a full day so that they could completely destroy the enemy. The Israelites then returned to their camp at Gilgal. The five Amorite kings that escaped were trapped in a cave and brought to Joshua. He hanged them and then had their bodies placed back in the cave and sealed it. Joshua then moved on and attacked Libnah, again taking no survivors. Then they moved on to Lachish and defeated the inhabitants as well as Horam, king of Gezer, who tried to come to the aid of Lachish. The Israelites also defeated Eglon, Hebron, and Debir. They took no prisoners and defeated all of the kings as the LORD commanded.

JOSHUA 11

Verse 23: *So Joshua took the entire land, just as the LORD had directed Moses, and he gave it as an inheritance to Israel according to their tribal divisions. Then the land had rest from war.*

Jabin, king of Hazor, assembled all of the northern kings and their armies to attack Israel. The LORD told Joshua that Israel would be victorious, and that Joshua should hamstring their horses and burn their chariots afterward. Again, they destroyed the entire army and killed Jabin himself. Finally, Joshua destroyed the Anakites and destroyed all of the remaining cities of the hill country. He captured the entire land, just as the LORD had directed. Then the Israelites rested.

JOSHUA 12

Verse 6: *Moses, the servant of the LORD, and the Israelites conquered them. And Moses the servant of the LORD gave their land to the Reubenites, the Gadites and the half-tribe of Manasseh to be their possession.*

This chapter reviews all of the kingdoms that Moses and the Israelites conquered east of the Jordan, and that Joshua and his armies defeated west of the Jordan.

JOSHUA 13

Verse 1: *When Joshua was old and well advanced in years, the LORD said to him, "You are very old, and there are still very large areas of land to be taken over."*

Joshua was growing old, but the LORD indicated that there were still large areas of land left for the Israelites to conquer. He also assigned the land to each of the twelve tribes. He assigned no land to the tribe of Levi so that they could concentrate on their priestly duties. The LORD God was their inheritance.

JOSHUA 14

Verse 12: *Now give me this hill country that the LORD promised me that day. You yourself heard then that the Anakites were there and their cities were large and fortified, but, the LORD helping me, I will drive them out just as he said.*

Much of the division of the land was decided by lot. The tribe of Judah, Caleb, and the Kenizzite approached Joshua and reminded him of the promises made to them. Caleb was sent to explore the land when they were still in the desert and brought back a good report unlike the others. For that, God had promised to give him and his descendants the very land he had explored. Caleb, now eighty-five years old, was anxious to do the LORD's will and drive out the Anakites who were living in that land.

JOSHUA 15

Verse 63: *Judah could not dislodge the Jebusites, who were living in Jerusalem; to this day the Jebusites live there with the people of Judah.*

The tribe of Judah was given a generous allotment. Caleb drove out the Anakites and of-fered his daughter in marriage for the man who captured Kiriath Sepher. Othniel did so and was married to Caleb's daughter. The tribe of Judah was unable to drive out the Jebusites from Jerusalem.

JOSHUA 16

Verse 10: *They did not dislodge the Canaanites living in Gezer, to this day the Canaanites live among the people of Ephraim but are required to do forced labor.*

Allotments were made for Ephraim next to the Jordan River.

JOSHUA 17

Verse 14: *The people of Joseph said to Joshua, "Why have you given us only one allotment and one portion for an inheritance? We are a numerous people and the LORD has blessed us abundantly."*

Joseph's firstborn child was given a very nice allotment. Joshua told the tribes of Ephraim and Manasseh to drive out the Canaanites who were in the forested land, if they needed more territory. The Israelites objected that the Canaanite had iron chariots, but Joshua told them to be strong and drive them out.

Joshua 18

Verse 3: *So Joshua said to the Israelites: "How long will you wait before you begin to take possession of the land that the LORD, the God of your fathers, has given you?"*

There were still seven Israelite tribes that had not received their land. The remaining land was divided during an assembly at the Tent of Meeting in Shiloh. Joshua sent out a survey team with three members of each of the seven tribes. The land was then distributed by lot in the presence of the LORD. The tribe of Benjamin received the first lot and took land adjacent to the Jordan.

Joshua 19

Verse 51: *These are the territories that Eleazar the priest, Joshua son of Nun and the heads of the tribal clans of Israel assigned by lot at Shiloh in the presence of the LORD at the entrance to the Tent of Meeting. And so they finished dividing the land.*

The tribe of Simeon was awarded the second lot, then Zebulun, Issachar, Asher, Naphtali, and finally Dan. The Danites had difficulty taking possession of their territory and attacked Leshem, finally capturing it. Finally, Joshua was given the town of Timnath Serah in the hill country of Ephraim. The land division was complete.

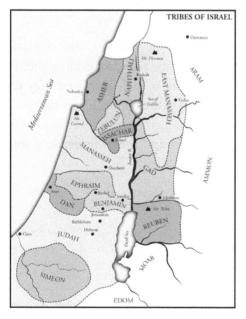

Figure 5: Division of Israel by Tribes

Joshua 20

Verse 3: *Tell the Israelites to designate the cities of refuge, as I instructed you through Moses....*

The LORD designated cities of refuge for those who accidentally committed a crime. Kedesh in Galilee, Shechem in Ephraim, and Kiriath Arba (Hebron) in Judah were chosen. Bezer in Reuben, Ramoth in Gilead and Golan in Bashan were also designated.

Joshua 21

Verse 44: *The LORD gave them rest on every side, just as he had sworn to their forefathers. Not one of their enemies withstood them; the LORD handed all their enemies over to them.*

The Levites were given towns and pastureland as promised. The LORD gave Israel all the land He had sworn to give to their forefathers, then He gave them rest. All promises were fulfilled.

Joshua 22

Verse 34: *And the Reubenites and the Gadites gave the altar this name: A Witness Between Us that the LORD is God.*

Joshua summoned the Reubenites, the Gadites, and the half-tribe of Manasseh and sent them on their way with words of encouragement, reminding them to obey the Laws of the LORD. They returned and built an imposing altar. Thinking that they did so in defiance of the LORD, the other tribes of Israel protested and threatened to go to war. The Reubenites insisted that the altar was an earnest offering to the LORD to show that they had a share in the LORD. This explanation pleased Phinehas the priest and the other leaders and was acceptable to them.

Joshua 23

Verse 14: *Now I am about to go the way of all the earth. You know with all your heart and soul that not one of all the good promises the LORD your God gave you has failed. Every promise has been fulfilled; not one has failed.*

After all the tribes were well settled in their new lands, Joshua summoned the leaders, gave them all final words of encouragement, warned them not to associate with their neighbors, and to always remember the LORD who had fulfilled His promise by giving them the land. He warned them that if they strayed, the LORD would punish them. He admonished them about worshiping other gods and reminded them of the anger that the LORD would show if they did so.

JOSHUA 24

Verse 31: Israel served the LORD throughout the lifetime of Joshua and of the elders who outlived him and who had experienced everything the LORD had done for Israel.

Joshua then assembled all of the Israelites at Shechem. He recounted the story from Exodus and reminded them of their leaders. He told them to fear the LORD and faithfully serve Him. He said to the people, "As for me and my house, we will serve the LORD." The people all agreed, promising to serve God. Joshua told them once again to throw away their foreign gods and accept only the LORD. The people promised to do so. Joshua recorded this and set it under a large stone under an oak tree as a witness to them. Joshua then died at the age of 110. He was buried at Timnath Serah, the land of his inheritance. Joseph's bones were laid to rest at Shechem in his offspring's land of inheritance. Aaron's son Eleazar was buried at Gibeah, which was the land allotted to him.

JUDGES

JUDGES 1

Verse 7: *Then Adoni-Bezek said, "Seventy kings with their thumbs and big toes cut off have picked up scraps under my table. Now God has paid me back for what I did to them." They brought him to Jerusalem, and he died there.*

After Joshua's death, the Israelites asked the LORD who should fight the Canaanites. The LORD told the tribe of Judah to do so. They enlisted the help of the Simeonites and attacked and defeated the Canaanites, taking Adoni-Bezek as a prisoner. They attacked and conquered Jerusalem and then the hill country. Caleb offered his daughter Acsah to the man who captured Kiriath Sepher; Othniel did so. Acsah later asked Othniel to ask her father for a field with springs of water and when he did, Caleb gave it to them. Judah then took Zephath, Gaza, Ashkelon, and Ekron. They were unable to drive the people from the plains, and the Benjamites were unable to dislodge the Jebusites in Jerusalem. Joseph attacked and conquered Bethel after they enlisted the support of a man leaving the city. The man and his family were spared. They then conquered the Hittites and built the city of Luz. Manasseh did not drive out a number of people, and Ephraim, Zebulun, Asher, and Naphtali all failed to drive out all of the inhabitants of their territories.

JUDGES 2

Verse 10: *After that whole generation had been gathered to their fathers, another generation grew up, who knew neither the LORD nor what he had done for Israel.*

The angel of the LORD appeared at Bokim and asked the people why they did not drive the enemy out completely, and indicated that these people would be thorns in their side, and their gods would snare the Israelites. After Joshua's generation had passed away, another generation grew up not knowing the LORD and all that was done for them. They worshiped idols and angered the LORD. The LORD did not protect them against their enemies. Therefore, the LORD raised up judges to rule them and restore order, but the people did not obey them. The LORD was angered and let their enemies attack them.

JUDGES 3

Verse 7: *The Israelites did evil in the eyes of the LORD; they forgot the LORD their God and served the Baals and the Asherahs.*

The Israelites' enemies included the Philistines, the Canaanites, the Sidonians, and the Hivites. The Israelites lived among the pagans and despite God's instructions, married them and served their gods. Because of their evil deeds, Aram, whose king ruled over them for eight years, overthrew them. When Othniel cried out to the LORD, He made him Israel's judge, and he defeated Aram, and the land had peace for forty years. After Othniel's death, the people again did evil, and Moab, whose king ruled them for eighteen years, defeated them. Again, they appealed to the LORD, and Ehud was appointed as the next judge. He presented a double-edged sword to Eglon, king of Moab, and stabbed the king in his upper room. Because Eglon was so fat, the Moabites did not discover that the king was impaled with the sword until Ehud got away. He then rallied the Israelites and they defeated Moab, and lived in the land in peace for eighty years. Shamgar was the next judge (a minor one), and he defeated the Philistines.

JUDGES 4

Verse 5: *She held court under the Palm of Deborah between Ramah and Bethel in the hill country of Ephraim, and the Israelites came to her to have their disputes decided.*

After Ehud (and Shamgar), the Israelites did evil again, so they were overtaken by Canaan. The Canaanites had nine hundred iron chariots and oppressed the Israelites for twenty years.

Deborah, who was the next judge of Israel, sent Barak and ten thousand men to Mount Tabor to overtake Jabin, king of Canaan. Barak said he would go only if Deborah went along with them, so she went, telling him that the honor of victory would go to a woman. They routed the Canaanites and overcame all nine hundred chariots, killing all of the men, even those who fled. Sisera, the commander of the Canaan army, escaped and sought refuge with Jael, the wife of Heber the Kenite. She stabbed him in the temple with a tent peg while he was asleep and killed him. Barak arrived and discovered what had occurred. Jabin, the Canaanite king was defeated by the Israelites.

JUDGES 5

Verse 2: *When the princes in Israel take the lead, when the people willingly offer themselves—praise the LORD!*

Deborah and Barak sang a song after their victory. The song was a tribute to the LORD for His victory. She recounted the events of the victory and thanked God for Jael. After the victory, there was peace for forty years.

JUDGES 6

Verse 15: *"But LORD," Gideon asked, "how can I save Israel? My clan is the weakest in Manasseh, and I am the least in my family."*

The Israelites again did evil, and the Midianites overtook them and ruled over them for seven years. They were oppressed and hid in caves during this time. The Midianites decimated the crops, the livestock, and the land. The Israelites appealed to the LORD who sent a prophet, telling them that they were evil despite what He had done for them. The angel of the LORD selected Gideon as the LORD's warrior. Gideon questioned the angel why the oppression had occurred. He was told to overcome the Midianites, but he questioned his ability to do so. He asked for a sign, and after he had prepared an offering and set it on a rock, fire flared from the rock. Gideon realized that the LORD Himself had called him, so he built an altar and prepared to do as he was instructed. The LORD told him to take a bull from his father's herd, tear down all of the pagan altars, and sacrifice the bull to the LORD. That night, Gideon did so. The next morning, the men in the town discovered what had occurred, and demanded that Joash (Gideon's father) bring out his son so they could kill him. Joash asked them why Baal needed them to help defend him, and they left expecting Baal to contend with Gideon. Gideon assembled the army to attack the Midianites and their allies the Amalekites. He asked God for another sign. If they were to be successful, he asked that the wool fleece he placed on the threshing floor be wet with dew and the ground dry. This occurred, and Gideon asked for one more sign from God—for the fleece to be dry and the ground wet. The next morning it was so, and Gideon knew that he would be victorious.

JUDGES 7

Verse 22a: *When the three hundred trumpets sounded, the LORD caused the men throughout the camp to turn on each other with their swords.*

As they prepared to fight the Midianites, the LORD told Gideon that he had too many men, because He wanted it clear that the LORD would deliver them from their oppression. Gideon announced that anyone who was afraid could return to camp, and twenty-two thousand men did so, leaving ten thousand to fight. The LORD said that there were still too many men. He instructed Gideon to take them to the water and allow them to drink. Three hundred men lapped the water with their tongues like a dog, and the others knelt to drink. The LORD told Gideon to take only those three hundred to fight the Midianites. Gideon went to the Midian camp and overheard the Midianites worrying about their attackers and was assured that he would be victorious. He divided the three hundred men into three companies, giving each trumpets and empty jars with torches inside. They went to the edge of the Midianite camp, blew their trumpets, smashed their jars, and cried out, "A sword for the LORD and for Gideon." The Midianites ran for their lives and turned on each other with their swords. The Israelites pursued the Midianites and killed their leaders.

JUDGES 8

Verse 23: *But Gideon told them, "I will not rule over you, nor will my son rule over you. The LORD will rule over you."*

The Ephraimites asked Gideon why he did not ask them to help him. Gideon smoothed things over by telling them that he did ask, and they helped by killing the enemy leaders. Gideon and his men continued to pursue Zebah and Zalmunna, the kings of Midian. When he asked the officials of Succoth for help, they refused, and Gideon told them that he would tear their flesh with thorns and briers. He went on the Peniel and asked for help, and they too refused. Gideon told them he would tear down their tower when he returned. Gideon cornered the kings and destroyed their remaining army. Upon his return, he made good on his promises to those who would not help. Gideon questioned the kings and realized they had killed his brothers. He ordered his oldest son Jether to kill them, but he was afraid; so Gideon killed them himself. The Israelites asked Gideon to rule over them, but Gideon refused, saying that neither he nor his son would be their ruler. He asked each for a gold earring from the plunder, and they gladly gave it to him. Gideon made the gold into an ephod, and as people later worshiped it as an idol, it became a snare to Gideon and his family. There was peace for forty years. Gideon had seventy sons not including Abimelech, whose mother was his concubine. Gideon died, and the people again returned to Baal worship.

JUDGES 9

Verse 56: Thus God repaid the wickedness that Abimelech had done to his father by murdering his seventy brothers.

Abimelech went to the citizens of Shechem and named himself as leader. He murdered all seventy of Gideon's other sons, except Jotham, who escaped. When he was about to be crowned king, Jotham interceded and warned the people that if Abimelech was not honorable, fire would come out of him and consume them and vice versa. Abimelech governed Israel three years. Some of the citizens who opposed him ambushed and robbed all that passed by Shechem. Gaal questioned the authority of Abimelech. Zebul, the governor of Shechem, told Abimelech of Gaal's attempts to stir up the city against him. Abimelech and his men surrounded Shechem and attacked the city, eventually destroying it. Some escaped to the tower and Abimelech set fire in the tower, killing all inside. Abimelech next captured Thebez and again all of the people hid in the tower. Abimelech started to set the tower on fire, but was struck by a millstone that a woman dropped on his head from the tower. He had his servant kill him so that no one could say that a woman killed him. Therefore, the LORD made both Abimelech and the people of Shechem pay for their wickedness.

JUDGES 10

Verse 16: Then they got rid of the foreign gods among them and served the LORD. And he could bear Israel's misery no long.

Tola, a minor judge from Shamir, ruled for twenty-three years. Jair of Gilead, who led Israel for twenty-two years, followed him. Again, the Israelites sinned and were overtaken by the Philistines and Ammonites, who oppressed them for eighteen years. When the people cried out to the LORD, He told them to let their pagan gods save them. They pleaded with the LORD getting rid of their idols. The Israelites prepared to fight the Ammonites in Gilead. They announced that anyone who led the attack against the Ammonites would be their new leader.

JUDGES 11

Verse 24: *Will you not take what your god Chemosh gives you? Likewise, whatever the LORD our God has given us, we will possess.*

The people approached Jephthah, the illegitimate son of Gilead, and asked him to lead the fight against the Ammonites. He questioned whether they would really make him the leader if he was successful because they did not support him when his half-brothers took away any claim to an inheritance from his father. Jephthah sent messengers to the Ammonite king outlining their claim to the territory, but they were ignored. The LORD backed Jephthah as he went to battle against the Ammonites. Jephthah promised, if successful, that he would sacrifice whatever first came out of his door when he returned, as a burnt offering. He devastated the Ammonites, returned home, and his daughter, his only child, was at the doorway. She asked for two months to roam the hills and weep, because she would never marry. He allowed her to go, and when she returned, he fulfilled his promise.

JUDGES 12

Verse 3: *When I saw that you wouldn't help, I took my life in my hands and crossed over to fight the Ammonites, and the LORD gave me the victory over them. Now why have you come up today to fight me?*

The Ephraimites were offended that they were not asked to help in the battle against the Ammonites. Jephthah said that he did ask them, but they would not help. Jephthah called on the men of Gilead and defeated the Ephraimites. They cut them off at the Jordan, identifying them because they could not pronounce the word "Shibboleth" correctly. Jephthah led Israel six years. Several minor judges ruled next, including Ibzan (seven years), Elon (ten years), and Abdon (eight years).

JUDGES 13

Verse 5b: *No razor may be used on his head, because the boy is to be a Nazirite, set apart to God from birth, and he will begin the deliverance of Israel from the hands of the Philistines.*

The Israelites did evil so they were delivered into the hands of the Philistines for forty years. Manoah had a wife who was sterile. The angel of the LORD appeared to her and told her that she would conceive a son who would deliver Israel from the Philistines. Manoah prayed to the LORD and asked Him to teach them how to bring up the boy. The angel returned to Manoah and his wife. Manoah asked the angel his name, but he said it was beyond understanding. Manoah offered a burnt sacrifice, and the angel ascended into the flame. Manoah and his wife fell to the ground and prayed. They had a boy and named him Samson, and the LORD blessed him and prepared him.

JUDGES 14

Verse 19: *Then the Spirit of the LORD came upon him in power. He went down to Ashkelon, struck down thirty of their men, stripped them of their belonging and gave their clothes to those who had explained the riddle. Burning with anger, he went up to his father's house.*

Samson met a Philistine woman and wanted to marry her. He went to meet her with his parents and killed a lion on the way. Later when he returned to marry the woman, he saw the carcass of the lion and there were bees and honey inside. He took some honey and gave some to his parents, but did not tell them about the lion. Samson made a wager with his companions that they could not solve a riddle he posed: "Out of the eater, something to eat; out of the strong, something sweet." They could not solve it and asked Samson's wife to help them. In fact, they threatened to burn her father's house down if she did not give them the answer. Samson's wife begged him for the answer, which he reluctantly gave her on the last day of the wager. She told her people, and they gave Samson the answer. He was angered, but fulfilled the terms of the wager by taking the items from the men of Ashkelon. He knew that his wife had been unfaithful and left the land of the Philistines enraged.

JUDGES 15

Verse 14: *As he approached Lehi, the Philistines came toward him shouting. The Spirit of the LORD came upon him in power. The ropes on his arms became like charred flax, and the bindings dropped from his hands.*

Samson later returned and asked to see his wife. His father-in-law thought that he had left her, and had given her to his friend. He offered his younger daughter, but Samson was angered. He caught three hundred foxes, tied them tail-to-tail in pairs, and fastened a torch to each of the tied tails. He then let them loose in the grain fields, and all of the grain was burned. When the people learned that Samson had done this, they burned his wife and father-in-law to death. Samson slaughtered many of those who assaulted them, and then retreated to a cave. The Philistines went to Judah looking for Samson. The Judahites went to the cave where Samson was hiding to hand him over. Samson made them promise that they would not kill him themselves, and they agreed. When the Philistines approached, he broke his ropes and killed a thousand Philistines with the jawbone of a donkey he found. He then asked the LORD for water, and a spring appeared and satisfied his thirst. Samson led Israel for twenty years.

JUDGES 16

Verse 17: *So he told her everything, "No razor has ever been used on my head," he said, "because I have been a Nazirite set apart to God since birth. If my head were shaved, my strength would leave me, and I would become as weak as any other man."*

Samson went to Gaza and the Philistines tried to capture him. He escaped by ripping off the doors of the city gate and carrying them to the top of the hill. Later he met a woman named Delilah, also a Philistine. The Philistine rulers tried to enlist her help in gaining the secret to Samson's strength, promising a great sum of money. Samson told her that if anyone tied him with seven fresh thongs, he would become as weak as any other man. The Philistines had her tie him with seven thongs and waited to capture him. He broke the bonds and escaped. Delilah told him he had made a fool of her and asked again. This time Samson said they needed new ropes, and they tried the same ploy again. Again it failed, and again she asked him. This time he told her that if she weaved the seven braids of his hair into the fabric of the loom, he would be as weak as any man. Again, she failed. Finally, she asked him how he could love her if he would not confide in her. After she continued to prod him, he finally told her the true secret—his hair. When he fell asleep, she told the rulers of the Philistines to shave his head, and his strength left him. Then they were able to overcome him. They gouged out his eyes, put him in bronze shackles, and sent him to prison. There, his hair began to grow again. The people were celebrating their victory over Samson and told the guards to bring him out to mock him. Samson was placed between two pillars that supported the pagan temple where they were. He prayed to the Lord for enough strength for one more act. Then Samson shook the pillars and the temple collapsed, killing him and three thousand Philistines inside.

Judges 17

Verse 6: *In those days Israel had no king; everyone did as he saw fit.*

Micah from Ephraim returned the silver that he had taken from his mother. She took a portion of the silver and had it made into an idol. Micah put this with his other idols in a shrine. He invited a young Levite from Bethlehem to stay with him and become his priest. Micah felt that he had earned the Lord's favor because the priest was living with him.

Judges 18

Verse 1b: *And in those days the tribe of the Danites was seeking a place of their own where they might settle, because they had not yet come into an inheritance among the tribes of Israel.*

The Danites, who were looking for a place to settle, sent out spies who came upon Micah's house. They recognized the priest who was staying with Micah and questioned him. They came upon Laish and found the land to be prosperous, then returned to their leaders and reported their findings. The six hundred Danites decided to attack Laish and stopped at Micah's house on the way. They stole all of the idols and the priest asked them what they were doing. The Danites encouraged him to come with them and be their priest, and so he agreed and left with them. Micah and his men pursued them, but turned away when they realized they were outnumbered. The Danites overtook Laish and made it their home. There they worshiped the idols that they had taken from Micah.

Judges 19

Verse 30: *Everyone who saw it said, "Such a thing has never been seen or done, not since the day the Israelites came up out of Egypt. Think about it! Consider it! Tell us what to do!"*

A Levite from a remote area of Ephraim took a concubine, but she was unfaithful to him and went back to her father's house in Bethlehem. The Levite went there to retrieve her and her father-in-law persuaded him to stay with them for several days. When they finally left, they made it to Gibeah in Benjamin by the time it was dark. An old man invited the Levite, his concubine, and their servant to stay with them. Some of the wicked men of the city came to the old man's house to rape the Levite. He sent out his concubine and the men raped her all night long. In the morning, the Levite set out and found her. He put her on a donkey, and when he reached home, he cut her up into twelve parts and sent them into all the areas of Israel. The people of Israel were upset and wondered what to do.

JUDGES 20

Verse 11: *So all the men of Israel got together and united as one man against the city.*

All of the Israelites assembled before the LORD in Mizpah. They asked the Levite how this awful thing happened. He explained what had occurred, stating that the wicked men of Gibeah in Benjamin killed his concubine and he sent the pieces to show them the disgraceful act that the Israelites had committed. They assembled an army to seek retribution against the men of Gibeah. The Benjamites disagreed with this action and assembled in Gibeah to oppose the other Israelites. The Israelites asked God who should fight first. The LORD replied that Judah should. In the first day of the battle, the Benjamites killed twenty-two thousand Israelites. The Israelites sought counsel from the LORD and again were told to go up against the Benjamites the next day. They did, and another eighteen thousand were killed. They fasted and again asked the LORD if they should continue. The LORD told them to fight again the next day and they would be victorious. They ambushed the Benjamites, killing 25,100 of them, and defeated them. Six hundred Benjamites escaped to the desert.

JUDGES 21

Verse 3: *"O LORD, the God of Israel," they cried, "why has this happened to Israel? Why should one tribe be missing from Israel today?"*

The Israelites grieved for their brothers the Benjamites. They had all taken an oath that none of the assembled tribes would give their daughters to be married to a Benjamite, but they were concerned that the Benjamites would not have wives from Israel. Then they realized that the tribe of Jabesh Gilead was not assembled with them. They sent twelve thousand soldiers to Jabesh Gilead with instructions to kill every male and every woman who was not a virgin.

They found four hundred virgins and took them to the remaining Benjamites, but there were not enough. They told the remaining Benjamites to seize a wife during the festival in Shiloh. In that way, they would not give them wives and the Benjamites could still procreate. Israel had no king, and the people did what they saw fit.

JUDGES—SUMMARY

Major Judge	Minor Judge	Defeated	Ruled	Interval
				8 years
Othniel		Aram	40 years	18 years
Ehud		Moab	80 years	20 years
	Shamgar			
Deborah		Canaan	40 years	7 years
Gideon (Abimelech)		Midian	40 years	18 years
	Tola		23 years	
	Jair		22 years	
Jephthah		Ammonites	6 years	40 years
	Ibzan		7 years	
	Elon		10 years	
	Abdon		8 years	
Samson		Philistines	20 years	

Chapter 8

RUTH

RUTH 1

Verse 16: *But Ruth replied, "Don't urge me to leave you or to turn back from you. Where you go I will go, and where you stay I will stay. Your people will be my people and your God my God."*

Elimelech and his wife Naomi went to live in Moab with their two sons Mahlon and Kilion because of the drought in their home in Bethlehem. Elimelech died and Naomi's two sons married Moabite women, one named Orpah and the other Ruth. Both of Naomi's sons died, leaving Ruth with the two widowed daughters-in-law. When the drought ended, Naomi planned to return to Judah. She bid her daughters-in-law goodbye and told them to return to their families. Orpah returned, but Ruth pleaded to go with her and make Naomi's home her home, and Naomi's God her God. The two women went on to Bethlehem. They arrived at harvest time and upon her return, Naomi told her people to call her Mara (bitter) because of her misfortune.

RUTH 2

Verse 20: *"The LORD bless him!" Naomi said to her daughter-in-law. "He has not stopped showing his kindness to the living and the dead." She added, "That man is our close relative, he is one of our kinsman-redeemers."*

Ruth went to the fields to pick up leftover grain. There she met Boaz, a wealthy landowner and relative of Naomi. Boaz was very nice to her, allowing her to work with his servants and offering her water from his jars. He had heard her story and asked that the LORD bless her, then he gave her some bread and wine and had his harvesters save some choice grain for her. She brought home grain to Naomi and told her of Boaz's kindness.

RUTH 3

Verse 9: *"Who are you?" he asked, "I am your servant Ruth," she said. "Spread the corner of your garment over me, since you are a kinsman-redeemer."*

Naomi instructed Ruth to meet Boaz on the threshing floor. She did so, and lay at his feet. Boaz discovered her in the middle of the night and promised to look after her. He gave her six measures of barley to take to Naomi.

RUTH 4

Verse 11: *Then the elders and all those at the gate said, "We are witnesses. May the LORD make the woman who is coming into your home like Rachel and Leah, who together built up the house of Israel. May you have standing in Ephrathah and be famous in Bethlehem."*

Boaz met with the elders and the other kinsman-redeemer and gained permission to marry Ruth and provide for Naomi. Boaz married Ruth and they had a son, Obed. Obed was the father of Jesse, who was the father of David.

Chapter 9

1 SAMUEL

1 SAMUEL 1

Verse 15: *"Not so, my lord," Hannah replied, "I am a woman who is deeply troubled. I have not been drinking wine or beer; I was pouring out my soul to the LORD."*

Elkanah, son of Jeroham, lived in the hill country of Ephraim and had two wives, Hannah and Peninnah. Peninnah had children, but Hannah did not. Hannah was very sad that she had no children and prayed to the LORD for a son. She promised that if He would give her one, she would turn him over to the LORD. Eli the priest observed Hannah praying and thought she was drunk. When Hannah assured him that she was not but was earnestly praying to the LORD, Eli asked God to grant her request. Hannah conceived and gave birth to a son, and named him Samuel. After he was weaned, Hannah took Samuel with a sacrifice offering to the temple at Shiloh. Hannah gave her son to Eli to serve the LORD.

1 SAMUEL 2

Verse 25: *"If a man sins against another man, God may mediate for him; but if a man sins against the LORD, who will intercede for him?" His sons, however, did not listen to their father's rebuke, for it was the LORD's will to put them to death.*

Hannah praised the LORD for her son, recognizing God's greatness. Eli's own sons were evil and did not obey the law regarding the priest's portions of sacrificed meat, and they were treating the LORD's offering with contempt. Eli prayed for Hannah, and she had three more sons and two daughters. Eli heard about his sons' evil deeds, which also included sleeping with women at the temple. When Eli confronted them, they ignored him and continued their wicked ways. A messenger of the LORD came to Eli and promised that they would be punished for their sins. He noted that his two sons would be killed on the same day and that the LORD would raise up a faithful priest to honor Him.

1 SAMUEL 3

Verse 1: *The boy Samuel ministered before the LORD under Eli. In those days the word of the LORD was rare; there were not many visions.*

Samuel ministered before the LORD under Eli. The LORD called to Samuel one night, but Samuel thought that Eli had called him, and he went to him. This happened three times. Then Eli realized that it was the LORD who was calling Samuel. Eli told Samuel to say, "Speak, for your servant is listening" when he was called again. The LORD told him about His plans to punish Eli and his sons. The next morning, after Eli insisted, Samuel told Eli about his vision. Eli accepted this word from God without protest. Samuel grew up as a prophet recognized throughout the land.

1 SAMUEL 4

Verse 22: *She said, "The glory has departed from Israel, for the ark of God has been captured."*

The Israelites were fighting the Philistines and were losing. Therefore, they sent for the Ark of the Covenant from Shiloh to help them in battle. Eli's two sons, Hophni and Phinehas arrived with the Ark to the sounds of cheers. The Philistines learned that the Ark had arrived and they were afraid. Nevertheless, the Philistines won the battle, killed thirty thousand Israelite soldiers including Eli's two sons, and captured the Ark. A soldier told Eli the news and he fell off his chair, broke his neck, and died. That same day, Eli's daughter-in-law, who was pregnant, heard the news that both her husband and father-in-law died, and went into labor. She died giving birth to a son, who was named Ichabod.

1 Samuel 5

Verse 11: *So they called together all the rulers of the Philistines and said, "Send the ark of the god of Israel away; let it go back to its own place, or it will kill us and our people. For death had filled the city with panic; God's hand was very heavy upon it."*

The Philistines took the Ark and put it in the temple of the pagan god Dagon in Ashdod. When they awoke the next morning, they found Dagon had fallen on his face in front of the Ark. They put him upright, but the same thing occurred the following day. This time Dagon's head and hands were broken off and lying on the threshold. The LORD brought devastation to the people of Ashdod; so they moved the Ark to Gath. Again, the Ark brought trouble to this city, so they moved it again, this time to Ekron. The people of Ekron had heard about the Ark and there was a public outcry.

1 Samuel 6

Verse 18b: *The large rock, on which they set the ark of the LORD, is a witness to this day in the field of Joshua of Beth Shemesh.*

The Philistines decided to return the Ark to Israel. The Philistine priests and diviners told them that they needed to send a guilt offering of gold along with it. They told them to place it in a cart hitched to two cows that have never been yoked. The Philistines did as they were told, and the cart went directly toward Israel and Beth Shemesh where a sacrifice of the cart and cows was made to the LORD. The LORD put seventy men from Beth Shemesh to death because they looked into the Ark. They sent word to the people of Kiriath Jearim asking them to come and pick up the Ark.

1 Samuel 7

Verse 12: *Then Samuel took a stone and set it up between Mizpah and Shen. He named it Ebenezer, saying, "Thus far has the LORD helped us."*

The Ark was picked up and taken to Abinadab's house, where it remained for twenty years. His son Eleazar was selected to guard it. Samuel told all the people that if they would give up all of their pagan gods and worship only the LORD, He would deliver them out of the hand of the Philistines. Samuel had them all assemble at Mizpah so he could appeal to the LORD. They did so, and the Philistines attacked just while Samuel was making a burnt offering. Loud thunder was heard and the Philistines were routed. Samuel placed a stone between Mizpah and Shen naming it Ebenezer (stone of help) and the Philistines did not invade again. Samuel served as a judge over Israel for his whole life and built an altar to the LORD in Ramah, his home.

1 Samuel 8

Verse 7: *And the LORD told him, "Listen to all that the people are saying to you; it is not you they have rejected, but they have rejected me as their king."*

When Samuel grew old, he appointed his sons as judges. They were not righteous, however, and the elders of Israel gathered and asked Samuel to appoint a king. Samuel was displeased and prayed to the LORD. The LORD told Samuel that it was not he who the people had rejected, but God, their true King, by asking for a king to be named. Based upon the LORD's instructions, Samuel told the people that if he named a king, the king would enlist their men to support the army and their daughters to support his household. He would take the best servants and animals for his use and tax their resources. The people still wanted a king.

1 Samuel 9

Verse 17: *When Samuel caught sight of Saul, the LORD said to him, "This is the man I spoke to about; he will govern my people."*

Kish, who lived in Benjamin, lost some donkeys so he sent his son Saul to find them. Saul, who was a foot taller than any other Israelite, set off with his servant and they journeyed through the land to find the donkeys. They eventually decided to ask Samuel for assistance before they returned to their home. Samuel was not surprised to see them because the LORD had told him that a man would arrive from Benjamin whom Samuel was to anoint as king. Samuel greeted Saul and asked him to stay with him. He assured Saul that the donkeys had been found. Saul and his servant stayed with Samuel and he escorted them to the edge of the town. Samuel told Saul's servant to go ahead, because Samuel wanted to deliver a message from God to Saul.

1 SAMUEL 10

Verse 9: *As Saul turned to leave Samuel, God changed Saul's heart, and all these signs were fulfilled that day.*

Samuel anointed Saul and gave him instructions for his return. He told Saul that two men would meet him telling him about the donkeys, others would offer him bread and wine, and that he would meet a procession of prophets. Saul did just as he was instructed and returned to his home. Samuel assembled all of the people of Israel in Mizpah to choose a king. He first selected the tribe of Benjamin, then Saul from that tribe. Saul was not immediately present and the LORD said he had hidden himself amongst the baggage. They brought him out and he was made king. Samuel explained the regulations of the kingship to the people; and he was accepted as king by most, but not all.

1 SAMUEL 11

Verse 6: *When Saul heard their words, the Spirit of God came upon him in power, and he burned with anger.*

Nahash led the Ammonites against Israel at Jabesh Gilead. The men of Jabesh offered to surrender, but Nahash refused unless he could gash out the right eye of every man in the city. Word came to Saul and he was angered. He cut up his pair of oxen and sent them to all of the territories of Israel, threatening the same to anyone who did not follow him. Three hundred thousand men of Israel mustered at Bezek to opposed thirty thousand Ammonites. Saul separated his men and slaughtered the Ammonites. All of the people went to Gilgal and Saul was confirmed as king in the presence of the LORD.

1 SAMUEL 12

Verse 23: *As for me, far be if from me that I should sin against the LORD by failing to pray for you. And I will teach you the way that is good and right.*

Samuel gave the people his farewell speech, first confirming to them that he did not owe anyone anything, then reminding them of their heritage. He reaffirmed Saul as king, and told them to obey the LORD. Samuel called down thunder and rain from the LORD so that they would realize what an evil thing it was to insist upon having a king. He told them that even though they have been evil, if they served the LORD with all their hearts and turned away from idols, the LORD would not reject them. He told them that if they persisted in doing evil both they and their king would be swept away.

1 SAMUEL 13

Verse 14: *But now your kingdom will not endure; the LORD has sought out a man after his own heart and appointed him leader of his people, because you have not kept the LORD's command.*

Saul was thirty years old when he became king and he reigned for forty-two years. He chose three thousand men for his army and attacked the Philistine outpost at Geba. A huge battle ensued and all the Israelite men were again called. A Philistine force with thousands of chariots and men assembled and prepared to attack. Saul, afraid of the impending attack, offered a burnt offering to the LORD. Samuel arrived and asked Saul what he had done. The offering was exclusively Samuel's to offer, and Saul did not keep the LORD's command. Samuel told Saul that if he had kept the command, the LORD would have established Saul's kingdom over Israel for all time; now it would not last. Samuel left with many of Saul's men, leaving Saul and his son Jonathan with six hundred men. The battle ensued, but the Israelites had nothing but plowshares, axes, and sickles as weapons.

1 SAMUEL 14

Verse 15: *Then panic struck the whole army—those in the camp and field, and those in the outposts and raiding parties—and the ground shook. It was a panic sent by God.*

Jonathan set out on his own to attack an outpost of the Philistines. He told his armor-bearer that if the Philistines told them to climb up to them it would be a sign from the LORD that they would overcome them. The Philistines told them to climb up, and they attacked and killed twenty Philistines. Saul assembled his army and attacked the Philistines. Panic and confusion struck the whole Philistine army, and they attacked each other, so the LORD rescued the Israelites. Saul had made his entire army promise under oath that as a tribute to God, they would not eat that day. Jonathan did not hear this, and ate honey and his eyes brightened. The soldiers warned Jonathan about his father's oath, but instead, Jonathan encouraged the soldiers to eat also. The men killed the Philistine livestock and began eating. Saul built an altar and had all of the meat brought to it. He cast lots and determined that it was Jonathan who had disobeyed his command. Saul was prepared to put his son to death for his disobedience, but his men pleaded to spare him because he had initiated the successful battle against the Philistines. Saul went on to fight other enemies—Moab, Amon, Edom, and Zobah. He fought valiantly for Israel. In addition to Jonathan, Saul's other sons were Ishvi and Malki-Shua. He was at war with the Philistines during the entire time of his reign and was always looking for brave men for his army.

1 SAMUEL 15

Verse 23: *For rebellion is like the sin of divination, and arrogance like the evil of idolatry. Because you have rejected the word of the LORD, he has rejected you as king.*

Samuel instructed Saul to completely destroy the Amalekites for what they had done to Israel. Saul mustered his men. He attacked and destroyed the kingdom, but spared the king of Agag and kept all of the livestock. The LORD was grieved because Saul did not carry out His instructions to *completely* destroy the Amalekites. Samuel told Saul that the LORD was angered. Saul said he did carry out His orders and that the soldiers took the livestock to make sacrifices to the LORD. Saul begged for forgiveness, but Samuel refused. They worshiped together, Samuel asked to see Agag, then put him to death by the sword. Saul and Samuel did not meet again, and the LORD was grieved that He had made Saul king.

1 SAMUEL 16

Verse 7: *But the LORD said to Samuel, "Do not consider his appearance or his height, for I have rejected him. The LORD does not look at the things man looks at. Man looks at the outward appearance but the LORD looks at the heart."*

The LORD told Samuel to quit mourning for Saul and prepare to anoint one of Jesse's sons from Bethlehem as king. He arrived in Bethlehem and invited all to a sacrifice to the LORD. Jesse's sons passed before him, but none were chosen. Samuel asked if that were all of his sons, and Jesse replied that the youngest was tending sheep. He was sent for, and when he arrived, the LORD instructed that he be anointed as king. Saul was being tormented by an evil spirit and had heard that Jesse's youngest son played the harp, so he sent for him. Saul liked him very much and asked that David be allowed to stay with him.

1 SAMUEL 17

Verse 47: *All those gathered here will know that it is not by sword or spear that the LORD saves; for the battle is the LORD's, and he will give all of you into our hands.*

The Philistines were preparing for battle against the Israelites and they stood on opposite hills. A nine-foot armored giant named Goliath came out of the Philistine camp challenging the Israelites to fight one-on-one with him—winner take all. David went back and forth between Saul's camp and home to tend sheep. His father, Jesse, sent him back to the front with bread for his oldest brothers who were in Saul's camp. David witnessed Goliath's challenge and heard that great wealth and the king's daughter was offered for anyone who would slay Goliath. David's oldest brother, Eliab, chastised David for coming to the front. When Saul overheard what David had said, he sent for him. David told Saul that he would fight Goliath. Saul responded that he was only a boy and Goliath had been fighting from his youth. David told Saul that he had killed lions and bears while tending sheep, and if the LORD delivered him from them, then surely He would do the same against the Philistine. The king outfitted David in his own armor, but David was not comfortable in the outfit, and took them off. He selected five stones and brought his sling. Goliath approached and asked if he was a dog because David came at him with sticks. David replied that he came against Goliath in the name of the LORD. He took a stone, slung it, hit Goliath in the forehead and knocked him down. Then David killed Goliath with Goliath's sword and cut off his head with it. The Philistines ran and the Israelites chased after them, killing them along the way. They plundered the Philistine camp and returned victorious. Saul asked David whose son he was, and he said he was the son of Jesse.

1 SAMUEL 18

Verse 1: *After David had finished with Saul, Jonathan became one in spirit with David, and he loved him as himself.*

Jonathan, Saul's son, became close friends with David and even gave him his robe. David was successful in all missions that Saul gave him, and he earned a high rank in the army. Saul saw that the people were praising David's feats, and became jealous of him. The next day, an evil spirit overcame Saul and he tried to kill David with a spear twice. Saul sent David away with a thousand men, and he was successful in all of his campaigns. Saul offered his first daughter, Merab, to David in marriage but David refused, asking who was he to become the king's son-in-law. Saul's second daughter, Michal, was in love with David, and so Saul gave David a second chance to be his son-in-law. Saul thought that David would fall to the Philistines trying to meet his demand, because he asked David to bring him one hundred of their foreskins in exchange for his daughter. David brought Saul two hundred foreskins and married Michal. Saul realized that the LORD was with David and remained his enemy. David continued to be a successful leader in battle, and his name became well known.

1 SAMUEL 19

Verse 4: Jonathan spoke well of David to Saul his father and said to him, "Let not the king do wrong to his servant David; he has not wronged you, and what he has done has benefited you greatly."

Saul told Jonathan and all of his attendants to kill David. Jonathan warned David of his father's plans. Jonathan promised to talk to his father, and Saul promised not to kill David. Later, Saul tried to spear David, but he escaped with Michal's help. Michal put an idol in David's bed under the covers. When Saul attempted to kill David, he discovered that he was not there and questioned Michal. David escaped to Naioth at Ramah. Saul sent three separate sets of men after him, but each time the men arrived, they were caught up with Samuel and a group of prophets there and began prophesying. Finally, Saul himself went to Naioth, but he himself was caught up and lay powerless all night.

1 SAMUEL 20

Verse 42: Jonathan said to David, "Go in peace, for we have sworn friendship with each other in the name of the LORD, saying, 'The LORD is witness between you and me, and between your descendants and my descendants forever.'" Then David left, and Jonathan went back to the town.

David fled and asked Jonathan what his crime was that Saul was attempting to take his life. Jonathan promised to warn David if his life was at stake. He arranged a signal to David regarding arrows that he would shoot at a target. When Saul saw that David was not at his table he was angered, and told Jonathan to find him and bring him to Saul so that he could kill him. Jonathan pleaded with Saul, but Saul threw his spear at him; so Jonathan knew his father was serious. Jonathan gave the signal to David that his life was in danger and bid goodbye to his friend.

1 Samuel 21

Verse 6: *So the priest gave him the consecrated bread, since there was no bread there except the bread of the Presence that had been removed from before the Lord and replaced by hot bread on the day it was taken away.*

David went to Nob and visited Ahimelech the priest, not telling him of his plight. The priest gave him food and the sword that David used to kill Goliath. David fled to Achish king of Gath. While there, he became concerned for his safety and feigned that he was insane, then left the territory.

1 Samuel 22

Verse 2: *All those who were in distress or in debt or discontented gathered around him, and he became their leader. About four hundred men were with him.*

David left Gath and escaped to the cave of Adullam. Four hundred men met with him there, including his family. From there he went to Moab and met with the king. With his permission, he left his parents with the king and returned to Judah, as the prophet Gad had told him. Saul learned that David had visited Ahimelech and sent for the priest. He confronted Ahimelech and the other priests and sentenced him to die for not telling him about David, but his guards refused to kill the priests. The king ordered Doeg, his Edomite servant to kill them, and he murdered all eighty-five priests. He also put to the sword the entire town of Nob. Ahimelech's son Abiathar escaped and joined David.

1 Samuel 23

Verse 16: *And Saul's son Jonathan went to David at Horesh and helped him find strength in God.*

David learned that the Philistines were attacking Keilah. He inquired of the Lord as to whether he should attack, and the Lord told him to do so. He asked a second time and again was told that the Lord would deliver the Philistines to him. He was successful in saving the town of Keilah and conquered the Philistines. Saul learned of this and assembled his men to trap and besiege David and his men at Keilah. After inquiring of the Lord, David and his men escaped and went on the run. Jonathan went to David at Horesh pledging his support. The Ziphites went to Saul and promised to hand David over to him, so Saul asked them to spy on David and let him know where he was hiding. Saul and his men pursued David and were about to catch him when word came to Saul that the Philistines were raiding the land. David escaped and went to the strongholds of En Gedi.

1 Samuel 24

Verse 6: *The Lord forbid that I should do such a thing to my master, the Lord's anointed, or lift my hand against him; for he is the anointed of the Lord.*

After pursuing the Philistines, Saul took three thousand men and went out after David again. While Saul was relieving himself in a cave, David snuck up and cut off a corner of Saul's robe, but spared his life. David pleaded with Saul to realize that he had done no wrong and was not his enemy. Saul told David that David was more righteous than he was. He asked that the Lord treat David well for the way he treated Saul. He recognized David as the new king and asked him to spare his family and him.

1 Samuel 25

Verse 25: *May my lord pay no attention to that wicked man Nabal. He is just like his name—his name is Fool, and the folly goes with him. But as for me, your servant, I did not see the men my master sent.*

Samuel died and all of Israel mourned. David moved on to Maon and asked for provisions for his men from Nabal, a wealthy landowner. The man refused, so David and his men armed themselves. In the meantime, Nabal's wife Abigail prepared food for David and his men and loaded it on donkeys. Abigail met David and humbled herself, asking for forgiveness for Nabal's foolishness. David thanked her, telling her that he was about to destroy Nabal's entire household. When Nabal learned later what had occurred, he became senseless, and died ten days later. David asked Abigail to become his wife. He also married Ahinoam of Jezreel. Saul gave David's first wife, Michal, away to another man.

1 Samuel 26

Verse 19: *Now let my lord the king listen to his servant's words. If the LORD has incited you against me, then may he accept an offering. If, however, men have done it, may they be cursed before the LORD! They have now driven me from my share in the LORD's inheritance and have said, "Go, serve other gods."*

The Ziphites told Saul that David was in Hakilah. Saul took three thousand men and set out after David. David went into Saul's camp and stood over Saul and Abner, his army commander. They were both sleeping. Again, David spared Saul's life, because he did not want to kill the one whom God had anointed. He took Saul's spear and water bottle and returned to his own camp. David then called out to Abner and admonished him for not taking better care of the king. Saul heard him and called out to David. David asked Saul why he was still pursuing him. Saul admitted that he had sinned and asked David to come back. David said that as surely as he valued Saul's life that day, so may the LORD value David's life and deliver him from all trouble. David went on his way, and Saul returned home.

1 Samuel 27

Verse 12: *Achish trusted David and said to himself, "He has become so odious to his people, the Israelites, that he will be my servant forever."*

David and his men were still concerned that Saul would eventually capture them and went to the Philistines for protection. When Saul learned what David had done, he did not pursue him. David asked Achish, king of the Philistines, for a place to settle, and he was given Ziklag where they lived for sixteen months. David and his men raided Israel and other areas, each time leaving no survivors so no one would know it was they. Achish believed that because of his actions, David would be his servant forever.

1 Samuel 28

Verse 15b: *"I am in great distress," Saul said, "The Philistines are fighting against me, and God has turned away from me. He no longer answers me, either by prophets or by dreams. So I have called on you to tell me what to do."*

The Philistines gathered to fight Israel. Achish told David that he must accompany them and made him his bodyguard. Saul gathered the Israelites and asked the LORD what to do, but received no answer. Therefore, he disguised himself and went to a medium in Endor who conjured up Samuel for him to consult. She then recognized that he was Saul and was afraid for her life. Samuel asked Saul why he had disturbed him. Saul asked for Samuel's help, but he said that the LORD had done what he had predicted and given the kingship to David because of Saul's disobedience. He told him that the LORD will hand over both Israel and Saul to the Philistines and that Saul and his sons would join him (in death) the next day. Saul was despondent, but the woman and Saul's men insisted that he eat, which he did, then they left.

1 SAMUEL 29

Verse 6: *So Achish called David and said to him, "As surely as the LORD lives, you have been reliable, and I would be pleased to have you serve with me in the army. From the day you came to me until now I have found no fault in you, but the rulers don't approve of you."*

The Philistines gathered for battle, and their commander asked about the Hebrews that were with King Achish. Achish told them that David had been with him for a year. The commander insisted that they send them back, and Achish asked David to return. David asked what he had done wrong, and Achish replied nothing, but the commanders had insisted. So David and his men returned to Philistia.

1 SAMUEL 30

Verse 6: *David was greatly distressed because the men were talking of stoning him; each one was bitter in spirit because of his sons and daughters. But David found strength in the LORD his God.*

When David and his men returned, they found that the Amalekites had raided Negev and Ziklag. All of their wives and children had been taken captive. David asked the LORD if he should pursue the raiders, and the LORD told him to do so. When they reached the Besor Ravine, two hundred of his men were too exhausted to continue, so they stayed and the other four hundred continued. They went after the Amalekites and came across one of their abandoned slaves. The slave promised to show them the way if they would not kill him. David found the Amalekites and recaptured all of the plunder. When they returned to the two hundred men they had left behind, some of the four hundred men did not want to share the Amalekite plunder with them. David ignored these protests, and gave an equal share to all of his men as well as sending some to the elders and his friends and neighbors.

1 SAMUEL 31

Verse 13: *Then they took their bones and buried them under a tamarisk tree at Jabesh, and they fasted seven days.*

The Philistines fought Israel and overtook them, killing all of Saul's sons. Saul himself was critically wounded. He asked his armor-bearer to kill him, but he refused, so Saul fell on his own sword. After seeing this, the armor-bearer did the same. The Philistines took Saul and put his armor in their temple and fastened his body to a wall. The Israelites later retrieved it and buried Saul. The Philistines ruled over all of Israel.

2 SAMUEL

2 SAMUEL 1

Verse 23: *Saul and Jonathan—in life they were loved and gracious, and in death they were not parted. They were swifter than eagles, they were stronger than lions.*

David and his men stayed in Ziklag. Three days after the Philistine victory, an Amalekite from Saul's camp arrived and told David the news that the king and his sons had died. David questioned him, and he recounted that he actually helped Saul kill himself. He brought David the king's crown and armband. David and his men mourned. David then killed the Amalekite for killing the LORD's anointed. David lamented Saul and Jonathan's death with a tribute that he had his men memorize.

2 SAMUEL 2

Verse 7: *Now then, be strong and brave, for Saul your master is dead, and the house of Judah has anointed me king over them.*

David asked the Lord if he should go to Judah, and the LORD told him to go to Hebron. When he arrived, the men of Judah anointed David king of Judah. Abner, the commander of Saul's army, made Saul's only remaining son, Ish-Bosheth, king over Israel. Abner, Ish-Bosheth and the other leaders went to Gibeon and met with David and his men, including Joab. Abner proposed to Joab that the young men should fight hand to hand in front of them. They agreed, but things quickly escalated. During the fight, Abner killed Joab's brother Asahel. David's men won the battle, killing three hundred and sixteen of Abner's men. Only nineteen of David's men were missing. Abner and his men marched through the night and arrived in Mahanaim the following day. David's men, led by Joab, marched through the night and returned to Hebron by daybreak.

2 SAMUEL 3

Verse 28: *Later, when David heard about this, he said, "I and my kingdom are forever innocent before the LORD concerning the blood of Abner son of Ner."*

The war between the tribes of northern Israel and Judah continued for years. David became stronger and the house of Saul weaker. David had six sons from six wives while he was in Hebron. His first son was Amnon. Ish-Bosheth accused Abner of sleeping with his father's concubine, and this angered Abner. Abner sent messengers to David, offering to come over to his side. David agreed, but insisted that Abner bring Michal back to him as his wife. Abner agreed and began preparations for David to become king over all of Israel. Joab arrived just as Abner was leaving from meeting with David. Joab questioned David, and asked why he let him go because Joab thought he was trying to deceive David. Joab sent word to Abner and met him in private. He then killed him to avenge the death of his brother. David was distraught and laid the guilt solely on Joab. David fasted, and all the people knew that David had nothing to do with Abner's murder.

2 SAMUEL 4

Verse 4: *Jonathan son of Saul had a son who was lame in both feet. He was five years old when the news about Saul and Jonathan came from Jezreel. His nurse picked him up and fled, but as she hurried to leave, he fell and became crippled. His name was Mephibosheth.*

Ricab and Bannah, who were leaders of raiding bands, snuck into the inner house of Ish-Bosheth and murdered him. There were no other surviving heirs, except for Jonathan's son Mephibosheth who was lame in both feet. The raiders brought Ish-Bosheth's head to David expecting a reward. David was angered, and had both of the raiders killed for murdering an innocent man.

2 SAMUEL 5

Verse 12: *And David knew that the LORD had established him as king over Israel and had exalted his kingdom for the sake of his people Israel.*

All of the tribes of Israel came to David and asked him to become king, so the elders came to Hebron and anointed him king over all of Israel. David was thirty years old when he became king and he reigned for forty years (including the seven and one half years that he reigned over Judah). David and his men attacked the Jebusites and overtook Jerusalem. He made Jerusalem the capital of Israel and lived there in the LORD's favor. Hiram, king of Tyre, helped build David a palace. David had more wives and children and was successful in Jerusalem. The Philistines gathered to attack the Israelites, and he consulted the LORD and was advised to attack them. He attacked them and carried off the plunder. The Philistines attacked again, and this time the LORD advised him to encircle them. When he did, he struck down the Philistines.

2 SAMUEL 6

Verse 21: *David said to Michal, "It was before the LORD, who chose me rather than your father or anyone from his house when he appointed me ruler over the LORD's people Israel—I will celebrate before the LORD."*

David picked thirty thousand men to bring the Ark of the Covenant to Jerusalem. En route, Uzzah, one of Abinadab's sons, grabbed the Ark to keep it from falling. Because he violated the instructions that the LORD had given regarding the Ark, the LORD struck him dead. When they reached Jerusalem, David, who was still upset about the death of Uzzah, left the Ark in the house of Obed-Edom for three months. After he heard of the blessings that the Ark had bestowed upon the house of Obed-Edom, he brought the Ark into Jerusalem (the City of David). There was a great celebration, and they made offerings to the LORD. When David arrived home, Michal was angry with him for dancing during the celebration. David justified his actions, and the LORD punished Michal by denying her any children during her lifetime.

2 SAMUEL 7

Verse 13: *He is the one who will build a house for my Name, and I will establish the throne of his kingdom forever.*

David spoke to the prophet Nathan and asked whether he should build a temple for the LORD. The LORD spoke to Nathan and told him to tell David not to build the temple. David would be a great ruler of Israel, but the task of building a temple would fall to his offspring. He was told that David's throne would be established forever. David praised the LORD, noting that His name would be great forever. He asked for His blessings over Israel.

2 SAMUEL 8

Verse 15: *David reigned over all Israel, doing what was just and right for all his people.*

During his reign, David defeated the Philistines, the Moabites, and many others. When he defeated Zobah, he hamstrung hundreds of their chariot horses. He also stuck down the Arameans and killed twenty-two thousand of them, taking their gold shields and bronze. He also defeated Edom and Ammon, and Amalek. The LORD gave David victory wherever he went. Joab was his commander, Jehoshaphat was his recorder, Zadok and Ahimelech were his priests, Seraiah was secretary, Benaiah was an assistant, and his sons were his royal advisors.

2 SAMUEL 9

Verse 13: *And Mephibosheth lived in Jerusalem, because he always ate at the king's table, and he was crippled in both feet.*

David asked if there was anyone left from Saul's household to whom he could show kindness. He was told of Jonathan's son Mephibosheth, and David sent for him. David promised him all of the land that belonged to Saul and a place at his table. Mephibosheth had a young son named Mica.

2 SAMUEL 10

Verse 2: *David thought, "I will show kindness to Hanun son of Nahash, just as his father showed kindness to me."*

David sent goodwill messengers to Hanun, the new king of the Ammonites when the old king died. When they arrived, the Ammonite nobles advised the king that the messengers were there to spy on them, so Hanun had half of the beards shaved off and their garments cut off the men. When they returned, David was upset. When the Ammonites realized how angry David was, they hired thousands of soldiers. David sent out his army and Joab realized that there were armies on both sides of them, the Ammonites in front of them and the Arameans behind them.

He split his army and sent his best troops against the Arameans. The Arameans fled and both sides then attacked the Ammonites, but they retreated to their city. The Arameans regrouped and attacked Israel, but David and his men easily routed them. Therefore, the Arameans did not help the Ammonites any more.

2 SAMUEL 11

Verse 27: *After the time of mourning was over, David had her brought to his house, and she became his wife and bore him a son. But the thing David had done displeased the LORD.*

In the spring, David was in Jerusalem while Joab was out fighting battles. David saw a beautiful woman bathing while he was on his roof and sent someone to find out about her. He discovered her name was Bathsheba, and she was the wife of one of his officers named Uriah. David sent for her, slept with her, and she became pregnant, so David sent word to Joab to send Uriah to him. David met with Uriah and told him to spend the night in his own home. The next morning David discovered that Uriah had slept at his door. When questioned, Uriah said that he could not sleep in his own home when his men and the Ark were staying in tents. David told him to stay one more day and David invited him to eat and drink with him. Uriah slept on a mat with the servants that night. David instructed Uriah to return to Joab with a letter. In the letter, David told Joab to put Uriah on the front line and then withdraw from him. He did so, and Uriah was killed in battle. Bathsheba mourned the death of her husband, and then became David's wife; but the LORD was displeased.

2 SAMUEL 12

Verse 9: *Why did you despise the word of the LORD by doing what is evil in his eyes? You struck down Uriah the Hittite with the sword and took his wife to be your own. You killed him with the sword of the Ammonites.*

The LORD sent Nathan the prophet to David. Nathan told David a parable about a rich man who took a poor man's only lamb instead of one of his own to serve to a traveler. David said that the rich man should pay for the lamb four times over. Nathan then told David that he was like the rich man, and the LORD was angered by his actions against Uriah. The LORD said the sword would never leave David's house, and He promised that his wives would be given to those close to him and that they would lie together in broad daylight. He also told David that Bathsheba's son would die. Seven days later, despite David's fasting and praying, the child died.

David took it well, and comforted Bathsheba. They had another son, Solomon, who pleased the LORD. Nathan instructed David to name him Jedidiah (loved by the LORD). Joab sent word to David that he was about to conquer the Ammonites, and David mustered the entire army, captured the city of Rabbah, and took the crown from the head of their king. They took the plunder and returned to Jerusalem.

2 SAMUEL 13

Verse 39: *And the spirit of the king longed to go to Absalom, for he was consoled concerning Amnon's death.*

David's first son, Amnon fell in love with Tamar, his half-sister and his brother Absalom's full sister. His friend Jonadab told Amnon to pretend to be ill and have Tamar prepare food for him. She did, but he refused to eat and sent everyone but Tamar out of the room. When she approached, he grabbed her and raped her. He then sent her away. David and Absalom were both furious when they heard what had happened. Two years later, when they were away from Jerusalem, Absalom had Amnon murdered. The word came back to David that Absalom had murdered all of David's sons, but later it was clarified that only Amnon was killed. The other sons returned, and they mourned the death of their brother with David. Absalom fled to Talmai, the king of Geshur.

2 SAMUEL 14

Verse 14: *Like water spilled on the ground, which cannot be recovered, so we must die. But God does not take away life; instead, he devises ways so that a banished person may not remain estranged from him.*

Joab knew that David missed Absalom, so he had a women dress as if she was in mourning. The woman approached King David and convinced him to forgive her son who had murdered her other son. Eventually, David caught on and realized that Joab was behind this, but he had already promised not to harm the son. Joab went to Geshur and brought Absalom back to Jerusalem, but David refused to see his face. After two years of persistence, to the point of burning Joab's field, Absalom convinced Joab to allow him to approach the king. Absalom was allowed to see David and was forgiven.

2 SAMUEL 15

Verse 6: *Absalom behaved in this way toward all the Israelites who came to the king asking for justice, and so he stole the hearts of the men of Israel.*

Absalom tried to appoint himself as a judge, and tried to serve as an intermediary for the king by speaking to people as they came through the city gate. He asked David if he could go to Hebron to fulfill a vow he had made. The king let him, and he went to Hebron and tried to appoint himself king of Hebron. A messenger came to David and told him that the men of Israel wanted to follow Absalom. David packed up his household and left Jerusalem. The king told Ittai that he did not need to go with them, but he insisted. The people wept as the procession passed by. Zadok, the priest, led the group that carried the Ark out of the city. When they were all out, David told Zadok to return the Ark. David stated that if the LORD found favor with him, He would let him return. David also asked Zadok and Abiathar to go back so that he could get word from them later. David continued on to the Mount of Olives. He prayed that Ahithophel, Absalom's counselor, would give him bad advice. David greeted his friend Hushai, and he agreed to return to Jerusalem to frustrate Ahithophel's advice to Absalom for David. He arrived at Jerusalem just as Absalom entered the city.

2 SAMUEL 16

Verse 11: *David then said to Abishai and all his officials, "My son, who is of my own flesh, is trying to take my life. How much more, then, this Benjamite! Leave him alone; let him curse, for the LORD has told him to."*

Ziba (Saul's servant) greeted David with plenty of food and donkeys waiting for him. David asked him where Mephibosheth (Jonathan's son) was. He replied that Mephibosheth stayed in Jerusalem, hoping that Absalom would reward him. David told Ziba that all that was Mephibosheth's now belonged to Ziba. As they approached Bahurim, Shimei threw stones at David and his group, saying that he was getting what he deserved for killing Saul's household. David told Abishai to leave the man alone, because the LORD told him to curse David. Absalom greeted Hushai and asked why he was not with his friend David. He replied that he would serve whomever the people had appointed. Absalom asked Ahithophel for advice on what to do, and he told him to lie with his father's concubines. He did so in a tent on the roof, in the sight of all of Israel.

2 SAMUEL 17

Verse 14: *Absalom and all the man of Israel said, "The advice of Hushai the Arkite is better than that of Ahithophel." For the LORD had determined to frustrate the good advice of Ahithophel in order to bring disaster on Absalom.*

Ahithophel then advised Absalom to select twelve thousand men and pursue David. He recommended that he kill only his father, then bring all of the followers back to Jerusalem. Absalom also asked Hushai what he thought of this plan. Hushai told him it was not a good plan, because if David overthrew them Absalom would look foolish. Hushai proposed that Absalom should lead the entire army into battle and kill all of the men, not just David. Hushai then sent word to David to cross the Jordan to avoid the approaching troops. When Ahithophel saw that his advice was not followed, he hung himself. David went to Mahanaim and Absalom crossed the Jordan with his men in pursuit of David. Amasa was placed in charge of the army in place of Joab. When David and his men came to Mahanaim, the Ammonites gave them food and lodging.

2 SAMUEL 18

Verse 33: *The king was shaken. He went up to the room over the gateway and wept. As he went, he said: "O my son Absalom! My son, my son Absalom! If only I had died instead of you—O Absalom, my son, my son!"*

David divided his army into three groups. The commanders insisted that David stay behind, because he was worth ten thousand of them. David told the commanders to be gentle with Absalom. David's men defeated the Israelite army, killing twenty thousand men. During the battle, Absalom was riding a mule, and he got caught in a tree and hanged himself. While he was still alive, Joab plunged three javelins into Absalom's heart, then men buried Absalom under a large heap of rocks. David heard the news and was saddened.

2 SAMUEL 19

Verse 20b: *For I your servant know that I have sinned, but today I have come here as the first of the whole house of Joseph to come down and meet my lord the king.*

David grieved for his dead son. Joab confronted him and told David that he was humiliating the men who had won the battle for him. He told him to go encourage the men. The Israelites who were with Absalom fled to their homes. David won over the Israelites and promised he would appoint Amasa over Joab as commander of the army. They crossed the Jordan as heroes, and even Shimei, who had thrown stones at them on their way out of Israel, praised David and begged for forgiveness. David confronted Mephibosheth and asked why he did not go with him. Mephibosheth replied that he was lame and Ziba, his servant betrayed him and did not help him mount his donkey. David told them to divide the fields between them. David invited his Mahanaim host, Barzillai, to come with him, but he declined, saying that he was too old. He offered his servant Kimham to go with David, and he did. The men of Judah and the men of Israel had an argument over who had the greater claim over David.

2 SAMUEL 20

Verse 19b: *We are the peaceful and faithful in Israel. You are trying to destroy a city that is a mother in Israel. Why do you want to swallow up the LORD's inheritance?*

Sheba, a Benjamite, rebelled against David, and the Israelites began to follow him. Judah, however, still followed David. When he returned to Jerusalem, he put his ten concubines under house guard and did not sleep with them. David told Amasa to summon the men, but Amasa took longer than David allotted, so he appointed Abishai (Joab's brother) to command the men and they set out after Sheba. Amasa met up with the group and Joab stabbed and killed him. Joab and Abishai then went after Sheba. They attacked Sheba at Abel Beth Maacah. A wise woman told Joab not to destroy the city. Joab said that they would stop their siege if the people handed Sheba over to them. She went to the people of the city, and they cut off the head of Sheba and delivered it to Joab, who returned home with it. Joab regained his position as head of the army.

2 SAMUEL 21

Verse 14: *They buried the bones of Saul and his son Jonathan in the tomb of Saul's father Kish, at Zela in Benjamin, and did everything the king commanded. After that, God answered prayer in behalf of the land.*

There was a three-year famine and David asked the LORD why. He responded that it was because Saul had put the Gibeonites to death. David assembled the Gibeonites and asked how he could make amends. They asked for seven of Saul's male descendants to be given to them to be killed. The king did so, sparing Mephibosheth. As a gesture of respect to Saul's family, he gathered Saul and Jonathan's bones and gave them a proper burial. The Israelites and Philistines continued to battle and David went with his men. A Philistine named Ishbi-Benob tried to kill David, but Abishai saved his life. David's men insisted that David should never again go to battle so that the lamp of Israel would not be extinguished. During the course of the battles, David's men killed four descendants of Rapha in Gath.

2 SAMUEL 22

Verse 47: *The LORD lives! Praise be to my Rock! Exalted be God, the Rock, my Savior!*

David was delivered from all of his enemies and offered a song to the LORD. He noted that the LORD was his Rock and he praised His name.

2 SAMUEL 23

Verse 5: *Is not my house right with God? Has he not made with me an everlasting covenant, arranged and secured in every part? Will he not bring to fruition my salvation and grant me my every desire?*

David offered his last words, praising the LORD, noting that his house was right with God. All of David's mighty men were reviewed and their actions chronicled.

2 SAMUEL 24

Verse 24: *But the king replied to Araunah, "No, I insist on paying you for it. I will not sacrifice to the LORD my God burnt offerings that cost me nothing."*

The LORD incited David to take a census of Israel and Judah, because He was angry with Israel. David enlisted the help of Joab who reluctantly spent almost ten months counting all of the men in the land. There were eight hundred thousand able-bodied fighting men in Israel and five hundred thousand in Judah. David realized his foolishness in counting the men and asked God for forgiveness. The LORD gave David three options: Three years of famine, three months of fleeing from their enemies, or three days of plague. After consulting with Gad, David chose the last option. When the three days were over, seventy thousand had died. David saw the angel of the LORD killing the people and asked the LORD to stop and to let His hand fall upon David and his family. Gad told David to build an altar where he saw the angel, on the threshing floor of Araunah. Araunah bowed to the king and asked what he could do. David asked him if he could buy his threshing floor to build the altar. Araunah gave it to him, as well as oxen for sacrifice. David insisted upon buying it, and he built an altar and sacrificed to the LORD. Then the plague stopped.

Chapter 11

1 KINGS

1 KINGS 1

Verse 30: *I will surely carry out today what I swore to you by the LORD, the God of Israel: Solomon your son shall be king after me, and he will sit on my throne in my place.*

King David was growing old, so his servants sought out a young virgin, Abishag, to take care of him. The girl did so but did not have sexual relations with him. Before David named a successor, one of his sons, Adonijah, proclaimed himself king with the approval of Abiathar the priest and Joab the commander of the army. Nathan the prophet told Bathsheba, Solomon's (David's son) mother, of this development, and encouraged her to approach David. The king commanded that Solomon be named king, and had Zadok the priest perform the ordination in Gihon. Abiathar's son informed Adonijah what had occurred and was afraid. Solomon said that if Adonijah was worthy his life would be spared.

1 KINGS 2

Verse 27: *So Solomon removed Abiathar from the priesthood of the LORD, fulfilling the word the LORD had spoken at Shiloh about the house of Eli.*

David instructed Solomon on his deathbed to be strong and to walk with the LORD as king. He told him to deal strongly with Joab (who had killed two of his commanders), to be kind to the sons of Barzillai of Gilead, and to deal strongly with Shimei son of Gera. David, who had ruled for forty years, then died. Adonijah asked Bathsheba to ask Solomon if he could take Abishag as his wife. Solomon was offended, and had Adonijah put to death. Solomon spared Abiathar the priest, but did remove him from the priesthood. He named Zadok to replace Abiathar. He then had Joab put to death, and replaced him with a new commander (Benaiah). Solomon told Shimei that he would be spared as long as he remained in the Kidron Valley. He obeyed Solomon for three years, but then disobeyed. He was killed.

1 KINGS 3

Verse 13: *Moreover, I will give you what you did not ask for—both riches and honor—so that in your lifetime you will have no equal among kings.*

Solomon made an alliance with Pharaoh, king of Egypt, and married his daughter. Solomon walked with the LORD, except that he, like many of the people, worshiped idols in high places. The LORD appeared to Solomon in a dream at Gibeon and told him to ask for whatever he wanted. Solomon asked for a discerning heart to determine right from wrong. The LORD was pleased with this request and granted it. Solomon showed wisdom when he was asked to make a decision about a dispute between two women regarding who was the mother of a boy. The king told the women that he would cut the child in half and give one half to each of the women. One of the women was distraught with this decision and told the king to give the boy to the other woman in order to save his life. The king then knew that she was the rightful mother and dismissed the other woman. Word of Solomon's wisdom spread throughout the kingdom.

1 KINGS 4

Verse 25: *During Solomon's lifetime Judah and Israel, from Dan to Beersheba, lived in safety, each man under his own vine and fig tree.*

Solomon's chief officials were as follows:

Azariah	High Priest
Elihoreph and Ahijah	Secretaries
Jehoshaphat	Recorder
Benaiah	Commander-In-Chief

Zadok and Abiathar	Priests
Azariah	District Officer Chief
Zabud	Priest and Personal Advisor
Ahishar	Palace Chief
Adoniram	Labor Chief

In addition, there were twelve district governors and their territories:

Ben-Hur	Ephraim
Ben-Deker	Makaz, Shaalbim, Beth Shemesh, Elon Bethhanan
Ben-Hesed	Arubboth
Ben-Abinadab	Napoth Dor
Baana	Tannach, Megiddo, Beth Shan
Ben-Geber	Ramoth Gilead
Ahinadab	Mahanaim
Ahimaaz	Naphtali
Baana	Asher and Aloth
Jehoshaphat	Issachar
Shimei	Benjamin
Gerber	Gilead

Solomon lived well with abundant provisions. Solomon ruled with wisdom, as the LORD had promised.

1 KINGS 5

Verse 5: *I intend, therefore, to build a temple for the Name of the LORD my God, as the LORD told my father David, when he said, "Your son whom I will put on the throne in your place will build the temple for my Name."*

Hiram, king of Tyre, was friendly with Solomon, and therefore Solomon asked for the neighboring king's help in building a new temple for the LORD. Hiram agreed to allow the cedars of Lebanon to be used to this end in exchange for grain. Timber and stone were prepared for the temple.

1 KINGS 6

Verse 12: *As for this temple you are building, if you follow my decrees, carry out my regulations and keep all my commands and obey them, I will fulfill through you the promise I gave to David your father.*

Solomon began to build the temple, 480 years after the exodus from Egypt and in his fourth year as king. The finest masonry and wood was used for the temple. The LORD spoke to Solomon, assuring him of His promise to David if he followed His decrees. Cedar was used on the interior, and an inner sanctuary was built to hold the holy objects. Courtyards and altars were included in the design. The temple took seven years to complete.

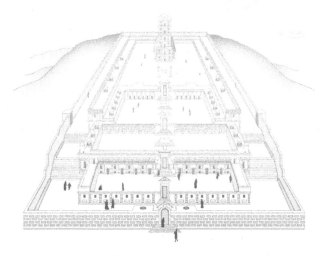

Figure 6: Solomon's Temple

1 KINGS 7

Verse 51: *When all the work King Solomon had done for the temple of the LORD was finished, he brought in the things his father David had dedicated—the silver and gold and the furnishings—and he placed them in the treasuries of the LORD's temple.*

After the temple was completed, Solomon spent the next 13 years constructing his palace. It also was made of cedar and had high-grade cut stone. Solomon had Huram do all of the bronze work for the temple including stands, basins, and pillars. The altar, table, lampstands, basins, and other items were made of gold.

1 Kings 8

Verse 30: *Hear the supplication of your servant and of your people Israel when they pray toward this place. Hear from heaven, your dwelling place, and when you hear, forgive.*

In a formal ceremony, the priests brought the Ark to the temple. Numerous sacrifices were made. The Ark held the two stone tablets that Moses was given. Then the glory of the Lord filled the temple. Solomon praised the Lord, and dedicated the temple. He asked God for forgiveness for the future transgressions of the Israelites. He then turned and blessed the whole assembly of Israel. Twenty-two thousand cattle and one hundred and twenty thousand sheep and goats were sacrificed.

1 Kings 9

Verse 8: *And though this temple is now imposing, all who pass by will be appalled and will scoff and say, "Why has the Lord done such a thing to this land and to this temple?"*

The Lord appeared to Solomon again and promised to continue to bless Israel as long as he followed His commands, but that the blessing would be taken away if he turned away from God. Solomon gave Hiram, king of Tyre, land and twenty towns in Galilee and 120 talents of gold as payment for all that he supplied to the building effort. Solomon used conscript labor from neighboring territories for the work. He made sacrifices at the temple three times a year. He also built ships and prospered.

1 Kings 10

Verse 9: *Praise be to the Lord your God, who has delighted in you and placed you on the throne of Israel. Because of the Lord's eternal love for Israel, he has made you king, to maintain justice and righteousness.*

The queen of Sheba visited Solomon and was impressed by the buildings and by the king's wisdom. The queen gave Solomon 120 talents of gold and precious stones and spices, and he gave the queen gifts in return. Solomon brought much gold to Israel on his ships and made gold shields, thrones, ornaments, and goblets. He prospered and accumulated much wealth, horses, chariots, and other splendor, and greatly expanded the territory of Israel.

Figure 7: Final Conquests of David and Solomon

1 KINGS 11

Verse 39: *I will humble David's descendants because of this, but not forever.*

King Solomon had many foreign wives, disobeying the LORD's instructions not to intermarry because of the risk of turning to their gods. Solomon did follow other gods and this angered the LORD. Solomon built high places for these gods. The LORD proclaimed to Solomon that his successor would be punished and that the kingdom would be divided because of his transgressions. Hadad, who also married into the family of Pharaoh of Egypt, planned to return to Edom and was an adversary to Solomon. Jeroboam, who was in charge of Solomon's labor force, also rebelled. Ahijah the prophet tore his cloak into twelve pieces, symbolic of the twelve tribes of Israel, and told Jeroboam that he would rule ten tribes. Ahijah told Jeroboam that the LORD promised him that he would be king of Israel (except for Judah) if he followed His ways. Solomon tried to kill Jeroboam, but he fled to Egypt and did not return until Solomon's death. Solomon ruled for forty years and was succeeded by his son, Rehoboam.

1 KING 12

Verse 28: *After seeking advice, the king made two golden calves. He said to the people, "It is too much for you to go up to Jerusalem. Here are your gods, O Israel, who brought you up out of Egypt."*

Rehoboam went to Shechem to be crowned king of all Israel. He was advised that he should lighten up on the people because they were worked so hard during his father's reign. Rehoboam consulted the elders, who recommended that he take this advice. He consulted his friends, and they advised that he make it even harder on the people. Rehoboam unwisely took the advice of the younger men, and the Israelites rebelled. They established Jeroboam as king of Israel (except for Judah). The tribe of Benjamin joined Judah, and they made plans to make war with Israel to reclaim the entire kingdom. God told Shemaiah to advise Rehoboam not to pursue the war. The people obeyed this advice. Jeroboam fortified the city of Shechem and lived there. Concerned that the people would return to Judah to worship at the temple, he made two golden calves for the people to worship instead, one in Bethel, and the other in Dan. He also built an altar in Bethel, and shrines to other gods in high places.

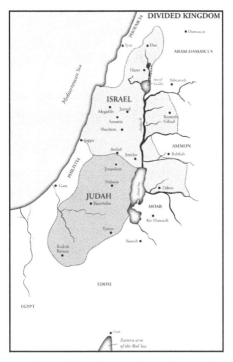

Figure 8: Divided Kingdoms and Neighboring Kingdoms

1 Kings 13

Verse 2: *He cried out against the altar by the word of the* Lord: *"O altar, altar! This is what the* Lord *says: 'A son named Josiah will be born to the house of David. On you he will sacrifice the priests of the high places who now make offerings here, and human bones will be burned on you.'"*

A man of God cried out against the altar and King Jeroboam and told him that he and his priests would be burned on that altar. He indicated that as a sign, the altar would split apart. Jeroboam ordered the man to be seized, but the altar split and Jeroboam's hand shriveled. Jeroboam pleaded with the man to intercede to the Lord on his behalf. He did, and Jeroboam's hand was restored. Jeroboam offered the man a reward and asked him to stay, but based upon the Lord's instructions, he replied that he must not eat or drink, but leave in a different direction than he came. An old prophet heard this story, and caught up with the man, telling him to return with him to eat and drink. When the man told the old prophet about his explicit instructions, the prophet told the man that an angel instructed him to have the man return with him, so he did. A lion killed the man on his trip home, and the prophet retrieved the body, mourned over it, and buried him. He instructed his sons to bury him next to the man when he died. Meanwhile, Jeroboam continued in his evil ways.

1 Kings 14

Verse 9: *You have done more evil than all who lived before you. You have made for yourself other gods, idols made of metal; you have provoked me to anger and thrust me behind your back.*

Jeroboam's son Abijah became ill and Jeroboam told his wife to disguise herself and seek counsel from the prophet Ahijah. Ahijah, warned by the Lord, recognized her, and told her that because of Jeroboam's evil ways her son would die when she returned home. The prophet also warned her of the woes to come for Israel. Abijah died at the exact time the woman got home, and he was buried. While Rehoboam reigned in Judah, idolatry, prostitution, and evil filled the land. Shishak, king of Egypt ransacked the temple and palace during Rehoboam's reign. There was continual warfare between Jeroboam and Rehoboam, who ruled for seventeen years until he died. He was succeeded by his son Abijah (not the son who died).

1 Kings 15

Verse 14: *Although he did not remove the high places, Asa's heart was fully committed to the LORD all his life.*

Abijah ruled for three years, and the evil ways continued. Asa became king of Judah, and did good in the eyes of the LORD. He reigned for forty-one years. War between Judah and Israel continued throughout Asa's reign. Asa made a treaty with Ben-Hadad of Aram, and Ben-Hadad broke his previous treaty with Israel, conquering many towns there. He also took all of the timber and stones that Baasha, king of Israel, was using in an attempt to fortify the city of Ramah. Nadab (Jeroboam's son) became king of Israel during the second year of Asa's reign in Judah. He was evil, and lasted less than two years. He was overthrown and killed by Baasha in a coup. Baasha killed the remainder of Jeroboam's family, and did evil as king of Israel. He reigned for twenty-four years.

1 Kings 16

Verse 30: *Ahab son of Omri did more evil in the eyes of the LORD than any of those before him.*

Elah succeeded Baasha but reigned for only two years. He also did evil in the LORD's eyes, and worshiped idols. Zimri, one of his officials, killed him and all of Baasha's family as foretold by the prophet Jehu. Zimri reigned for only seven days. Omri, the commander of the Israelite army, besieged Tirzah, where Zimri was encamped. Zimri set fire to his palace and died in the fire. Omri became king after he was chosen over Tibni and reigned for twelve years. Omri built the city of Samaria but did evil and sinned more than his predecessors. His son, Ahab, who was even more evil in the eyes of the LORD, succeeded him. He took a foreign wife, Jezebel and worshiped Baal. During his reign, Hiel rebuilt Jericho, losing two sons in the process (as prophesied by Joshua).

1 Kings 17

Verse 14: *For this is what the LORD, the God of Israel, says: "The jar of flour will not be used up and the jar of oil will not run dry until the day the LORD gives rain on the land."*

Elijah prophesied to Ahab that according to the LORD a major drought and famine would occur. God instructed Elijah to hide in the Kerith Ravine. He did so, drinking from the ravine and being fed by ravens. When the water dried up, the LORD told Elijah to proceed to Zarephath of Sidon. He did so and instructed a widow there to bring him water and a small piece of bread. The woman was preparing what she thought to be the last meal for herself and her son with the small bit of flour that she still had, but she obeyed Elijah. For this she was rewarded with a never-ending supply of flour and oil for her family. Elijah stayed with her for some time. At one point the widow's son became ill and died, but with the LORD's help, Elijah brought him back to life.

1 KINGS 18

Verse 37: *Answer me, O LORD, answer me, so these people will know that you, O LORD are God, and that you are turning their hearts back again.*

Based on the LORD's instructions, Elijah returned to Ahab and told him God would bring rain. Obadiah, a devout believer, was in charge of the King's palace. He had hidden 100 prophets in caves because Jezebel had sought to rid the kingdom of prophets, and chief amongst them was Elijah. Elijah and Obadiah met, and fearing for his own life, Obadiah was reluctant to bring Elijah to Ahab as he had asked. Elijah eventually persuaded him, and Elijah met Ahab. Elijah asked Ahab to assemble the people on Mount Carmel including the hundreds of prophets of the false gods Baal and Asherah. Ahab did so, and Elijah addressed the people. Elijah had two sacrifices prepared, one for Baal and one for the LORD. He had Baal's prophets ask their god to set fire to their sacrifice, but they were unsuccessful. As the only prophet of the LORD, he made a stone altar and then had the people throw water on the wood that he had prepared for his sacrifice. Elijah then called on the LORD, and fire burned the sacrifice and lapped up the water in the trenches. Elijah proclaimed that the LORD is God and had the Baal prophets seized and slaughtered. Elijah then told Ahab that rain would come, and the skies became black and it rained.

1 KINGS 19

Verse 10: *I have been very zealous for the LORD God Almighty. The Israelites have rejected your covenant, broken down your altars, and put your prophets to death with the sword. I am the only one left, and now they are trying to kill me too.*

Jezebel heard what had occurred, and she vowed revenge. Fearing for his life, Elijah fled. While in Beersheba in Judah he asked the LORD to take his life. An angel saved him and he traveled for 40 days and nights until he reached Horeb. The LORD appeared to him in a gentle whisper, following a wind, an earthquake and a fire. Elijah explained that the Israelites rejected His covenant, had false gods, and were trying to kill him, the only true prophet who remained. The LORD instructed him to go to the desert of Damascus and to appoint Hazel as king of Aram, Jehu as king of Israel, and Elisha to succeed Elijah as prophet. He noted that Jehu will put to death anyone who escapes from Hazel, and Elisha will put to death anyone who escapes from Jehu, except for the 7,000 Israelites who did not worship Baal. Elijah found Elisha plowing a field and told him to leave with him. Elisha became Elijah's attendant once he said good-bye to his parents.

1 KINGS 20

Verse 42: *He said to the king, "This is what the LORD says: 'You have set free a man I had determined should die. Therefore it is your life for his life, your people for his people.'"*

Ben-Hadad king of Aram attacked Samaria and sent word to Ahab to surrender. He was willing to do so until he met with the elders, and then he refused. A prophet instructed him to attack before Ben-Hadad was ready. Ahab defeated the Arameans, and then, based on advice from the prophet, strengthened his position for a repeat attack. They attacked again in the spring, and again the LORD allowed him to be victorious. Ben-Hadad pleaded with him for mercy, and promised that he would return all land previously captured in return. The LORD spoke through a prophet and informed Ahab that because he set Ben-Hadad free, he would die.

1 KINGS 21

Verse 25a: *There was never a man like Ahab, who sold himself to do evil in the eyes of the LORD, urged on by Jezebel his wife.*

Ahab asked to buy some property next to his palace to plant a garden, but Naboth the owner refused, indicating that the LORD forbade it. Jezebel learned of this and had Naboth killed. When Ahab took possession of the vineyard, The LORD instructed Elijah to visit him and tell him that he would perish. Ahab humbled himself before the LORD, and because of this, the LORD deferred his punishment to his heirs.

1 Kings 22

Verse 8: *The king of Israel answered Jehoshaphat, "There is still one man through whom we can inquire of the LORD, but I hate him because he never prophesies anything good about me, but always bad. He is Micaiah son of Imlah."*

There was no war between Aram and Israel for three years. However, the land that Aram promised to return was not turned over. Ahab asked Jehoshaphat, the king of Judah, what he should do about that situation. Jehoshaphat indicated that he would join him, but suggested that they consult the LORD first. Four hundred prophets all supported the decision to attack Aram, but Jehoshaphat suggested that they consult a true prophet. Ahab reluctantly agreed, because the prophet, Micaiah, always delivered bad news. When they called in Micaiah he agreed with the other prophets at first, but was not sincere. When questioned further, he predicted the defeat of the Israelites if they attacked Aram. He also told Ahab that an angel of the LORD put a lying spirit in all of the mouths of his prophets. Ahab had Micaiah imprisoned until their return, but Micaiah told them they never would return. Ahab disguised himself as a common soldier because he knew that the Arameans were trying to kill him. He was killed by a random arrow and was buried in Samaria. Jehoshaphat was king of Judah for 25 years and did good in the eyes of the LORD except that he did not remove all of the idols. He also built a fleet of ships but they were wrecked. His son Jehoram succeeded him. Ahab's son, Ahaziah, succeeded him and he also did evil in the eyes of the LORD.

2 KINGS

2 KINGS 1

Verse 3b: Is it because there is no God in Israel that you are going off to consult Baal-Zebub, the god of Ekron?

Moab rebelled after Ahab's death. Ahaziah, Ahab's son, was injured when he fell through the lattice of his upper room in Samaria. Ahab sent messengers to Baal-Zebub (a pagan deity) to ask him if he would recover. An angel interceded and sent the prophet Elijah to tell the messengers to return with the message that Ahaziah would never recover because he consulted the pagan god rather than the true God. Ahaziah sent a captain with 50 men to bring Elijah to him, but Elijah called down fire from heaven to consume them. Ahaziah sent another contingent and the same thing happened. Ahaziah sent a third group, and the captain begged Elijah to spare them. The angel told Elijah to go with them and he met with the king. He told Ahaziah that he would die for his transgressions, and shortly afterward, he did. Ahaziah had no son, so Joram succeeded him as king.

2 KINGS 2

Verse 10: *"You have asked for a difficult thing,"* Elijah said, *"yet if you see me when I am taken from you, it will be yours—otherwise not."*

Elijah and Elisha were traveling together. Elijah was about to be called up to heaven. He told Elisha to stay while he went to Bethel, then Jericho, and then the Jordan River. Each time Elisha insisted on going with him, and each time the people in the region asked Elisha if he knew that God was going to take Elijah that day. When they reached the Jordan, Elijah struck the water with his rolled up cloak and it parted, allowing them to cross. Elijah asked Elisha what he could do for him before he departed. Elisha asked for a double portion of his spirit. A chariot of fire and horses then arrived and took Elijah away. Elisha returned to the Jordan, found Elijah's cloak, and struck the water. Again, it parted, and Elisha crossed over. The men witnessed this searched for Elijah for three days to no avail. Elisha then made the water of the region pure and went to Bethel where he was jeered by some youths. Elisha called down a curse from the LORD and bears mauled the youths. Elisha continued on to Mount Carmel.

2 KINGS 3

Verse 17: *For this is what the LORD says: "You will see neither wind nor rain, yet this valley will be filled with water, and you, your cattle and your other animals will drink."*

Joram, king of Israel, committed evil in the sight of the LORD, but not like his parents. He got rid of the Baal stone but did not turn from other pagan gods. Mesha, king of Moab, rebelled against Israel and refused to deliver the lambs and wool that he owed to Israel. Joram mobilized his army and asked Jehoshaphat, king of Judah, to be his ally. The two kings also allied with the king of Edom and they set off through the desert of Edom. After seven days of futility, they consulted Elisha. The LORD instructed him to tell the kings to dig moats in the land and He would fill them with water. They did, and the moats were filled. Then they overtook Moab after the Moabites were fooled into thinking that the attackers were all slaughtered because the pools appeared to be filled with blood. Mesha tried a counter attack but was thwarted and he even sacrificed his son to the pagan gods as a last ditch effort to save his kingdom. The LORD was not happy with Joram, however, and sent the Israelites back to their home.

2 KINGS 4

Verse 43b: *But Elisha answered, "Give it to the people to eat. For this is what the LORD says: 'They will eat and have some left over.'"*

Elisha helped a woman whose husband had died and her creditors had threatened to take away her sons. He had her collect jars from all of her neighbors, then filled all of them with oil even though they started with very little oil. He instructed them to sell the oil to satisfy her debts. Elisha then performed two miracles for a Shunammite woman who was hospitable to him. He allowed her to have a son even though she and her husband were old, and when the son became ill and died, Elisha told them to lay his staff on the boy. This did not work, so Elisha prayed to the LORD and the boy was restored to life. Elisha also saved several prophets from being poisoned by adding flour to a contaminated pot of stew. Then he fed one hundred men with twenty small loaves of bread.

2 KINGS 5

Verse 18: *But may the LORD forgive your servant for this one thing: When my master enters the temple of Rimmon to bow down and he is leaning on my arm and I bow there also—when I bow down in the temple of Rimmon, may the LORD forgive your servant for this.*

Because he had heard of the feats of Elisha, the king of Aram sent Naaman, his army commander, to the king of Israel to cure his leprosy. Elisha had the man wash himself seven times in the Jordan. He reluctantly did so and was cured. Naaman acknowledged the God of Israel as the only God and offered Elisha a gift, but Elisha refused. Elisha's servant Gehazi pursued Naaman when he left and asked for some of the silver that Elisha had refused. Elisha learned of this and Gehazi and his descendants were punished with leprosy.

2 KINGS 6

Verse 16: *"Don't be afraid," the prophet answered. "Those who are with us are more than those who are with them."*

Elisha and his followers moved to the Jordan and began to build a community. An ax head fell into the water and Elisha performed another miracle, allowing the iron ax head to float so that it could be retrieved. Elisha reported to the king of Israel the Arameans' plans to attack them, and when the king of Aram found out, he sent his men to capture Elisha. When they attempted to do so, Elisha, protected by a spiritual army, prayed to the LORD that the men would be blinded, and they were. He led them to Samaria where the Israelite king fed them and sent them back to Aram. For some time after that the Arameans stopped raiding Israel. Later, Aram besieged Samaria and famine swept the city. A woman complained to the king of Israel that she and another woman were so hungry that they ate her son the day before with the agreement that they would eat the other woman's son the following day' but the other woman hid her son. The king was distraught and sent his servants to kill Elisha, whom he held responsible.

2 KINGS 7

Verse 2: *The officer on whose arm the king was leaning said to the man of God, "Look, even if the LORD should open the floodgates of the heavens, could this happen?" "You will see it with your own eyes," answered Elisha, "but you will not eat any of it!"*

Elisha told the servants that flour and barley would be available at a cheap price in Samaria the following day. In the morning, four lepers found the Aramean camp empty. They ate from their tents, carried away clothes, silver and gold, and hid them. They reported their findings to the gatekeepers, and after some men confirmed the findings, the people raided the camp, and Elisha's prophecy held true. The gatekeeper, who had been told by Elisha that he would not eat any of this food, was trampled by the people at the gate, fulfilling this prophecy as well.

2 KINGS 8

Verse 11: *He stared at him with a fixed gaze until Hazael felt ashamed. Then the man of God began to weep.*

Elisha told the Shunammite women whose son he brought back to life, to leave the area for seven years because of a famine that was about to begin. She did so, then returned seven years later, appearing before the king to ask for her land back. Gehazi was with the king telling him about the miracle of the woman's son just then. When she confirmed the story, the king gave back all of her land and income from it. Ben-Hadad, king of Aram, fell ill, and he sent his servant Hazael with gifts to meet Elisha. When asked, Elisha told Hazael that he should tell the king that he would not die of his illness, but in truth, he would. Elisha wept because he knew that Hazael would become king and inflict much punishment upon Israel. When Hazael returned, he murdered Ben-Hadad, and became king of Aram. Jehoshaphat's son Jehoram became king of Judah. He married a daughter of Ahab and did evil in the eyes of the LORD. The LORD spared Judah because of His promise to David. Edom rebelled against Judah and Jehoram was surrounded by the Edomites, but escaped. His son Ahaziah succeeded him as king after eight years. Ahaziah reigned for only one year. He joined Joram son of Ahab to fight against Aram. Joram was wounded and Ahaziah went to Jezreel to see him.

2 Kings 9

Verse 22: *When Joram saw Jehu he asked, "Have you come in peace, Jehu?" "How can there be peace," Jehu replied, "as long as all the idolatry and witchcraft of your mother Jezebel abound?"*

Elisha sent a messenger to anoint Jehu, son of Jehoshaphat and the commander of the army, as king. He was instructed to inflict the judgment of Elijah on the house of Ahab. He went to Jezreel and Joram and Ahaziah rode out to meet him. They were both killed, fulfilling the prophecy. Jehu then went to Jezreel and sought Jezebel, who was killed and trampled by horses and eaten by dogs, also fulfilling prophecy.

2 Kings 10

Verse 30: *Because you have done well in accomplishing what is right in my eyes and have done to the house of Ahab all I had in mind to do, your descendants will sit on the throne of Israel to the fourth generation.*

Jehu then set after Ahab's seventy descendants. He sent a letter to the elders and guardians of Ahab's children and instructed them to name the strongest of them and make him king. The elders were afraid and responded that they would do anything that Jehu asked, but they would not appoint a king. Jehu told them to behead all seventy of the princes and send him their heads. They did so and Jehu made peace with the remainder of the people. He then went to Samaria. He met relatives of Ahaziah king of Judah at Beth Eked and killed all forty-two men. He then met Jehonadab, son of Recab, and made him an ally. Then he proceeded to Samaria and killed all remaining descendants of Ahab's family. Jehu then called all of the priests of Baal together, allegedly to hold a great sacrifice. When all had assembled in the temple, he had them all killed and then destroyed the temple. Jehu did not, however, destroy the golden calves. Jehu remained as king of Israel for twenty-eight years. The LORD promised Jehu that his descendants would sit on the throne for four generations.

2 KINGS 11

Verse 17: *Jehoiada then made a covenant between the LORD and the king and people that they would be the LORD's people. He also made a covenant between the king and the people.*

Athaliah, Ahaziah's mother, saw that her son was dead and proceeded to destroy the whole royal family, so that she could serve as ruler of Judah. Ahaziah's sister Jehosheba took Joash (Ahaziah's son) and hid him for six years. In his seventh year, Jehoiada, the high priest, introduced Joash to all of the commanders and organized them to guard the king during the Sabbath. On the Sabbath, Joash was anointed and crowned as king. Athaliah heard the commotion and realized too late what was happening. She was put to death. Joash destroyed all of the pagan temples and altars and served as a righteous king.

2 KINGS 12

Verse 5: *Let every priest receive the money from one of the treasurers, and let it be used to repair whatever damage is found in the temple.*

Joash reigned for forty years and did what was right in the eyes of the LORD, except that he did not destroy the high places. He collected money and used it to repair the temple. Hazael, king of Aram, attacked Gath and prepared to attack Jerusalem. Joash sent Hazael all of the gold his predecessors had collected and the army withdrew. At the end of his reign, his officials assassinated Joash, and his son Amaziah succeeded him.

2 KINGS 13

Verse 2: *He did evil in the eyes of the LORD by following the sins of Jeroboam son of Nebat, which he had caused Israel to commit, and he did not turn away from them.*

At the midpoint of Joash's reign in Judah, Jehoahaz, son of Jehu, became king of Israel in Samaria and reigned seventeen years. He was evil, and the LORD kept Israel under the power of Aram during much of this time. Finally, Jehoahaz sought the LORD's favor and Israel was delivered from Aram. Jehoahaz, however, did not follow through and destroy the pagan altars, including the Asherah pole. His son Jehoash, who reigned sixteen years, succeeded him. He was also evil, and at one point went to war against Amaziah, king of Judah. During his reign, Jehoash visited Elisha. Elisha told him to hold his bow and shoot an arrow to the East. He did so, and Elisha proclaimed that he would have victory over Aram. Elisha then told Jehoash to take the arrows and strike the ground. Jehoash did so, but only three times. Elisha then told him he would be victorious over Aram only three times rather than completely destroying it (which he would have if he struck the ground five or six times). Elisha died shortly after this and was buried. On one occasion when a man was being buried near his tomb, his dead body touched the tomb and he was brought back to life. Hazael, king of Aram, was succeeded by his son Ben-Hadad. They were defeated by the Israelites three times during the reign of Jehoash. Following his death, Jehoash was succeeded by Jeroboam.

2 Kings 14

Verse 10: *You have indeed defeated Edom and now you are arrogant. Glory in your victory, but stay at home! Why ask for trouble and cause your own downfall and that of Judah also?*

Amaziah began his reign in Judah in the second year of Jehoash's reign in Israel. He was righteous and reigned for twenty-nine years. Like his father, he did not remove the high places. Once he established his reign, he executed his father's murderers. He also defeated Edom, captured Sela, and renamed it Joktheel. Afterwards he challenged Jehoash of Israel to meet with him, but Jehoash refused, trying to avoid war. Amaziah would not listen and they went to war with each other. Israel routed Judah and Jehoash captured Amaziah and broke down the wall of Jerusalem and looted the palace and temple. After the death of Jehoash, the officials in Judah conspired against Amaziah. He escaped to Lachish, but was sought out and killed. Jeroboam began his reign in Israel in the middle of Amaziah's reign in Judah. He reigned for forty-one years, restoring the boundaries of Israel. He was evil and the LORD spared Israel only because of His promises. His son Zechariah succeeded Jeroboam.

2 Kings 15

Verse 4: *The high places, however, were not removed; the people continued to offer sacrifices and burn incense there.*

Two-thirds of the way through Jeroboam's reign in Israel, Azariah began his reign in Judah. He was a righteous king for fifty-two years, but again did not remove the high places. He was afflicted with leprosy and had to live in a separate house. His son, Jotham, was in charge of the palace during this time, and eventually succeeded his father as king. Three-fourths of the way through Azariah's reign in Judah, Zechariah, Jeroboam's son, became king of Israel, but only for six months. He was assassinated by Shallum, son of Jabesh, who then proclaimed himself king. Shallum's reign lasted only one month, however, when Menahem assassinated him. Menahem made himself king and did evil, ransacking several towns. Pui, Assyria's king, invaded and Menahem gathered money from the people and paid him off, so Assyria withdrew. He reigned for ten years until his son, Pekahiah succeeded him. Pekahiah was assassinated by one of his chief officers, Pekah. Pekah became king and reigned for twenty years, and was also evil. The Assyrians attacked and took much of Israel's territory. Hoshea, who succeeded him as king assassinated Pekah. Jotham began his reign as king of Judah during Pekah's reign. He reigned for sixteen years. He was righteous, rebuilt the Upper Gate, but did not get rid of the high places.

2 KINGS 16

Verse 2: Ahaz was twenty years old when he became king, and he reigned in Jerusalem sixteen years. Unlike David his father, he did not do what was right in the eyes of the LORD his God.

Jotham's son Ahaz began his reign over Judah in the seventeenth year of Pekah's reign over Israel. Ahaz was only twenty years old when he became king and reigned for sixteen years. He did not walk in the ways of the LORD; worshiped pagan gods, and even sacrificed his own son to a pagan god. Rezin, king of Aram (Syria) and Pekah attempted unsuccessfully to conquer Jerusalem, but Aram did overtake Elath in Judah. Ahaz attempted to make a treaty with Tiglath-Pileser, king of Assyria, sending him gifts from the palace and temple. In support of the treaty, Assyria overtook Damascus and put the king of Syria to death. Ahaz went to Damascus to visit the victorious Tiglath-Pileser, saw a pagan altar that he liked, and sent a sketch of it to Jerusalem so that a copy could be constructed in the temple of the LORD. He instructed Uriah, the chief priest, to make offerings on the new altar. He told Uriah that the original bronze altar of the temple would be used for seeking guidance. Upon his death, his son Hezekiah succeeded Ahaz.

2 KINGS 17

Verse 15: They rejected his decrees and the covenant he had made with their fathers and the warnings he had given them. They followed worthless idols and themselves became worthless. They imitated the nations around them although the LORD had ordered them, "Do not do as they do," and they did the things the LORD had forbidden them to do.

Hoshea became king of Israel in Samaria towards the end of Ahaz's reign in Judah. He was an evil king who reigned for nine years. Shalmaneser, king of Assyria, attacked Hoshea. Hoshea had been a vassal to Assyria, but changed his allegiance to So, king of Egypt. This angered Shalmaneser, who attacked and put Hoshea in prison. Assyria laid siege to Israel for three years, captured Samaria, and deported the Israelites to Assyria. This occurred because the Israelites had sinned against the LORD. They worshiped other gods, built high places for them, ignored the warnings of the prophets, and did other things detestable to God. The LORD gave up on Israel, and only Judah remained. Judah, however, would also succumb to evil. Israel's sins began with the division of the kingdoms under Jeroboam and continued throughout their nation's existence. The king of Assyria repopulated Samaria with his own citizens. They worshiped their own gods, and therefore the LORD sent lions to kill them. The Assyrian king sent an Israelite priest to teach the people how to worship God, but the people continued to worship their other gods as well.

2 KINGS 18

Verse 4: *He removed the high places; smashed the sacred stones and cut down the Asherah poles. He broke into pieces the bronze snake Moses had made, for up to that time the Israelites had been burning incense to it. (It was called Nehushtan.)*

Hezekiah became king of Judah in the third year of Hoshea's reign. He was twenty-five years old when he became king and reigned for twenty-nine years. He did what was right in the eyes of the LORD, by destroying idols and the high places, and the LORD was with him. He rebelled against the king of Assyria, and defeated the Philistines. Assyria defeated Israel during the early part of his reign. Sennacherib, king of Assyria, attacked and occupied several of Judah's cities in the fourteenth year of Hezekiah's reign. Hezekiah paid him gold and silver from the temple to withdraw. The Assyrian king sent his chief commander to Jerusalem to persuade the people to lay down their arms and not resist their conquest of Judah. Hezekiah told the people that the LORD would deliver them, but the Assyrian commander persisted in trying to convince the people, claiming that their LORD had sent him.

2 KINGS 19

Verse 34: *I will defend this city and save it, for my sake and for the sake of David my servant.*

Hezekiah and his advisors sent for the prophet Isaiah who assured them that the LORD was indeed with them. He told them not to be afraid, and that the LORD would punish the Assyrian king for the blasphemy he told his commander to tell the people. Sennacherib again sent word to Hezekiah to surrender, warning him not to depend upon his God. Hezekiah prayed to the LORD. The LORD responded through Isaiah, telling Hezekiah that the insults and blasphemy of the Assyrians angered Him. Isaiah reminded them of the power of the LORD and that He would punish the Assyrians. He offered a sign, saying that in three years Judah would be able to plant and harvest again. He also noted that Assyria would not enter Jerusalem. That night, the angel of death killed a hundred and eighty-five thousand Assyrian soldiers. Sennacherib withdrew, and was later assassinated by two of his sons, and succeeded by another son.

2 KINGS 20

Verse 19: *"The word of the LORD you have spoken is good," Hezekiah replied. For he thought, "Will there not be peace and security in my lifetime?"*

Hezekiah became ill and Isaiah visited him and told him to get his affairs in order because he was about to die. Hezekiah appealed to the LORD in prayer, and God instructed Isaiah to return to him and tell him that he would let him live fifteen more years. Hezekiah was given a sign—a shadow traveling backwards, that he would be well in three days. Hezekiah received envoys from Babylon who brought gifts because they had heard of his illness. Hezekiah showed them everything in the palace. Isaiah questioned why he had done that, and foretold of the eventual fall of Jerusalem to Babylon. Manasseh, Hezekiah's son, succeeded him as king.

2 KINGS 21

Verse 12: *Therefore this is what the LORD, the God of Israel, says: I am going to bring such disaster on Jerusalem and Judah that the ears of everyone who hears of it will tingle.*

Manassah became king of Israel at age 12, and reigned for fifty-five years. He did evil by rebuilding the high places, erected altars to Baal, and made an Asherah pole. He even built pagan altars in the temple and sacrificed his own son to the pagan gods. He killed many innocent people and did much evil. He angered the LORD, who promised to punish all of Judah. Manasseh's son Amon succeeded him as king. Amon lasted only two years and was also evil. His officials conspired against him and assassinated him in his palace. The people killed all of the officials and appointed Josiah, Amon's son as king.

2 KINGS 22

Verse 13: Go and inquire of the LORD for me and for the people and for all Judah about what is written in this book that has been found. Great is the LORD's anger that burns against us because our fathers have not obeyed the words of this book; they have not acted in accordance with all that is written there concerning us.

Josiah was only eight years old when he became king of Judah. He was righteous and reigned for thirty-one years. Midway through his reign, he commissioned repairs to the temple. Hilkiah, the high priest, found the Book of the Law, which had been lost for many years. Upon reading it, Josiah realized how evil the sins of his forefathers were. He sent messengers to the prophetess, Huldah, who told them that Judah was about to be punished severely for their evil, but that Josiah would be buried in peace and spared seeing it.

2 KINGS 23

Verse 25: Neither before nor after Josiah was there a king like him who turned to the LORD as he did—with all his heart and with all his soul and with all his strength, in accordance with all the Law of Moses.

Josiah called all of the people of Jerusalem and all of the elders of Judah together and read the Book of the Covenant. In their presence, he renewed the covenant, and ordered Hilkiah to remove all of the pagan altars from the temple and the land. He purged the land of all priests, altars, and temples to the pagan gods. He then renewed the custom of celebrating the Passover. Despite all that Josiah had done, the LORD was still angered and only postponed the judgment against Judah and Jerusalem. Josiah's reign ended when Pharaoh Neco of Egypt killed him in battle. Josiah's son Jehoahaz was made king. Jehoahaz was evil and lasted only three months. He was imprisoned by Neco, who made his brother, Eliakim, king after changing his name to Jehoiakim. Neco imposed a tax upon Israel and took Jehoahaz to Egypt, where he died. Jehoiakim had to tax the people in order to pay Neco. He reigned for eleven years and was evil.

Kings and Prophets Chronology

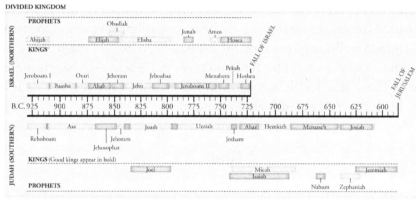

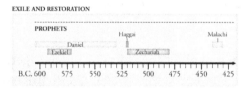

Figure 9: Chronology of Kings and Prophets

2 Kings 24

Verse 20: *It was because of the LORD's anger that all this happened to Jerusalem and Judah, and in the end he thrust them from his presence.*

Nebuchadnezzar, king of Babylon invaded Judah. Aram, Moab, and Ammon also raided Judah. Jehoiakim's son Jehoiachin became king after Jehoiakim's death and reigned three months. Nebuchadnezzar overtook Jerusalem and removed all of the treasures and men. He made Mattaniah, Jehoiachin's uncle, king and changed his name to Zedekiah. He reigned for eleven years, doing evil.

2 Kings 25

Verse 21b: *So Judah went into captivity, away from her land.*

Zedekiah rebelled against Babylon, so Nebuchadnezzar marched against Jerusalem, besieging the city. After several months, the king and the army fled, but were caught and killed by the Babylonians, including all of Jehoiachin's sons (who were killed in front of him). The temple and all of Jerusalem was set on fire and destroyed. The Babylonians removed anything of worth and returned it to Babylon. Judah went into captivity in Babylon. Nebuchadnezzar appointed Gedaliah, son of Ahikam to be governor of what remained of Judah. Gedaliah told the people to obey the rules of the Babylonians and they would do well. Gedaliah was assassinated along with his men, and the people fled to Egypt for fear of the Babylonians. Jehoiachin, who had been imprisoned in Babylon, was set free after thirty-seven years of exile.

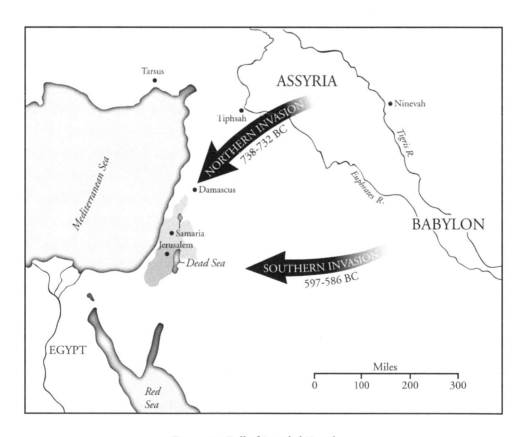

Figure 10: Fall of Divided Kingdoms

Chapter 13

1 CHRONICLES

1 CHRONICLES 1

Verse 34: *Abraham was the father of Isaac. The sons of Isaac: Esau and Israel.*

The genealogy from Adam to Abraham and his son Isaac is detailed, along with the people of Edom and their rulers.

1 CHRONICLES 2

Verses 1,2: *These were the sons of Israel: Reuben, Simeon, Levi, Judah, Issachar, Zebulun, Dan, Joseph, Benjamin, Naphtali, Gad and Asher.*

The genealogy of the twelve tribes of Israel is given. David is listed as the seventh son of Jesse.

1 CHRONICLES 3

Verse 9: *All these were the sons of David, besides his sons by his concubines. And Tamar was their sister.*

David's sons are listed as well as the kings of Judah, before and after exile.

1 Chronicles 4

Verse 9: *Jabez was more honorable than his brothers. His mother had named him Jabez, saying, "I gave birth to him in pain."*

This chapter lists the other descendants of Judah. Included is Jabez, who asked God to bless him and enlarge his territory. He also asked that the Lord's hand be with him and keep him from harm so that he would be free from pain. The genealogy of Simeon is also given.

1 Chronicles 5

Verse 20: *They were helped in fighting them, and God handed the Hagrites and all their allies over to them, because they cried out to him during the battle. He answered their prayers, because they trusted in him.*

The genealogy of the tribes Reuben, Gad, and the half-tribe of Manasseh are listed along with their military victory over the Hagrites.

1 Chronicles 6

Verse 32: *They ministered with music before the tabernacle, the Tent of Meeting, until Solomon built the temple of the Lord in Jerusalem. They performed their duties according to the regulations laid down for them.*

The descendants of the tribes Levi, including the temple musicians, are detailed.

1 Chronicles 7

Verse 15b: *Another descendant was named Zelophehad, who had only daughters.*

Issachar, Benjamin, Naphtali, Manasseh, Ephraim and Asher genealogies are detailed.

1 Chronicles 8

Verse 33: *Ner was the father of Kish, Kish the father of Saul, and Saul the father of Jonathan, Malki-Shua, Abinadab and Esh-Baal.*

The descendants of Benjamin in the line of Saul are provided.

1 CHRONICLES 9

Verse 1: *All Israel was listed in the genealogies recorded in the book of the kings of Israel.*

This chapter lists the members of the tribes that returned to Jerusalem following their return from Babylonian captivity. The genealogy of Saul, the first king of Israel, is detailed. Jeiel was the father of Gibeon who was the father of Ner, who was the father of Kish, who was the father of Saul.

1 CHRONICLES 10

Verse 13: *Saul died because he was unfaithful to the LORD; he did not keep the word of the LORD and even consulted a medium for guidance....*

The Philistines were fighting Israel and killed Saul's sons Jonathan, Abinadab, and Malki-Shua on Mount Gilboa. Saul himself was wounded by an arrow and asked his armor-bearer to kill him with his sword. When he refused, Saul fell on his own sword and killed himself. His armor-bearer then did the same. The Israelites fled and the Philistines captured the cities. The next day they took Saul's head and hung it in their pagan temple. The inhabitants of Jabesh Gilead buried the body of Saul and his sons and fasted for seven days. The LORD punished Saul for his unfaithfulness and made David king.

1 CHRONICLES 11

Verse 7: *David then took up residence in the fortress, and so it was called the City of David.*

David became king of Israel and enjoyed the support of the entire nation. They recaptured Jerusalem under the leadership of Joab, who became commander-in-chief. David built up the city and became very powerful because the LORD was with him. David's mighty men included Jashobeam, Eleazar, Abishai, Benaiah, and thirty others—all famous for their heroism.

1 CHRONICLES 12

Verse 18: *Then the Spirit came upon Amasai, chief of the Thirty, and he said: "We are yours, O David! We are with you, O son of Jesse! Success, success to you, and success to those who help you, for your God will help you." So David received them and made them leaders of his raiding bands.*

Many other warriors joined David while he was banished during Saul's reign. David assembled a volunteer army of over 340,000 in Hebron. After Saul's death, even more people joined David, determined to make him king.

1 CHRONICLES 13

Verse 2: *He then said to the whole assembly of Israel, "If it seems good to you and if it is the will of the LORD our God, let us send word far and wide to the rest of our brothers throughout the territories of Israel, and also to the priests and Levites who are with them in their town and pasturelands to come and join us."*

David consulted with the leaders of his army, as well as the Levites, and proclaimed that they would bring back the Ark of the Covenant to Jerusalem, if it was the will of God. They went to Kiriath Jearim (where the Philistines had returned it) to retrieve it. As they were transporting the Ark, Uzzah, a descendant of Abinadab, reached out to steady the Ark with his hand when the oxen stumbled. The LORD killed him on the spot. David was concerned about the wrath of God, and therefore the Ark was kept outside of Jerusalem, at the home of Obed-Edom for three months.

1 CHRONICLES 14

Verse 16: *So David did as God commanded him, and they struck down the Philistine army, all the way from Gibeon to Gezer.*

Hiram, king of Tyre sent gifts to David, including materials and workers to build a palace. David prospered and had many children. The Philistines assembled for battle, and David asked the LORD if he should attack. The LORD promised him victory. They defeated the Philistines with the help of the LORD and David's fame spread throughout the land.

1 CHRONICLES 15

Verse 13: *It was because you, the Levites, did not bring it up the first time that the LORD our God broke out in anger against us. We did not inquire of him about how to do it in the prescribed way.*

David constructed a tent for the Ark and instructed the Levites to bring the Ark into the city. David assembled the Israelites and appointed Zadok and Abiathar the priests, and other leaders of the Levites to preside over the ceremony. Gatekeepers, doorkeepers, and musicians were assigned and the Ark was triumphantly returned to Jerusalem. David was seen dancing during the procession by Saul's daughter Michal, who despised him in her heart.

1 CHRONICLES 16

Verse 36: *"Praise be to the LORD, the God of Israel, from everlasting to everlasting." And all the people said "Amen" and "Praise the LORD."*

Offerings were made to the LORD and David gave cakes to everyone in attendance. David then offered a psalm of thanks to the LORD. He praised the LORD for all He had done and asked for the LORD's continued blessings.

1 CHRONICLES 17

Verse 16: *Then King David went in and sat before the LORD, and said: "Who am I, O LORD God, and what is my family, that you have brought me this far?"*

David returned to his palace and began planning for a new temple. The prophet Nathan told David that the LORD had instructed him not to build the temple. He shared that his son would build His temple. David prayed to the LORD thanking Him for his blessings.

1 CHRONICLES 18

Verse 6b: *The LORD gave David victory everywhere he went.*

David defeated the Philistines, the Moabites, and Hadadezer, king of Zobah. He also defeated the Arameans who came to help Hadadezer, taking their gold shields and bronze. Surrounding kings sent him gifts. His army, lead by Abishai, defeated the Edomites. David dedicated all of the victories to the LORD and he did what was just and right.

1 CHRONICLES 19

Verse 13: *Be strong and let us fight bravely for our people and the cities of our God. The LORD will do what is good in his sight.*

David sent his men on a goodwill mission to Ammon when Nahash, their king, died. The new king, Hanun, believed that David's men were spies so he had their beards shaved and further humiliated them. This escalated into a battle against the Ammonites and their allies the Arameans. Joab split his men to fight on two fronts and they won handily. The Arameans regrouped and were defeated by David's men again. They vowed never to help the Ammonites again.

1 CHRONICLES 20

Verse 2a: *David took the crown from the head of their king—its weight was found to be a talent of gold, and it was set with precious stones—and it was placed on David's head.*

Joab led the army in the spring and again defeated the Ammonites and then Rabbah. War broke out again with the Philistines and the Israelites prevailed in several battles.

1 CHRONICLES 21

Verse 3: *But Joab replied, "May the LORD multiply his troops a hundred times over. My lord the king, are they not all my lord's subjects? Why does my lord want to do this? Why should he bring guilt on Israel?"*

David had Joab take a census of his army against the LORD's wishes. Joab reported back that there were 1,100,000. However, he did not include the tribes of Levi and Benjamin because he was angry with David. The LORD was also angry and, through the prophet Gad, gave David three options for punishment: Three years of famine, three months of defeat by their enemies, or three days of plague. David chose the last option, and lost seventy thousand men to the plague. David pleaded with the LORD, asking that the punishment be his alone, and the LORD had mercy on him. This happened on the threshing floor of Araunah. They built an altar to the LORD on that spot and offered sacrifices to Him.

1 CHRONICLES 22

Verse 8: *But this word of the LORD came to me: "You have shed much blood and have fought many wars. You are not to build a house for my Name, because you have shed much blood on the earth in my sight."*

David began preparations for the building of the temple. He then summoned his son, Solomon, and charged him with the task of building a magnificent house for the LORD. He asked that the LORD be with Solomon and enlisted the help and support of all of Israel.

1 CHRONICLES 23

Verse 28: *The duty of the Levites was to help Aaron's descendants in the service of the temple of the LORD: to be in charge of the courtyards, the side rooms, the purification of all sacred things and the performance of other duties at the house of God.*

David grew old and made Solomon king of Israel. He organized all the Levites and assigned them responsibilities for the temple.

1 CHRONICLES 24

Verse 5: *They divided them impartially by drawing lots, for there were officials of the sanctuary and officials of God among the descendants of both Eleazar and Ithamar.*

The priests were divided and given specific responsibilities.

1 CHRONICLES 25

Verse 1a: *David, together with the commanders of the army, set apart some of the sons of Asaph, Heman, and Jeduthun for the ministry of prophesying, accompanied by harps, lyres and cymbals.*

David assigned men to prophesying and appointed musicians.

1 CHRONICLES 26

Verse 13: *Lots were cast for each gate, according to their families, young and old alike.*

David designated gatekeepers for the temple and appointed treasurers and other officials.

1 Chronicles 27

Verse 23: *David did not take the number of the men twenty years old or less, because the LORD had promised to make Israel as numerous as the stars in the sky.*

David's army was arranged in twelve divisions of 24,000 men each. Each of the twelve tribes was assigned a leader. The king also had several overseers.

1 Chronicles 28

Verse 9: *And you, my son Solomon, acknowledge the God of your father, and serve him with whole-hearted devotion and with a willing mind, for the LORD searches every heart and understands every motive behind the thoughts. If you seek him, he will be found by you; but if you forsake him, he will reject you forever.*

David assembled all of the leaders of Israel and announced that he had planned to build the temple, but the LORD instructed him to leave the task to his son, Solomon. He asked the people to follow the word of the LORD and to serve Solomon. David gave Solomon all of the plans for the temple that the Spirit had inspired. He told his son to be strong and courageous and assured him that the LORD was with him.

1 Chronicles 29

Verse 9: *The people rejoiced at the willing response of their leaders, for they had given freely and wholeheartedly to the LORD. David the king also rejoiced greatly.*

David announced gifts that he made personally to the temple, and others also gave willingly. David then offered a prayer of praise and exaltation to the LORD. They all praised the LORD and Solomon was acknowledged as king. David, who ruled Israel for forty years, died at a good old age and was succeeded by his son Solomon.

Chapter 14

2 CHRONICLES

2 CHRONICLES 1

Verse 12b: *...wisdom and knowledge will be given you. And I will also give you wealth, riches and honor, such as no king who was before you ever had and none after you will have.*

Solomon became a great king and the LORD was with him. He made a thousand burnt offerings to the LORD and He asked him what he wanted. Solomon requested wisdom and knowledge, and because he did not ask for anything selfish, the LORD granted his request. Solomon and all of Israel became rich and successful.

2 CHRONICLES 2

Verse 6: *But who is able to build a temple for him, since the heavens, even the highest heavens, cannot contain him? Who then am I to build a temple for him, except as a place to burn sacrifices before him?*

Solomon began preparing to build the temple. He sent word to Hiram king of Tyre to send cedar logs and craftsmen. Hiram obliged Solomon and praised the LORD and Solomon for his wisdom. Solomon assigned all the foreigners to be carriers and stonecutters for the temple.

2 Chronicles 3

Verse 1: *Then Solomon began to build the temple of the LORD in Jerusalem on Mount Moriah, where the LORD had appeared to his father David. It was on the threshing floor of Araunah the Jebusite, the place provided by David.*

Solomon began building the temple on Mount Moriah. He spared no expense, using the finest gold and precious stones. He included ornate pillars and cherubim.

2 Chronicles 4

Verse 18: *All these things that Solomon made amounted to so much that the weight of the bronze was not determined.*

The temple furnishings were also made of the finest materials. Altars, basins, lampstands, tables, and stands were all lavishly designed and made of bronze and gold.

2 Chronicles 5

Verses 13b, 14: *Then the temple of the LORD was filled with a cloud, and the priests could not perform their service because of the cloud, for the glory of the LORD filled the temple of God.*

Solomon brought in all of the items his father David had dedicated to the LORD. He then had the Levites bring in the Ark of the Covenant. Sacrifices were made to the LORD, trumpeters played, and everyone sang to Him. Then the temple was filled with a cloud and the glory of the LORD filled the temple.

2 Chronicles 6

Verse 21: *Hear the supplications of your servant and of your people Israel when they pray toward this place. Hear from heaven, your dwelling place; and when you hear, forgive.*

Solomon offered words of praise to the LORD. He thanked Him for keeping His promise to his father David. Solomon asked for God's continued presence in the temple. He asked for mercy when the people sinned. He asked that the temple be a sanctuary for all the people.

2 CHRONICLES 7

Verse 14: *...if my people, who are called by my name, will humble themselves and pray and seek my face and turn from their wicked ways, then will I hear from heaven and will forgive their sin and will heal their land.*

Fire came from heaven and consumed the burnt offerings and the glory of the LORD filled the temple. The people knelt and worshiped the LORD. Solomon made an offering of twenty-two thousand head of cattle and an equal number of sheep and goats. The dedication was observed for seven days and the festival another seven days. The LORD appeared to Solomon and told him that if the people would humble themselves and if Solomon would follow His commands they would never fail. He warned that if they turn away, then Israel will be uprooted from the land and He would reject the temple.

2 CHRONICLES 8

Verse 11: *Solomon brought Pharaoh's daughter up from the City of David to the palace he had built for her, for he said, "My wife must not live in the palace of David king of Israel, because the places the ark of the LORD has entered are holy."*

Solomon also rebuilt the villages that Hiram had given him, captured Hamath Zobah, built Tadmor, rebuilt Upper and Lower Beth Horon, and accomplished many things during his reign. He conscripted all the foreigners into slave labor. He made a separate palace for his wife, Pharaoh's daughter, because David's palace was considered holy. He celebrated the Feasts and kept the Levites organized in their duties. The temple of the LORD was finished.

2 CHRONICLES 9

Verse 22: *King Solomon was greater in riches and wisdom than all the other kings of the earth.*

The queen of Sheba visited Solomon. She asked him difficult questions, but Solomon was able to answer all of them. The queen was impressed and gave Solomon gold, precious stones, and spices. Solomon made two hundred gold shields, and an ornate throne. He had an impressive army with thousands of chariots and horses and a large fleet of ships that brought him even more riches. Solomon ruled Israel in prosperity for forty years. When he died his son Rehoboam succeeded him as king.

2 Chronicles 10

Verse 4: *Your father put a heavy yoke on us, but now lighten the harsh labor and the heavy yoke he put on us, and we will serve you.*

Rehoboam foolishly took the advice of the young men and not the elders and promised to rule with even more oppression that his father. This angered the people, who stoned his labor enforcer Adoniram to death, and Israel rebelled against Rehoboam's rule.

2 Chronicles 11

Verse 16: *Those from every tribe of Israel who set their hearts on seeking the LORD, the God of Israel, followed the Levites to Jerusalem to offer sacrifices to the LORD, the God of their fathers.*

Rehoboam mustered his army to fight the Israelites, led by Jeroboam who opposed him. However, his prophet Shemaiah told him not to march against Jeroboam and Rehoboam listened to him. Rehoboam fortified Judah. The Levites allied with Rehoboam as Jeroboam rejected them and worshiped idols. Rehoboam had eighteen wives, sixty concubines and fathered twenty-eight sons and sixty daughters. He loved Maacah, daughter of Absalom, the most. He appointed Maacah's son Abijah as the crown prince.

2 Chronicles 12

Verse 12: *Because Rehoboam humbled himself, the LORD's anger turned from him, and he was not totally destroyed. Indeed, there was some good in Judah.*

Rehoboam strayed from the ways of the LORD and Shishak, king of Egypt, attacked Judah. He conquered all of the fortified cities and closed in on Jerusalem. The prophet Shemaiah came to Rehoboam and he and the other leaders humbled themselves before God. The LORD spared their lives, but Shishak plundered the city. Rehoboam reigned for seventeen years and was continually at battle with Jeroboam. When he died he was laid to rest with his father Solomon and his grandfather David.

2 CHRONICLES 13

Verse 12: *God is with us; he is our leader. His priests with their trumpets will sound the battle cry against you. Men of Israel, do not fight against the LORD, the God of your fathers, for you will not succeed.*

Abijah became king but reigned for only three years in Judah. He also fought with Jeroboam. Abijah appealed to all of Israel on the battlefield, asking that they come together and worship the LORD again. Jeroboam surrounded the outnumbered men from Judah and attacked them. The LORD intervened and routed Jeroboam and the Israelites. Jeroboam did not regain power but Abijah grew in strength until his death.

2 CHRONICLES 14

Verse 11: *Then Asa called to the LORD his God and said, "LORD, there is no one like you to help the powerless against the mighty. Help us, O LORD our God, for we rely on you, and in your name we have come against this vast army, O LORD, you are our God; do not let man prevail against you."*

Abijah's son Asa succeeded him as king. Asa did what was right in the eyes of the LORD, and there was peace for ten years. He destroyed all the pagan altars and turned the people back to the LORD. The Cushites, led by Zerah, attacked Judah, but with the help of the LORD, they successfully defended their home and pursued the Cushites, returning with much plunder.

2 CHRONICLES 15

Verse 15: *All Judah rejoiced about the oath because they had sworn it wholeheartedly. They sought God eagerly, and he was found by them. So the LORD gave them rest on every side.*

The prophet Azariah encouraged Asa to bring about reform in Judah. Asa destroyed all the pagan altars including an Asherah pole belonging to the queen mother Maacah.

2 CHRONICLES 16

Verse 9: *For the eyes of the LORD range throughout the earth to strengthen those whose hearts are fully committed to him. You have done a foolish thing, and from now on you will be at war.*

Baasha, king of Israel, attacked Judah in the thirty-sixth year of Asa's reign. Asa allied with Ben-Haddad, king of Aram, against Israel. However, because Asa did not consult the LORD first, the alliance did not hold up, and Asa was at war for the rest of his reign. Asa was also afflicted with a disease of his feet. He reigned for forty-one years.

2 Chronicles 17

Verse 9: *They taught throughout Judah, taking with them the Book of the Law of the LORD; they went around to all the towns of Judah and taught the people.*

After Asa's death, his son Jehoshaphat became king. Jehoshaphat fortified Judah's defenses and the LORD was with him. Jehoshaphat sent out his priests to teach the Law, and the fear of the LORD prevented anyone from attacking Jehoshaphat and Judah. Jehoshaphat became powerful and his army strong.

2 Chronicles 18

Verse 22: *So now the LORD has put a lying spirit in the mouths of these prophets of yours. The LORD has decreed disaster for you.*

Ahab, king of Israel asked Jehoshaphat to be his ally against Ramoth Gilead. Jehoshaphat insisted they first consult the prophet Micaiah. Although all of the other prophets that Ahab consulted encouraged them to attack, Micaiah, when pressed, told them they would be defeated if they attacked Ramoth Gilead. Ahab had Micaiah imprisoned and attacked Ramoth Gilead with Jehoshaphat. Jehoshaphat cried to the LORD for help and he was spared, but Ahab was killed by an arrow in battle.

2 Chronicles 19

Verse 6: *He told them, "Consider carefully what you do, because you are not judging for man but for the LORD, who is with you whenever you give a verdict."*

When Jehoshaphat returned, the prophet Jehu appealed to him to seek God and do good to avoid the wrath of the LORD. Jehoshaphat turned back to the LORD and appointed priests and judges throughout Judah.

2 CHRONICLES 20

Verse 17: *You will not have to fight this battle. Take up your positions; stand firm and see the deliverance the LORD will give you, O Judah and Jerusalem. Do not be afraid; do not be discouraged. Go out to face them tomorrow, and the LORD will be with you.*

The Moabites and Ammonites came to attack Judah. Jehoshaphat appealed to the LORD. The prophet Jahaziel told the people not to be afraid or discouraged but to march out against the enemy the next day. They did so, praising the LORD. The LORD ambushed the enemy soldiers who began fighting each other until they all perished. It took three days for Jehoshaphat and his men to carry off all the plunder. They then praised the LORD and returned to Jerusalem. Jehoshaphat reigned for twenty-five years, doing mostly good. He did make an alliance with Ahaziah, the wicked king of Israel, to build a fleet of trading ships. Because of this, the LORD destroyed all the ships prior to them sailing.

2 CHRONICLES 21

Verse 20: *Jehoram was thirty-two years old when he became king, and he reigned in Jerusalem eight years. He passed away, to no one's regret, and was buried in the City of David, but not in the tombs of the kings.*

Jehoshaphat died and his son Jehoram succeeded him. He reigned for eight years in Judah and did evil in the eyes of the LORD. He put all of his brothers to death and married a daughter of Ahab. Edom rebelled against Judah and Jehoram barely escaped. Jehoram led Judah astray. The prophet Elijah wrote Jehoram warning him that the LORD was about to strike him and the people of Judah. He told Jehoram that he would be very ill. The Philistines and Arabs attacked and plundered Judah and killed all of Jehoram's sons except for Ahaziah, the youngest. Jehoram suffered from his illness and eventually died in great pain.

2 CHRONICLES 22

Verse 3: *He also walked in the ways of the house of Ahab, for his mother encouraged him in doing wrong.*

Ahaziah became king and reigned for only one year. He too was evil and followed the bad counsel of his father's advisors. He allied with Joram son of Ahab, king of Israel, and was defeated by Hazael king of Aram at Ramoth Gilead. Joram was wounded in battle and Ahaziah went to visit him. Based on the LORD's instructions, Jehu executed judgment on the house of Ahab and put Ahaziah and his relatives to death. Jehosheba, the daughter of King Jehoram, hid Ahaziah's son Joash from Ahaziah's mother Athaliah who was attempting to destroy the entire royal family after Ahaziah's death. He remained hidden for six years while Athaliah ruled Judah.

2 CHRONICLES 23

Verse 16: *Jehoiada then made a covenant that he and the people and the king would be the LORD's people.*

Jehoiada, the high priest, made a covenant with the commanders of the army, the heads of the Levites and other leaders to protect Joash and bring him to power. They organized their followers and appointed Joash king of Judah. Athaliah discovered this too late and cried treason. Jehoiada had her seized and put to death. Jehoiada then tore down all the pagan altars, restored worship in the temple, and placed Joash on the throne.

2 CHRONICLES 24

Verse 20: *Then the Spirit of God came upon Zechariah son of Jehoiada the priest. He stood before the people and said, "This is what God says: 'Why do you disobey the LORD's commands? You will not prosper. Because you have forsaken the LORD, he has forsaken you.'"*

Joash was seven years old when he became king and he ruled for forty years. He initially did what was right in the LORD's eyes and restored the temple. The people were asked to help pay for repairs, which they gladly did. Offerings and worship continued as long as Jehoiada remained as chief priest. He eventually died at the age of a hundred and thirty, and then Judah returned to its evil ways. The LORD sent prophets but Joash and the people did not listen. The Spirit of God spoke through Jehoiada's son Zechariah, but the people did not listen to him either, and stoned him to death by order of the king. Zechariah held the king accountable in the LORD's eyes as his last words. Aram attacked Jerusalem, killed all the leaders, and plundered the city. Joash was severely wounded. His own officials (Zabad and Jehozabad) then finished the job as punishment for murdering Zechariah. His son Amaziah then became king.

2 CHRONICLES 25

Verse 9: *Amaziah asked the man of God, "But what about the hundred talents I paid for these Israelite troops?" The man of God replied, "The LORD can give you much more than that."*

Amaziah was twenty-five years old when he became king and he reigned in Judah for twenty-nine years. He was righteous but not committed to doing good in the eyes of the LORD. He put Zabad and Jehozabad to death for killing his father. He restored the army and hired another one hundred thousand warriors from Israel. Upon advice from his priest, he released the Israelite soldiers, because the LORD was not with them. Amaziah's army defeated the Edomites at Seir. Amaziah worshiped the pagan gods that he captured from Sier, invoking the wrath of the LORD. In the meantime, the hundred thousand troops that Amaziah had released attacked Judah. A prophet warned Amaziah that the LORD would destroy him, but he disregarded this advice. Amaziah challenged Jehoash, king of Israel in battle, but Jehoash told him to stay at home. Amaziah would not listen, and his army was defeated by Israel. Jehoash captured Amaziah and plundered the city of Jerusalem, leveling a six hundred foot section of the city wall. His own men eventually killed Amaziah when he fled to Lachish.

2 CHRONICLES 26

Verse 19: *Uzziah, who had a censer in his hand ready to burn incense, became angry. While he was raging at the priests in their presence before the incense altar in the LORD's temple, leprosy broke out on his forehead.*

The people of Judah made Amaziah's son Uzziah king. He was sixteen years old when he became king and he ruled for fifty-two years. He did what was right in the eyes of the LORD. He became powerful, defeating the Philistines and the Arabs. He built towers and fortified the walls of Jerusalem. His army was powerful and well equipped. Ultimately, Uzziah's pride led to his downfall. He was unfaithful to the LORD and burned incense in the temple, which was something that only the Levites were allowed to do. Azariah the priest confronted Uzziah and the king was afflicted with leprosy. Jotham, his son, succeeded him as king.

2 CHRONICLES 27

Verse 6: *Jotham grew powerful because he walked steadfastly before the LORD his God.*

Jotham became king of Judah at age twenty-five and reigned for sixteen years. Like his father, Uzziah, he did right in the eyes of the LORD. He did not enter forbidden areas in the temple of the LORD, but the people continued to be corrupt. Jotham rebuilt the Upper Gate of the temple and did much work to rebuild surrounding towns. He conquered the Ammonites who paid Judah with silver and grain. He grew powerful because he walked with the LORD. His son Ahaz succeeded him as king.

2 CHRONICLES 28

Verse 13: *"You must not bring those prisoners here," they said, "or we will be guilty before the LORD. Do you intend to add to our sin and guilt? For our guilt is already great, and his fierce anger rests on Israel."*

Ahaz was twenty when he became king. He also reigned for sixteen years, but he did not do what was right in the eyes of the LORD. He worshiped Baal and sacrificed his own sons to pagan gods. He offered sacrifices and burned incense in high places. The LORD was angered, and so Aram defeated Ahaz. Many of his people were captured and exiled in Damascus. Israel also defeated Ahaz, inflicting heavy casualties (Judah lost one hundred twenty thousand soldiers in one day). An Ephraimite named Zicri killed two of his sons, Maaseiah and Elkanah. The Israelites plundered Judah and took the spoils, including two hundred thousand women and children back to Samaria. A prophet named Oded confronted Israel on behalf of the LORD, however, and the women and children were returned. Ahaz asked the king of Assyria for help, because the Edomites and the Philistines continued the attack of Judah because of the LORD's anger against Ahaz. Tiglath-Pileser, king of Assyria, came, but did not help. Instead, he also pillaged Judah. Rather than appealing to the LORD, Ahaz offered sacrifices to the gods of his enemies and shut down the temple, further angering the LORD. Hezekiah, his son, succeeded him as king.

2 CHRONICLES 29

Verse 10: *Now I intend to make a covenant with the LORD, the God of Israel, so that his fierce anger will turn away from us.*

Hezekiah was twenty-five when he became king and he reigned for twenty-nine years. He did what was right in the eyes of the LORD. He reopened the temple and ordered the Levites to consecrate themselves and the temple. He reminded the people of Judah's sins, and made a covenant with the LORD. When the Levites had completed their work in purifying and consecrating the temple, King Hezekiah had the Levites give an offering of seven bulls, seven rams, seven male lambs, and seven male goats. They prayed to the LORD on their knees and then made additional offerings to the LORD. The service of the temple of the LORD was thus reestablished.

2 CHRONICLES 30

Verse 26: *There was great joy in Jerusalem, for since the days of Solomon son of David king of Israel there had been nothing like this in Jerusalem.*

Hezekiah invited all of Israel, Judah, Ephraim, and Manasseh to celebrate the Passover in Jerusalem. Many people scorned and ridiculed Hezekiah's messengers who delivered the invitations, but many others came to the celebration. Hezekiah prayed to the LORD to forgive them for not strictly following the Passover laws, and the LORD healed the assembled people. They celebrated for two weeks, and the Levites reassumed their duties, as did the priests. There was much joy in Jerusalem.

2 CHRONICLES 31

Verse 10b: *Since the people began to bring their contributions to the temple of the LORD, we have had enough to eat and plenty to spare, because the LORD has blessed his people, and this great amount is left over.*

After the celebration, all of the pagan altars were destroyed, even in the high places. King Hezekiah organized the Levites and the people brought tithes and abundant offerings. Hezekiah was obedient to the LORD, and he and all of Judah prospered.

2 CHRONICLES 32

Verse 8: *"With him is only the arm of flesh, but with us is the LORD our God to help us and to fight our battles." And the people gained confidence from what Hezekiah the king of Judah said.*

Sennacherib, king of Assyria, invaded Judah. Hezekiah repaired the walls, upgraded his defenses, and secured the water supply to Jerusalem. He reassured the people that they would be safe because the LORD was with them. Sennacherib sent word to all of Judah telling them that no god could protect them against his armies, and wrote letters insulting the LORD. King Hezekiah and the prophet Isaiah prayed to God. The LORD sent an angel and annihilated Sennacherib and his armies. They retreated in disgrace, and his own sons killed Sennacherib. Hezekiah became ill and prayed for health. The LORD offered a miraculous sign, but Hezekiah was too proud to respond, angering the LORD. When he repented, the LORD's wrath was lifted from him and Judah. Hezekiah became very wealthy and successful during his reign as king of

Judah. However, he did receive envoys from Babylon, a decision that would later be considered unwise. Hezekiah's son, Manasseh, succeeded him as king.

2 CHRONICLES 33

Verse 13: *And when he prayed to him, the LORD was moved by his entreaty and listened to his plea; so he brought him back to Jerusalem and to his kingdom. Then Manasseh knew that the LORD is God.*

Manasseh became king when he was twelve years old and reigned for fifty-five years. He was evil, building altars in high places, and worshiping Baal and other pagan gods. He even built altars in the LORD's temple and sacrificed his sons in pagan rituals. He led all of Judah astray. The LORD spoke to him, but he ignored the warnings. Finally, the LORD allowed Assyria to conquer him and he was imprisoned in Babylon. Manasseh humbled himself and prayed to the LORD, who later restored him as king of Judah. When he returned, he rebuilt the walls of Jerusalem and rid it of the foreign gods. His son Amon succeeded him. He was twenty-two when he became king. He reigned for only two years. Amon did evil in the eyes of the LORD, but did not humble himself before the LORD. Amon was assassinated by his officials. The people punished those who assassinated him and then appointed his son Josiah as king.

2 CHRONICLES 34

Verse 32: *Then he had everyone in Jerusalem and Benjamin pledge themselves to it; the people of Jerusalem did this in accordance with the covenant of God, the God of their fathers.*

Josiah became king when he was eight years old and reigned for thirty-one years. He was a righteous king. He began to seek God in his eighth year as king, and in his twelfth year he began purging Judah of all pagan altars and high places. In his eighteenth year he sent Shaphan, Maaseiah and Joah to repair the temple. They went to Hilkiah, the high priest, and commissioned the repairs. During the repairs, Hilkiah found the missing Book of the Law and gave it to Shaphan, who took it to Josiah. When the king heard the words of the Book read to him, he tore his robes. The king ordered Hilkiah, Shaphan, and his son Ahikam, Abdon, and his attendant Asaiah to go ask the LORD what he should do. They went to the Prophetess Huldah who told them that because they had forsaken Him, the LORD was going to bring disaster upon Judah. The LORD also told them that Josiah would be spared from seeing the disaster because he humbled himself. The king assembled all the people of Judah and read from the Book, renewing the covenant with the LORD.

2 CHRONICLES 35

Verse 18: The Passover had not been observed like this in Israel since the days of the prophet Samuel; and none of the kings of Israel had ever celebrated such a Passover as did Josiah, with the priests, the Levites and all Judah and Israel who were there with the people of Jerusalem.

Josiah celebrated the Passover at the appointed time and renewed all of the rituals prescribed for the Levites. All of the celebrations were observed as outlined in the Book of the Law. Neco, king of Egypt, went up to the Euphrates River to help the king of Assyria against the Babylonians. Josiah marched out to meet him in battle. Neco told him that he was not attacking Judah, but Josiah stayed and fought against the Egyptians. Josiah was shot with an arrow and returned to Jerusalem to die. Jeremiah composed laments (Lamentations) for Josiah.

2 CHRONICLES 36

Verse 21: The land enjoyed its sabbath rests; all the time of its desolation it rested, until the seventy years were completed in fulfillment of the word of the LORD spoken by Jeremiah.

Jehoahaz, Josiah's 23-year-old son, was made king. He reigned for only three months. The king of Egypt dethroned him, imposed a heavy fine on Judah, and appointed Jehoahaz's brother Eliakim (whom he renamed Jehoiakim) as king. Jehoiakim was twenty-five when he was appointed as king, and he reigned eleven years. He was evil, and Nebuchadnezzar eventually defeated him. Jehoiakim was taken to Babylon and held in captivity. His son, Jehoiachin, who was eighteen at the time, succeeded him. He was also evil, and was quickly replaced by his uncle, Zedekiah. Zedekiah was twenty-one when he became king and reigned for eleven years. He also did evil and refused to listen to the prophet Jeremiah. He led the people into total disobedience to the LORD. Because the people refused to listen to the LORD, despite numerous warnings, Jerusalem was attacked and conquered by the Babylonians. The temple was pillaged and burned, and the people killed or taken into captivity. The remnant spent seventy years in exile until the LORD moved Cyrus, king of Persia, to make a proclamation that they could return to Jerusalem to rebuild the temple.

Year (BC)	Judah King	Length of Reign	Character	Israel King	Length of Reign	Character
930	Rehoboam	17 years	Bad	Jeroboam I	22 years	Bad
913	Abijah	3 years	Bad			
910	Asa	41 years	Good			
909				Nadab	2 years	Bad
908				Baasha	24 years	Bad
886				Elah	2 years	Bad
885				Zimri	7 days	Bad
885				Omri	11 years	Real Bad
874				Ahab	21 years	Very Bad
Year (BC)	Judah King	Length of Reign	Character	Israel King	Length of Reign	Character
872	Jehoshaphat	25 years	Good			
853				Ahaziah	2 years	Bad
852				Joram	12 years	Bad
848	Jehoram	8 years	Bad			
841	Ahaziah	1 year	Bad	Jehu	28 years	Bad
841	Athaliah	7 years	Murderer			
835	Joash	40 years	Good			
814				Jehoahaz	17 years	Bad
798				Jehoash	16 years	Bad
796	Amaziah	29 years	Good			
793				Jeroboam II	41 years	Bad
792	Azariah	52 years	Good			
753				Zechariah	6 months	Bad
752				Shallum	1 month	Bad
752				Menahem	10 years	Bad
(742)				Pekahiah	2 years	Bad
752				Pekah	20 years	Bad
750	Jotham	16 years	Good			
735	Ahaz	16 years	Bad			
732				Hoshea	9 years	Bad
715	Hezekiah	29 years	Good	[Assyria]		

697	Manasseh	55 years	Bad			
642	Amon	2 years	Bad			
640	Josiah	31 years	Good			
609	Jehoahaz	3 months	Bad			
609	Jehoiakim	11 years	Bad			
598	Jehoiachin	3 months	Bad			
597	Zedekiah	11 years	Bad			
586	[Babylon]					

Chapter 15

EZRA

EZRA 1

Verse 1: *In the first year of Cyrus king of Persia, in order to fulfill the word of the LORD spoken by Jeremiah, the LORD moved the heart of Cyrus king of Persia to make a proclamation throughout his realm and to put it in writing....*

Cyrus, King of Persia, made a proclamation that a temple should be built for the LORD at Jerusalem. This was because the LORD moved him and instructed that the Israelites should be allowed to go construct it. The people prepared to build the temple, and all of the neighbors provided gold, silver, livestock and other gifts. Cyrus provided all of the building materials from when Nebuchadnezzar had raided the temple. There were 5,400 articles of gold and silver.

EZRA 2

Verse 62: *These searched for their family records, but they could not find them and so were excluded from the priesthood as unclean.*

There were 42,360 Israelites and 7,337 servants who returned from exile to build the temple. Descendants of priests had to be able to prove their lineage to participate in the priesthood. When the people arrived, there were freewill offerings made to the LORD at the site of the temple. All the people settled in their own towns.

Ezra 3

Verse 12: *But many of the older priests and Levites and family heads, who had seen the former temple, wept aloud when they saw the foundation of this temple being laid, while many others shouted for joy.*

The people assembled and Jeshua and his fellow priest Zerubbabel along with the other priests began to build the altar to the LORD, and they sacrificed a burnt offering to the LORD. They celebrated the Feast of Tabernacles in accordance with the Law of Moses. Then they employed masons and carpenters and began construction of the temple. Zerubbabel and the rest of the priests appointed Levites to supervise the building of the temple. They celebrated when the foundation was laid, shouting and weeping; and they praised God.

Ezra 4

Verse 5: *They hired counselors to work against them and frustrate their plans during the entire reign of Cyrus king of Persia and down to the reign of Darius king of Persia.*

Judah and Benjamin's enemies came to Zerubbabel and asked to help build the temple because they wished to worship their LORD. Zerubbabel, Jeshua, and the heads of families declined. Then the people around them tried to oppose and discourage them. The commanding officer and others wrote a letter to Artaxerxes, who was then king of Persia, telling them that the Jews were rebuilding the rebellious and wicked city. He also told him that after it was built, the Jews would pay no more taxes, and they would revolt. The king replied that he had researched the city, and that indeed there was a long history of revolt from Jerusalem and they should stop work on the rebuilding. The rebuilding came to an abrupt halt.

Ezra 5

Verse 5: *But the eye of their God was watching over the elders of the Jews, and they were not stopped until a report could go to Darius and his written reply be received.*

The prophets Haggai and Zechariah prophesied to the Jews in Judah. Then Zerubbabel and Jeshua set to work again rebuilding the temple. Tattenai, the governor of the region, and Shethar-Bozenai, asked them who had authorized the rebuilding project. They ignored this question, and kept up their work. Tattenai and Shethar-Bozenai wrote to King Darius, telling him that the temple building was proceeding. Darius told them what he had been told regarding whether King Cyrus had authorized the rebuilding.

Ezra 6

Verse 11: *Furthermore, I decree that if anyone changes this edict, a beam is to be pulled from his house and he is to be lifted up and impaled on it. And for this crime his house is to be made a pile of rubble.*

King Darius confirmed that King Cyrus had initiated the temple rebuilding with the costs to be paid by the royal treasury. He further instructed Tattenai and Shethar-Bozenai to stay away. He endorsed the work and instructed them to support it with funds and whatever else was needed, including animals for sacrifice. The king promised punishment if his orders were not obeyed. Work continued on the temple and it was completed in the sixth year of the reign of Darius. The Israelites celebrated and dedicated the temple to the LORD. They celebrated the Passover Feast just as the Law of Moses instructed.

Ezra 7

Verse 27: *Praise be to the LORD, the God of our fathers, who has put it into the king's heart to bring honor to the house of the LORD in Jerusalem in this way....*

Ezra, the chief priest, came from Babylon after the temple was completed. He was a descendant of Aaron and well-versed in the Law of Moses. He had a letter from the king with him, giving him permission to return to Jerusalem with the Israelites, and he was given gold and silver for the temple. The king gave him authority to spend money, and do whatever was necessary to support the temple. He also told him that no taxes would be collected from any of the workers or worshipers of the temple. Ezra gathered all of the leading men of Israel to go with him.

Ezra 8

Verse 23: *So we fasted and petitioned our God about this, and he answered our prayer.*

Ezra took approximately 1,500 men with him. He made sure he had many Levites and temple servants with him prior to his departure. They fasted and prayed. Ezra then divided the gold and silver between twelve priests to guard and protect. They arrived in Jerusalem and rested three days. They returned all of the gold and silver and sacrificed burnt offerings to God.

EZRA 9

Verse 13: *What has happened to us is a result of our evil deeds and our great guilt, and yet, our God, you have punished us less than our sins have deserved and have given us a remnant like this.*

Ezra learned that the Israelites had been intermarrying with the neighboring people. He then prayed for the forgiveness of their sins.

EZRA 10

Verse 14: *Let our officials act for the whole assembly. Then let everyone in our towns who has married a foreign woman come at a set time, along with the elders and judges of each town, until the fierce anger of our God in this matter is turned away from us.*

A large crowd gathered while Ezra was praying and weeping, and they wept also. They asked Ezra to make a covenant before God, and they all took an oath. A proclamation was made to all of the Israelites throughout Jerusalem and Judah to assemble within three days or forfeit all of their land. After they assembled, Ezra announced to them that they needed to make a confession to the LORD and separate themselves from their neighbors. They agreed and asked for all that had intermarried to assemble separately. Everyone but Jonathan, Jahzeiah, Meshullam, and Shabbethai agreed to this. When they met, everyone who had married foreign women was discovered.

Chapter 16

NEHEMIAH

NEHEMIAH 1

Verse 7: *We have acted very wickedly toward you. We have not obeyed the commands decrees and laws you gave your servant Moses.*

Nehemiah, a cupbearer for the king of Babylon, learned from his brother Hanani that the Jewish remnant that survived the exile was back in the province and that they were in trouble and disgrace. The wall of Jerusalem was broken down and its gates burned. When he heard this he wept, mourned, fasted, and prayed. He confessed the sins of Israel and asked for success when he was with the king.

NEHEMIAH 2

Verse 3: *…but I said to the king, "May the king live forever! Why should my face not look sad when the city where my fathers are buried lies in ruins, and its gates have been destroyed by fire?"*

Artaxerxes, king of Babylon, asked Nehemiah why he was sad. He was afraid, but told him, and the king asked what he could do. Nehemiah asked permission from the king to go and rebuild Jerusalem. The king asked how long it would take. Nehemiah answered him and asked for letters for safekeeping and for timber to rebuild the city. He was granted what he requested. When Sanballat the Horonite and Tobiah the Ammonite official heard, however, they were disturbed. Nehemiah went to Jerusalem and found that the walls and many of the gates were destroyed. Nehemiah assembled the leaders and gained their support to start rebuilding the walls. They began the work, despite the protest of the local officials. Nehemiah told the people that the God of heaven would give them success.

NEHEMIAH 3

Verse 12: *Shallum son of Hallohesh, ruler of a half-district of Jerusalem, repaired the next section with the help of his daughters.*

Eliashib the high priest and his fellow priests began work on the Sheep gate and the wall adjoining. The men of Jericho built next to them, and Zaccur built next to them. The sons of Hassenaah rebuilt the Fish gate, and many other groups built sections and gates that adjoined them. The Jeshanah Gate was repaired by Joiada, the Valley gate by Hanun, the Fountain Gate by Shallum, and so on. Many different groups, some of them leaders and rulers, rebuilt portions of the walls around Jerusalem.

NEHEMIAH 4

Verse 14: *After I looked things over, I stood up and said to the nobles, the officials and the rest of the people, "Don't be afraid of them. Remember the Lord, who is great and awesome, and fight for your brothers, your sons and your daughters, your wives and your homes."*

Sanballat remained angry regarding the rebuilding of Jerusalem, and ridiculed the Jews, as did Tobiah. The Jews prayed to the Lord and asked that their insults be turned back on these men. The walls were rebuilt to half of their original height, and the opposition increased. Nehemiah posted guards, and encouraged the people to continue building, telling them to remember the Lord who would protect them. They continued work with half of the men standing guard, while the other half worked. Nehemiah told them to assemble and prepare for battle at the sound of the trumpet. They carried their weapons with them while they worked.

NEHEMIAH 5

Verse 13: *I also shook out the folds of my robe and said, "In this way may God shake out of his house and possessions every man who does not keep the promise. So may such a man be shaken out and emptied!" At this the whole assembly said, "Amen," and praised the LORD. And the people did as they had promised.*

Many of the men complained to Nehemiah that they were having trouble making enough money to eat and stay alive. Nehemiah went to the officials and asked for their help. He told them to give the people back their land and crops, and to stop taxing the people. The officials agreed, and did as they promised. Unlike previous governors, Nehemiah did not ask the people to pay taxes, but devoted all of the resources toward repairing the wall.

NEHEMIAH 6

Verse 9: *They were all trying to frighten us, thinking, "Their hands will get too weak for the work, and it will not be complete." But I prayed, "Now strengthen my hands."*

When the wall was complete except for the doors on the gates, Sanballat and Geshem sent word to Nehemiah to meet with them. Fearing a trap, Nehemiah sent messengers on five separate occasions saying that he could not meet with them because he was working on the wall. Sanballat told Nehemiah he heard that the Jews were revolting and Nehemiah had plans to claim to be king of Judah. Nehemiah replied this was not true, and asked God for help. Nehemiah was not afraid of death threats and continued building the wall. The wall was finished in fifty-two days, and all of the surrounding nations were afraid because they had seen what God had done.

NEHEMIAH 7

Verse 5a: *So my God put it into my heart to assemble the nobles, the officials and the common people for registration by families. I found the genealogical record of those who had been the first to return.*

Nehemiah appointed his brother Hanani to be in charge of Jerusalem and Hananiah as his commander. Nehemiah gave instructions not to open the gates each day until late morning. He also appointed guards for the city. Nehemiah took a census, and found that there were 42,360 people and approximately 7,500 servants and singers.

NEHEMIAH 8

Verse 12: *Then all the people went away to eat and drink, to send portions of food and to celebrate with great joy, because they now understood the words that had been made known to them.*

Nehemiah assembled all of the people and Ezra the priest read the Book of the Law. They then praised the LORD and celebrated the Feast of the Tabernacle, reading the book of the Law each day and observing the traditional celebration for seven days.

NEHEMIAH 9

Verse 33: *In all that has happened to us, you have been just; you have acted faithfully, while we did wrong.*

On the eighth day they assembled and confessed their sins. The Levites led the praise of the LORD. They recalled the plight of their forefathers, from slavery, to their exodus, and the Law given to Moses. They reminded the assembly that their ancestors were stubborn and did not follow the Law. They noted how God was patient and compassionate during their desert wanderings and entry into the Promised Land. They recalled their disobedience and rebellion that led to their eventual downfall. They reminded the group, however, that the LORD had now released them from exile and they appealed to the assemblage to follow Him and His Laws.

NEHEMIAH 10

Verse 39: *The people of Israel, including the Levites, are to bring their contributions of grain, new wine and oil to the storerooms where the articles for the sanctuary are kept and where the ministering priests, the gatekeepers and the singers stay. We will not neglect the house of our God.*

The Levites made a binding agreement and asked everyone to sign the document. The agreement included specifics about following the Law, not allowing intermarriages with non-Jewish natives, keeping the Sabbath, giving offerings, and obeying other Laws and traditions.

NEHEMIAH 11

Verse 2: *The people commended all the men who volunteered to live in Jerusalem.*

The people cast lots to repopulate the city, and the leaders moved to the city as well.

NEHEMIAH 12

Verse 43: *And on that day they offered great sacrifices, rejoicing because God had given them great joy. The women and children also rejoiced. The sound of rejoicing in Jerusalem could be heard far away.*

Priests and Levites also lived in the city of Jerusalem. A dedication of the wall was celebrated, led by the Levites. Choirs sang praises to the LORD and great sacrifices were made.

NEHEMIAH 13

Verse 14: *Remember me for this, O my God, and do not blot out what I have so faithfully done for the house of my God and its services.*

Nehemiah made other reforms including forbidding foreigners from worshiping with them. Nehemiah returned to Babylon, but heard that Eliashib the priest had allowed his enemy, Tobiah, entry into a storage room meant for offerings. Therefore, Nehemiah came back to Jerusalem and removed all of Tobiah's possessions from the room. He also learned that the Levites were not receiving their share of the offerings and rectified this problem. Then he reinstated the Sabbath, which was being ignored, and once again forbade intermarriages. He rectified all of the wrongs that had occurred since they had signed their binding agreement.

ESTHER

ESTHER 1

Verse 20: *Then when the king's edict is proclaimed throughout all his vast realm, all the women will respect their husbands, from the least to the greatest.*

Xerxes, king of Persia, held a great banquet during the third year of his reign. He held the feast for seven days, and spared no expense. Queen Vashti also held a banquet for the women in the royal palace of King Xerxes. The king sent for the queen, but she refused to come. The king was furious and consulted with his advisors. Memucan advised the king to punish the queen for her disobedience. In order to make an example of her, the king issued an edict that expelled Vashti from the kingdom.

ESTHER 2

Verse 17: *Now the king was attracted to Esther more than to any of the other women, and she won his favor and approval more than any of the other virgins. So he set a royal crown on her head and made her queen instead of Vashti.*

The king then had his attendants search the land for a new queen. Esther, a Jew from the tribe of Benjamin, was among the women selected to be taken to the palace for the king to choose from. Mordecai, Esther's uncle who raised her from childhood, instructed Esther to keep her heritage secret. When it was Esther's turn to be presented to the king, he took an instant liking to her and selected her to become the new queen. He proclaimed a holiday and had a banquet in her honor. Mordecai overheard two of the king's officers conspiring to assassinate the king. He told Esther, who warned the king, giving Mordecai credit. The two officials were discovered and hanged.

ESTHER 3

Verse 7: *In the twelfth year of King Xerxes, in the first month, the month of Nisan, they cast the pur (that is, the lot) in the presence of Haman to select a day and month. And the lot fell on the twelfth month, the month of Adar.*

The king promoted Haman to be the chief of all the nobles and instructed everyone to kneel in his presence. Mordecai refused to do so, and Haman conspired to kill not only Mordecai, but also all of the Jews. Haman received the king's endorsement and put a bounty on all Jews. A decree was sent out with the king's signature ordering the annihilation of all Jews in the country on a chosen day.

ESTHER 4

Verse 14: *For if you remain silent at this time, relief and deliverance for the Jews will arise from another place, but you and your father's family will perish. And who knows but that you have come to royal position for such a time as this?*

Mordecai and all of the Jews were anguished when they learned of the decree. Esther learned that her uncle was upset, but did not know why. She sent a servant to visit him and he returned to her with all the details of the king's order. She was reluctant to appeal to the king because he had a rule that anyone who approached him without being summoned would be put to death unless he immediately gave a pardon. Mordecai sent word to her that it was her duty to her people to approach the king. Esther instructed Mordecai to gather all of the Jewish people and fast, and she would appeal to the king, fully aware of the possible consequences.

ESTHER 5

Verse 14: *His wife Zeresh and all his friends said to him, "Have a gallows built, seventy-five feet high, and ask the king in the morning to have Mordecai hanged on it. Then go with the king to the dinner and be happy." This suggestion delighted Haman, and he had the gallows built.*

Esther prepared a banquet for the king and Haman. Haman was pleased that he alone was invited to the banquet but was angered when Mordecai again refused to show him respect.

Upon his wife and friend's suggestions, he had gallows built so that he could ask the king to hang Mordecai on it.

ESTHER 6

Verse 11: *So Haman got the robe and the horse. He robed Mordecai, and led him on horseback through the city streets, proclaiming before him, "This is what is done for the man the king delights to honor!"*

That night the king reviewed the record of his reign and discovered that Mordecai had never been recognized for exposing the assassination plot against him. The king asked Haman what he should do to honor someone he favored. Haman, thinking it was he who was to be honored, suggested that the king give this person a royal robe and parade him throughout the city on a royal horse proclaiming that the king was honoring him. The king ordered that Mordecai be so honored, and Haman was devastated.

ESTHER 7

Verse 9: *Then Harbona, one of the eunuchs attending the king, said, "A gallows seventy five feet high stands by Haman's house. He had it made for Mordecai, who spoke up to help the king." The king said, "Hang him on it!"*

King Xerxes, Esther, and Haman took part in the royal banquet and the king asked Esther what she wanted. Esther asked that her life and that of her people be spared. The king asked who was responsible for this action and Esther said that Haman was. Xerxes left the room and returned to find Haman begging Esther (who was lying on the couch) to spare his life. This further infuriated the king who ordered Haman to be hanged on the very gallows that he had constructed for Mordecai.

ESTHER 8

Verse 17: *In every province and in every city, wherever the edict of the king went, there was joy and gladness among the Jews, with feasting and celebrating. And many people of other nationalities became Jews because fear of the Jews had seized them.*

Esther was given Haman's estate and she appointed Mordecai to oversee it. Mordecai was also given Haman's position. Esther asked King Xerxes to rescind the previous order, but he could not because it was sealed with his ring. A new order was written and sealed, however, that gave the Jews the right to assemble and defend themselves. All of the Jews celebrated the new edict.

ESTHER 9

Verse 28: *These days should be remembered and observed in every generation by every family, and in every province and in every city. And these days of Purim should never cease to be celebrated by the Jews, nor should the memory of them die out among their descendants.*

The Jews successfully defended themselves on the date of the original order. They killed over seventy-five thousand men and, with the king's approval, hanged the ten sons of Haman. The Jews celebrated what would become an annual celebration observing Purim (named for the lots cast by Haman for their bounty). Another edict was written by Queen Esther, and signed and sealed by King Xerxes, commemorating this occasion.

ESTHER 10

Verse 3: *Mordecai the Jew was held in high esteem by his many fellow Jews, because he worked for the good of his people and spoke up for the welfare of all the Jews.*

Xerxes went on to be known as a great and powerful king and Mordecai the Jew was second in rank and held in high esteem.

Wisdom and Poetry

Chapter 18

JOB

JOB 1

Verse 12: *The LORD said to Satan, "Very well, then everything he has is in your hands, but on the man himself do not lay a finger." Then Satan went out from the presence of the LORD.*

Job lived in Uz and was considered the greatest man among all the people of the East. He was loyal to God and to his seven sons and three daughters. Satan met with God, and God told him about His blameless and upright servant Job. Satan suggested that if Job's wealth and success were taken away that even Job would curse God. Job was immediately tested. His animals were stolen, his possessions were burned, and his children were killed. Job was distraught, yet fell to the ground in worship and praised God. He noted that, "The LORD gave and the LORD has taken away; may the name of the LORD be praised."

JOB 2

Verse 10: *He replied, "You are talking like a foolish woman. Shall we accept good from God, and not trouble?" In all this, Job did not sin.*

Satan again met with the LORD, acknowledging that Job passed the first test, but suggesting that if Job were physically smitten he would forsake the LORD. Job was then inflicted with horrible sores, and his wife told him to curse God, but Job refused. Job's three friends, Eliphaz the Temanite, Bildad the Shuhite, and Zophar the Naamathite came to comfort Job. They sat with him in silence for seven days and seven nights.

Job 3

Verse 26: *I have no peace, no quietness; I have no rest, but only turmoil.*

Job spoke and cursed the day of his birth, but did not curse God. He embarked on a long oration indicating that he wished he would die so he could rest.

Job 4

Verse 6: *Should not your piety be your confidence and your blameless ways your hope?*

Job's friend, Eliphaz, replied to Job, first encouraging him and then suggesting that he must have sinned in order to evoke this response from God. He asked Job if a mortal man could be more righteous or more pure than God.

Job 5

Verse 2: *Resentment kills a fool, and envy slays the simple.*

Eliphaz continued, telling Job not to be resentful. He encouraged Job to appeal to God, and assured Job that God would eventually rescue him.

Job 6

Verse 10: *Then I would still have this consolation—my joy in unrelenting pain—that I had not denied the words of the Holy One.*

Job told Eliphaz how much pain and suffering he was enduring. He prayed that God would end his life, criticized his friends for being of no help, and pleaded for relief.

Job 7

Verse 16: *I despise my life; I would not live forever. Let me alone; my days have no meaning.*

Job continued to bemoan his very existence. He asked God why he was targeted and why his sins had not been forgiven.

Job 8

Verse 20: *Surely God does not reject a blameless man or strengthen the hands of evildoers.*

Bildad the Shuhite (Job's other friend) tried to comfort Job and suggested that he should not blame God. However, he echoed the sentiment of Eliphaz that Job would not have been punished if he were blameless.

Job 9

Verse 33-35: *If only there were someone to arbitrate between us, to lay his hand upon us both, someone to remove God's rod from me, so that his terror would frighten me no more. Then I would speak up without fear of him, but as it now stands with me, I cannot.*

Job replied to Bildad, recognizing the power of God. He asked rhetorically how he could argue with God. He noted that he was blameless, but that he was no longer concerned about his own life. Job wished that he could speak to God through an arbitrator.

Job 10

Verse 15: *If I am guilty—woe to me! Even if I am innocent, I cannot lift my head, for I am full of shame and drowned in my affliction.*

Job continued stating that he loathed his life and asked God to tell him how he had sinned. He felt ashamed (even in innocence).

Job 11

Verse 7: *Can you fathom the mysteries of God? Can you probe the limits of the Almighty?*

Zophar the Naamathite next tried to console Job. He also suspected that Job had wronged God and encouraged him to go to God for help.

Job 12

Verse 5: *Men at ease have contempt for misfortune as the fate of those whose feet are slipping.*

Job replied to Zophar that he was indeed blameless and criticized his friends for assuming that his misfortune was his fault. He then praised God for all of His power.

Job 13

Verse 15: *Though he slay me, yet will I hope in him; I will surely defend my ways to his face.*

Job continued to praise God. He asked for an audience with God instead of his "friends." He asked for the LORD to withdraw His terrors and for a chance to present his case to Him.

Job 14

Verse 14: *If a man dies, will he live again? All the days of my hard service I will wait for my renewal to come.*

Job noted that man's days on earth are numbered, and asked that he be allowed to pass away until God's wrath was over.

Job 15

Verse 6: *Your own mouth condemns you, not mine; your own lips testify against you.*

Eliphaz again addressed Job, asking him why he was so angry with God. He explained that Job was suffering because of the inherent evil of man.

Job 16

Verse 19: *Even now my witness is in heaven; my advocate is on high.*

Job criticized his friends for being "miserable comforters," and accused them of being long-winded. He acknowledged that God had turned against him, yet he did not forsake Him.

Job 17

Verse 3: *Give me, O God, the pledge you demand. Who else will put up security for me?*

Job asked where his hope was and challenged his friends and God to help him.

Job 18

Verse 2: *When will you end these speeches? Be sensible, and then we can talk.*

Bildad tried again to comfort Job. He turned the long-winded accusation back at him, and told Job that he must be evil to be receiving this punishment.

Job 19

Verse 25: *I know that my Redeemer lives, and that in the end he will stand upon the earth.*

Job criticized his friends for tormenting him. He again proclaimed that he had done no wrong, asked his friends for pity, and acknowledged God's power.

Job 20

Verse 27: *The heavens will expose his guilt; the earth will rise up against him.*

Zophar talked to Job again, indicating that all men sin, and that God would punish all. He again implied that Job had sinned.

Job 21

Verse 7: *Why do the wicked live on, growing old and increasing in power?*

Job asked why he was punished, but the wicked were not. He asked what the reward for believing in God was if people who have not accepted Him live and prosper.

Job 22

Verse 21: *Submit to God and be at peace with him; in this way prosperity will come to you.*

Eliphaz asked Job if a man could be of benefit to God. He again implied that Job, like all men, had sinned. He told Job to submit to God and return to the Almighty.

Job 23

Verse 10: *But he knows the way that I take; when he has tested me, I will come forth as gold.*

Job wished that he could submit his case to God, but stated that he could not find Him. He indicated that he continued to fear God.

Job 24

Verse 24: *For a little while they are exalted, and then they are gone; they are brought low and gathered up like all others; they are cut off like heads of grain.*

Job asked why God had not set times for judgment. He wondered why the poor believers must look in vain, and wondered about the power of God.

Job 25

Verse 4: *How then can a man be righteous before God? How can one born of a woman be pure?*

Bildad replied to Job that no man is righteous before God.

JOB 26

Verse 14: *And these are but the outer fringe of his works; how faint the whisper we hear of him! Who then can understand the thunder of his power?*

Job commented (rhetorically) on what good advice his friends had offered. He then went on to describe the power and destructive capability of God.

JOB 27

Verse 6: *I will maintain my righteousness and never let go of it; my conscience will not reproach me as long as I live.*

Job noted that God had denied him justice, but stopped short of forsaking the LORD. He promised that as long as he continued to live, no matter how miserably, he would not speak against Him. He again proclaimed the power of God.

JOB 28

Verse 23: *God understands the way to it and he alone knows where it dwells....*

Job wondered aloud where wisdom and understanding dwell. He noted that man, despite his capabilities, could not find them; only God knew. Job recognized that "the fear of the LORD is wisdom."

JOB 29

Verse 2: *How I long for the months gone by, for the days when God watched over me....*

Job reminisced about the good old days. He had been a very prominent and successful citizen, but this was all taken away from him.

JOB 30

Verse 16: *And now my life ebbs away; days of suffering grip me.*

Job went on to describe all that had been taken away from him. He was mocked and detested by the same people who had looked up to him before. He was tired, sore, and fearful, and he felt like he was dying, and felt that even the LORD had turned away from him. He was desolate.

JOB 31

Verse 23: *For I dreaded destruction from God, and for fear of his splendor I could not do such things.*

Job reiterated that he was blameless; he had not lusted for other women or denied justice to his servants. He had given to the poor, not coveted money, or enjoyed another's misfortune. He discussed his lack of sin and asked God again for an audience. He asked for punishment if he had sinned in any way.

JOB 32

Verse 5: *But when he saw that the three men had nothing more to say, his anger was aroused.*

Job's other three friends no longer answered Job, but Elihu, son of Barakel the Buzite did speak. He indicated that although he was young, he felt obliged to speak.

JOB 33

Verse 13: *Why do you complain to him that he answers none of man's words?*

Elihu said that Job was not right in proclaiming his innocence, because God is greater than man. He noted that God does not have to answer to man.

Job 34

Verse 10: *So listen to me, you men of understanding. Far be it from God to do evil, from the Almighty to do wrong.*

Elihu continued, instructing Job to listen closely to him. He proclaimed that Job had gotten what he deserved, and that it was unthinkable that God could or would do wrong. Elihu said that God is all-powerful, just, and fair. He told the group that Job spoke without knowledge, and believed that Job should be tested.

Job 35

Verse 12: *He does not answer when men cry out because of the arrogance of the wicked.*

Elihu told Job that God does not have to answer him. He again accused Job of sinning.

Job 36

Verse 21: *Beware of turning to evil, which you seem to prefer to affliction.*

Elihu continued, claiming that he was talking on God's behalf. He told Job that God is just and that there was a reason for his suffering. He noted that God would forgive him if he would repent. He went on to espouse the power of the Lord.

Job 37

Verse 23: *The Almighty is beyond our reach and exalted in power; in his justice and great righteousness, he does not oppress.*

Elihu expounded on God's power, indicating that He is beyond man's reach.

Job 38

Verse 18: *Have you comprehended the vast expanses of the earth? Tell me, if you know all this.*

The LORD answered Job out of the storm. He challenged Job (and Elihu) about their irreverence to Him, then asked them where they were when He made the Earth. God went on to ask if they (he) could do a number of things that only the LORD could do.

Job 39

Verse 1: *Do you know when the mountain goats give birth? Do you watch when the doe bears her fawn?*

The LORD continued His admonition, asking rhetorically if they could do the things He has done or if they know the things that He knows.

Job 40

Verse 2: *Will the one who contends with the Almighty correct him? Let him who accuses God answer him!*

God commanded Job to answer Him with his accusations. Job replied that he was unworthy. He said that he had spoken, but he would say no more. The LORD again rebuked him for challenging His authority.

Job 41

Verse 1: *Can you pull in the leviathan with a fishhook or tie down his tongue with a rope?*

The LORD told of His power, citing His control over leviathan as an example. He challenged Job again. God concluded that He looks down on all that are haughty, because He is King over all that are proud.

Job 42

Verse 3: *You asked, "Who is this that obscured my counsel without knowledge?" Surely I spoke of things I did not understand, things too wonderful for me to know.*

Job responded that he knew God could do all things and that no plan of His could be thwarted. Job concluded that he despised himself and repented in dust and ashes. The LORD spoke to Eliphaz and expressed His anger with him and his friends. He commanded him to make a sacrifice on Job's behalf. Job prayed for his friends, and the LORD made him prosperous again, giving him twice what he had before. All of his brothers and sisters joined him, bringing him gifts and consoling him. He had ten more children, seven sons and three beautiful daughters. He had countless livestock and possessions. Job lived to be one hundred and forty, and he prospered.

Chapter 19

PSALMS

THE FIRST BOOK OF PSALMS, Psalms 1-41: Similar to Genesis, this first book presents a theme of humans being blessed by God, falling, and then being redeemed by God.

PSALM 1 *Author: Anonymous*

Verse 3: *He is like a tree planted by streams of water, which yields its fruit in season and whose leaf does not wither. Whatever he does prospers.*

The author writes that the man who does not associate with sinners, who is righteous, and who obeys the Law, is blessed, and compares him to a healthy tree bearing fruit. The wicked are like chaff that the wind blows away. The author states that the wicked will not stand in judgment or assemble with the righteous. He declares that the LORD watches over the righteous and the wicked will perish.

PSALM 2 *Author: David*

Verse 12: *Kiss the Son, lest he be angry and you be destroyed in your way, for his wrath can flare up in a moment. Blessed are all who take refuge in him.*

David asks why the earthly rulers try to overthrow the LORD and His anointed King (David [and Christ]). The Lord scoffs at them and then shows His wrath. The LORD proclaims that if His King asks, He will give Him all the nations of the world. David admonishes the earthly rulers to obey the LORD or they will perish.

PSALM 3 *Author: David*

Verse 3: *But you are a shield around me, O LORD; you bestow glory on me and lift up my head.*

David appeals to the LORD for help when he was fleeing from his son Absalom. He acknowledges that the LORD is his shield and his only hope. Even though his enemies surround him, David knows that the LORD will save him, for salvation and joy come from the LORD.

PSALM 4 *Author: David*

Verse 4: *In your anger do not sin; when you are on your beds, search your hearts and be silent.*

David writes that one must put his trust in the LORD and not in idols. He knows that the LORD has set apart the redeemed for Himself. He states that the LORD will keep him safe and at peace.

PSALM 5 *Author: David*

Verse 3: *In the morning, O LORD, you hear my voice; in the morning I lay my requests before you and wait in expectation.*

David appeals to the LORD for protection against his wicked and lying enemies. He asks that they be punished for their sins, but also asks for joy to come to those who put their trust in Him. David states that the LORD blesses and protects the godly man with His "shield of love."

PSALM 6 *Author: David*

Verse 3: *My soul is in anguish. How long, O LORD, how long?*

David asks for forgiveness and restoration. He asks for God's help in turning away his enemies. He declares that God will turn them back in shame.

PSALM 7 *Author: David*

Verse 14: *He who is pregnant with evil and conceives trouble gives birth to disillusionment.*

David asks to be saved from his persecutors. He asks for justice against those who persecute the innocent. He asks for an end to all wickedness and blessings to those who truly worship the righteous LORD. David states that God is a shield to defend the innocent and a fair and righteous judge. David is grateful and thankful.

PSALM 8 *Author: David*

Verse 2: *From the lips of children and infants you have ordained praise because of your enemies, to silence the foe and the avenger.*

David contemplates how the all-powerful Creator of the moon and stars still pays attention to a lowly human. He knows that God has put man in charge of everything He made, and placed him just below the angels. David declares the majesty and glory of His name that fills the earth.

PSALM 9 *Author: David*

Verse 10: *Those who know your name will trust in you, for you, LORD, have never forsaken those who seek you.*

David praises and thanks the LORD for victory over his enemies. The LORD had rebuked his enemies and destroyed the wicked. David declares that the merciful LORD rules the world and does not ignore calls of help from the righteous. David asks for mercy and salvation. He also asks the LORD to judge and punish the evil nations.

PSALM 10 *Author: Anonymous [probably David]*

Verse 14: *But you, O God, do see trouble and grief; you consider it to take it in hand. The victim commits himself to you; you are the helper of the fatherless.*

The author asks that the wicked men who persecute the poor be punished. He states that although the LORD appears not to be watching at times, He is aware of every injustice.

The author appeals to the LORD to act on these injustices stating that God is the "helper of the helpless."

PSALM 11 *Author: David*

Verse 4: *The LORD is in his holy temple; the LORD in on his heavenly throne. He observes the sons of men; his eyes examine them.*

Surrounded by his enemies, David does not panic, but puts his faith in the LORD. God is in control and tests both the righteous and the wicked. God loves goodness and will punish the wicked.

PSALM 12 *Author: David*

Verse 8: *The wicked freely strut about when what is vile is honored among men.*

David wonders where the honest and righteous are, but is confident that liars and evil men will be punished. The LORD will defend the oppressed, the poor, and the needy. He will protect His own from the evil men that surround them.

PSALM 13 *Author: David*

Verse 1: *How long, O LORD? Will you forget me forever? How long will you hide your face from me?*

David prays for relief from despair and is discouraged that the LORD has not answered him immediately. Nevertheless, he puts his trust in God's mercy and rejoices in His salvation. He sings to the LORD for His rich blessings.

PSALM 14 *Author: David*

Verse 7: *Oh, that salvation for Israel would come out of Zion! When the LORD restores the fortunes of his people, let Jacob rejoice and Israel be glad!*

David declares that anyone who denies the presence of God is a fool. He says that the LORD is looking for those who are wise and want to please Him; that God is with those who love Him, but will terrorize those who do not.

PSALM 15 *Author: David*

Verse 1: *LORD, who may dwell in your sanctuary? Who may live on your holy hill?*

David writes that the LORD will reward those who are blameless and sincere. He says that men who refuse to slander others, do not harm their neighbors, avoid sin, and are faithful and fair, will stand firm with the LORD forever.

PSALM 16 *Author: David*

Verse 6: *The boundary lines have fallen for me in pleasant places; surely I have a delightful inheritance.*

David is thankful for the company of God, and godly men and women. He calls the LORD a "wonderful inheritance." The joy and pleasure of God's presence is exalted.

PSALM 17 *Author: David*

Verse 3: *Though you probe my heart and examine me at night, though you test me, you will find nothing; I have resolved that my mouth will not sin.*

David appeals to the LORD for help while Saul is persecuting him. He asserts that he has been righteous and asks for God's love and protection. He asks for help to fend off his enemies, who surround him like young lions ready to pounce. David recognizes that the men who pursue him are after earthly treasures, but his treasure is in heaven.

PSALM 18 *Author: David*

Verse 46: *The LORD lives! Praise be to my Rock! Exalted be God my Savior!*

This is a song of David after he was delivered from his enemies. He praises the LORD for His protection. He tells that the LORD's intervention was swift and mighty with thunder and lightning from heaven; that the LORD blessed him for his righteousness. David praises God for His mercy and light. He thanks Him for filling him with strength and salvation. The LORD clothed David in armor and gave him His shield of salvation. He praises the Almighty for victory over his enemies. God has rescued him—God is alive!

PSALM 19 *Author: David*

Verse 13: Keep your servant also from willful sins; may they not rule over me. Then will I be blameless, innocent of great transgression.

David writes that the heavens are a marvelous display of God's glory. He states that God's laws are perfect—they protect those who follow them and give joy and light. David asks for the LORD's help in following these laws and asks that he be pleasing to the LORD—his Rock and Redeemer.

PSALM 20 *Author: David*

Verse 7: Some trust in chariots and some in horses; but we trust in the name of the LORD our God.

David prays for victory in battle. He places his trust in the LORD exclaiming, "God save the king."

PSALM 21 *Author: David*

Verse 2: You have granted him the desire of his heart and have not withheld the request of his lips.

David praises the LORD for victory. He declares that God has given life, fame, honor, splendor, majesty, and eternal happiness. David praises the LORD for His future and eternal victories.

PSALM 22 *Author: David*

Verse 22: My God, my God, why have you forsaken me? Why are you so far from saving me, so far from the words of my groaning?

The psalm begins with an expression of suffering and despair, and asks for the LORD's help in overcoming his enemies. He asks for God's strength and to be rescued. He promises to publicly bring glory to God for His help. He concludes that "dominion belongs to the LORD and he rules the nations." He promises that he, his children, and generations to come will worship Him.

PSALM 23 *Author: David*

Verse 6: *Surely goodness and love will follow me all the days of my life, and I will dwell in the house of the LORD forever.*

David states: "The LORD is my shepherd;" He makes me rest in the meadow, gives me strength, and helps me to honor Him. He protects me from danger, provides for me, and blesses me. He will be with me all my life and then allow me to live with Him forever.

PSALM 24 *Author: David*

Verse 10: *Who is he, this King of glory? The LORD Almighty—he is the King of glory.*

David declares that everything on earth belongs to God the Creator, and that only the pure and righteous may stand before Him. He urges that the ancient gates be open wide to let the King of Glory, the Commander of all of heaven's armies, in.

PSALM 25 *Author: David*

Verse 11: *For the sake of your name, O LORD, forgive my iniquity, though it is great.*

This is a prayer for victory, guidance, and forgiveness of sin. David asks the LORD to guide him on the right path. He says that the man who obeys and fears the LORD will inherit the earth, and friendship with God is reserved for those who reverence Him. David asks God to rescue Israel from distress, sorrows and enemies.

PSALM 26 *Author: David*

Verse 12: *My feet stand on level ground; in the great assembly I will praise the LORD.*

Declaring loyalty to God, David asks to be cross-examined because he has walked the straight and narrow path. He praises the LORD for keeping him from slipping.

PSALM 27 *Author: David*

Verse 13: *I am still confident of this: I will see the goodness of the LORD in the land of the living.*

David states that unwavering confidence in the LORD makes him fearless. He knows that when troubles come, the answer is to be in the presence of the LORD. He asks the LORD for guidance and to be rescued from his enemies. He advises: Do not be impatient, wait for the LORD and He will come and save you.

PSALM 28 *Author: David*

> Verse 7: *The LORD is my strength and my shield; my heart trusts in him, and I am helped. My heart leaps for joy and I will give thanks to him in song.*

David pleads for help from the LORD, his Rock of safety. He asks for the wicked to be punished. He knows that the LORD protects His people.

PSALM 29 *Author: David*

> Verse 3: *The voice of the LORD is over the waters; the God of glory thunders, the LORD thunders over the mighty waters.*

David praises the LORD, who reveals His great power in nature. He acknowledges that God brings both peace and strength to the storms of life.

PSALM 30 *Author: David*

> Verse 5: *For his anger lasts only a moment, but his favor lasts a lifetime; weeping may remain for a night, but rejoicing comes in the morning.*

David praises the LORD for saving him from his enemies. He praises the LORD for saving his life. David declares that self-reliance results in despair and that only the LORD can rescue.

PSALM 31 *Author: David (or Jeremiah)*

> Verse 6: *I hate those who cling to worthless idols; I trust in the LORD."*

This psalm is a plea: Rescue us from our enemies, LORD, for You are our Rock. Have mercy on us in times of stress, sin, and sadness. The psalmist states that the LORD alone is his God and that there are great blessings for those who trust and reverence Him. He tells the saints to bless and love the LORD who protects them.

PSALM 32 *Author: David*

Verse 7: *You are my hiding place; you will protect me from trouble and surround me with songs of deliverance.*

David writes that those who confess their sins to the LORD will have happiness and relief. He states that abiding love surrounds those who trust in the LORD and obedience to Him makes one rejoice.

PSALM 33 *Author: Anonymous*

Verse 12: *Blessed is the nation whose God is the LORD, the people he chose for his inheritance.*

The author states that the LORD is to be praised for He is trustworthy; He is the Creator and everyone should stand in awe of Him. The author declares that God alone can save and protect; He is faithful even in the worst of times. The reader is urged to trust in His holy name.

PSALM 34 *Author: David*

Verse 18: *The LORD is close to the brokenhearted and saves those who are crushed in spirit.*

David praises and exalts the LORD. He states that the LORD rescues the oppressed and that those who reverence Him will never lack any good thing. David proclaims that the good man does not escape all his troubles, but he has the LORD to help him with every one. It is clear to David that He will redeem those who serve Him.

PSALM 35 *Author: David*

Verse 10: *My whole being will exclaim, "Who is like you O LORD?"*

David asks the LORD to fight those who are fighting him. He asks for victory over his enemies who are unjustly accusing him. He states that he will rejoice in the LORD for He will rescue the righteous.

PSALM 36 *Author: David*

Verse 5: *Your love, O LORD, reaches to the heavens, your faithfulness to the skies.*

David sees that sin lurks in the hearts of evil and wicked men but that God's faithfulness, love, and justice overcome all evil. He states that God is the fountain of life that pours out love and blessings to those who do His will.

PSALM 37 *Author: David*

Verse 4: *Delight yourself in the LORD and he will give you the desires of your heart.*

David gives this exhortation: Never envy the wicked—trust and delight in the LORD. The wicked will be destroyed, but those who trust in the LORD shall be given every blessing. David states that if someone wants an eternal home, he must leave his evil ways and live a good life—the good man will eventually prevail over the evil one. David declares that the LORD will rescue godly men from the plots of evil men.

PSALM 38 *Author: David*

Verse 4: *My guilt has overwhelmed me like a burden too heavy to bear.*

David brings a petition before the LORD, recognizing that his sin has brought him sorrow and sickness. He states that God alone is the true source of healing and protection to those who confess their sins to Him and that the LORD will protect those who believe in Him from those who attempt to slander them.

PSALM 39 *Author: David*

Verse 12: *Hear my prayer, O LORD, listen to my cry for help; be not deaf to my weeping. For I dwell with you as an alien, a stranger, as all my fathers were.*

David recognizes how short life is and that his only hope is in the LORD. He sees himself as a guest of the LORD, as a traveler through the earth, and he asks for God's mercy.

PSALM 40 *Author: David*

Verse 3: *He put a new song in my mouth, a hymn of praise to our God. Many will see and fear and put their trust in the LORD.*

David had waited patiently for God's help. He states that many blessings are given to those who trust in the LORD, and that life-long service to the LORD is pleasing to Him. To David the Good News is that God forgives sins, and His people should spread the word. David declares how great God is because to the weak, He is strong.

PSALM 41 *Author: David*

Verse 13: *Praise be to the LORD, the God of Israel, from everlasting to everlasting. Amen and Amen.*

David asserts that God blesses those who are kind to the poor, and even when the sick are abandoned, the Lord is there for them. David blesses the LORD who has existed from everlasting ages past and into everlasting eternity ahead.

THE SECOND BOOK OF PSALMS, Psalms 42-72. This collection, written mostly by David and the sons of Korah (Temple musicians and assistants), is similar to Exodus—the story of a nation ruined and recovered.

PSALM 42 *Author: Sons of Korah*

Verse 2: *My soul thirsts for God, for the living God. When can I go and meet with God?*

The author thirsts for God as the deer pants for water. In the midst of despair, he takes courage and receives his happiness from the LORD. He expects God to act and will praise Him for all that He does.

PSALM 43 *Author: Sons of Korah*

Verse 5: *Why are you downcast, O my soul? Why so disturbed within me? Put your hope in God, for I will yet praise him, my Savior and my God.*

The author puts his trust in God to defend him from the charges of merciless and deceitful men. He has hope in times of discouragement—for the LORD is his God.

PSALM 44 *Author: Sons of Korah*

Verse 8: *In God we make our boast all day long, and we will praise your name forever.*

This is a plea for victory. The author states that he does not trust his weapons, for only God can grant victory. He thanks God, remembering His victories in the past. He asks God why it seems that He is opposing His people now; the word "Jew" has become a name of contempt and shame. The author pleads with the LORD and notes that the people's hearts are pure. He says that they are being persecuted for their faith and he asks God to awaken and save them with His constant love.

PSALM 45 *Author: Sons of Korah*

Verse 1: *My heart is stirred by a noble theme as I recite my verses for the king; my tongue is the pen of a skillful writer.*

This is a poem to a king (Solomon?) on his wedding day. The poet calls the king the fairest of all and blessed by God. He encourages the king to go on to victory defending truth, humility, and justice. The writer states that God has given the king gladness because he is just, loves what is good, and hates what is wrong. The richly dressed bride is encouraged to reverence her new husband and told that she will be rewarded; their sons will sit on thrones around the world, and the king's name will be honored for generations.

PSALM 46 *Author: Sons of Korah*

Verse 10: *Be still, and know that I am God; I will be exalted among the nations, I will be exalted in the earth.*

The author writes that God is the refuge and strength of the people even if the mountains crumble. It is stated that the Commander of the armies of heaven supports Jerusalem, and He will rescue the city (from the attacking Assyrian army). The author declares that the LORD wants it known that He is God and He will be honored in every nation in the world.

PSALM 47 *Author: Sons of Korah*

Verse 1: *Clap your hands, all you nations; shout to God with cries of joy.*

This is a joyous and triumphant praise to the LORD. It contains exaltations to the King who reigns over all the earth. It tells that He is highly honored everywhere, even among the Gentiles who were once attacking God's people.

PSALM 48 *Author: Sons of Korah*

Verse 1: *Great is the LORD, and most worthy of praise, in the city of our God, his holy mountain.*

This is a declaration of how great the LORD is who resides in Mount Zion above the Holy City. The author states that God Himself is the defender of Jerusalem; that God has defeated the enemies of Jerusalem and has established the city forever. The reader is told to rejoice and praise God!

PSALM 49 *Author: Sons of Korah*

Verse 20: *A man who has riches without understanding is like the beasts that perish.*

The psalmist writes that he will not fear in times of trouble, and it is God's forgiveness—not all the money in the world—that will grant salvation. He says that wealth should be left to others; the power of wealth is gone with death. He declares that God will redeem the souls of believers from the power of death, for a man with all his pomp must die like any animal.

PSALM 50 *Author: Asaph, one of David's chief musicians*

Verse 9: *I have no need of a bull from your stall or of goats from your pens....*

Asaph writes of God gathering all of His people for judgment; the LORD does not ask for sacrifices, but for their true thanks. Asaph states that God requires that His people trust Him so that He may rescue them and bring glory to Himself. It is written that God gives evil men one last chance before He tears them apart. It is also stated that true praise is a worthy sacrifice and salvation is the reward for walking His path.

PSALM 51 *Author: David*

Verse 17: *The sacrifices of God are a broken spirit; a broken and contrite heart, O God, you will not despise.*

David asks for mercy and pity following his adultery with Bathsheba and murder of Uriah, her husband. He asks for cleansing. He asks for a new, clean heart and the joy of God's salvation. He pleads for forgiveness and rescue while praising God.

PSALM 52 *Author: David*

Verse 8: *But I am like an olive tree flourishing in the house of God; I trust in God's unfailing love for ever and ever.*

David protests the evil of his enemy Doeg. He predicts God's punishment against him and recognizes that the LORD shelters him.

PSALM 53 *Author: David*

Verse 6: *Oh, that salvation for Israel would come out of Zion! When God restores the fortunes of his people, let Jacob rejoice and Israel be glad!*

David writes that everyone has sinned and because of sin, no one can find God without God's help. David asks God to save Israel and for restoration of the people.

PSALM 54 *Author: David*

Verse 6: *I will sacrifice a freewill offering to you; I will praise your name, O LORD, for it is good.*

David asks for the LORD's help in defending himself against his enemies who tried to betray him to Saul. David declares that because God is his helper, these wicked men will fail, and God will rescue him.

PSALM 55 *Author: David*

Verse 22: *Cast your cares on the LORD and he will sustain you; he will never let the righteous fall.*

David is anguished over the treachery of a friend and asks the LORD for refuge. He asks that his wicked and dishonest enemies be defeated and for God to save him and to carry his burdens.

PSALM 56 *Author: David*

Verse 4: *In God, whose word I praise, in God I trust; I will not be afraid. What can mortal man do to me?*

With his enemies closing in on him, David puts his trust in the LORD. He thanks God for His help in defeating his enemies. He states that the LORD saved him from death so that he may walk before Him.

PSALM 57 *Author: David*

Verse 5: *Be exalted, O God, above the heavens; let your glory be over all the earth.*

David hides behind the shadow of the LORD's wings for protection. As his enemies dug a pit to trap David, they themselves fell into it. David exalts the LORD and sings His praises. He asks that His glory shine throughout the earth.

PSALM 58 *Author: David*

Verse 1: *Do you rulers indeed speak justly? Do you judge uprightly among men?*

David asks that all those be punished who were in authority and unjust. He states that the godly shall rejoice in the triumph of right; good is rewarded and God judges justly here on the earth.

PSALM 59 *Author: David*

Verse 16: *But I will sing of your strength, in the morning I will sing of your love; for you are my fortress, my refuge in times of trouble.*

David asks the LORD to save him from his enemies. He sings the LORD's praises, and asks that God bring his enemies to their knees. He sings praises to the Lord, his tower of refuge and safety.

PSALM 60 *Author: David*

Verse 12: *With God we will gain the victory, and he will trample down our enemies.*

David asks for the LORD's help in the midst of battle. He rallies around God who has given Israel a banner. He exalts the LORD, shouts in triumph, and knows that God will bring him victory over Edom. David states that with God's help the people will do mighty things, for He will trample their foes.

PSALM 61 *Author: David*

Verse 2: *From the ends of the earth I call to you, I call as my heart grows faint; lead me to the rock that is higher than I.*

David praises the LORD as his source of strength and refuge. He promises to live before the LORD forever.

PSALM 62 *Author: David*

Verse 6: *He alone is my rock and my salvation; he is my fortress, I will not be shaken.*

David proclaims the LORD as his rock and rescuer; his protection and success come from God alone. He tells his people to trust in the LORD; that power belongs to Him and He rewards everyone according to what his or her works deserve.

PSALM 63 *Author: David*

Verse 7: *Because you are my help, I sing in the shadow of your wings.*

David searches for the LORD. He praises and blesses the Him. He states that his enemies who seek to destroy him are doomed to die. David rejoices in God, saying that all who trust in Him will exalt, while liars will be silenced.

PSALM 64 *Author: David*

Verse 9: *All mankind will fear; they will proclaim the works of God and ponder what he has done.*

David asks to be rescued from wicked men who pursue him. He states that God Himself will shoot them down. He writes that everyone will recognize the greatness of God, rejoice, and trust in the LORD.

PSALM 65 *Author: David*

Verse 8: *Those living far away fear your wonders; where morning dawns and evening fades you call forth songs of joy.*

This is a prayer to God. David writes that even though sin fills the people's hearts, God will forgive. David declares that He is the only hope for all of mankind; He is mighty and strong; He provides and maintains the earth and the entire world sings with joy.

PSALM 66 *Author: Anonymous*

Verse 18: *If I had cherished sin in my heart, the Lord would not have listened....*

This psalm praises the Lord following a great victory in battle. It declares that God has done glorious and miraculous things like when He parted the Red Sea, and that He will deflate the pride of rebel lands. It exhorts the people to sing praises to God because He brought them through trials and tribulations and in the end brought abundance. The author brings many offerings to the temple to thank the Lord. The Lord answered his prayers.

Psalm 67 *Author: Anonymous*

Verse 3: *May the peoples praise you, O God; may all the peoples praise you.*

This psalm is asking for the LORD's blessing during a harvest festival. It tells of the people's responsibility to spread the word of His greatness, thus experiencing great joy. The author says that all the people will give thanks to God who blesses; all people from the most remote lands will worship Him.

Psalm 68 *Author: David*

Verse 5: *As father to the fatherless, as defender of widows, is God in his holy dwelling.*

David appeals to the LORD to scatter his wicked enemies. David states that the godly man should exalt and sing praises because God the Father is just and holy. David recalls the abundance from God throughout the history of the Israelites and states that the glorious LORD lives with His people and gives them salvation. It is stated that God rescues His people from death, but crushes His enemies. David writes of a victorious procession of praise to the LORD with the little tribe of Benjamin leading the way. He declares that power belongs to God and He gives it to His people.

Psalm 69 *Author: David*

Verse 6: *May those who hope in you not be disgraced because of me, O Lord, the LORD Almighty; may those who seek you not be put to shame because of me, O God of Israel.*

David appeals to the LORD for help as his enemies attempt to punish him unjustly. David's enemies mock him for his steadfast belief in the LORD, and David asks for help. He asks to be rescued from his enemies who are drowning him. He asks the LORD to pour out His fury on them. He promises to praise the LORD if He would rescue him. He declares that God will save Jerusalem and rebuild the cities of Judah, and their children will inherit the land.

Psalm 70 *Author: David*

Verse 4: *But may all who seek you rejoice and be glad in you; may those who love your salvation always say, "Let God be exalted!"*

Again, David asks to be rescued. He asks God to rush to his aid and for all who love His salvation to exclaim what a wonderful God He is.

PSALM 71 *Author: Anonymous*

Verse 19: *Your righteousness reaches to the skies, O God, you who have done great things. Who, O God, is like you?*

The author writes that the LORD is the people's refuge. He asks for rescue and protection. Praise and honor is given to God. The author asks that God destroy their enemies who say that God has forsaken them. Praises are given to God with promises to proclaim His glory. The author states that all who have tried to hurt him have been disgraced and dishonored.

PSALM 72 *Author: Solomon*

Verse 19: *Praise be to his glorious name forever; may the whole earth be filled with his glory. Amen and Amen.*

Solomon asks the LORD for justice, even to the poor. He asks for God's help in the reign of his son so that he may flourish, but also to take care of the poor and weak. He blesses the God of Israel, who only does wonderful things.

THE THIRD BOOK OF PSALMS, Psalms 73-89: This section, written mainly by Asaph (a temple choir leader), is similar to the book of Leviticus. The temple, deliverance, and praise are common themes.

PSALM 73 *Author: Asaph*

Verse 28: *But as for me, it is good to be near God. I have made the Sovereign LORD my refuge; I will tell of all your deeds.*

This psalm is a warning not to envy the proud and wicked who scoff at God because they are on a *slippery slope* and may fall into an eternity of terror. It is stated that God represents strength, and those refusing to worship Him will perish.

PSALM 74 *Author: Asaph (or a descendant)*

Verse 12: *But you, O God, are my king from of old; you bring salvation upon the earth.*

This is a plea to God to restore Jerusalem after it was destroyed. The author states that God is all-powerful and should punish those who destroyed Israel. He goes on to ask for both protection and retribution.

PSALM 75 *Author: Asaph*

Verse 8: *In the hand of the LORD is a cup full of foaming wine mixed with spices; he pours it out, and all the wicked of the earth drink it down to its very dregs.*

In this psalm God declares that He will punish the wicked when He chooses to do so. He warns the arrogant and the wicked that they will be punished. As for the author, he praises the LORD.

PSALM 76 *Author: Asaph*

Verse 10: *Surely your wrath against men brings you praise, and the survivors of your wrath are restrained.*

Asaph praises God because He punishes evildoers for His own glory. He asks who can stand before God when He is angry and states that God should be reverenced and feared by everyone.

PSALM 77 *Author: Asaph*

Verse 2: *When I was in distress, I sought the Lord; at night I stretched out untiring hands and my soul refused to be comforted.*

This is a plea to the Lord for help. The author asks if He has forgotten him. He takes solace in the wonderful deeds of God in the past. He recalls the glory of the LORD when He parted the Red Sea during the exodus from Egypt.

PSALM 78 *Author: Asaph*

Verse 32: *In spite of all this, they kept on sinning; in spite of his wonders, they did not believe.*

This psalm begins with the admonition to obey God's Laws. It includes a review of Israel's history. The author recalls the exodus from Egypt, God's provision and glory, and the rebellion of the Israelites despite gifts of manna, quail, water, etc. The psalm relates how they forgot the power of God during the plagues on Egypt, the Passover, and their deliverance into the Promised Land. The psalmist states that because of the people's disobedience, God abandoned the temple and allowed the Ark to be captured and that the servant David restored obedience and conquest.

PSALM 79 *Author: Asaph or a descendant*

Verse 1: *O God, the nations have invaded your inheritance; they have defiled your holy temple, they have reduced Jerusalem to rubble.*

This is a plea to God for forgiveness following the Babylonian conquest. The author asks for vengeance against their captors and promises praise from the sheep of His pasture.

PSALM 80 *Author: Asaph or a descendant*

Verse 19: *Restore us, O LORD God Almighty; make your face shine upon us, that we may be saved.*

This is a request to God to restore Israel. The author asks for mercy and promises to continue God's work. The author also promises not to forget the LORD again. He asks his brethren to trust in God and for God to turn to them, His face aglow, with joy and love.

PSALM 81 *Author: Asaph*

Verse 8: *Hear, O my people, and I will warn you—if you would but listen to me, O Israel!*

This is a song of rejoicing. The author again reminds the reader of the Jewish exodus. He offers an admonition against idol worship. The LORD counsels that if His people would only listen to Him, He would destroy all of their enemies.

PSALM 82 *Author: Asaph*

Verse 4: *Rescue the weak and needy; deliver them from the hand of the wicked.*

This is an admonishment to the judges of Israel for not ruling fairly. The psalm states that God will judge the wicked.

PSALM 83 *Author: Asaph or descendant*

Verse 16: *Cover their faces with shame so that men will seek your name, O LORD.*

This psalm contains prayers to God for deliverance from the enemies who hate God. The author asks for defeat against all who have aligned themselves against God's people, as has happened so many times. He asks for defeat and disgrace of the enemies who do not recognize God's power.

PSALM 84 *Author: Sons of Korah*

Verse 10: *Better is one day in your courts than a thousand elsewhere; I would rather be a doorkeeper in the house of my God than dwell in the tents of the wicked.*

This is a psalm of happiness while praising the LORD in the temple. The author gives glory to the LORD.

PSALM 85 *Author: Sons of Korah*

Verse 2: *You forgave the iniquity of your people and covered all their sins.*

This is a prayer of praise for restoring Israel and for the forgiveness of sins. The author asks to be brought back to the LORD—a revival. He states that salvation is near to those who reverence God.

PSALM 86 *Author: David*

Verse 11: *Teach me your way, O LORD, and I will walk in your truth; give me an undivided heart, that I may fear your name.*

David asks for protection from death. He also asks for mercy and happiness. He states that all nations will bow before God, and promises reverence and glory to His name. David asks to be saved from his enemies.

PSALM 87 *Author: Sons of Korah*

Verse 5: *Indeed, of Zion it will be said, "This one and that one were born in her, and the Most High himself will establish her."*

The author writes that some day the highest honor will be to be called a native of Jerusalem. He writes that God personally blesses this city.

PSALM 88 *Author: Heman (a son of Korah)*

Verse 10: *Do you show your wonders to the dead? Do those who are dead rise up and praise you?*

This is a deathbed prayer to God. In his despair, Heman pleads with God. He asks God to save him because he cannot praise God in death.

PSALM 89 *Author: Ethan (Levite leader)*

Verse 24: *My faithful love will be with him, and through my name his horn will be exalted.*

Ethan offers praises to the LORD. He recalls God's oath to David and his descendants. He praises the LORD for His miracles and faithfulness. He declares that heaven and earth are the LORD's and that God sits on a throne surrounded by pillars of justice and righteousness. He asks God for restoration of the Davidic covenant. He goes on to plead with God to honor this covenant and restore Israel. He asks where the promised love is. He concludes with blessings to the LORD.

THE FOURTH BOOK OF PSALMS, Psalms 90-106: This book of Psalms, written mostly by unknown authors, is similar to Numbers. There is discussion regarding the relationship of God's kingdom to other nations.

PSALM 90 *Author: Moses*

Verse 2: *For a thousand years in your sight are like a day that was just gone by, or like a watch in the night.*

This is the oldest psalm and Moses starts by proclaiming that God is all-powerful and all knowing. He writes that people are given a limited time on earth, much of which is spent with emptiness and pain. Moses asks the LORD to help His people to spend their days as they should. He asks for blessings and prosperity.

PSALM 91 *Author: Anonymous*

Verse 11: *For he will command his angels concerning you to guard you in all your ways....*

The author states that God is his refuge and his protector who shields His people. He knows that God will rescue his people because they love Him.

PSALM 92 *Author: Anonymous*

Verse 4: *For you make me glad by your deeds, O LORD; I sing for joy at the works of your hands.*

This is a Sabbath Day temple song; praise and thanks are given to the LORD. The author relates how good it is to rejoice in His faithfulness, and reflects on the miracles and deep thoughts of the LORD. The goodness and blessings of God refresh him.

PSALM 93 *Author: Anonymous*

Verse 1: *The LORD reigns, he is robed in majesty; the LORD is robed in majesty and is armed with strength. The world is firmly established; it cannot be moved.*

The author writes that the LORD is the King and the world is His throne; He is powerful, and holiness is the keynote of His reign.

PSALM 94 *Author: Anonymous*

Verse 18: *When I said, "My foot is slipping," your love, O LORD, supported me.*

The author asks for vengeance against the unholy and insolent enemies. He asks for just punishment and defense of the righteous. He declares that the LORD saves those who ask and will make the sins of evildoers boomerang upon them.

PSALM 95 *Author: David*

Verse 7a: *…He is our God and we are the people of his pasture, the flock under his care.*

This is a praise song to the King and Shepherd declaring that the people should kneel before their Maker. David warns against hardened hearts like the Israelites had in the desert following their exodus from Egypt.

PSALM 96 *Author: [David?]*

Verse 1: *Sing to the LORD a new song; sing to the LORD, all the earth.*

This is another praise song declaring that the LORD is great beyond description. The author sings that He is glorious and strong; that Jehovah reigns! He declares that the LORD is coming to judge the earth.

PSALM 97 *Author: Anonymous*

Verse 9: *For you, O LORD, are the Most High over the earth; you are exalted far above all gods.*

This psalm is rejoicing in the King who is righteous and just. It states that idols should be disgraced and those who love the LORD should hate evil and praise His name.

PSALM 98 *Author: Anonymous*

Verse 4: *Shout for joy to the LORD, all the earth, burst into jubilant song with music....*

This is a song to the LORD praising His mighty deeds and expressing joy for victory and the promises of the LORD to Israel. The author gives glory to the LORD.

PSALM 99 *Author: Anonymous*

Verse 5: *Exalt the LORD our God and worship at his footstool; he is holy.*

This is an exclamation of God's greatness—He is King! The author praises His justice, fairness, and holiness. He recalls how God guided Moses, Aaron, and Samuel and exclaims: Exalt His name!

PSALM 100 *Author: Anonymous*

Verse 4: *Enter his gates with thanksgiving and his courts with praise, give thanks to him and praise his name.*

This is a joyful praise to God. The author is thankful for His majesty, kindness, love, and faithfulness.

PSALM 101 *Author: David*

Verse 7: *No one who practices deceit will dwell in my house; no one who speaks falsely will stand in my presence.*

This is a song of praise and a request for help in avoiding sin. David says that he will not tolerate evil amongst his people and asks that they be good servants.

PSALM 102 *Author: Anonymous*

Verse 18: *Let this be written for a future generation that a people not yet created may praise the LORD.*

This is a plea for help in a time of distress and despair. Destitute and near death, the author asks for God's mercy in restoring Jerusalem from ashes. He promises to praise God in the restored temple. He states that God will never grow old and that future generations will be preserved through God's protection.

PSALM 103 *Author: David*

Verse 12: *...as far as the east is from the west, so far has he removed our transgressions from us.*

This psalm is filled with blessings to God; He is kind, loving, just, and good. It states that He revealed His will and nature to Moses. David declares that the LORD is slow to anger and never remains angry and that He removes sin. He writes that, unlike man, God is everlasting and must be obeyed. David proclaims: Bless the ruler of Heaven!

PSALM 104 *Author: Anonymous*

Verse 34: *May my meditation be pleasing to him, as I rejoice in the LORD.*

This is a blessing to the Great God who made heaven and earth. It is a song of praise to God, the LORD who has created all of the wonders of the earth. The author notes that sinners will perish but that he will praise God.

PSALM 105 *Author: David*

Verse 8: *He remembers his covenant forever, the word he commanded, for a thousand generations....*

David gives praise and glory to God. In his search for strength, he remembers all of God's mighty deeds. David recalls the Abrahamic covenant, Joseph in Egypt, Israel's captivity in Egypt, the plagues, their exodus, Moses' leadership, and entry into the Promised Land. He knows that all of this was done to make the Israelites more faithful and obedient—Hallelujah!

PSALM 106 *Author: Anonymous*

Verse 47: *Save us, O LORD our God, and gather us from the nations, that we may give thanks to your holy name and glory in your praise.*

The author gives thanks and glory to God and then asks to be remembered by Him. He reminds the reader of the parting of the Red Sea and the restoration of the people's faith (although only temporarily). He comments on the Israelites return to sin, Dathan's demise and Moses' intercession. He also recalls the Israelites' idol worship, sinful acts, and Phinehas' action that halted the LORD's punishment. The author recounts the impatience of the people at Meribah. He notes the Israelites' failure to follow God's instructions in the conquest of the Promised Land and their constant idol worship that led to their eventual demise. He relates the recurrent theme of God's delivery of the people from slavery and His renewal of promises. The author concludes with a plea for deliverance once again.

FIFTH BOOK OF THE PSALMS, Psalm 107-150: This book, written mainly by David, is often compared to Deuteronomy. It includes numerous songs of praise and thanksgiving for God and His Word.

PSALM 107 *Author: Anonymous*

Verse 31: *Let them give thanks to the LORD for his unfailing love and his wonderful deeds for men.*

The author thanks God for His goodness and love (following the release of the Israelites from Babylonian captivity). He gives praise to the LORD who rescues those who ask for His help, no matter what their plight. He states that good men rejoice in His glory, but evil men are stricken and made silent.

PSALM 108 *Author: David*

Verse 13: *With God we will gain the victory, and he will trample down our enemies.*

This is a song of praise to the LORD. David rejoices after a victory over his enemies. He states that with the help of God, Israel can do mighty acts of valor.

PSALM 109 *Author: David*

Verse 28: *They may curse, but you will bless; when they attack they will be put to shame, but your servant will rejoice.*

This is a plea for retribution against David's enemies who mercilessly persecuted him. He asks for deliverance and to be treated as God's child. He gives thanks and praise to the LORD.

PSALM 110 *Author: David*

Verse 4: *The LORD has sworn and will not change his mind: "You are a priest forever, in the order of Melchizedek."*

This psalm refers to the Messiah, who will make His enemies bow before Him. It states that the Messiah will be like the Priest Melchizedek (Genesis 14) and will protect the believers and strike down His enemies. David writes that God will be refreshed by springs along the way and He judges the nations and crushes the rulers.

PSALM 111 *Author: Anonymous*

Verse 10: *The fear of the LORD is the beginning of wisdom; all who follow his precepts have good understanding. To him belongs eternal praise.*

This is a public thanksgiving to God for His mighty miracles, mercy, grace, power, and justice. The author declares that God paid a full ransom for His people and that wisdom comes through reverence to God.

PSALM 112 *Author: Anonymous*

Verse 9: *He has scattered abroad his gifts to the poor, his righteousness endures forever; his horn will be lifted high in honor.*

The author offers blessings for all who fear the LORD and writes that God will care for those who believe, but evil-minded men will be infuriated by jealousy.

PSALM 113 *Author: Anonymous*

Verse 3: *From the rising of the sun to the place where it sets, the name of the LORD is to be praised.*

This is a psalm of praise to God who is high above the nations and whose glory is greater than the heavens. God is praised as the One who helps the poor and oppressed.

PSALM 114 *Author: Anonymous*

Verse 3: *The sea looked and fled, the Jordan turned back....*

This psalm recalls the exodus of the Israelites, God's parting of the Red Sea, and the nation's crossing of the Jordan. It states that the earth trembles at the presence of the LORD who allowed water to gush from a rock.

PSALM 115 *Author: Anonymous*

Verse 8: *Those who make them will be like them, and so will all who trust in them.*

That author declares that God should be glorified and there is no reason to worship idols. He tells Israel to trust the LORD as a helper and shield; God will bless those who reverence Him. It is written that the heavens belong to the LORD, but He has given the earth to all mankind. The author exclaims, "Praise the Lord!"

PSALM 116 *Author: Anonymous*

Verse 15: *Precious in the sight of the LORD is the death of his saints.*

The author describes his love for the LORD because He answers his prayers. The LORD saved the author from death. He promises to worship God and give Him a thankful offering of praise.

PSALM 117 *Author: Anonymous*

Verse 1: *Praise the LORD, all you nations; extol him, all you peoples.*

This is the shortest chapter in the Bible and is a "mini" Doxology of praise to the LORD.

PSALM 118 *Author: Anonymous*

Verse 24: *This is the day the LORD has made; let us rejoice and be glad in it.*

This is a praise of thankfulness. The LORD rescued the author and he encourages Israel to have confidence in the LORD. He states that the LORD will protect His people from their enemies if they carry His flag. He tells of the rejected stone that has become the capstone.

He declares: Blessed is the One who is coming. He gives thanks and praise for the LORD's sacrifice.

PSALM 119 *Author: Anonymous [Ezra?]*

Verse 105: *Your word is a lamp to my feet and a light for my path.*

This is the longest psalm and the longest chapter in the Bible. In it, the author tells of finding happiness in following God's laws and staying pure by following God's word. He says that there are blessings in obedience and the LORD should rebuke those who refuse His commands. In discouragement, the author finds revival in His word. He asks for help in being obedient. He asks to substitute God's kindness and love for those who oppress and mock Him. He says that obedience results in lovingkindness, and offers praise, asks for mercy, and requests that his persecutors be punished. He states that the LORD's words are perfect and wise. The author promises obedience until death. He asks for the LORD's blessing mercy and justice.

PILGRIM PSALMS, Psalms 120-134: These psalms provided a cadence for journeys by foot.

PSALM 120 *Author: Anonymous [Hezekiah?]*

Verse 7: *I am a man of peace; but when I speak, they are for war."*

The author asks for help and deliverance from liars and warlike heathens who do not welcome peace.

PSALM 121 *Author: Anonymous [Hezekiah?]*

Verse 2: *My help comes from the LORD, the Maker of heaven and earth.*

The author states that he looks to the one true God, and not false gods, for help. He declares that God is always watching, caring, defending, and guarding His people.

PSALM 122 *Author: David*

Verse 1: *I rejoiced with those who said to me, "Let us go to the house of the LORD."*

This is a prayer for peace and prosperity for Jerusalem and the temple of the LORD.

PSALM 123 *Author: Anonymous [Hezekiah?]*

Verse 2: *As the eyes of slaves look to the hand of their master, as the eyes of a maid look to the hand of her mistress, so our eyes look to the LORD our God, till he shows us his mercy.*

This is a request for mercy and kindness for God's people, in the face of the contempt and scoffing of the rich and proud.

PSALM 124 *Author: David*

Verse 8: *Our help is in the name of the LORD, the Maker of heaven and earth.*

David expresses blessing and thankfulness to God for victory (over the Philistines).

PSALM 125 *Author: Anonymous [Hezekiah?]*

Verse 3: *The scepter of the wicked will not remain over the land allotted to the righteous, for then the righteous might use their hands to do evil.*

The author states that the LORD surrounds and protects His people like the mountains surround and protect Jerusalem. He also declares that God brings good to the good and bad to the bad. The author asks for quietness and peace to Israel.

PSALM 126 *Author: Anonymous*

Verse 6: *He who goes out weeping, carrying seed to sow, will return with songs of joy, carrying sheaves with him.*

This is a joyful song of celebration following the release from Babylonian captivity.

PSALM 127 *Author: Solomon*

Verse 1: *Unless the LORD builds the house, its builders labor in vain. Unless the LORD watches over the city, the watchmen stand guard in vain.*

Solomon writes that without God as a foundation, all hard work is for naught. He states that children are a gift from God and families should be honored.

PSALM 128 *Author: Anonymous [Hezekiah?]*

Verse 1: *Blessed are all who fear the LORD, who walk in his ways.*

The author states that those who reverence and obey the LORD are blessed and will be rewarded with a happy home.

PSALM 129 *Author: Anonymous [Hezekiah?]*

Verse 4: *But the LORD is righteous; he has cut me free from the cords of the wicked.*

The psalmist writes that Israel has been persecuted and discriminated against but not destroyed; the LORD is good and defeats Israel's enemies.

PSALM 130 *Author: Anonymous [Hezekiah?]*

Verse 4: *But with you there is forgiveness; therefore you are feared.*

This is a plea for help from the depths of despair. The author recognizes that the LORD is awesome because He forgets sins and forgives, and that God will ransom Israel from their slavery to sin.

PSALM 131 *Author: David*

Verse 1: *My heart is not proud, O LORD, my eyes are not haughty; I do not concern myself with great matters or things too wonderful for me.*

David advises not to be boastful and arrogant but to trust quietly in the LORD.

PSALM 132 *Author: Anonymous*

Verse 10: *For the sake of David your servant, do not reject your anointed one.*

The author reflects on the day when the Ark of the Covenant was brought from Ephrathah to Jerusalem. He recalls the celebration welcoming the LORD to His new home. The author remembers the LORD's covenant to David.

PSALM 133 *Author: David*

Verse 1: *How good and pleasant it is when brothers live together in unity!*

David asks for the joy of harmony and eternal blessings for Jerusalem.

PSALM 134 *Author: Anonymous [Hezekiah?]*

Verse 1: *Praise the LORD, all you servants of the LORD who minister by night in the house of the LORD.*

This is a blessing for the Temple watchmen.

PSALM 135 *Author: Anonymous*

Verse 6: *The LORD does whatever pleases him, in the heavens and on the earth, in the seas and all their depths.*

This is a hymn of praise to the LORD who has chosen Israel as His personal possession. It tells of the LORD's control over nature and how He delivered the Israelites from Egypt and smote great nations, giving their lands to His people. The psalm gives glory to God who is far greater than the idols that heathens worship.

PSALM 136 *Author: Anonymous*

Verse 1: *Give thanks to the LORD, for he is good. His love endures forever.*

This psalm gives thanks to God for His lovingkindness. It recalls Israel's history, including this thankful refrain.

PSALM 137 *Author: Anonymous*

Verse 4: *How can we sing the songs of the LORD while in a foreign land?*

This is a sad psalm describing the fall of Jerusalem. It includes a plea to God to punish the Edomites for not coming to aid the city and, in fact, celebrating her destruction by the Babylonians.

PSALM 138 *Author: David*

Verse 8: *The LORD will fulfill his purpose for me; your love, O LORD, endures forever—do not abandon the works of your hands.*

David offers a prayer of thanksgiving to the LORD for His lovingkindness and faithfulness. He states that even kings will give thanks to the LORD who respects the humble but not the proud. David says that God will bring him to safety through his troubles and work out His plan for his life.

PSALM 139 *Author: David*

Verse 14: *I praise you because I am fearfully and wonderfully made; your works are wonderful, I know that full well.*

David writes that the LORD knows everything about him, everything that he thinks and does, and even darkness cannot hide from God. David states that the Lord made him and was with him in his mother's womb. It is precious for David to know that the LORD is constantly thinking about him. David concludes that he hates those who hate the LORD.

PSALM 140 *Author: David*

Verse 4: *Keep me, O LORD, from the hands of the wicked; protect me from men of violence who plan to trip my feet.*

David asks for deliverance from evil and proud men who were conspiring against him.

PSALM 141 *Author: David*

Verse 5: *Let a righteous man strike me—it is a kindness; let him rebuke me—it is oil on my head. My head will not refuse it.*

This is a prayer to resist evil things and evil desires. David seeks the LORD's refuge.

PSALM 142 *Author: David*

Verse 3: *When my spirit grows faint within me, it is you who know my way. In the path where I walk men have hidden a snare for me.*

David pleads with God to help him against his enemies who are trying to trap him, because the LORD is his only place of refuge. He asks to be rescued from his persecutors so that he can thank God.

PSALM 143 *Author: David*

Verse 1: *O LORD, hear my prayer, listen to my cry for mercy; in your faithfulness and righteousness come to my relief.*

This is a prayer born out of hopelessness and depression. David recalls God's glorious miracles and asks to be saved from his enemies. He notes that by saving him, God will bring more glory to His holy name.

PSALM 144 *Author: David*

Verse 2: *He is my loving God and my fortress, my stronghold and my deliverer, my shield, in whom I take refuge, who subdues peoples under me.*

David offers a blessing to the LORD, his Rock, Tower of Strength, and Deliverer. He briefly contemplates man's role on earth. He then asks God to rescue him. He offers a song that describes a happy and bountiful land where the people worship the LORD.

PSALM 145 *Author: David*

Verse 9: *The LORD is good to all; he has compassion on all he has made.*

David offers praise for the glory, splendor, and majesty of the LORD. He proclaims God's greatness, thanks Him, and promises to pass this on to future generations. David states that God rules and helps the oppressed and that He protects all who love Him, but destroys the wicked.

PSALM 146 *Author: Anonymous*

Verse 2: *I will praise the LORD all my life; I will sing praise to my God as long as I live.*

The author gives praise to God. He advises the reader not to look to man for help, but to the LORD. He writes that God made the earth and heaven, He is just, feeds the hungry, and loves man. He declares that the LORD will reign forever.

PSALM 147 *Author: Anonymous*

Verse 3: *He heals the brokenhearted and binds up their wounds.*

This is a psalm of praise to the LORD for rebuilding Jerusalem and returning the exiles. The author offers thankfulness and praise for the God who sends peace and who rules the world.

PSALM 148 *Author: Anonymous*

Verse 5: *Let them praise the name of the LORD, for he commanded and they were created.*

The author gives praise for everything that God has made because His glory is greater than that of all earth and heaven. He exclaims: Hallelujah!

PSALM 149 *Author: Anonymous*

Verse 3: *Let them praise his name with dancing and make music to him with tambourine and harp.*

This is a song of praise and exaltation to the LORD. The author declares that God enjoys His people, and will save the humble. The author asks that He execute His punishment on Israel's enemies.

PSALM 150 *Author: Anonymous*

Verse 6: *Let everything that has breath praise the LORD. Praise the LORD.*

The psalm exhorts the reader to praise to the LORD and His mighty power, works, and greatness, and to offer praises with musical instruments. The message is: YOU praise Him!

PROVERBS

PROVERBS 1

Verse 8: *Listen, my son, to your father's instruction and do not forsake your mother's teaching.*

The beginning of Proverbs states that they were mainly written by Solomon and provide advice about wisdom, discipline, and justice. He states that the fear of the LORD is the beginning of knowledge and wisdom. Solomon warns the reader not to be enticed by sinners, because they only hurt themselves. He instructs us not to reject wisdom, for the LORD will not have mercy on those who do not fear Him. He states that the complacency of fools will destroy them, but whoever listens to the LORD will live in safety.

PROVERBS 2

Verse 11: *Discretion will protect you, and understanding will guard you.*

Solomon writes to his son, telling him if he searches for wisdom, he will find the knowledge of God and that God protects the faithful. He states that wisdom will protect him and save him from evil and adultery. He continues by saying that only the upright and blameless will live in the land.

PROVERBS 3

Verse 5: *Trust in the LORD with all your heart and lean not on your own understanding....*

Solomon writes that obedience to the LORD will prolong his son's life and bring prosperity, and that if he trusts in the LORD, He will keep his path straight. Solomon tells his son that if he honors the LORD, there will be abundance, and reminds him that the LORD disciplines those that He loves. Solomon declares that the man who finds wisdom is blessed because wisdom is a precious commodity. He tells his son that if he preserves sound judgment and discernment, they will be life and safety to him. He tells him to be good to those who deserve it, and to honor his neighbor. He declares that the wise man inherits honor, but fools will be shamed.

PROVERBS 4

Verse 7: *Wisdom is supreme; therefore get wisdom. Though it cost all you have, get understanding.*

Solomon says to his sons: Wisdom is supreme—get some! Wisdom will honor you and guide you—guard and protect it. Do not follow wicked men, but take the righteous path. Guard your heart, avoid corruptions, and stay focused.

PROVERBS 5

Verse 5: *Her feet go down to death; her steps lead straight to the grave.*

Solomon teaches to avoid adultery, which can seduce a man onto a crooked path. He says that a man should be happy with his own wife. He declares that the LORD sees all, and lack of discipline will lead to death.

PROVERBS 6

Verse 32: *But a man who commits adultery lacks judgment; whoever does so destroys himself.*

Solomon's instruction to his son was this: If you take responsibility for other's debts, free yourself. Scoundrels and villains will stir up dissension, but disaster will overtake them in an instant. The LORD detests pride, lies, murder, wickedness, evil, false witnesses, and those who stir up dissension. Stay away from immoral women, otherwise you will pay the price. Adultery is worse than a hungry man who steals food.

PROVERBS 7

Verse 21: *With persuasive words she led him astray; she seduced him with her smooth talk.*

Solomon tells his son to embrace wisdom; it will keep him from adultery. He tells him not to fall prey to seduction, for it is a highway to the grave.

PROVERBS 8

Verses 10,11: *Choose instruction instead of silver, knowledge rather than choice gold, for wisdom is more precious than rubies, and nothing you desire can compare with her.*

Solomon tells the reader to listen when wisdom calls; she speaks of righteousness, justice, and truth. He says that wisdom is more valuable than gold or precious gems, and it includes prudence, knowledge, and discretion. He states that the LORD hates arrogance, evil behavior, and perverse speech, but counsel, sound judgment, understanding, and power come from wisdom. He writes that kings who rule with wisdom prosper and that wisdom was present from the beginning of creation. Solomon states: Blessed is the man who finds wisdom, for he will find life and receive favor from the LORD.

PROVERBS 9

Verse 9: *Instruct a wise man and he will be wiser still; teach a righteous man and he will add to his learning.*

Solomon writes that wisdom prepares a feast and invites all who are willing, and that the fear of the LORD is the beginning of wisdom. He states that wisdom will reward the wise, but mockers will suffer, and folly will lead to death.

PROVERBS 10

Verse 19: *When words are many, sin is not absent, but he who holds his tongue is wise.*

This chapter begins a series of Solomon's proverbs that are short statements giving direction to the reader. Many of the proverbs are phrases of contrast—what is good and right is contrasted with what is bad and wrong—giving the same message from two different angles.

The wise son will bring joy. Ill-gotten treasures are worthless. The righteous will not go hungry. Diligent hands bring wealth. The wise gather crops in summer for the winter. The righteous will be blessed. The memory of the righteous is a blessing. The wise accepts commands. A man of integrity walks securely. The mouth of the righteous is a fountain of life. Love conquers all wrongs. Wisdom is on the lips of the discerning. Wise men love knowledge. Wealth is a fortified city. The wages of righteousness bring life. Discipline shows the way to life. Holding one's tongue is wise. The lips of the righteous nourish many. The LORD's blessing brings wealth. Men of understanding delight in wisdom. The righteous stand firm. Fear of the LORD adds length to life. The prospect of righteousness is joy. The LORD is a refuge. The righteous ones are wise.

PROVERBS 11

Verse 31: *If the righteous receive their due on earth, how much more the ungodly and the sinner?*

Solomon continues with the following proverbs: Honesty, humility, and integrity are wise. Righteousness delivers from death, makes path straight, and rescues from trouble. The blessing of the upright exalts the city. A man of understanding holds his tongue. The trustworthy person keeps a secret. The kindhearted individual commands respect. The righteous life is good. The LORD delights in blamelessness. One who gives freely will gain more. The righteous only seek good. There is no inheritance for one who brings trouble to his family. He who wins souls is wise.

PROVERBS 12

Verse 14: *From the fruit of his lips a man is filled with good things as surely as the work of his hands rewards him.*

The following proverbs describe the ways of the wise and righteous. Discipline is knowledge. A good man obtains favor from the LORD. The righteous will not be uprooted. The wife of a noble character is her husband's crown. The plans and words of the righteous are just. A house of righteousness stands firm. Wisdom is praised. It is better to be nobody than to pretend to be somebody without foundation. The righteous care for animals. Those who work will prosper. The righteous will flourish. A good man practices righteous talk, listens to advice, and overlooks insults. The righteous are honest, offer healing words, and are truthful. Joy comes to those who promote peace. The righteous man will keep his words to himself and be cautious in friendship. He will be kindhearted and a good steward. The way of righteousness is life.

PROVERBS 13

Verse 24: *He who spares the rod hates his son, but he who loves him is careful to discipline him.*

The following proverbs tell of a wise man's good life. The wise son heeds his father's instruction. One who guards his lips guards his life. The desires of the diligent are satisfied. The righteous hate falsehoods. The righteous guard integrity. Riches are not beneficial, but it is good to be frugal. The wise accept advice, teaching, and correction. Rewards come from respecting commands. Good understanding wins favor and a prudent man acts out of knowledge. A trustworthy messenger brings healing. It is wise to walk with the wise. A good man leaves an inheritance for his children. Discipline is good for children (*Spare the rod...*). The righteous ones are rewarded.

PROVERBS 14

Verse 12: *There is a way that seems right to a man, but in the end it leads to death.*

Solomon continues to share his wisdom with the reader. The one who fears the LORD will walk uprightly. Wisdom protects. A truthful witness does not deceive. Knowledge comes easily to the discerning. Stay away from fools. The wise will think about their actions. The upright practice goodwill. The wise will be patient, not quick-tempered, and shun evil. The prudent make plans and work hard. A heart at peace gives life. Being kind to the needy honors God. Righteousness exalts a nation and wisdom delights a king.

PROVERBS 15

Verse 3: *The eyes of the LORD are everywhere, keeping watch on the wicked and the good.*

Solomon continues writing: It is important to be gentle and caring. The LORD is constantly watching the earth. A son should heed his father's discipline. The righteous gain treasure. The wise spread knowledge and accept criticism. A happy and discerning heart is beneficial. Fear of the LORD is better than wealth. Patience calms quarrels. Being upright and pure makes for a better life. The fear of the LORD teaches wisdom. Humility comes before honor.

PROVERBS 16

Verse 3: *Commit to the LORD whatever you do, and your plans will succeed.*

Solomon gives more insights: The LORD weighs the motives of a man. Commit to the LORD, and go to Him with your plans. The LORD hates a proud heart. Love and faithfulness atone for sin. A man may plan a course in his heart but the LORD will determine his steps. Honesty pleases a ruler. Wisdom and understanding are better than riches. *Pride goeth before a fall*. He who heeds instructions will prosper. The wise in heart is discerning. Pleasant words are like a honeycomb. Evil and perversity stir up dissension. Violence leads to no good.

PROVERBS 17

Verse 9: *He who covers over an offense promotes love, but whoever repeats the matter separates close friends.*

Solomon explains the virtues of peace and quiet. The wise servant is greater than a disgraceful son. The LORD tests the heart. A wicked man listens to evil. Do not mock the poor or gloat over evil. Grandchildren are a crown to their grandparents. Be careful how you speak, avoid arrogance or lies. Solomon admonishes bribes, rebellion, fools and their folly. He advises to drop quarrels. Acquittal of the guilty and condemnation of the innocent are equally bad. Money is no use to a fool. A cheerful heart is good medicine. A discerning man keeps wisdom in view. A foolish son brings disgrace to his father. Use words with restraint: Be even-tempered.

PROVERBS 18

Verse 12: *Before his downfall a man's heart is proud, but humility comes before honor.*

An unfriendly man is selfish. Wickedness is contemptible. Do not be partial to the wicked. A fool's speech will bring man strife. The name of the LORD is a strong tower. Humility comes before honor. Seek knowledge. Words are powerful, use them carefully.

PROVERBS 19

Verse 18: *Discipline your son, for in that there is hope; do not be a willing party to his death.*

Zeal is no good without knowledge—get wisdom. Do not blame God for your troubles. False witnesses will be punished. Do not shun the poor. It is not fitting for a fool to live in luxury. Wisdom gives patience. A quarrelsome wife is like a constantly dripping tap. Be kind to the poor. Punish your son. A hot-tempered man must pay the penalty. Listen to good advice. The LORD's purpose will prevail. Fear the LORD. Do not disgrace your parents.

PROVERBS 20

Verse 22: *Do not say, "I'll pay you back for this wrong!" Wait for the LORD, and he will deliver you.*

Alcohol can lead you astray. Avoid strife. A sluggard will pay the price for his laziness. Be righteous and faithful. The LORD detests liars and cheaters. You will be known for your actions. Seek advice. Do not gossip. Do not take matters upon yourself, seek guidance from the LORD. Practice love and faithfulness. Punishment restrains evil.

PROVERBS 21

Verse 2: *All man's ways seem right to him, but the LORD weighs the heart.*

The LORD weighs what is right. Do what is just and right. Plan ahead, do not be hasty. Do not lie or be violent or guilty. A wise man gets knowledge. Justice brings joy to the righteous. A quarrelsome, ill-tempered wife is bad for a home. An arrogant man is a mocker. A sluggard, false witness, and wicked man are condemned by their actions. The LORD cannot be outwitted.

PROVERBS 22

Verse 6: *Train a child in the way he should go, and when he is old he will not turn from it.*

A good man is more desirable than riches. A prudent man avoids dangers. Humility brings a good life. Wickedness can be avoided by the guarding of the soul. Train a child and he will not stray. Sow wickedness and reap trouble. Be generous. Drive out mockers. God protects those who have knowledge. Those who oppress the poor will become poor. Solomon implores the reader to obey the sayings of the wise.

Sayings of the Wise:

1. Do not exploit the poor.
2. Do not befriend a hot-tempered man.

3. Do not assume other's debts.
4. Do not change the boundaries of another's land.
5. A skilled worker is valuable.

PROVERBS 23

Verse 4: *Do not wear yourself out to get rich; have the wisdom to show restraint.*

6. Eat carefully at the table of a superior.
7. Do not crave wealth.
8. Do not accept hospitality of a man eager to become rich.
9. Do not speak to a fool.
10. Do not take advantage of others.
11. Seek knowledge.
12. Discipline your children.
13. Have a wise heart.
14. Do not envy sinners.
15. There is hope in the future.
16. Do not be a drunkard or a glutton.
17. Honor your father and mother.
18. Get truth, wisdom, discipline and understanding.
19. The parents of the righteous are proud.
20. Prostitutes and wayward wives are evil.
21. Alcohol is dangerous.

PROVERBS 24

Verses 19,20: *Do not fret because of evil men or be envious of the wicked, for the evil man has no future hope, and the lamp of the wicked will be snuffed out.*

22. Do not envy the wicked.
23. Seek wisdom and knowledge.
24. A schemer is sinful.
25. Be strong in times of trouble.
26. Rescue those punished wrongly.
27. Wisdom is sweet.
28. Do not ambush a righteous man.
29. Do not gloat when your enemy fails.
30. Do not envy the wicked.

Further sayings of the wise: Judge impartially. Be honest. Work the fields first and then the home. Do not testify against your neighbor without cause. Do not pay back for a wrong. A sluggard lacks judgment and should be punished.

PROVERBS 25

Verse 28: *Like a city whose walls are broken down is a man who lacks self-control.*

The following are sayings of Solomon that were copied by the men of Hezekiah, king of Judah: God can conceal matters. Remove wickedness and a king can be righteous. Do not exalt yourself. Do not argue in front of others. Watch your tongue. Do not boast. Be patient. Eat judiciously. Limit your infringement upon another's hospitality. False testimony, unfaithfulness, and those without compassion for the sadness of others are to be condemned. Treat your enemy well. Righteousness, humility, and self-control are virtuous.

PROVERBS 26

Verse 11: *As a dog returns to its vomit, so a fool repeats his folly.*

Honor is not fitting for a fool. Avoid a fool's folly. Being a sluggard is bad. Do not meddle in another's quarrels. Gossip is bad. Malice in a man disguises itself but will eventually be revealed.

PROVERBS 27

Verse 11: *Be wise, my son, and bring joy to my heart; then I can answer anyone who treats me with contempt.*

Do not boast—let others praise you. Provocation by a fool is heavy. Do not stray from your nest. Do not forsake your friends. It is prudent to take refuge when you see danger. You will be rewarded if you help strangers. Iron sharpens iron like one man sharpens another. A man's heart reflects the man. Man is tested by the praise he receives. Watch out for your flocks.

PROVERBS 28

Verse 13: *He who conceals his sins does not prosper, but whoever confesses and renounces them finds mercy.*

The wicked man flees, but the righteous are bold. Do not oppress the poor or forsake the law. Evil men do not understand justice. Better to be poor and blameless than rich and perverse. If you charge exorbitant interest, you will end up giving it to the poor. Those who do not follow the law will not have their prayers heard. Stay on a straight path, be discerning. The righteous confess their sins and fear the LORD. Wicked tyrannical rulers lack judgment and hurt their people. Be blameless, work the land, be faithful, be impartial, and be generous. Be honest, be wise, give to the poor, and be righteous.

PROVERBS 29

Verse 25: *Fear of man will prove to be a snare, but whoever trusts in the LORD is kept safe.*

A person who does not accept criticism will be destroyed. The righteous and those who love wisdom will prosper. Seek justice and righteousness. Mockers and fools will be punished. The righteous and wise have integrity, keep their temper under control, judge the poor fairly, discipline their children, and keep the law. Speaking in haste is worse than a being a fool. Anger, pride, and thievery, are all bad. Do not fear a man, fear the LORD.

PROVERBS 30

Verse 8: *Keep falsehood and lies far from me; give me neither poverty nor riches, but give me only my daily bread.*

These are the sayings of Agur: He calls himself an ignorant man who does not know the LORD. He declares that every word of God is flawless. He asks the LORD to give him only what he needs and to keep lies from him. Agur states that it is wrong to slander a servant and that parents should be honored. He says that the grave, the barren womb, and land are never satisfied and that fire never says enough. He also says that some things are too amazing and difficult to understand.

PROVERBS 31

Verse 30: *Charm is deceptive, and beauty is fleeting; but a woman who fears the LORD is to be praised.*

These are the sayings of King Lemuel that were told to him by his mother: Do not spend your strength on women. Kings should not drink alcohol, but give it to those in anguish so they can forget their problems. Speak up for those who are oppressed and judge fairly. The wife of a noble character is worth more than rubies. She provides all and does many noble things. A woman who fears the LORD is to be praised.

Chapter 21

ECCLESIASTES

ECCLESIASTES 1

Verse 9: *What has been will be again, what has been done will be done again; there is nothing new under the sun.*

Everything is meaningless without God. Men come and go, but the earth remains forever. Nothing is new; wisdom is meaningless—a chasing after the wind. With wisdom comes sorrow—the more knowledge, the more grief.

ECCLESIASTES 2

Verse 14: *The wise man has eyes in his head, while the fool walks in the darkness; but I came to realize that the same fate overtakes them both.*

Pleasures are also meaningless; laughter is foolish. After amassing great fortune and possessions, the author concludes that everything is meaningless. Wisdom is better than folly, but both the wise man and fool will die. Toil and labor is worthless. All is meaningless without God.

ECCLESIASTES 3

Verse 11: *He has made everything beautiful in its time. He has also set eternity in the hearts of men; yet they cannot fathom what God has done from beginning to end.*

There is a time for everything. There is nothing better for men than to be happy and to do good while they are alive. Everything that God does will endure forever; He does this so that men will revere Him. God will judge the righteous and the wicked. There is nothing better for a man than for him to enjoy his work.

ECCLESIASTES 4

Verse 12*: Though one may be overpowered, two can defend themselves. A cord of three strands is not quickly broken.*

The oppressed have no comforter. The dead are happier than the living. Better still is he who has not been born, for he has not seen evil. Labor and achievement come from envy and are meaningless. Advancement is worthless. It is better not to be alone.

ECCLESIASTES 5

Verse 12: *The sleep of a laborer is sweet, whether he eats little or much, but the abundance of a rich man permits him no sleep.*

The author gives more advice to the reader: Guard your steps in the house of God. Also, be careful what you say—be patient. Fulfill your vows. Stand in awe of God. Riches are meaningless. A man leaves the world the same way he entered it—with nothing. Happiness with work is a gift from God.

ECCLESIASTES 6

Verse 11: *The more the words, the less the meaning, and how does that profit anyone?*

God does not enable men to enjoy the fruits of their labor. No matter how long a man lives and how many children he fathers, if he cannot enjoy his property and possessions he is no better off than if he were never born. All of man's efforts are to feed himself yet his appetite is never satisfied. What advantage does a wise man have over a fool? What man learns is already known, and there will always be someone stronger than he. Who knows what is good for man in life? What good are his possessions after he is gone?

ECCLESIASTES 7

Verse 14: *When times are good, be happy; but when times are bad, consider: God has made the one as well as the other. Therefore, a man cannot discover anything about his future.*

A good name is valuable. Death is the destiny of every man. Sorrow is better than laughter; the wise mourn, fools seek pleasure. It is better to follow a wise man's criticism than to listen to the song of fools. The laughter of fools is meaningless. The end of a matter is better than the beginning—patience is better than pride. Do not be easily provoked, do not long for the good old days. Wisdom is a good thing—it preserves the life of its possessor. Man cannot change what God determines. Be righteous but not overrighteous, wise but not overwise. The man who fears God will avoid all extremes. Do not pay attention to every word the people say. The importance of wisdom and the stupidity of wickedness are noted. The woman who is a snare will trap the sinner, but the man who pleases God will escape her. God made mankind upright, but men have gone in search of many schemes

ECCLESIASTES 8

Verse 11: *When the sentence for a crime is not quickly carried out, the hearts of the people are filled with schemes to do wrong.*

Wisdom brightens a man's face. Obey the king's commands. No man knows the future. No man has power over the wind. The sentence for a crime must be quickly carried out. Because the wicked do not fear God, their days are numbered. It is meaningless when righteous men get what the wicked deserve and wicked men get what the righteous deserves. The author commends the enjoyment of life. Man cannot appreciate all of God's glory—even a wise man cannot comprehend it.

ECCLESIASTES 9

Verse 12: *Moreover, no man knows when his hour will come: As fish are caught in a cruel net, or birds are taken in a snare, so men are trapped by evil times that fall unexpectedly upon them.*

The righteous and the wise and what they do are in God's hands; no man knows whether love or hate awaits him. A common destiny awaits everyone, but anyone who is among the living has hope. The author encourages the reader to enjoy life. No man knows when his hour will come. Wisdom is better than strength. The quiet words of the wise are much more valuable than the shouts of a ruler of fools. Wisdom is better than weapons of war, but one sinner destroys much good.

ECCLESIASTES 10

Verse 12: *The heart of the wise inclines to the right, but the heart of the fool to the left.*

Fools and folly are destructive. A man may fall into the pit that he digs. Heed the words of a wise man; a fool is consumed by his own words. Woe to those whose kings were usurpers. Lazy men are disparaged. Do not speak negatively of the king, as word will get back to him.

ECCLESIASTES 11

Verse 9: *Be happy, young man, while you are young, and let your heart give you joy in the days of your youth. Follow the ways of your heart and whatever your eyes see, but know that for all these things God will bring you to judgment.*

Cast your bread upon the water (do not always play it safe). Go about life with industry, because you cannot know what God will do. Enjoy life: Be happy. Follow the ways of your heart, and know that God will bring you judgment.

ECCLESIASTES 12

Verse 13: *Now all has been heard; here is the conclusion of the matter: Fear God and keep his commandments, for this is the whole duty of man.*

Remember your Creator, because some day you will go to your eternal home. Remember Him, because your spirit will return to God who gave it. The words of the wise, from the shepherd, should be followed. Fear God and His commandments, for God will judge everything, determining whether it is good or evil.

Chapter 22

SONG OF SONGS

SONG OF SONGS 1

Verse 4b: *We rejoice and delight in you; we will praise your love more than wine.*

The book begins with a profession of love for King Solomon. The beloved has adoration for the king. She is sensitive about her dark skin. As a shepherdess she seeks her lover. Her lover tells of her beauty and the strength of their love.

SONG OF SONGS 2

Verse 4: *He has taken me to the banquet hall, and his banner over me is love.*

The beloved compares herself to flowers and her lover to an apple tree, and then a gazelle. She warns the daughters of Jerusalem not to awaken or arouse love until it so desires. Her lover calls on her to frolic in the spring. There are more professions of love.

Song of Songs 3

Verse 5: *Daughters of Jerusalem, I charge you by the gazelles and by the does of the field: Do not arouse or awaken love until it so desires.*

The beloved misses her lover at night and then searches the streets of the city for him. When she eventually finds him, she will not let him go. She warns the daughters of Jerusalem again not to awaken or arouse love until it so desires. The wedding day of the king and his beloved is described in detail. The king's ornate carriage carries the couple.

Song of Songs 4

Verse 9: *You have stolen my heart, my sister, my bride; you have stolen my heart with one glance of your eyes, with one jewel of your necklace.*

The lover describes the beauty of his wife. There is no flaw in her beauty. She has stolen his heart. She is described as a garden fountain.

Song of Songs 5

Verse 16: *His mouth is sweetness itself; he is altogether lovely. This is my lover, this my friend, O daughters of Jerusalem.*

The beloved's lover knocks, but she hesitates to answer the door. When she does, he is gone and she again searches the city for him. She describes the beauty and wonderful attributes of her lover.

Song of Songs 6

Verse 10: *Who is it that appears like the dawn, fair as the moon, bright as the sun, majestic as the stars in procession?*

The woman's lover has gone to his garden. He again describes her beauty, stating that there may be sixty queens, but she is the most beautiful and praised by all others.

SONG OF SONGS 7

Verse 6: *How beautiful you are and how pleasing, O love, with your delights!*

The lover continues to describe the beauty of his beloved. They proclaim their love and desire for each other.

SONG OF SONGS 8

Verse 6: *Place me like a seal over your heart, like a seal on your arm; for love is as strong as death, its jealousy unyielding as the grave. It burns like blazing fire, like a mighty flame.*

The beloved warns the daughters of Jerusalem for the third time not to awaken or arouse love until it so desires. The beloved asks to be placed like a seal over her lover's heart. She saved herself for him.

Major Prophets

ISAIAH

ISAIAH 1

Verse 18: *"Come let us reason together," says the LORD. "Though your sins are like scarlet, they shall be as white as snow; though they are red as crimson, they shall be like wool."*

Isaiah saw a vision concerning Judah and Jerusalem. He stated that this rebellious nation was sinful and had forsaken the LORD. In the vision, Israel and Judah had been defeated by their neighbors and lay in ruin. The LORD abhorred the worship of idols and their wrongdoings. The LORD offered another chance if the people would be obedient. He promised to bring a revival to the nation, but only if there was repentance.

ISAIAH 2

Verse 11: *The eyes of the arrogant man will be humbled and the pride of men brought low; the LORD alone will be exalted in that day.*

Isaiah described another vision concerning Judah and Jerusalem. He saw a mountain of the LORD's temple with all people coming to worship. He described a time of peace. He also described a day of reckoning for all of the sinners and idol worshipers. In this day, they will run from, but not escape, the wrath of the LORD.

Isaiah 3

Verse 9: *The look on their faces testifies against them; they parade their sin like Sodom; they do not hide it. Woe to them! They have brought disaster upon themselves.*

Isaiah foretold of the impending destruction of Jerusalem and Judah. He noted they will bring disaster upon themselves. The LORD will administer judgment against the sins of the people. Isaiah warned of women being punished with baldness and sores for all of their flirtations and of men who will be killed in battle. Zion will be destroyed.

Isaiah 4

Verse 4: *The LORD will wash away the filth of the women of Zion; he will cleanse the bloodstains from Jerusalem by a spirit of judgment and a spirit of fire.*

The vision the LORD gave Isaiah showed that in these hard times women will look for ways to be rid of their disgrace and Israel will ask for redemption. The glory of God will return and the pillar of cloud and fire will reappear.

Isaiah 5

Verse 20: *Woe to those who call evil good and good evil, who put darkness for light and light for darkness, who put bitter for sweet and sweet for bitter.*

Isaiah shared a song about a vineyard that was planted on the most fertile soil with the finest vines, yet yielded only bad fruit. He was making an analogy about Israel. The LORD declared that He would destroy the vineyard. Six woes were expressed: they were against selfishness (coveters), carousers; those who welcome the LORD but do not believe (scoffers); those who do not understand good from evil (perverted); those who think they are too clever (arrogant), and drunkards. These were followed by three judgments: Fire because the people had rejected the law; the mountains will shake because of the LORD's anger; and their enemies will overrun the people.

ISAIAH 6

Verse 9: *He said, "Go and tell this people: 'Be ever hearing, but never understanding; be ever seeing, but never perceiving.'"*

Isaiah described a vision that he saw at the end of the reign of Uzziah (Azariah) [740 BC]. The LORD was seated on a throne with angels whose wings covered their hands and feet. Isaiah was afraid because he saw the LORD and knew his fate, however one of the angels touched his sinful lips with a coal from the altar to cleanse him. Isaiah volunteered to be the messenger (Here am I, send me!). The LORD instructed Isaiah to go and warn the people of their impending destruction, but told Isaiah that they would not understand and, ultimately his mission would fail. He was told to continue his efforts until all of the land was laid to waste except for a remnant (10%—a holy seed). Isaiah was told that even this remnant would not escape attack.

ISAIAH 7

Verse 14: *Therefore the LORD himself will give you a sign: The virgin will be with child and will give birth to a son, and will call him Immanuel.*

When Ahaz (Uzziah's grandson) was king of Judah, King Rezin of Aram (Syria) and Pekah, king of Israel tried unsuccessfully to conquer Jerusalem. Israel and Aram were allies and all the people of Judah were alarmed prior to the attack. The LORD told Isaiah to meet with Ahaz and tell him that they would be unsuccessful in conquering Judah. Isaiah told Ahaz to ask the LORD for a sign. Ahaz refused (which did not please the LORD), but Isaiah announced that as a sign, a virgin would bear a son, Immanuel. He foretold of the destruction of both Aram and Israel by Assyria. The Assyrian invasion would devastate the land and turn it into briars and thorns.

ISAIAH 8

Verse 10: *Devise your strategy, but it will be thwarted; propose your plan, but it will not stand, for God is with us.*

Isaiah related that the LORD instructed him to record that a prophetess would bear a son named Maher-Shalal-Hash-Baz (foretelling of the defeat of Ahaz's enemies but also of the suffering of Judah). He retold the people that Damascus and Assyria would defeat Samaria before the boy was old enough to talk. Assyria would also prevail over Israel and Judah, because the people worshiped idols. Isaiah told them to fear God. He pondered why the people consulted spirits and forsook the LORD.

ISAIAH 9

Verse 7: *Of the increase of his government and peace there will be no end. He will reign on David's throne and over his kingdom, establishing and upholding it with justice and righteousness from that time on and forever. The zeal of the LORD Almighty will accomplish this.*

Isaiah foretold of the gift of Christ for all people, including the Gentiles. He declared that the Christ child would be a great light, and would be called, "Wonderful Counselor, Mighty God, Everlasting Father, and Prince of Peace." He would reign on David's throne and accomplish the will of God. Isaiah told of the anger of the LORD and the destruction that awaits Israel. He stated that the elders and prophets (the head and the tail) would be cut off and the people would be defeated for not following God.

ISAIAH 10

Verse 15: *Does the ax raise itself above him who swings it, or the saw boast against him who uses it? As if a rod were to wield him who lifts it up, or a club brandish him who is not wood!*

Isaiah proclaims the woes of the LORD and asks where the Israelites will turn in the day of reckoning. Although the LORD planned to use Assyria to destroy Israel and Judah, He planned to punish them with a wasting disease after the invasion is completed. The remnant of Israel will remain and will return to God and they will regain their land.

ISAIAH 11

Verse 1: *A shoot will come up from the stump of Jesse; from his roots a Branch will bear fruit.*

A branch of Jesse (and David) will grow and the spirit of the LORD, wisdom, power, and knowledge will rest on Him. He will judge with righteousness and fairness. The wolf will live with the lamb and a little child will lead them. Children will be safe from harm. He will be glorious and will gather all exiles. Judah's enemies will be cut off. He will create a highway for the return of exiles to Israel.

ISAIAH 12

Verse 2: *Surely God is my salvation; I will trust and not be afraid. The LORD, the LORD, is my strength and my song; he has become my salvation.*

The LORD declares that once He redeems Israel, the people will sing songs of praise to Him. They will say that although God was angry, He now gives comfort and there is no need to fear. They will give thanks to the LORD and call on His name because the Holy One of Israel is great.

ISAIAH 13

Verse 11: *I will punish the world for its evil, the wicked for their sins. I will put an end to the arrogance of the haughty and will humble the pride of the ruthless.*

Isaiah saw an oracle concerning Babylon. The oracle said to raise a banner because the LORD is mustering an army for war. The day of the LORD will come like destruction. It will destroy the sinners of the earth. There will be darkness. The ruthless will be humbled. The heavens will tremble and the earth will shake at the LORD's wrath. The LORD will send the Medes to destroy Babylon. Babylon will be slaughtered like Sodom and Gomorrah were. Her days are numbered.

ISAIAH 14

Verse 12: *How you have fallen from heaven, O morning star, son of the dawn! You have been cast down to the earth, you who once laid low the nations!*

The oracle continued that the LORD will restore Israel and she will rule over her oppressors. Israel will be able to taunt Babylon. Babylon will be like a star that will fall from heaven into a deep pit and be covered with the slain. The offspring of the wicked will be forgotten. The LORD will rise up and cut off Babylon. The LORD will also crush Assyria and the Philistines. The LORD will establish Zion where His people can find refuge.

ISAIAH 15

Verse 5: *My heart cries out over Moab; her fugitives flee as far as Zoar, as far as Eglath Shelishi-yah. They go up the way to Luhith, weeping as they go; on the road to Horonaim they lament their destruction.*

Isaiah was given an oracle concerning Moab, stating that Moab will also be destroyed. The people will be decimated and the fugitives will flee. There will be famine and drought and all wealth will disappear. A lion will destroy what was left of Moab and its fugitives.

ISAIAH 16

Verse 5: *In love a throne will be established; in faithfulness a man will sit on it—one from the house of David—one who in judging seeks justice and speeds the cause of righteousness.*

The oracle continued. Moab must send lambs to Israel as a tribute. The Moabites will ask Judah for refuge. The oppressor will come to an end and a throne will be established. A man from the house of David will sit on the throne and seek justice and righteousness. Isaiah laments the destruction of Moab brought on by their pride and boastfulness. The LORD declared that Moab would be destroyed within three years.

ISAIAH 17

Verse 9: *In that day their strong cities, which they left because of the Israelites, will be like places abandoned to thickets and undergrowth. And all will be desolation.*

This was an oracle against Damascus (Aram [Syria]). Damascus will be a heap of ruins. Israel's glory will fade, but some gleanings will remain. Strong cities will be in desolation because they had forgotten their Savior. Despite the finest plantings, the harvest will be barren. The raging and uproar of nations will be rebuked.

ISAIAH 18

Verse 5: *For, before the harvest, when the blossom is gone and the flower becomes a ripening grape, he will cut off the shoots with pruning knives, and cut down and take away the spreading branches.*

The oracle continued, changing the focus to Cush (near Egypt). The LORD warned Cush. The LORD declared that when the banner is raised and the trumpet sounds, all will pay attention. He will cut off the fruits of harvest. Gifts will be brought to Mount Zion as a tribute.

ISAIAH 19

Verse 6: *In that day there will be an altar to the LORD in the heart of Egypt, and a monument to the LORD at its border.*

This was a prophesy about Egypt. The LORD will come to Egypt and idols will tremble. Egyptians will destroy themselves and be handed over to Assyria. Drought will come and fishermen will not find fish. All workers will be dejected. Pharaoh's counselors will give senseless advice. The LORD will punish them and they will be able to do nothing. The land of Judah will bring terror to the Egyptians. Five cities will swear allegiance to God. One will be called the City of Destruction. There will be altars to the LORD and He will send a Savior. There will be a highway between Egypt and Assyria and the two countries will be blessed, along with Israel.

ISAIAH 20

Verse 6: *In that day the people who live on this coast will say, "See what has happened to those we relied on, those we fled to for help and deliverance from the king of Assyria! How then can we escape?"*

This is a prophesy against Egypt and Cush, given to Isaiah the year the Assyrians attacked and captured Ashdod. The LORD had Isaiah go around stripped and barefoot for three years as a sign to Egypt and Cush that Assyria will defeat them. Those who trusted them in the past will be put them to shame. They will not know where to go for deliverance.

ISAIAH 21

Verse 4: *My heart falters, fear makes me tremble; the twilight I longed for has become a horror to me.*

This is an oracle concerning Babylon. An invader from the land of terror will destroy the nation. Pain and terror will overtake the people. Word will come to the lookout that Babylon has fallen and their idols were shattered. An oracle concerning Edom announced that Assyrian oppression was almost over. An oracle concerning Arabia foretold that a sword would defeat them.

ISAIAH 22

Verse 11: *You built a reservoir between the two walls for the water of the Old Pool, but you did not look to the One who made it, or have regard for the One who planned it long ago.*

This is a prophecy concerning Jerusalem. In Jerusalem, there will be a commotion. The leaders will flee and Israel will be destroyed. The LORD will have His day. The people will prepare to defend their city, but will forget to ask the LORD for help. Foreigners will occupy the city and put the Israelites to shame.

ISAIAH 23

Verse 9: *The LORD Almighty planned it, to bring low the pride of all glory and to humble all who are renowned on the earth.*

This is a prophecy against Tyre (the capital of Phoenicia). Tyre will be destroyed. The sea merchants of Tarshish and the city of Sidon will mourn. The LORD planned the destruction of the fortresses of Phoenicia because of her pride. The Phoenicians will find no comfort in Babylon because the Assyrians will have turned Babylon into a desert. Tyre will be forgotten for 70 years. When the LORD remembers her again, her profits will go to the LORD.

ISAIAH 24

Verse 7: *The new wine dries up and the vine withers; all the merry makers groan.*

The LORD will lay waste to the earth and *all* inhabitants, and completely plunder it. A curse will consume the earth because of the people's disobedience of the Law. Desolation and gloom will replace all joy—the city will be in ruins. The godly remnant will shout with joy to the LORD, but others will perish in terror. The LORD will punish powers in heaven and on earth. He will reign gloriously on Mount Zion.

ISAIAH 25

Verse 1: *O LORD, you are my God; I will exalt you and praise your name, for in perfect faithfulness you have done marvelous things, things planned long ago.*

Isaiah praised the LORD for His strength and refuge. He declared that God will silence the foreigners and remove disgrace from His people who will rejoice. Isaiah then prophesied about a banquet that the LORD will give for all people, when people's eyes will be opened, death will be defeated forever, and the LORD will wipe away everyone's tears. The LORD stated that in that day people will be blessed because they trust God, but Moab will be trampled because of her pride.

ISAIAH 26

Verse 3: *You will keep in perfect peace him whose mind is steadfast, because he trusts in you.*

On the day of the LORD's coming, a song of praise will be sung in Judah. Peace, righteousness, and trust in the LORD will be rewarded. The arrogant will be humbled. The LORD will teach righteousness and establish peace. The people are encouraged to honor only the LORD. The evil will be punished. Oppression will end and the innocent and righteous will prevail.

ISAIAH 27

Verse 11: *When its twigs are dry, they are broken off and women come and make fires with them. For this is a people without understanding; so their Maker has no compassion on them, and their Creator shows them no favor.*

Prophecy continued. In the day of the LORD, He will punish wicked nations and protect Israel. Israel will blossom and atone for her guilt. No pagan altars will remain. All of Israel will gather in Jerusalem to worship the LORD.

Isaiah 28

Verse 5: *In that day the LORD Almighty will be a glorious crown, a beautiful wreath for the remnant of his people.*

The Word of the LORD continued. Ephraim is warned because it did not destroy its drunkards. God will rule the remnant in glory. The LORD will punish the unbelievers and He warns the rulers of Jerusalem. The righteous will survive the destruction of the land. The LORD is wonderful in counsel and magnificent in wisdom.

Isaiah 29

Verse 13: *The LORD says: "These people come near to me with their mouth and honor me with their lips, but their hearts are far from me. Their worship of me is made up only of rules taught by men."*

The prophecy continued with a woe to Jerusalem. Her enemies will besiege Jerusalem, but in time the LORD will turn them into dust. Isaiah warned of the LORD's impending judgment. The LORD will confound the nations. Warning is given to those who worship with their lips but not their hearts. Isaiah stated that the humble and needy would again rejoice with the LORD. Ruthless men and murderers will vanish. Those who worship the LORD will not be ashamed.

Isaiah 30

Verse 11: *Leave this way, get off this path, and stop confronting us with the Holy One of Israel!*

The Word of the LORD continued with words of woe to the obstinate children—the nation that does not carry out the LORD's plans, but looks to Egypt for help, paying Pharaoh tribute. The people were told not to listen to false prophets and that sin would come to those who reject the LORD's true message. He declared that those who did not repent would be punished. They were told that the LORD longs to be gracious and show compassion if only they would ask! It is stated that the LORD will bless the faithful and destroy Israel's enemies—Assyria and the Ammonites.

ISAIAH 31

Verse 5: *Like birds hovering overhead, the LORD Almighty will shield Jerusalem; he will shield it and deliver it, he will "pass over" it and will rescue it.*

The LORD continued with words of woe to those who ask Egypt for help instead of asking the Holy One. The LORD will protect Jerusalem and "pass over" it. Isaiah made a plea to the people to return to the LORD. Assyria will be destroyed, but not by man.

ISAIAH 32

Verse 17: *The fruit of righteousness will be peace; the effect of righteousness will be quietness and confidence forever.*

The prophecy given to Isaiah continued. A king will rule in righteousness; he will open eyes and ears. Fools and scoundrels will flounder, but wise men will listen. Isaiah appealed to the women of Jerusalem for humility, justice, and righteousness.

ISAIAH 33

Verse 10: *"Now will I arise," says the LORD. "Now will I be exalted; now will I be lifted up."*

The LORD spoke another woe—this time to the destroyer and traitor (Assyria?), who will eventually be destroyed and betrayed. Isaiah cried out to the LORD with longing for Israel, and declared that the LORD will fill Zion with justice and righteousness. The LORD said that He would arise and be exalted. Sinners in Zion will be consumed with fire. The righteous will be rewarded and will see the King. Jerusalem will prosper and her sins will be forgiven.

ISAIAH 34

Verse 4: *All the stars of the heavens will be dissolved and the sky rolled up like a scroll; all the starry host will fall like withered leaves from the vine, like shriveled figs from the fig tree.*

Isaiah continued to speak for the LORD. The LORD was angry at all nations and said that He would destroy all the armies. The judgment for Edom is that it will be slaughtered by the sword and blazing fire. The LORD's Day of vengeance over Edom will occur and Edom will be decimated. Isaiah read from a scroll of the LORD that states that He has given this order against Edom.

ISAIAH 35

Verse 8: *And a highway will be there; it will be called the Way of Holiness. The unclean will not journey on it; it will be for those who walk in that Way; wicked fools will not go about on it.*

Isaiah continued to read the scroll of the LORD. He read of the splendor and glory of the redeemed that will shine. The LORD will save the righteous and God will come. Miracles will be performed. The redeemed will walk on the highway and enter Zion singing with joy.

ISAIAH 36

Verse 20: *Who of all the gods of these countries has been able to save his lands from me? How then can the LORD deliver Jerusalem from my hand?*

Sennacherib, king of Assyria, attacked Judah and surrounded Jerusalem. Word was sent from the field commander to Hezekiah, king of Judah, asking how he was planning to defend himself. Sennacherib discounted Egypt's help and asked Hezekiah if he thought his God would save them. Sennacherib's messenger claimed their LORD told him to conquer Jerusalem, and appealed to the Israelites who lined the wall of the city not to believe Hezekiah's assurance that their LORD would save them. The people obeyed Hezekiah's instruction to remain silent. Hezekiah was then informed of what was said.

ISAIAH 37

Verse 32: *For out of Jerusalem will come a remnant, and out of Mount Zion a band of survivors. The zeal of the LORD Almighty will accomplish this.*

Hezekiah humbled himself and went to the temple of the LORD. Isaiah reassured the king and promised him that the LORD would cut down his enemies with the sword. Sennacherib sent a letter to Hezekiah asking him where the gods of the other countries he had conquered were when he attacked them. Hezekiah took the letter to the Temple and prayed over it. Isaiah reminded Hezekiah of the LORD's power. He foretold of the remnant from Israel that would survive. He told Hezekiah that the LORD promised that Sennacherib would not enter the city. That night, the Angel of Death destroyed the Assyrian camp and 185,000 men were killed. What remained of the Assyrian army withdrew. His own sons later murdered Sennacherib.

ISAIAH 38

Verse 18: *For the grave cannot praise you, death cannot sing your praise; those who go down to the pit cannot hope for your faithfulness.*

Hezekiah became ill and Isaiah told him to organize his affairs because he was about to die. Hezekiah appealed to the LORD and was granted fifteen more years to live. As a sign, a shadow backed up ten steps on the stairway. Hezekiah praised the LORD and promised to be humble.

ISAIAH 39

Verse 2: *Hezekiah received the envoys gladly and showed them what was in his storehouses—the silver, the gold, the spices, the fine oil, his entire armory and everything found among his treasures. There was nothing in his palace or in all his kingdom that Hezekiah did not show them.*

Hezekiah received envoys from Babylon and showed them everything in his palace. When Isaiah heard this, he prophesied that all of the treasures of his palace, including some of his own descendants, would be carried off to Babylon.

ISAIAH 40

Verse 31: *...but those who hope in the LORD will renew their strength. They will soar on wings like eagles; they will run and not grow weary, they will walk and not be faint.*

The LORD told Isaiah to comfort His people. Jerusalem will have payment for her sin. Isaiah prophesied about one who will prepare the way for the glory of God to be revealed. Isaiah was told to cry out that the grass withers and the flowers fall, but the glory of God stands forever. The people were exhorted to announce the coming of the Sovereign LORD. It was stated that nothing can compare to the LORD. The LORD sits enthroned above the circle of the earth. The LORD has no equal. The Creator's strength and understanding are unfathomable. Those with hope in the LORD will not grow weary.

ISAIAH 41

Verse 4: *Who has done this and carried it through, calling forth the generations from the beginning? I, the LORD—with the first of them and with the last—I am he.*

Isaiah continued to prophesy about Israel. God will use Cyrus, the king of Persia (from the East), for righteous acts. The other heathen nations will fear. Israel was instructed not to fear because the LORD is their God. He will protect them and help them defeat their enemies. They were told to rejoice in the LORD. The LORD will water the deserts and help them prosper. Those who worship idol gods, however, will amount to nothing.

ISAIAH 42

Verse 1: *Here is my servant, who I uphold, my chosen one in whom I delight; I will put my Spirit on him and he will bring justice to the nations.*

Isaiah continued prophesying. The LORD's servant, the Chosen One, will bring justice to all nations. The LORD calls the righteous to offer a song of praise to the LORD. The LORD will lay waste to the mountains and dry up the waters. He will lead the blind and turn darkness into light. Israel was blind and deaf and would be punished for that.

ISAIAH 43

Verse 19: *See, I am doing a new thing! Now it springs up; do you not perceive it? I am making a way in the desert and streams in the wasteland.*

The Word of the LORD continued. The LORD is the Creator and Israel's only Redeemer. He will bring His people, who were scattered in all directions, back to the land so that others may witness His power. He will bring down Babylon. The LORD is making a way in the desert for His people, but Israel has not honored Him.

ISAIAH 44

Verse 6: *This is what the LORD says—Israel's King and Redeemer, the LORD Almighty: I am the first and I am the last; apart from me there is no God.*

The LORD continued through Isaiah. Israel is His chosen nation. God will pour out His Spirit and blessings. There is no other God besides Him—there is no other Rock! Even those who make idols use God's resources to do so. Idols are detestable. Israel's sins have been forgiven and they are redeemed—sing for joy! The LORD will allow Jerusalem and the Temple to be rebuilt.

ISAIAH 45

Verse 19: *I have not spoken in secret, from somewhere in a land of darkness; I have not said to Jacob's descendants, "Seek me in vain." I, the LORD, speak the truth; I declare what is right.*

The prophecy continued. The LORD will allow Cyrus to conquer Israel's enemies, and He will strengthen him even though he will not acknowledge the LORD. The LORD is the Creator of all things and He will raise up Cyrus in His righteousness and will rebuild His city. All idol worshipers will be shamed. The LORD urged His people to turn to the One True God and be saved. Every knee will bow, every tongue will swear. In the LORD, all descendants of Israel will be found righteous.

ISAIAH 46

Verse 10: *I make known the end from the beginning, from ancient times, what is still to come. I say: My purpose will stand, and I will do all that I please.*

The prophecy continued. The gods of Babylon will bow to the LORD God. The LORD is the one who will sustain and rescue Israel. Idol worshipers cannot get answers from their gods. There is no God like the LORD. The LORD will bring righteousness and salvation.

ISAIAH 47

Verse 4: *Our Redeemer—the LORD Almighty is his name—is the Holy One of Israel.*

The fall of Babylon is foretold. Her shame will be uncovered. Vengeance will be the LORD's. God will use Babylon as an instrument of His will, but Babylon would be cruel to His people.

Disaster will come upon them because of their wickedness. Babylon's sorcerers and idolaters will not be able to help them—no one will be able to save them.

ISAIAH 48

Verse 18: *If only you had paid attention to my commands, your peace would have been like a river, your righteousness like the waves of the sea.*

Israel was stubborn and did not listen to the LORD. The people worshiped idols, rebelled against God, and so the LORD tested them. The LORD told them ahead of time what He was planning to do so that they would recognize Him. Israel's eventual freedom was prophesied. The LORD reminded Israel that He is the LORD, and that if they had listened to Him they would have prospered beyond imagination. He will tell His people to leave Babylon. There will be no peace for the wicked.

ISAIAH 49

Verse 25: *But this is what the LORD says: "Yes, captives will be taken from warriors, and plunder retrieved from the fierce; I will contend with those who contend with you, and your children I will save."*

The prophecy foretold of the LORD's soon coming servant. God's people felt that they had labored in vain, but God assured them that their reward is with Him. Through His servant, the LORD will bring back the people to their land. He will include the Gentiles and spread the word. Kings will bow down before the restored Israel. He will restore the nation. There will be rejoicing in the LORD for His compassion. The LORD will lift up their banner, beckon to the Gentiles, and make Israel great. The LORD will protect them and make all nations know His greatness.

ISAIAH 50

Verse 4: *The Sovereign LORD has given me an instructed tongue, to know the word that sustains the weary. He wakens me morning by morning, wakens my ear to listen like one being taught.*

The LORD continued through Isaiah concerning Israel's sin. Israel was punished because of these sins. Israel was deaf to God despite His awesome power and glory. The LORD's servant does not sin. He will trust completely in the LORD in all circumstances. The LORD will always help him. The LORD gave Israel a choice: Trust in Him and obey His word or be self-reliant and lie down in torment.

ISAIAH 51

Verse 7: *Hear me, you who know what is right, you people who have my law in your hearts: Do not fear the reproach of men or be terrified by their insults.*

The LORD spoke to the righteous. He will comfort Zion and will make her wastelands like gardens of the LORD. His justice will become a light to the nations. The earth will wear out but His righteous salvation will last forever. He will comfort those who have feared mortal men and will welcome them back to Jerusalem. The great and powerful LORD will acknowledge His people and will defend them against their tormentors.

ISAIAH 52

Verse 7: *How beautiful on the mountains are the feet of those who bring good news, who proclaim peace, who bring good tidings, who proclaim salvation, who say to Zion, "Your God reigns!"*

The LORD continued to speak to Zion. He will redeem her and will not allow Jerusalem to be defiled again. The people will proclaim that the God of Israel reigns. When the LORD returns to Zion, all nations will see the glory and salvation of the Almighty God. The LORD will be the Israelites' rear guard on their return to Jerusalem. God's servant will be raised up to service the nations. What they were not told they will see, and what they have not heard they will understand.

ISAIAH 53

Verse 6: *We all, like sheep, have gone astray, each of us has turned to his own way; and the LORD has laid on him the iniquity of us all.*

The arm of the LORD (the Messiah) will grow up from a root. He will be despised and rejected, but will carry our sorrows. He will accept the punishment for all our sins. The LORD laid the iniquity of all of us on Him. He quietly accepted our punishment though He, Himself, had done no violence. The LORD made His life a guilt offering. After suffering, He will see the light (resurrection). He will bear the sin of many.

ISAIAH 54

Verse 5: *For your Maker is your husband—the LORD Almighty is his name—the Holy One of Israel is your Redeemer; he is called the God of all the earth.*

The LORD continued to encourage Jerusalem. In the future, she will grow and prosper. The LORD, with deep compassion, will bring her people back. The LORD swore not to be angry or rebuke them again. He will rebuild Jerusalem with precious stones. The LORD will teach their children. Peace, righteousness, and protection will be enjoyed. The LORD will vindicate them.

ISAIAH 55

Verse 2: *Why spend money on what is not bread, and your labor on what does not satisfy? Listen, listen to me, and eat what is good, and your soul will delight in the richest of fare.*

The LORD invited all who are thirsty to come and drink. He renewed His covenant with the Israelites. He invited all the nations to know the LORD. All were encouraged to turn toward the LORD. He encouraged His people to go out in joy and peace as they return to Israel.

ISAIAH 56

Verse 1: *This is what the LORD says: "Maintain justice and do what is right, for my salvation is close at hand and my righteousness will soon be revealed."*

The LORD continued to speak to His people. Be just and righteous and the LORD's salvation will be at hand. Keep the Sabbath and hold fast to God's covenant and all believers, including foreigners, will be rewarded in Heaven. *All* who believe in the LORD will be included. The evil and wicked, however, will be punished.

ISAIAH 57

Verse 1: *The righteous perish, and no one ponders it in his heart; devout men are taken away, and no one understands that the righteous are taken away to be spared from evil.*

The LORD continued His instruction through Isaiah. The righteous who perish will find peace. Those who worship idols will inherit nothing. Those who take refuge in the LORD will inherit His holy mountain. Prepare the road for the LORD. He will revive the spirit of the lowly and contrite. God was angry with Israel but will restore and comfort His people. There will be no peace for the wicked.

ISAIAH 58

Verse 6: *Is not this the kind of fasting I have chosen: to loose the chains of injustice and untie the cords of the yoke, to set the oppressed free and break every yoke?*

The LORD told Isaiah to shout out the sins of His people. The LORD accused His people of insincere worship of Him. He told them to feed and clothe the poor and honor their families, so that righteousness will go before them. The LORD will answer their prayers. The LORD will guide the righteous and rebuild the ruins. Those who honor the Sabbath will find joy in the LORD.

ISAIAH 59

Verse 8: *The way of peace they do not know; there is no justice in their paths. They have turned them into crooked roads; no one who walks in them will know peace.*

The Word of God continued through Isaiah. He told the people their sins have separated them from the LORD. The sinners do not know peace or justice. They look for light, but all is darkness. Isaiah acknowledged the sins of Israel and declared that the LORD's own salvation and righteousness sustained Him. God will put on armor of righteousness, salvation, and vengeance, and will repay His wrath upon His enemies. The Redeemer will come to Zion. The LORD's Spirit and words will not depart from the citizens of Zion.

ISAIAH 60

Verse 1: *Arise, shine, for your light has come, and the glory of the LORD rises upon you.*

The LORD continued to speak to Israel. The glory of the LORD shines. Nations will come to Zion's light. All will come from afar. People will bring silver and gold to honor the LORD. The gates will remain open day and night and the LORD will protect and honor Israel. The cedars of Lebanon will be brought to rebuild the Temple. All enemies will bow before Zion. Peace and righteousness will rule. There will be no violence, but salvation in the land. The LORD will be Zion's light. The remnant will grow and prosper in the LORD's glory.

ISAIAH 61

Verse 10: *I delight greatly in the LORD; my soul rejoices in my God. For he has clothed me with garments of salvation and arrayed me in a robe of righteousness, as a bridegroom adorns his head like a priest, and as a bride adorns herself with her jewels.*

Isaiah prophesied again about Messiah and why He will be sent to Israel. The year of the LORD's favor was proclaimed for Zion. All of the oppressed will be honored. All sorrow will be replaced with joy. The ancient ruins will be rebuilt. They will inherit a double portion of land and everlasting joy will be theirs. The LORD blessed them and renewed His covenant with them. Salvation and righteousness will be upon Zion before all of the nations.

ISAIAH 62

Verse 2: *The nations will see your righteousness, and all kings your glory; you will be called by a new name that the mouth of the LORD will bestow.*

Prophecy continued. Zion will be called by a new name—Hephzibah—and the land will be called Beulah. God will rejoice over Israel. The LORD will make Jerusalem the praise of the earth. Israel will not be defeated again. A way will be prepared for the people. A banner will be raised to tell the nations. The Holy People will be redeemed—the city will no longer be deserted.

ISAIAH 63

Verse 9: *In all their distress he too was distressed, and the angel of his presence saved them. In his love and mercy he redeemed them; he lifted them up and carried them all the days of old.*

Isaiah prophesied concerning God's day of vengeance and year of redemption. Isaiah praised the LORD for all the good things that He has done. Isaiah recalled the oppression in Egypt and the days of Moses, remembering that God was there. The LORD is the Father and redeemer of Israel, but the enemies have trampled the sanctuary.

ISAIAH 64

Verse 6: *All of us have become like one who is unclean, and all our righteous acts are like filthy rags; we all shrivel up like a leaf, and like the wind our sins sweep us away.*

This is a call to the LORD to humble His enemies. Isaiah asked God to act on the behalf of His people. They have been punished for their sins. Isaiah acknowledged that He is the potter, and they are the clay. He asked for forgiveness and action from the LORD.

ISAIAH 65

Verse 25: *"The wolf and the lamb will feed together, and the lion will eat straw like the ox, but dust will be the serpent's food. They will neither harm nor destroy on all my holy mountain," says the LORD.*

The LORD responded to the people's plea. He had been patient with an obstinate people. He did not destroy them because there was some good in them. He declared that the chosen will inherit Israel, but the sword will be for those who forsake the LORD. He who takes an oath to the LORD will have his past troubles forgotten. A new heaven and a new earth will be created. There will be joy in Jerusalem. People will all live more than 100 years. The LORD will bless His people. There will be peace.

ISAIAH 66

Verse 2: *"Has not my hand made all these things, and so they came into being?" declares the LORD. "This is the one I esteem: he who is humble and contrite in spirit, and trembles at my word."*

The LORD asked where His dwelling place would be. He declared that He esteems the humble and contrite in spirit, but will punish evil. Jerusalem will be reborn. The LORD will protect His child. He is coming with fire to judge all. Punishment will fall upon those who do not follow the Law. He will send survivors as messengers to distant lands. People will gather from all nations in Jerusalem to worship the LORD. A new heaven and a new earth will be formed.

JEREMIAH

JEREMIAH 1

Verse 5: *Before I formed you in the womb I knew you, before you were born I set you apart; I appointed you as a prophet to the nations.*

Jeremiah, a priest, received the word of the LORD and became a prophet in the middle of Josiah's reign as king of Judah. The LORD touched his mouth and appointed him over all nations. The LORD told Jeremiah that disaster would come from the north because of Judah's wickedness. He told Jeremiah to be His spokesman, and He would stand behind him.

JEREMIAH 2

Verse 13: *My people have committed two sins: They have forsaken me, the spring of living water, and have dug their own cisterns, broken cisterns that cannot hold water.*

The LORD instructed Jeremiah to ask Israel why she had forsaken Him. The Israelites were worshiping idols and depending on themselves instead of the LORD. Jeremiah reminded them that the LORD led them out of Egypt. The LORD was frustrated with their lack of loyalty to Him when He had done so much for them.

JEREMIAH 3

Verse 11: *The LORD said to me, "Faithless Israel is more righteous than unfaithful Judah."*

The LORD asked that if a man divorces his wife and she marries another man should he return to her? Likewise, if the Israelites prostitute themselves with idols, could they return to the LORD? He stated that the land was barren and a drought underway because of their wickedness. He recounted that when Israel was unfaithful, it led to her demise. He was upset that Judah was doing the same thing. She had not learned from her sister. God would be more sympathetic to Israel, if she would repent, than Judah. He urged the unfaithful to return to Him.

JEREMIAH 4

Verse 3: *This is what the LORD says to the men of Judah and to Jerusalem: "Break up your unplowed ground and do not sow among thorns."*

The LORD urged Israel to repent and return to Him. He foretold of Judah's impending wrath from the north. He warned of an advancing army from the north. He described the destruction that was in store for them.

JEREMIAH 5

Verse 31: *The prophets prophesy lies, the priests rule by their own authority, and my people love it this way. But what will you do in the end?*

The LORD told Jeremiah that if he could find one righteous person, he would spare the city of Jerusalem. He continued with his condemnation of Judah and the unfaithfulness of His people. He described the impending invasion against them. He asked rhetorically if he should punish them for their evil and deceit.

JEREMIAH 6

Verse 16: *This is what the LORD says: "Stand at the crossroads and look; ask for the ancient paths, ask where the good way is, and walk in it, and you will find rest for your souls." But you said, "We will not walk in it."*

The LORD continued telling them that He will destroy Jerusalem. The greatest to the least all practice deceit and He foretells of the disaster that loomed from the north. He described how the siege on Jerusalem would be done. He also described the wrath of the LORD.

JEREMIAH 7

Verse 11a: *"Has this house, which bears my Name, become a den of robbers to you? But I have been watching!" declares the LORD.*

The LORD instructed Jeremiah to stand at the gate of the temple and proclaim the word of the LORD to the people. He told them to reform their ways, and He would let them continue to live in the land. The LORD had called them, but they did not come; they continued to worship foreign gods. He declared that His anger and wrath would be poured out on Judah. He recalled that their forefathers had not obeyed Him, and now their descendants were not obeying Him either. The LORD told Jeremiah that the people would not listen to him; therefore, he should say that the LORD has rejected this generation that is under His wrath. He will bury the dead in places where the people had sacrificed their sons to pagan gods. There will be no joy or gladness and the land will become desolate.

JEREMIAH 8

Verse 20: *The harvest is past, the summer is ended, and we are not saved.*

Then the LORD declared that the bones of all who have been buried in Judah would be exposed like refuse on the ground. Any survivors of the wrath to come would prefer death. The LORD lamented the sins of Judah and their refusal to listen to Him. He announced His plans for the destruction of the land, the women, the harvest, and the water. He described the terror of the enemy's horses, venomous snakes, and torment to come. He again questioned why Judah provoked Him and lamented saying that He was crushed and mourning along with His people.

JEREMIAH 9

Verse 16: *I will scatter them among nations that neither they nor their fathers have known, and I will pursue them with the sword until I have destroyed them.*

The LORD spoke of weeping over the fate of the people. They were in the midst of deception and refused to acknowledge the LORD. He told them again of the ruins that would be the result of their defiance. He foretold of death and destruction that would follow.

JEREMIAH 10

Verse 5: *Like a scarecrow in a melon patch, their idols cannot speak; they must be carried because they cannot walk. Do not fear them; they can do no harm nor can they do any good.*

Jeremiah concluded his temple message contrasting idols with the one true God. He made a contrast between man-made objects that will fade and the LORD. He proclaimed the power of God. He concluded that the people should gather up their belongings for the wrath of God was near. Finally, Jeremiah prayed for divine justice on the people's behalf.

JEREMIAH 11

Verse 14: *Do not pray for this people nor offer any plea or petition for them, because I will not listen when they call to me in the time of their distress.*

The LORD instructed Jeremiah to tell the people they are cursed if they do not obey the terms of the covenant and obey His word. He was distraught that the people did not do so. He promised a disaster as punishment for breaking the covenant. He noted that they have as many idols as they have towns in Judah and their altars are shameful. He stated that He would not listen to their pleas in the time of distress. The LORD warned Jeremiah about the plot against him. The men of Anathoth were planning to kill Jeremiah, but the LORD promised retribution against them.

JEREMIAH 12

Verse 17: *"But if any nation does not listen, I will completely uproot and destroy it," declares the LORD.*

Jeremiah asked the LORD why the way of the wicked prospered (why do the godless invaders prosper?). The LORD responded that they would take over the land but would not prosper. He implied that He would eventually bring back the exiles from Judah and, if the people repented, they would prosper.

JEREMIAH 13

Verse 11: *"For as a belt is bound around a man's waist, so I bound the whole house of Israel and the whole house of Judah to me," declares the LORD, "to be my people for my renown and praise and honor. But they have not listened."*

The LORD illustrated the uselessness of Judah by instructing Jeremiah to buy a white linen belt, bury it in the dirt for several days, and then retrieve it. He did so, and it was useless. The LORD indicated that in the same way the pride of Judah and their stubbornness had made them useless. He then told Jeremiah that God's wrath would be like drunkenness on all of the officials of Judah. He gave one last warning to the people to listen or they would be taken into captivity. He warned them to look up and see the invasion from the north. He proclaimed: "Woe to you Jerusalem!"

JEREMIAH 14

Verse 7: *Although our sins testify against us, O LORD, do something for the sake of your name. For our backsliding is great; we have sinned against you.*

The LORD told Jeremiah of the impending drought. Jeremiah pleaded with the LORD on behalf of the people, but He did not accept this, because He remembered their wickedness. He told Jeremiah that the false prophets who proclaimed there would be no sword or famine in the land would perish by the sword and famine. Again, Jeremiah prayed for the people of Judah, and asked that the LORD would not despise them, but remember His covenant.

JEREMIAH 15

Verse 19: *If you repent, I will restore you that you may serve me; if you utter worthy, not worthless, words, you will be my spokesman. Let this people turn to you, but you must not turn to them.*

The LORD responded that even if Moses and Samuel came to Him, He would not spare Judah. He went on to describe four kinds of destroyers: The sword to kill, the dogs to drag them away, and the birds and beasts to devour them. He attributed this all to what Manasseh, king of Judah had done. He went on to describe the destruction that awaited Judah. Jeremiah pleaded with the LORD about his own fate, his mission, and God's faithfulness. God told Jeremiah to repent, and He would save him from the wicked.

JEREMIAH 16

Verse 17: *My eyes are on all their ways; they are not hidden from me, nor is their sin concealed from my eyes.*

The LORD told Jeremiah not to marry or have children because all wives and children would die of deadly diseases and birds and beasts would consume their carcasses. He told him not to attend funerals because He would have no pity. All joy and gladness would be gone. The LORD explained that the people had acted even more wickedly than their forefathers. He again promised to eventually restore Israel, but not until vengeance was done. He declared that he would teach His people that His name is the LORD.

JEREMIAH 17

Verse 5: *Cursed is the one who trusts in man, who depends on flesh for his strength and whose heart turns away from the LORD.*

The LORD stated that Judah's sin was engraved on the tablets of their hearts. He explained the curse of depending on man and the blessings that come from depending on God. He told them that those who turned away from Him would be written in dust. The LORD told Jeremiah to stand at the city gate telling the people to keep the Sabbath day holy and if they obeyed, then King David's destiny would last forever; but if they did not, the gates would be consumed in fire.

JEREMIAH 18

Verse 6: *"O house of Israel, can I not do with you as this potter does?" declares the LORD. "Like clay in the hand of the potter, so are you in my hand, O house of Israel."*

The LORD then instructed Jeremiah to go to the potter's house and asked why He could not mold the people as the potter molds the clay. He declared that the actions of His people could change his mind from punishing or blessing a nation. He told Jeremiah again to tell the people of the disaster that was in their future. He again lamented over the sins of Judah. Plans were made against Jeremiah; and the people jeered him. Jeremiah then asked the LORD not to forgive their sins and to let them be overthrown.

JEREMIAH 19

Verse 15: *This is what the LORD Almighty, the God of Israel, says: "Listen! I am going to bring on this city and the villages around it every disaster I pronounced against them, because they were stiff-necked and would not listen to my words."*

The LORD told Jeremiah to buy a clay jar from a potter and to meet with the elders explaining that the wrath of God was near. He instructed him to smash the jar at the end of his meeting, telling them that the LORD would smash their nation. Jeremiah did this and then announced to the people at the temple that the LORD was about to bring disaster to the city because they would not listen.

JEREMIAH 20

Verse 13: *Sing to the LORD! Give praise to the LORD! He rescues the life of the needy from the hands of the wicked.*

Pashhur, the chief priest, heard the prophesies of Jeremiah and had him beaten. When he was released, Jeremiah told him that his new name was Magor-Missabib (terror on every side). He warned him that the LORD would make him a terror to himself and all of his friends. He told him that Babylon would plunder the city and Pashhur and his family would go into exile in Babylon. Jeremiah then complained to the LORD that He deceived him and that he was ridiculed all day long. He exalted the LORD, then was despondent and cursed the day he was born.

JEREMIAH 21

Verse 13: *I am against you, Jerusalem, you who live above this valley on the rocky plateau, declares the LORD—you who say, "Who can come against us? Who can enter our refuge?"*

King Zedekiah sent the priests Pashhur and Zephaniah to ask Jeremiah to ask the LORD to help them from the attack of King Nebuchadnezzar of Babylon. Jeremiah told them that even the weapons they were using to defend themselves would be turned against them and then God would turn over any survivors to Nebuchadnezzar. He told them that anyone who wants to save his life should surrender to the Babylonians. He said that the LORD would punish them for their deeds.

JEREMIAH 22

Verse 21: *I warned you when you felt secure, but you said, "I will not listen!" This has been your way from your youth; you have not obeyed me.*

The LORD told Jeremiah to go to the king's palace and announce to the king and his officials to do what is right or the palace will become a ruin. The LORD declared that people from other nations will ask why the city was destroyed, and the answer will be because the people did not obey the LORD. The LORD proclaimed that Shallum (Jehoahaz), Josiah's son, and next in line for king, would die in captivity. Josiah's son Jehoiakim would not be mourned. He proclaimed that none of the royal family would ever return to Judah.

JEREMIAH 23

Verse 5: *"The days are coming," declares the LORD, "when I will raise up to David a righteous Branch, a King who will reign wisely and do what is just and right in the land."*

The LORD addressed the rulers and priests (shepherds) and told them of their pending punishment. He noted that new shepherds would eventually lead the flock. The new King (Jesus) will do what is just and right. The LORD addressed the prophets noting that they were godless and wicked and they would be banished into darkness. The LORD was angry with them for prophesying things that He did not tell them and things that were from pagan gods. Likewise, He declared that the false oracles and prophets would receive everlasting disgrace.

JEREMIAH 24

Verse 7: *I will give them a heart to know me, that I am the LORD. They will be my people, and I will be their God, for they will return to me with all their heart.*

After the Babylonians had carried off the spoils, two baskets of figs were shown to Jeremiah. One basket had ripe good fruit, the other had rotten figs. The LORD proclaimed that like the figs, He would watch over the good citizens of Judah who were in captivity and eventually bring them back to Judah. The bad figs would be destroyed.

JEREMIAH 25

Verse 29: *See I am beginning to bring disaster on the city that bears my Name, and will you indeed go unpunished? You will not go unpunished, for I am calling down a sword upon all who live on the earth, declares the LORD Almighty.*

Jeremiah told the people that he had warned them to repent for twenty-three years, but they did not listen. He announced they would be in exile for seventy years, and then the Babylonians would be enslaved and decimated. The LORD proclaimed that He would give the cup of His wrath to all of the surrounding kingdoms, and all would eventually be punished. They will all be slaughtered for their deeds.

JEREMIAH 26

Verse 11: *Then the priests and the prophets said to the officials and all the people, "This man should be sentenced to death because he has prophesied against this city. You have heard it with your own ears!"*

Jeremiah was again instructed by the LORD to stand in the courtyard and tell the people of the disaster that He was planning. The priests and prophets seized Jeremiah and they tried to have him killed. Jeremiah gave them one more chance to reform their ways. He told them to do what they wished with him, but that his innocent blood would be on their hands. Some of the elders advised that they release Jeremiah or they would bring a terrible disaster upon themselves, so he was released. Uriah, another prophet who prophesied the same message as Jeremiah, also avoided death by escaping. King Jehoiakim pursued him, brought him out of Egypt, and had him put to death.

JEREMIAH 27

Verse 5: *With my great power and outstretched arm I made the earth and its people and the animals that are on it, and I give it to anyone I please.*

Early in Zedekiah's reign, the LORD told Jeremiah that Judah would be handed over to Nebuchadnezzar, king of Babylon. If Judah and the other nations refused to serve Nebuchadnezzar, the LORD would punish them. He advised Zedekiah to serve the king of Babylon and not listen to false prophets. He also advised the priests to serve the king of Babylon so they would live. He proclaimed that all articles that remained in the temple and palace would be taken to Babylon and would be returned when the LORD called for them.

JEREMIAH 28

Verse 9: *But the prophet who prophesies peace will be recognized as one truly sent by the LORD only if his prediction comes true.*

The false prophet Hananiah told Zedekiah the LORD would allow them to go out of Babylonian exile within two years. The LORD told Jeremiah that the wooden yoke that Hananiah had used as an illustration would be an iron yoke, and because of the false prophesies he gave, he would die that very year.

JEREMIAH 29

Verse 13: *You will seek me and find me when you seek me with all your heart.*

Jeremiah sent a letter from Jerusalem to the surviving elders and priests in exile in Babylon. Elasah delivered the letter. In it, Jeremiah told the people to go on about their lives and not to listen to prophets. He told them that it would be seventy years until they returned to Judah. He told them to pray to the LORD, and He will bring them back at that time. He announced that the LORD would punish the Babylonians and that the false prophets would be put to death. Shemaiah, a false prophet, disagreed with the letter and started a rebellion but the LORD learned of this and promised that he and his descendants would be punished.

JEREMIAH 30

Verse 24: *The fierce anger of the LORD will not turn back until he fully accomplishes the purposes of his heart. In days to come you will understand this.*

The LORD gave Jeremiah a look forward to the days when the Israelites would be released from captivity. The LORD declared that in that day, they would serve the LORD and all would be good. He would destroy their enemies and deal justly with them. He would plunder the plunderers, and heal their wounds. Jerusalem would be rebuilt on its ruins. Their new leader would come from among them.

JEREMIAH 31

Verse 13: *Then maidens will dance and be glad, young men and old as well. I will turn their mourning into gladness; I will give them comfort and joy instead of sorrow.*

The LORD declared that at that time He would be God over all of Israel, and would rebuild them again. The LORD would gather them and shepherd them. There would be rejoicing and the land would be bountiful. He offered hope for their future. He indicated that He would make a new covenant with Israel and Judah that would be written on their hearts. All would know the LORD and His greatness. Jerusalem would be restored.

JEREMIAH 32

Verse 17: *Ah Sovereign LORD, you have made the heavens and the earth by your outstretched arm. Nothing is too difficult for you.*

Jeremiah was instructed to buy a field in Anathoth before the invasion was complete. He protected the deed to the land in a jar. The LORD promised that this land, and other lands, would be reclaimed by the Israelites when they returned.

JEREMIAH 33

Verse 3: *Call to me and I will answer you and tell you great and unsearchable things you do not know.*

The LORD once more promised restoration, and joy and gladness would eventually be present again in the city. He told His people of His gracious promise of a Savior from the line of David that would do right in the land. Judah would be saved and righteous.

JEREMIAH 34

Verse 17: *Therefore, this is what the LORD says: You have not obeyed me; you have not proclaimed freedom for your fellow countrymen. So I now proclaim "freedom" for you, declares the LORD—"freedom" to fall by the sword, plague and famine. I will make you abhorrent to all the kingdoms of the earth.*

The LORD told Jeremiah to go to King Zedekiah while the siege was underway and tell him that the LORD was about to hand over the city and that the king would be handed over to

Nebuchadnezzar and go to Babylon. Jeremiah told the king that he would not die by the sword, and Zedekiah told the people to release their Hebrew slaves. They did so, but then took them back again. This angered the LORD and He promised death by the sword, plague, and famine.

JEREMIAH 35

Verse 16: *The descendants of Jonadab son of Recab have carried out the command their forefather gave them, but these people have not obeyed me.*

The LORD instructed Jeremiah to go to the Recabite family. He did so and brought them to the temple and served them wine. The Recabites refused because their forefather Jonadab told them to never drink wine and they obeyed. The LORD used this as an illustration of how the Judahites should have obeyed Him. The LORD told them that they would be punished for their disobedience, but the Recabites would always be allowed to serve Him.

JEREMIAH 36

Verse 6: *So you go to the house of the LORD on a day of fasting and read to the people from the scroll the words of the LORD that you wrote as I dictated. Read them to all the people of Judah who come in from their towns.*

Based upon the LORD's instructions, Jeremiah dictated to Baruch to write on a scroll all of the punishments that God intended to inflict upon Judah. After he was done, Jeremiah had Baruch read the scroll to the people at the temple. The officials of Judah asked that Baruch bring the scroll to them, and he did. They told Baruch that Jeremiah and he should go and hide. They brought the scroll to the king who threw it into the fire and ordered that Baruch and Jeremiah be arrested. The LORD told Jeremiah to make a second scroll and tell the king that he would be punished for his actions and that he would have no one to sit on the throne after him.

JEREMIAH 37

Verse 2: *Neither he nor his attendants nor the people of the land paid any attention to the words the LORD had spoken through Jeremiah the prophet.*

Nebuchadnezzar made Zedekiah, Josiah's son, king of Judah. Zedekiah asked Jeremiah to pray for him. Jeremiah was arrested when he was leaving the city and was accused of deserting to the Babylonians. He protested, but the officials had him beaten and imprisoned. Zedekiah eventually called for him, and asked what their fate would be, because the Babylonian's attack was temporarily halted because the Egyptians were advancing. Jeremiah told him that the Babylonians would still conquer them. Jeremiah then asked if he could be released from prison, and the king let him stay in the courtyard and have fresh bread daily.

JEREMIAH 38

Verse 27: *All the officials did come to Jeremiah and question him, and he told them everything the king had ordered him to say. So they said no more to him, for no one had heard his conversation with the king.*

King Zedekiah again sent for Jeremiah after he had been thrown into a cistern for speaking the word of the LORD. Jeremiah told the king that his life would be spared if he surrendered to Babylon. He urged the king to obey the LORD and hand the city over to the Babylonians, or their wives and children would perish and the city would be burned down. The king made Jeremiah promise to tell no one of their conversation.

JEREMIAH 39

Verse 18: *I will save you; you will not fall by the sword but will escape with your life, because you trust in me, declares the LORD.*

The Babylonians besieged Jerusalem and eventually the wall was broken through. Zedekiah tried to escape, but the Babylonian army overtook him. Zedekiah's sons were killed in front of him and Zedekiah himself was blinded and shackled. The Babylonians set fire to the city and the remaining people were carried into exile. Jeremiah was allowed to remain amongst his own people.

JEREMIAH 40

Verse 9: *Gedaliah son of Ahikam, the son of Shaphan, took an oath to reassure them and their men. "Do not be afraid to serve the Babylonians," he said. "Settle down in the land and serve the king of Babylon, and it will go well with you."*

Nebuzaradan, the Babylonian commander of the imperial guard, found Jeremiah in chains and released him. Jeremiah went back to Gedaliah, son of Ahikam, who was the interim governor of Judah as Nebuzaradan had suggested. Gedaliah gathered all of the remaining men in

Judah and instructed them to settle down in the land and serve the Babylonians. He indicated that he would stay at Mizpah. Many of the Jews who were in neighboring countries returned and worked the land. Johanan and the army officers warned Gedaliah that Baalis king of the Ammonites was sending Ishmael to assassinate him. Johanan offered to quietly kill Ishmael so that the plot would not be carried out, but Gedaliah did not believe that he was in jeopardy.

JEREMIAH 41

Verse 13: *When all the people Ishmael had with him saw Johanan son of Kareah and the army officers who were with him, they were glad.*

Ishmael and ten of his men visited Gedaliah and killed him, along with all of the Jews who were with him, and all of the Babylonian soldiers that were there. Ishmael slaughtered seventy men who were bringing grain and incense and threw them into a trench. He saved ten of them because they had more grain, oil, and honey hidden in the field. Ishmael then made captives of the rest of the people in Mizpah. Johanan learned about Ishmael's crimes and set out with his men to fight him. Ishmael and eight of his men escaped. Johanan and his officers led the survivors to Egypt because they were worried that the Babylonians would blame them for what had happened.

JEREMIAH 42

Verse 5: *Then they said to Jeremiah, "May the LORD be a true and faithful witness against us if we do not act in accordance with everything the LORD your God sends you to tell us."*

The officers sought help from Jeremiah promising to do what the LORD commanded them to do. Ten days later, the LORD spoke to Jeremiah and he shared it with Johanan and his men. Jeremiah told them that the LORD would protect them if they stayed in the land. He promised to build them up and to protect them from the king of Babylon. If they proceeded on to Egypt, then they would perish from the sword, famine, and plague. Jeremiah pleaded with the remnant of Judah to not go to Egypt.

JEREMIAH 43

Verse 11: *He will come and attack Egypt, bringing death to those destined for death, captivity to those destined for captivity, and the sword to those destined for the sword.*

Azariah and Johanan accused Jeremiah of lying and led the people to Egypt, disobeying the LORD's commands. The LORD told Jeremiah to lay stones at the entrance of Pharaoh's palace in Egypt. He would have Nebuchadnezzar, king of Babylon defeat Egypt and set his throne on those stones.

JEREMIAH 44

Verse 14: *None of the remnant of Judah who have gone to live in Egypt will escape or survive to return to the land of Judah, to which they long to return and live; none will return except a few fugitives.*

The LORD was angered by the remnant's exodus to Egypt. He noted the destruction that He had brought on Judah would now befall the remnant. Jeremiah warned the people in Egypt, but they ignored him and continued to worship other gods. He promised that Hophra, king of Egypt would be handed over to his enemies as a sign of what was about to occur.

JEREMIAH 45

Verse 5: *Should you then seek great things for yourself? Seek them not. For I will bring disaster on all people, declares the LORD, but wherever you go I will let you escape with your life.*

Jeremiah's scribe, Baruch, complained that the LORD had added sorrow to his pain and that he was worn out. The LORD told Jeremiah to tell Baruch that even though He was destroying Judah, He would spare Baruch's life.

JEREMIAH 46

Verse 27: *Do not fear, O Jacob my servant; do not be dismayed, O Israel. I will surely save you out of a distant place, your descendants from the land of their exile. Jacob will again have peace and security, and no one will make him afraid.*

Nebuchadnezzar defeated the Egyptians, just as the LORD promised. The LORD had warned that the warriors who were preparing to defend Egypt would fall. Jeremiah warned the Egyptians regarding the approach of the Babylonians and their impending defeat. The LORD promised defeat to all of the pagan gods of the land. The LORD promised that He would not completely destroy what remains of Judah to allow His people to rise again.

JEREMIAH 47

Verse 1: *This is the word of the LORD that came to Jeremiah the prophet concerning the Philistines before Pharaoh attacked Gaza.*

Jeremiah announced that the LORD would next destroy the Philistines.

JEREMIAH 48

Verse 13: *Then Moab will be ashamed of Chemosh, as the house of Israel was ashamed when they trusted in Bethel.*

Jeremiah announced that Moab would also be destroyed. Moab would be punished for its false pride and idol worship.

JEREMIAH 49

Verse 16: *"The terror you inspire and the pride of your heart have deceived you, you who live in the clefts of the rocks, who occupy the heights of the hill. Though you build your nest as high as the eagle's, from there I will bring you down," declares the LORD.*

Jeremiah promised that the LORD would destroy Ammon and Edom. He also promised that destruction would come upon Damascus, Kedar and Hazor, and Elam.

JEREMIAH 50

Verse 34: *Yet their Redeemer is strong; the LORD Almighty is his name. He will vigorously defend their cause so that he may bring rest to their land, but unrest to those who live in Babylon.*

Finally, Jeremiah announced the LORD's plans for Babylon. Babylon would be captured and laid to waste. He promised to bring Israel back to its own pasture and to forgive the remnant of Judah.

JEREMIAH 51

Verse 47: *For the time will surely come when I will punish the idols of Babylon; her whole land will be disgraced and her slain will all lie fallen within her.*

The LORD continued to describe the defeat of Babylon. He encouraged the Israelites to run for their lives. He announced that Babylon must fall because of Israel's slain. Jeremiah gave a scroll to Seraiah describing the disasters that would befall Babylon. He told him to read the words aloud in Babylon, and when finished he was to tie a rock around the scroll and throw it into the Euphrates. He was told to announce that Babylon would sink like the scroll because of the disaster that would occur.

JEREMIAH 52

Verse 3a: *It was because of the LORD's anger that all this happened to Jerusalem and Judah, and in the end he thrust them from his presence.*

In this chapter, the fall of Jerusalem is described. The Babylonians surrounded the city and laid siege upon it. The wall was broken through and Zedekiah and his men escaped, but the Babylonians who pursued them caught them. His sons and officials were killed in front of him and he was blinded and imprisoned. The Babylonians brought most of the Jews back to their country but left a small group. They destroyed the city, broke up the bronze pillars, plundered the temple, and brought all of the goods to Babylon. A total of 4,600 people were taken into Babylonian captivity. Jehoiachin was released in his thirty-seventh year of captivity and was allowed to sit at the Babylonian king's table.

Chapter 25

LAMENTATIONS

LAMENTATIONS 1

Verse 14: *My sins have been bound into a yoke; by his hands they were woven together. They have come upon my neck and the Lord has sapped my strength. He has handed me over to those I cannot withstand.*

The author described the defeated and deserted city of Jerusalem. The saddened people were taken into exile, because the Lord had brought them grief for their great sins. The enemy destroyed the city and plundered all of its treasures. The desperate people were dirty, hungry, and ill from the siege. They grieved, but there was no one to comfort them. The author praised the LORD in spite of the turmoil.

LAMENTATIONS 2

Verse 13: *What can I say for you? With what can I compare you, O Daughter of Jerusalem? To what can I liken you, that I may comfort you, O Virgin Daughter of Zion? Your wound is as deep as the sea. Who can heal you?*

The author recalled how the LORD's wrath was carried out upon the city. Jerusalem was leveled and burned by the Lord because they would not listen and repent. The people, some of whom were forced into cannibalism, lay dead in the streets. No one escaped the LORD's punishment.

LAMENTATIONS 3

Verses 22,23: *Because of the LORD's great love we are not consumed, for his compassions never fail. They are new every morning; great is your faithfulness.*

The anguished author mourned. He and Jerusalem were the targets of the LORD's anger. Nevertheless, the author praised the LORD and looked forward to better days. He pleaded with the LORD to redeem the people and punish their enemies.

LAMENTATIONS 4

Verse 2: *How the precious sons of Zion, once worth their weight in gold, are now considered as pots of clay, the work of a potter's hands!*

The author described the utter destruction of the city and all of its precious metal and jewels. People lay dead in the streets. Those who survived were starving and lying in rubble and waste. Their punishment was worse than that of Sodom. The people failed to believe that they could be conquered and did not heed the LORD's warnings.

LAMENTATIONS 5

Verse 20: *Why do you always forget us? Why do you forsake us so long?*

The author asked the LORD to remember their disgrace because they were hungry, cold, ill, and desolate. They were disgraced because they had sinned. He concluded with praise to the LORD and a plea for restoration.

EZEKIEL

EZEKIEL 1

Verse 20: *Wherever the spirit would go, they would go, and the wheels would rise along with them, because the spirit of the living creatures was in the wheels.*

Ezekiel, who was a prophet exiled in Babylon prior to the final defeat of Judah, saw a vision from the LORD. He described four winged creatures that came from the north. The creatures had features of men, lions, oxen, and eagles. They had wheels that represented the presence of God. A sapphire throne with fire and a rainbow shown above them, and the glory of the LORD appeared.

EZEKIEL 2

Verse 5: *And whether they listen or fail to listen—for they are a rebellious house—they will know that a prophet has been among them.*

The LORD spoke to Ezekiel and told him that He was sending him to the rebellious Israelites. The LORD instructed him not to be afraid, but to teach them and to pass on His message to them. The LORD gave Ezekiel a scroll.

EZEKIEL 3

Verse 17: *Son of man, I have made you a watchman for the house of Israel; so hear the word I speak and give them warning from me.*

The LORD told Ezekiel to eat the scroll, and he did, noting that it tasted as sweet as honey. The LORD said that he would make Ezekiel as unyielding and hardheaded as the Israelites, and He gave him instructions to teach them. The Spirit then lifted Ezekiel, left him with the exiles, where he sat for seven days until the LORD moved him and charged him to warn the people when they strayed from righteousness. Ezekiel was told that he would be able to speak only when he had a message from God.

EZEKIEL 4

Verse 16: *He then said to me: "Son of man, I will cut off the supply of food in Jerusalem. The people will eat rationed food in anxiety and drink rationed water in despair…."*

The LORD instructed Ezekiel to construct a model symbolizing Jerusalem's siege. He told him to eat only bread, and sacrifice for 390 days for the house of Israel and 40 days for the house of Judah. The LORD told Ezekiel of Jerusalem's sins.

EZEKIEL 5

Verse 12: *A third of your people will die of the plague or perish by famine inside you; a third will fall by the sword outside your walls; and a third I will scatter to the winds and pursue with drawn sword.*

Ezekiel was instructed to shave his head and to burn his hair. The LORD recounted the disobedience of Jerusalem. The LORD shared His plans to punish Israel for her idolatry and detestable practices. He promised plague, famine, and bloodshed.

EZEKIEL 6

Verse 10: *And they will know that I am the LORD; I did not threaten in vain to bring this calamity on them.*

The LORD instructed Ezekiel to prophesy against Israel. He promised to destroy the high places, idol altars, and the people themselves. He also promised to spare a remnant. He declared that this would be done so that all people would know that He is the LORD. He described His wrath toward the nation.

EZEKIEL 7

Verse 19: *They will throw their silver into the streets, and their gold will be an unclean thing. Their silver and gold will not be able to save them in the day of the LORD's wrath. They will not be able to satisfy their hunger or fill their stomachs with it, for it has made them stumble into sin.*

Ezekiel was told that the end had come to the four corners of the earth. The LORD described His wrath and the doom of the Israelites. He said that those who survived would be weakened and shamed, then He described the plunder and destruction of the city with terror and violence.

EZEKIEL 8

Verse 12: *He said to me, "Son of man, have you seen what the elders of the house of Israel are doing in the darkness, each at the shrine of his own idol? They say, 'The LORD does not see us; the LORD has forsaken the land.'"*

An angel of the LORD appeared to Ezekiel while he was with the elders of Judah. The Spirit, shrouded in fire and bright light, lifted Ezekiel and took him into Jerusalem. The angel showed him a large idol prominently displayed in the city, then explained how detestable that was and showed him a vision of Israelites worshiping idols. The angel then showed Ezekiel a vision of Israelites worshiping the sun inside the inner court of the Temple. The angel also explained that the people of Judah would be punished for their detestable practices.

EZEKIEL 9

Verse 4b: *Go throughout the city of Jerusalem and put a mark on the foreheads of those who grieve and lament over all the detestable things that are done in it.*

The LORD called forward the seven guardian angels of Jerusalem and asked the one clothed in linen to put a mark on the forehead of any who lamented over the detestable practices going on there. All who did not have the mark were to be killed by the other six angels. Ezekiel cried out for mercy for Judah, but the LORD explained that their sin was too great, and the punishment was carried out.

EZEKIEL 10

Verse 18: *Then the glory of the LORD departed from over the threshold of the temple and stopped above the cherubim.*

Ezekiel saw a throne of sapphire that was above the cherubim and the LORD told the man clothed in linen to scatter coals over the city of Jerusalem. Four wheels from amongst the cherubim began to spin and the cherubim moved. Each had four faces; a cherub, a man, a lion, and an eagle, and was full of eyes. Then the glory of the LORD departed from the temple. Ezekiel realized that the creatures were the same as what he had seen by the Kebar River (Ezekiel 1).

EZEKIEL 11

Verse 19: *I will give them an undivided heart and put a new spirit in them; I will remove from them their heart of stone and give them a heart of flesh.*

The Spirit brought Ezekiel to the East Gate of the Temple where twenty-five men awaited him. The LORD told Ezekiel that the men were plotting evil, and He instructed him to prophesy against them. Ezekiel did this, telling them that the sword would drive them out of the city. One of the twenty-five died, and Ezekiel prayed to the LORD that the remnant be saved. The LORD promised that He would bring back the remnant that was scattered amongst the nations in the future. Then the cherubim, with the wheels beside them and the glory of God departed. The Spirit took Ezekiel to the exiles in Babylon. There, Ezekiel told them everything the LORD had shown him.

EZEKIEL 12

Verse 2: *Son of man, you are living among a rebellious people. They have eyes to see but do not see and ears to hear but do not hear, for they are a rebellious people.*

The LORD told Ezekiel that he was living amongst a rebellious people. He was instructed to bring out his things packed for exile in the morning, and to take his belongings through a hole dug in the wall in the evening, signifying what was about to happen to Jerusalem. The Israelites were obstinate and the LORD promised that He would scatter them among the nations; but He promised to spare a few of them. The LORD told Ezekiel to warn the people that the time of their exile was near.

EZEKIEL 13

Verse 9: *My hand will be against the prophets who see false visions and utter lying divinations. They will not belong to the council of my people or be listed in the records of the house of Israel, nor will they enter the land of Israel. Then you will know that I am the Sovereign LORD.*

Ezekiel was told to speak against false prophets who were claiming that all was well. He did so, promising them punishment and destruction. Based upon the LORD's instructions, he also prophesied against women who gave prophecies with magic charms, declaring that they would also be punished.

EZEKIEL 14

Verse 11: *Then the people of Israel will no longer stray from me, nor will they defile themselves anymore with all their sins. They will be my people, and I will be their God, declares the Sovereign LORD.*

Ezekiel was instructed to tell idolaters to repent and that they would be cut off like the false prophets. The LORD indicated that His judgment was unavoidable and that even Noah, Daniel, and Job could not save them. Four dreadful punishments were promised—sword, famine, wild beasts, and plague. All punishment would be rendered with just cause.

EZEKIEL 15

Verse 7: *I will set my face against them. Although they have come out of the fire, the fire will yet consume them. And when I set my face against them, you will know that I am the LORD.*

The LORD told Ezekiel that the people of Jerusalem would be useless like burnt vines and that the land would be desolate.

EZEKIEL 16

Verse 6: *Then I passed by and saw you kicking about in your blood, and as you lay there in your blood I said to you, "Live!"*

The LORD recounted the history of Jerusalem and how He raised the city like a child. He related how He had clothed Jerusalem and gave her costly jewelry. The LORD said that Jerusalem's fame spread because of the splendor that He gave her, but Jerusalem prostituted herself, sacrificing her own sons and daughters to idols. The LORD warned the idol worshipers and those who prostituted themselves with foreigners. Vengeance was promised for their sins—foreign powers would destroy them. He said that He would hand them over naked to their foreign lovers, and the lovers would destroy them. He told them that His wrath would be upon them. The LORD declared that their disgraces were worse than that of Sodom and Samaria. He promised to renew His covenant after their repentance.

EZEKIEL 17

Verse 24: *All the trees of the field will know that I the LORD bring down the tall tree and make the low tree grow tall. I dry up the green tree and make the dry tree flourish. "I the LORD have spoken, and I will do it."*

The LORD told Ezekiel to tell a parable about an eagle that broke off the topmost shoot of a cedar and carried it off to a city of traders where he planted it. The eagle also took some seed and planted it and it grew into a vine. The parable told of another eagle that was unable to help the vine. God explained that the first eagle was Nebuchadnezzar, who took Israel from its land. The other eagle symbolized an Egyptian pharaoh that Zedekiah went to unsuccessfully for help against the Babylonians. The LORD told Ezekiel that Zedekiah would be defeated because he broke his oath to Nebuchadnezzar. He promised that He would break off a shoot of the cedar and plant it on a mountain where it would flourish.

EZEKIEL 18

Verse 23: *Do I take any pleasure in the death of the wicked? declares the Sovereign LORD. Rather, am I not pleased when they turn from their ways and live?*

The LORD explained that the Israelites could no longer blame their sins on their ancestors, because they themselves had sinned. He explained that if the son of a righteous man was evil, then the son would be put to death and his blood would be on his own head. Alternatively, if the son of an evil man were righteous, then he would not die for his father's sins. The soul who sins will be the one to die. If a wicked man turns away from all of his sins and becomes righteous, he will not die; if a righteous man becomes wicked, he will die. The LORD will judge each person according to his ways. He encouraged the Israelites to repent and live. He noted that He does not take pleasure in punishing them.

EZEKIEL 19

Verse 14: *Fire spread from one of its main branches and consumed its fruit. No strong branch is left on it fit for a ruler's scepter. This is a lament and is to be used as a lament.*

Ezekiel shared a lament for Israel's princes. It described a lioness (Israel) and one of her cubs (Jehoahaz) that devoured men and was led away to Egypt. Another of her cubs (Jehoiachin or Zedekiah) was also caught and made a prisoner in Babylon. The vine (Israel) was uprooted and shriveled.

EZEKIEL 20

Verse 44: *You will know that I am the LORD, when I deal with you for my name's sake and not according to your evil ways and your corrupt practices, O house of Israel, declares the Sovereign LORD.*

Ezekiel reminded some of the elders of Israel's rebelliousness. He reminded them of the unfaithfulness of their forefathers during their exodus from Egypt and their failure to obey the Sabbath in the desert. He also told them of the second chance that God gave to the children to enter the Promised Land, and the fact that the children also rebelled against Him. Ezekiel described the present, continual pagan worship and failure to keep God's laws. He promised the wrath of God for their sins, and noted that they would loathe themselves. He shared a prophecy of invasion of the southern portion of Israel (Judah) from the north (Babylon).

EZEKIEL 21

Verse 6: *Therefore groan, son of man! Groan before them with broken heart and bitter grief.*

The LORD told Ezekiel to prophesy against Israel and tell the people that the LORD had drawn His sword to punish them and that they would groan in grief. Ezekiel told them that they should prepare for a slaughter because the king of Babylon will lead his army and choose to proceed to Jerusalem rather than Ammon. He will surround Jerusalem and besiege the city. Ezekiel told the people that they would be soundly defeated and taken captive because of their sins. Jerusalem will be ruined until the one who rightfully owns Jerusalem comes. After Jerusalem is dealt with, the foreigners will be punished.

EZEKIEL 22

Verse 30: *I looked for a man among them who would build up the wall and stand before me in the gap on behalf of the land so I would not have to destroy it, but I found none.*

The LORD detailed Jerusalem's sin to Ezekiel. The people had disobeyed their parents, mistreated the poor, desecrated the Sabbath, and honored false gods. They had slept with prostitutes and other family members, accepted bribes, practiced extortion, and forgotten God. The LORD said that He would make an example of Jerusalem by scattering the people throughout the countries. He said they would become the leftover waste at the bottom of a smelting pot, and would be burned. The LORD declared that their rulers were unjust and their priests profaned holy things; they believed false prophets, they committed extortion, robbery, and they oppressed the poor. The LORD had looked for a man to stand in the gap, but found no one. Therefore, He decided to pour out His wrath on the people.

EZEKIEL 23

Verse 49: *You will suffer the penalty for your lewdness and bear the consequences of your sins of idolatry. Then you will know that I am the Sovereign LORD.*

Samaria and Jerusalem were characterized as two sisters that became prostitutes in Egypt. Oholah was Samaria and Oholibah was Jerusalem. Oholah prostituted with the Assyrians, so the LORD gave her over to them and they punished her. Oholibah saw this but did not repent and did even more evil. She lusted after the Babylonians and defiled herself. Therefore, the LORD was going to turn her over to her lovers. They would destroy her and plunder the city because she must pay the consequences of her action. The people of Jerusalem committed adultery with their idols, sacrificed their children, defiled the sanctuary, and desecrated the Sabbath. The LORD promised to put an end to the lewdness in the land.

EZEKIEL 24

Verse 27: *At that time your mouth will be opened; you will speak with him and will no longer be silent. So you will be a sign to them, and they will know that I am the LORD.*

The LORD announced the date that Babylon would besiege Jerusalem. He relayed a parable about a cooking pot (Jerusalem) that would be brought to a boil and burned. The LORD told

Ezekiel that his wife would die, but that he should not mourn. When asked, Ezekiel told the people that Jerusalem would die and that they should not mourn so that they would acknowledge the Sovereign LORD. God told Ezekiel that he would learn of the fall of Jerusalem from a foreign messenger and would no longer be silent.

EZEKIEL 25

Verse 17: *I will carry out great vengeance on them and punish them in my wrath. Then they will know that I am the LORD, when I take vengeance on them.*

Ezekiel prophesied against the Ammonites that people from the East would destroy them. They would be punished because they reveled in Jerusalem's destruction. Moab would suffer a similar fate. The LORD promised to punish the Edomites because they took revenge on Judah. Ezekiel also prophesied against the Philistines for their prolonged hostilities.

EZEKIEL 26

Verse 13: *I will put an end to your noisy songs, and the music of your harps will be heard no more.*

The LORD told Ezekiel that Tyre, the Phoenician capital renowned for its shipping industry, would also be punished because it planned to take advantage of Jerusalem's misfortune. Babylon (and other armies) would conquer Tyre and plunder the land. Tyre would collapse into the sea and the people would never return but "dwell in the earth below."

EZEKIEL 27

Verse 27: *Your wealth, merchandise and wares, your mariners, seamen and shipwrights, your merchants and all your soldiers, and everyone else on board will sink into the heart of the sea on the day of your shipwreck.*

The LORD gave Ezekiel a lament for Tyre. The song exalted her domain on the high seas, and Tyre's great history as a merchant was noted. It told how Tyre did business with all nations and was tremendously successful, but that the east wind would break her and she would sink.

EZEKIEL 28

Verse 17: *Your heart became proud on account of your beauty, and you corrupted your wisdom because of your splendor. So I threw you to the earth; I made a spectacle of you before kings.*

This is a prophecy against the king of Tyre. The king thought of himself as a god and not a man. Because of this, the LORD said that He would bring foreigners to draw their swords against him. A lament to the king of Tyre was offered espousing his greatness and wealth and declaring the punishment for his sins. Ezekiel also prophesied against Sidon, saying that she would be punished with a plague and defeat. The LORD told Ezekiel that Israel would not have any more malicious neighbors, and when He restores Israel and gathers all of her people who were scattered among all of the nations, they will live in safety and know the LORD.

EZEKIEL 29

Verse 19: *Therefore this is what the Sovereign LORD says: I am going to give Egypt to Nebuchadnezzar king of Babylon, and he will carry off its wealth. He will loot and plunder the land as pay for his army.*

This is a prophecy against Pharaoh in Egypt. The LORD declared that he would be made like a fish that was hooked and fed to wild beasts and birds and that a sword would punish the Egyptians for their sins against Israel. The LORD promised to destroy Egypt and scatter her people. In forty years, He would bring them back, but only as a lowly nation who could not threaten her neighbors. The Babylonians would have difficulty with their campaign against Tyre and therefore the LORD would give them Egypt as a reward for their efforts on His behalf.

EZEKIEL 30

Verse 3: *For the day is near, the day of the LORD is near—a day of clouds, a time of doom for the nations.*

The LORD told Ezekiel that the day is near when Egypt will fall by the sword. Babylon will conquer the Egyptians and the LORD will dry up all of the streams of the Nile. The LORD will destroy all of their idols. Egypt will be burned and destroyed. The arms of the Pharaoh will be broken and Babylon will be strengthened.

EZEKIEL 31

Verse 18: *Which of the trees of Eden can be compared with you in splendor and majesty? Yet you, too, will be brought down with the trees of Eden to the earth below; you will lie among the uncircumcised, with those killed by the sword. This is Pharaoh and all his hordes, declares the Sovereign LORD.*

The LORD told Ezekiel to speak to Pharaoh in Egypt about what happened to Assyria. Assyria had been a great power, a mighty cedar. The land, however, became too proud and so the LORD handed it over to other nations. Ezekiel also told of how the LORD brought gloom to Lebanon. Egypt would likewise be toppled and killed by the sword.

EZEKIEL 32

Verse 10: *I will cause many peoples to be appalled at you, and their kings will shudder with horror because of you when I brandish my sword before them. On the day of your downfall each of them will tremble every moment for his life.*

Ezekiel offers a lament for Pharaoh. The LORD will capture Egypt, a giant sea monster, and throw it up onto land for birds and beasts to devour. He will annihilate him and there will be darkness. The sword of Babylon will destroy Egypt. Through their destruction, the Egyptians will come to know the Sovereign LORD. They will lay with the uncircumcised of Assyria, Elam, Meshech and Tubal. The Pharaoh will be killed, will join the uncircumcised who were killed by the sword, and will go down to the pit.

EZEKIEL 33

Verse 32: *Indeed, to them you are no more than one who sings love songs with a beautiful voice and plays an instrument well, for they hear your words but do not put them into practice.*

The LORD compared Ezekiel's mission to that of a watchman. If the watchman warns the people of approaching armies and the people do not heed his warning, it is their own fault. If the watchman fails to warn the people, then blame is with the watchman. Since Ezekiel had been a faithful watchman, he would be saved even though the people did not heed his warning. Ezekiel pleaded with Israel to turn from their ways, but they did not listen. He told them that if the righteous man becomes wicked, he will surely die and if the wicked man becomes righteous, he would be saved. Each will be judged according to his own ways. The LORD foretold of the desolation of Judah. He said that even those who survived the attack would die of plague or be attacked by wild animals. He would punish them for their sins, and told Ezekiel that the people would hear him, but not put his words into practice. The LORD declared that when Judah was conquered, they would recognize Ezekiel as a true prophet.

EZEKIEL 34

Verse 31: *You my sheep, the sheep of my pasture, are people, and I am your God, declares the Sovereign LORD.*

The LORD instructed Ezekiel to prophesy against the shepherds who take care of themselves but not the flock. The LORD declared that He would rescue the flock, which would be scattered about the countryside and attacked by wild animals because they had no shepherd. He said that He would pasture them on the mountains of Israel and tend them in good pasture. He would rescue the lost sheep, strengthen, and heal them. He would judge the sheep and David would be their shepherd. The LORD would bless them and protect them, and they would recognize Him as their God.

EZEKIEL 35

Verse 9: *I will make you desolate forever; your towns will not be inhabited. Then you will know that I am the LORD.*

Ezekiel went on to prophesy about the destruction of Mount Seir (Edom). The LORD said that He would bring death to the entire country because of its hostility against Israel.

EZEKIEL 36

Verse 24: *Therefore say to the house of Israel, "This is what the Sovereign LORD says: It is not for your sake, O house of Israel, that I am going to do these things, but for the sake of my holy name, which you have profaned among the nations where you have gone."*

The LORD told Ezekiel to speak to the mountains of Israel. He promised to bring His wrath on the conquerors of Israel. Ezekiel prophesied that the people of Israel would return and re-build the nation. He promised to do this for the sake of His holy name. Ezekiel declared that the LORD would gather the people and cleanse them and then they would follow the LORD, prosper, and be ashamed of their prior conduct. Then the nations that surround them would see this and recognize the work of the LORD.

EZEKIEL 37

Verse 4: *Then he said to me, "Prophesy to these bones and say to them, 'Dry bones, hear the word of the LORD!'"*

The LORD instructed Ezekiel to prophesy in the valley of dry bones. As he did, the bones reassembled and they came to life. He told Ezekiel that He was going to open the graves of the Israelites and bring them back to the land of Israel so that then they would know that He is LORD. He told Ezekiel to take two sticks, symbolizing Israel and Judah, and bind them together. He explained that Israel would again be one nation with one king (David). They would no longer worship idols or be unrighteous. The LORD renewed His covenant promise with Israel.

EZEKIEL 38

Verse 23: *And so I will show my greatness and my holiness, and I will make myself known in the sight of many nations. Then they will know that I am the LORD.*

The LORD told Ezekiel to prophesy against Gog of Meshech and Tubal, declaring that the LORD would summon His army against Israel. Persia, Cush, and Put will be with Gog, along with Gomer, and they will march together from the north. There will be a great earthquake. The LORD will summon a sword against Gog. Plague, bloodshed, hail, and burning sulfur will rain upon the people and they will know that He is the LORD.

EZEKIEL 39

Verse 29: *I will no longer hide my face from them, for I will pour out my Spirit on the house of Israel, declares the Sovereign LORD.*

Ezekiel was told again to prophesy against Gog. He told Ezekiel to say that the people will fall, and birds and wild animals will feed upon them. The LORD declared that He would send fire on Magog. He said that the day is coming when all nations will know the LORD. Ezekiel prophesied that those living in Israel would use their weapons for fuel because they would not need to defend themselves—they would plunder the plunderers. All the men of Gog will be buried. Men of Israel would be paid to cleanse the land by finding human bones and burying them. Birds and wild animals will have a feast and all will acknowledge the LORD. The LORD will bring His people back from captivity. They will live in safety and know the LORD God.

EZEKIEL 40

Verse 40: *The man said to me, "Son of man, look with your eyes and hear with your ears and pay attention to everything I am going to show you, for that is why you have been brought here. Tell the house of Israel everything you see."*

The LORD took Ezekiel to Jerusalem and sat him on a mountain overlooking the city. A man whose appearance was like bronze told Ezekiel to pay attention to what he was about to show him. The man proceeded to take measurements of the North gate and then the South gate. The gateways to the inner court were then measured. The rooms for preparing sacrifices were described. The inner court was measured and two rooms for the priests were described. The portico to the temple was also measured.

EZEKIEL 41

Verse 4b: *He said to me, "This is the Most Holy Place."*

Ezekiel and the man toured the outer sanctuary and the inner sanctuary, and the Most Holy Place was measured. The Temple wall and side rooms were described. The outer measurements of the Temple were given. The Temple was covered with wood, and ornate designs were carved in the wood, including a cherub with two faces—a man and a lion. A wooden altar was in the Most Holy Place. The man told Ezekiel that the altar is the table that is before the LORD.

EZEKIEL 42

Verse 20: *So he measured the area on all four sides. It had a wall around it, five hundred cubits long and five hundred cubits wide, to separate the holy from the common.*

The priest's rooms encompassed three floors surrounding the Temple. The man explained to Ezekiel that the priests had to change their clothes before leaving the inner court. He then proceeded to measure the perimeter of the Temple and courtyard.

EZEKIEL 43

Verse 12: *This is the law of the temple: All the surrounding area on top of the mountain will be most holy. Such is the law of the temple.*

Ezekiel was led back to the East Gate and the Glory of the LORD roared from the East and filled the Temple. Ezekiel fell face down. The LORD spoke to Ezekiel showing him that this is where His throne would be. He noted that Israel would never again dishonor His name, and instructed Ezekiel to describe the Temple to His people so that they would be ashamed of their sins. All of the area surrounding the Temple would be holy. The altar measurements were then recorded. Regulations for sacrifice were detailed. Sin offerings, burnt offerings, and fellowship offerings would be made for seven days and then the LORD would accept them.

EZEKIEL 44

Verse 28: *I am to be the only inheritance the priests have. You are to give them no possession in Israel; I will be their possession.*

Ezekiel was led back to the East Gate, which was shut. The LORD proclaimed that it would remain shut because the LORD God passed through it. Only the prince could sit inside the gateway. Ezekiel went by the North Gate, saw the Glory of the LORD, and fell face down. He told him to remember all of the details of the Temple so that he could tell the rebellious Israelites who desecrated His Temple. The LORD proclaimed that no foreigner, uncircumcised in heart and flesh, would enter His Temple. Levites who sinned may work in the outer court, but only the loyal and righteous Zadokites (Levites who were descendants of Zadok) could work in the inner Sanctuary. They were to wear linen robes and turbans. They must change their clothes before leaving the inner court, keep their hair trimmed, refrain from drinking wine in the inner court, and they were only allowed to marry a virgin. They must teach the people about holiness and cleanliness. They will also serve as judges for disputes. The priests must own nothing except for what the LORD supplies.

EZEKIEL 45

Verse 9: *This is what the Sovereign LORD says: "You have gone far enough, O princes of Israel! Give up your violence and oppression and do what is just and right. Stop dispossessing my people, declares the Sovereign LORD."*

The LORD continued to tell Ezekiel that the land will be divided and an area for the sanctuary and rooms for the priests surrounding the sanctuary will be set aside. Bordering this sacred district will be an area for the princes running lengthwise from east to west. The LORD admonished the princes of Israel for their dishonesty with weights and measures during trade. He described the requirements for offerings, Passover, and the Feast of Tabernacles.

EZEKIEL 46

Verse 9b: *No one is to return through the gate by which he entered, but each is to go out the opposite gate.*

The LORD stated that the East Gate was to be opened on the Sabbath for the prince to enter. The prince's offerings were detailed. The inheritance from the prince would first go to his family. Ezekiel was then shown where offerings were to be prepared.

EZEKIEL 47

Verse 12: *Fruit trees of all kinds will grow on both banks of the river. Their leaves will not wither, nor will their fruit fail. Every month they will bear, because the water from the sanctuary flows to them. Their fruit will serve for food and their leaves for healing.*

Ezekiel was then shown a river coming from under the Temple. The river flowed to the sea, providing fresh water out into the sea. Ezekiel was told that fish would prosper in this area. Fruit trees will line the river and they will bear fruit all year long. The boundaries of the land were described and instructions given to divide it amongst the twelve tribes.

EZEKIEL 48

Verse 14: *They must not sell or exchange any of it. This is the best of the land and must not pass into other hands, because it is holy to the LORD.*

Ezekiel was told that Dan, Asher, and Naphtali would be given land in the north. Manasseh, Ephraim, Reuben and Judah would also be in the north. The special area for the Temple and surroundings will be next to Judah. This area is to be used by the priests and will never be sold. Benjamin, Simeon, Issachar, Zebulun, and Gad would be farther south. The Gates of Jerusalem would all be named after the twelve tribes. The City will be renamed "THE LORD IS THERE."

Chapter 27

DANIEL

DANIEL 1

Verse 20: *In every matter of wisdom and understanding about which the king questioned them, he found them ten times better than all the magicians and enchanters in his whole kingdom.*

King Nebuchadnezzar of Babylon defeated Jehoiakim, king of Judah, and took the spoils of Jerusalem, including articles from the temple of God, and brought them to the temple of his pagan god in Babylonia. Nebuchadnezzar took the best and brightest of his captives and trained them for three years. Daniel, who was among these young men, chose not to defile himself with food from the royal table. He, Hananiah, Mishael, and Azariah asked that they be tested. They would be given only vegetables to eat and water to drink for ten days and then be compared to the rest of the youths. At the end of the ten days, they were healthier than the others, so the guard allowed them to continue to eat vegetables and drink water. Daniel was given knowledge and understanding as well as visions from the LORD. At the end of their training, the king chose Daniel and the other three over all of the others for the king's service.

DANIEL 2

Verse 27, 28a: *Daniel replied, "No wise man, enchanter, magician or diviner can explain to the king the mystery he has asked about, but there is a God in heaven who reveals mysteries."*

Nebuchadnezzar had dreams that troubled him, and he asked his magicians and sorcerers to tell him what he dreamed, and then interpret the dream for him, but they were unable to do so. The king was frustrated and ordered that all the wise men of Babylon (including Daniel) be put to death. When the king's men came to Daniel, he asked that the king allow him to interpret the dream. Daniel and his friends prayed, and he was given a vision that night. He prayed to God, thanking Him. The next day Daniel asked for an audience with the king and explained his dream to him. Daniel explained that his interpretation came directly from God. He proceeded to tell Nebuchadnezzar that he dreamt of a large statue with a head of gold, a chest of silver, a belly and thighs of bronze, legs of iron, and feet of clay. A rock, not cut from

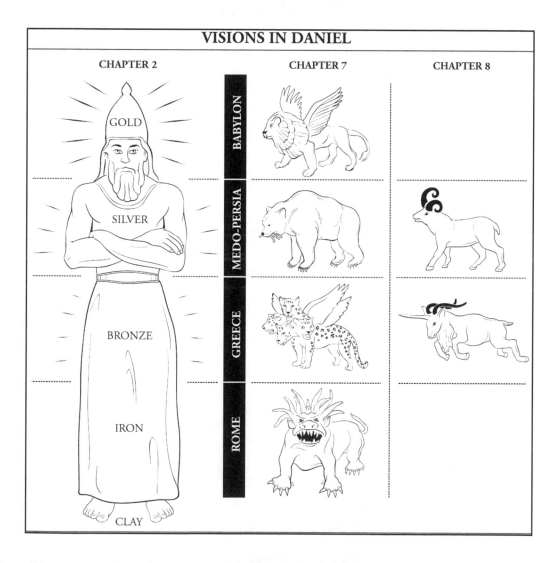

Figure 11: Daniel's Visions

human hands, smashed the statue and became a mountain. Daniel went on to interpret the dream, noting that the king was the head of gold, and that the kingdoms that followed his would be inferior, made of silver, bronze, and iron. Daniel told him God would crush all the kingdoms and reign as King over all. Nebuchadnezzar thanked Daniel, rewarded him with a high position, and recognized his God. At Daniel's request, the king named Shadrach, Meshach, and Abednego as administrators for him.

DANIEL 3

Verse 17: *If we are thrown into the blazing furnace, the God we serve is able to save us from it, and he will rescue us from your hand, O king.*

King Nebuchadnezzar made a huge statue of all gold, and instructed all in his kingdom to worship it whenever they heard the sound of music. Daniel's three friends refused to do so, and the king threw them into a blazing furnace. The three were seen walking in the furnace with a fourth figure. The king summoned them, and they came to him, completely unharmed by the furnace. The king praised their God for sending an angel to rescue them and promoted them to a position of higher authority.

DANIEL 4

Verse 37: *Now I, Nebuchadnezzar, praise and exalt and glorify the King of heaven, because everything he does is right and all his ways are just. And those who walk in pride he is able to humble.*

Nebuchadnezzar addressed all people telling them about his experience with the LORD and praising the wonders of the Most High God. Nebuchadnezzar had another dream, and again his magicians could not interpret it for him. He dreamt of an enormous tree that reached the sky and provided fruit for all. He was instructed by a holy one to cut down the tree, but let the stump remain for seven times. Daniel told the king the tree was Nebuchadnezzar himself, and his kingdom would be cut down until he acknowledged that the Most High is sovereign over all the kingdoms of man. The dream came true, and Nebuchadnezzar was stripped of all authority and slept in the fields with the cattle. Finally, Nebuchadnezzar looked up and praised the Most High. He was brought back to the throne and became even greater than before.

DANIEL 5

Verse 23: *Instead, you have set yourself up against the LORD of heaven. You had the goblets from his temple brought to you, and you and your nobles, your wives and your concubines drank wine from them. You praised the gods of silver and gold, of bronze, iron, wood, and stone, which cannot see or hear or understand. But you did not honor the God who holds in his hand your life and all your ways.*

Nebuchadnezzar's son, Belshazzar, became king and ordered that the gold and silver goblets his father had taken from the temple in Jerusalem be brought to him and his nobles to drink from. As they drank, they praised their pagan gods. Then, the fingers of a human hand wrote something on the wall of the palace. Belshazzar and his guests were terrified and asked his magicians to interpret what the writing meant, but again they were unsuccessful. Finally, Daniel was summoned, and he was promised riches and power to interpret it. Daniel told the king to keep his reward but agreed to tell him what it meant. Daniel reminded Belshazzar of his father's plight until he acknowledged God. He noted that Belshazzar had not humbled himself as did his father, and had failed to honor God by drinking from the goblets of the temple, praising his own gods. He then explained the words on the wall—Mene, Mene, Tekel, and Parsin. Mene—God has numbered the days of your reign; Tekel—You have been measured and have come up short; Parsin—Your kingdom will be divided amongst the Medes and Persians. Belshazzar was slain that very night and Darius, a Mede, took over the kingdom.

DANIEL 6

Verse 10: *Now when Daniel learned that the decree had been published, he went home to his upstairs room where the windows opened toward Jerusalem. Three times a day he got down on his knees and prayed, giving thanks to his God, just as he had done before.*

Daniel was appointed as one of the chief administrators over the kingdom. The other administrators plotted against him. They asked the king to issue a decree saying that anyone who worshiped any god other than the king for the next thirty days would be thrown into the lions' den. Darius put out the decree, and Daniel was arrested for worshiping God. Darius reluctantly had Daniel thrown into the lions' den, telling him that he would have to ask his God to rescue him. When Darius opened the den the following morning, he found Daniel alive. Daniel explained that an angel had saved him. Darius had the men who had accused Daniel, along with their families, thrown to the lions. They quickly perished. Darius issued a decree that everyone in his kingdom fear and worship the God of Daniel.

DANIEL 7

Verse 18: But the saints of the Most High will receive the kingdom and will possess it forever—yes, forever and ever.

Daniel had a dream in which four great beasts came out of the sea. The first was a lion with wings that were torn off and it was given the heart of a man. The second was a bear with three ribs in its mouth. The third was a leopard with four wings on its back. It also had four heads and was given authority to rule. A fourth beast was terrifying and frightening. It had ten horns and iron teeth and trampled anything left from the other beasts. A small horn among the other horns was boasting. The Ancient of Days took His seat on a throne with a river of fire flowing around Him and thousands upon thousands standing before Him. The last beast was slain and thrown into the fire. The Son of Man appeared and approached the Ancient of Days and was given glory and power. Daniel was given the interpretation of his dream. The four great beasts were the four kingdoms of the earth, but the saints of the Most High would eventually receive the kingdom. The fourth beast is the fourth kingdom that will appear on the earth that will devour the other kingdoms. The ten horns are the ten kings who will come from that kingdom. The small horn represents a king who will arise, subdue three kings, and speak against the Most High. The saints will be handed over to him for three and one-half times. Then the saints of the Most High will live in an everlasting kingdom, worshiping and obeying Him. (see Figure 11 Daniel 2)

DANIEL 8

Verse 26: The visions of the evenings and mornings that has been given you is true, but seal up the vision, for it concerns the distant future.

Daniel had another vision of a ram with two horns, one larger than the other. The ram charged in all directions, and was all-powerful. A goat with one central horn charged and overcame the ram, but his horn was broken off and replaced with four smaller horns. Another horn grew out of one of these four and grew until it reached the heavens. It threw some of the starry hosts to the earth and trampled them. It set itself up as a Prince and took away the daily sacrifice. When asked how long it will take for the vision to be fulfilled, the answer was 2,300 days. Daniel was given the interpretation of this dream, this time by the angel Gabriel. He explained that the two-horned ram represented the kings of Media and Persia. The goat was the king of Greece, and the large horn, its king. The four smaller horns represent the four lesser kingdoms that will arise from Greece. One evil king will arise from one of those kingdoms and destroy the holy people. He will be destroyed, but not by human power. Daniel was exhausted after these two visions, but eventually went back to the king's business. (see Figure 11 Daniel 2)

DANIEL 9

Verse 19: *O Lord, listen! O Lord, forgive! O Lord, hear and act! For your sake, O my God, do not delay, because your city and your people bear your Name.*

Daniel read and understood from the Scriptures that Israel's captivity would last seventy years. This caused Daniel to pray to the LORD, first acknowledging his sins and the sins of Israel. He recounted the shame of all of the Israelites for not obeying God. He noted they had not turned from their sins and obeyed the Law. He asked the Lord to turn away His anger and wrath from them. After Daniel was done praying, Gabriel came to him again. He explained Israel must wait for seventy sevens to atone for their sins prior to rebuilding Jerusalem and sixty-nine sevens from the issuing of a decree to rebuild the city until the Anointed One comes. He was also told of another ruler who will destroy Jerusalem. This ruler will make a seven-year covenant with Israel and set up an "abomination that causes desolation," until the end that is decreed is poured out on him.

DANIEL 10

Verse 19a: *"Do not be afraid, O man highly esteemed," he said. "Peace! Be strong now; be strong."*

Daniel was given another vision concerning a great war. Three weeks later, he saw a man dressed in linen with a gold belt, a face like lightning, eyes like flaming torches, and arms and legs like bronze. Daniel was terrified, but a hand touched him and told him to stand and listen. He was told not to be afraid. The man explained he was detained for almost three weeks by the king of Persia and was eventually helped by the archangel Michael. He noted he had an important message regarding Daniel's people in the future. After Daniel was given strength, the man went on to tell him he had to return to fight the Prince of Persia and Greece, but first he had to give Daniel the message.

DANIEL 11

Verse 32: *With flattery he will corrupt those who have violated the covenant, but the people who know their God will firmly resist him.*

He explained that three more kings would appear in Persia, and then a fourth who would be strong and powerful. He will lead the fight against Greece. Then a mighty king will appear. After this king, his empire will be divided into four parcels. The king of the South and his successors will become powerful and defeat the armies of the king of the North. Later, the king of the North will conquer the forces of the South. The king of the North will then attempt to conquer the coastlines but will be defeated. The successor of the king of the North will collect taxes for a few years but then will be defeated. His successor, in turn, will not be given power but will seize it. He will attack and plunder the countryside. Eventually, the king of the South will attempt to fight him but will fail. The king of the North will then return and persecute believers and set up the "abomination that causes desolation." The king will exalt himself over God and will worship false gods. The king of the South will again challenge him, and the king of the North will conquer all of the land.

DANIEL 12

Verse 2: *Multitudes who sleep in the dust of the earth will awake; some to everlasting life, others to shame and everlasting contempt.*

The angel told Daniel that at that time the archangel Michael will arise and there will be a time of distress. Then, everyone whose name is written in the Book will be delivered. Those who are worthy will have everlasting life. Then two other angels appeared and asked when these things will take place. The man clothed in linen said that it will be a time, times, and a half time when the power of the holy people has been finally broken. When questioned by Daniel, the angels told him that it would be 1,290 days from the "abomination that causes desolation." Daniel was told to rest, and at the end of the days he would receive his inheritance.

Minor Prophets

HOSEA

HOSEA 1

Verse 2: When the LORD began to speak through Hosea, the LORD said to him, "Go take to yourself an adulterous wife and children of unfaithfulness, because the land is guilty of the vilest adultery in departing from the LORD."

Hosea was a prophet during the time of Jeroboam II, during the last days of Israel. The LORD instructed Hosea to marry an adulterous wife. Hosea married Gomer, who later bore Hosea a son whom the LORD named Jezreel (God scatters). Gomer went on to give birth to two other children (of questionable lineage): a daughter Lo-Ruhamah (no mercy) and another daughter Lo-Ammi (not my people). The LORD told Hosea he was very unhappy with Israel but loved Judah. He promised a future reunion of the two countries.

HOSEA 2

Verse 19: I will betroth you to me forever; I will betroth you in righteousness and justice, in love and compassion.

The LORD told Hosea of the impending punishment for Israel and the restoration that would follow. God told Hosea's children and Hosea himself to leave Gomer. He described Israel's foreboding future, comparing it to that of Gomer.

HOSEA 3

Verse 4: *For the Israelites will live many days without king or prince, without sacrifice or sacred stones, without ephod or idol.*

The LORD encouraged Hosea to reconcile with his wife despite her infidelity. Hosea actually had to buy Gomer out of slavery to get her back. The comparison of the Israelites returning to God is made.

HOSEA 4

Verse 12: *They consult a wooden idol and are answered by a stick of wood. A spirit of prostitution leads them astray; they are unfaithful to their God.*

The LORD spoke through Hosea and made charges against Israel. He accused them of lack of faith and love, prostitution, adultery, idolatry, drunkenness, and failure to obey the Laws of the LORD. He also warned them not to spread their sins to Judah.

HOSEA 5

Verse 4: *Their deeds do not permit them to return to their God. A spirit of prostitution is in their heart; they do not acknowledge the LORD.*

Hosea proclaimed the LORD's judgment against Israel. He warned of God's discipline and told them the LORD had withdrawn from them. He declared they would be devoured by their false gods and conquered by their neighbors. He said the LORD would be like a lion and tear Israel into pieces.

HOSEA 6

Verse 6: *For I desire mercy, not sacrifice, and acknowledgment of God rather than burnt offerings.*

Hosea prophesied that once the LORD had destroyed Israel He would revive them in two days, and restore them on the third day if they would turn back to Him. He stated that the LORD desires loyalty not sacrifice.

HOSEA 7

Verse 13: *Woe to them, because they have strayed from me! Destruction to them, because they have rebelled against me! I long to redeem them but they speak lies against me.*

Hosea went on to predict that the sins of Ephraim and Israel would engulf them. He then described the destruction Israel would face.

HOSEA 8

Verse 11: *Though Ephraim built many altars for sin offerings, these have become altars for sinning.*

Hosea described how the LORD was angered by their idols. He indicated that Israel had forgotten his Maker.

HOSEA 9

Verse 7: *The days of punishment are coming, the days of reckoning are at hand. Let Israel know this. Because your sins are so many and your hostility so great, the prophet is considered a fool, the inspired man a maniac.*

Hosea continued to recount the sins of Israel and tell the punishment that awaited them. He told them they would be banished from the Promised Land; that God remembered their wickedness and would punish them for their sins. He noted that the sins of Israel would be accounted for and pregnancies would result in miscarriages.

HOSEA 10

Verse 12: *Sow for yourselves righteousness, reap the fruit of unfailing love, and break up your unplowed ground; for it is time to seek the LORD, until he comes and showers righteousness on you.*

Hosea promised that the LORD would destroy their altars to idols as well as their wickedness.

HOSEA 11

Verse 9: *I will not carry out my fierce anger, nor will I turn and devastate Ephraim. For I am God, and not man—the Holy One among you. I will not come in wrath.*

Through Hosea, God declared that He had loved Israel, but Israel strayed away and made sacrifices to Baal. The LORD had raised Ephraim, but they would return to Egypt and would be ruled by Assyria because they refused to repent. Their city would be destroyed. He told them that even if they called out to God, He would not exalt them. However, the LORD's heart had changed, and He spoke of Israel's eventual deliverance.

HOSEA 12

Verse 6: *But you must return to your God; maintain love and justice, and wait for your God always.*

The LORD was displeased with all of Israel's actions, including its treaties that were made without consulting God. He made a comparison between the people of Israel and Jacob with his struggles in the womb with Esau, and his fight with God at Bethel. The LORD was showing Israel their need to return to God.

HOSEA 13

Verse 14: *I will ransom them from the power of the grave; I will redeem them from death. Where, O death, are your plagues? Where, O grave, is your destruction?*

Again, Hosea recounted the many sins of Israel including dishonesty, deceit, and Baal worship. He referred to the LORD as a lion, a leopard, and a bear, and promised vengeance. He prophesied that plague, drought and defeat awaited Israel.

HOSEA 14

Verse 2: *Take the words with you and return to the LORD. Say to him: "Forgive all our sins and receive us graciously, that we may offer the fruit of our lips."*

Hosea pleaded with the Israelites to return to God. He asked the people to repent and admit their need for God's salvation. God promised to heal them and love them freely.

JOEL

JOEL 1

Verse 14: *Declare a holy fast; call a sacred assembly. Summon the elders and all who live in the land to the house of the LORD your God, and cry out to the LORD.*

Joel, a prophet, heard the Word of the LORD. He described the devastation caused by swarms of locusts on the land. The joy of mankind had withered away. He called on the people to repent and fast, and noted that the day of the LORD was near. He called out to the LORD. Even livestock and wild animals would suffer.

JOEL 2

Verse 25: *I will repay you for the years the locusts have eaten—the great locust and the young locust, the others locusts and the locust swarm—my great army that I sent among you.*

Joel continued to speak to Judah for the LORD. The day of the LORD was close at hand. Darkness and gloom would spread over the land. The army of the LORD is a swarm of locusts that will gallop like horses and devastate the land. They will advance like warriors. The earth will shake and the sky tremble in their wake. The day of the LORD is great. Joel encouraged Judah to repent. He told them to return to the gracious LORD, for He may have pity upon them. Joel called for an assembly to call upon the LORD so the LORD will take pity on them. Then the LORD will restore the land and they will rejoice and praise God. Then He will pour out His Spirit and anyone who calls upon His name will be delivered.

JOEL 3

Verse 21: *Their bloodguilt, which I have not pardoned, I will pardon. The LORD dwells in Zion!*

Joel declared that when the LORD restores Judah and Jerusalem, He would gather all nations and recount all the sins against Israel, and hold the other nations accountable for their actions. He told the nations to be prepared to battle against the LORD's army. The day of the LORD was near. The LORD will roar from Zion with thunder and the earth will shake. He will be a refuge and stronghold for Israel. Jerusalem will be holy and He will dwell in it. Egypt will become a desert waste. He will pardon Israel and the LORD will dwell in Zion.

Chapter 30

AMOS

AMOS 1

Verse 2: *He said: "The LORD roars from Zion and thunders from Jerusalem; the pastures of the shepherds dry up, and the top of Carmel withers."*

Amos was a shepherd from Tekoa (south of Jerusalem) during the time when Jeroboam II was king of Israel and Uzziah was king of Judah (2 Kings). He prophesied to the Israelites two years before a major earthquake, and chastised the people for their sins, including idolatry. He detailed the sins of Damascus, Gaza, Tyre, Edom, and Ammon.

AMOS 2

Verse 10: *I brought you up out of Egypt, and I led you forty years in the desert to give you the land of the Amorites.*

Amos continued to prophesy the wrath of the LORD for the sins of Moab, Judah, and Israel. He listed seven sins committed by the Israelites. He criticized the people for not following the LORD after all that He had done for them.

Amos 3

Verse 2: *You only have I chosen of all the families of the earth; therefore I will punish you for all your sins.*

Amos foretold of the fall of Israel. The people had been forewarned of the Lord's plan through His prophets, but had not listened. Amos noted that the Lord would punish all of Israel for her sins, saving only a few, just like a shepherd can save only a part of the sheep from the lion's mouth.

Amos 4

Verse 9: *"Many times I struck your gardens and vineyards, I struck them with blight and mildew. Locusts devoured your fig and olive trees, yet you have not returned to me," declares the Lord.*

Amos told the people the Lord was punishing them for not returning to Him. Despite His warnings and punishments, the people had not listened. Amos admonished the people for their sinful ways and warned them to prepare to meet their God—the Lord God Almighty.

Amos 5

Verse 24: *But let justice roll on like a river, righteousness like a never-failing stream!*

Amos offered a lament and a call to repentance. He noted that only ten percent of Israel would survive and instructed the people to seek the Lord and live. He detailed their sins, including not being righteous, trampling on the poor, and promoting evil. He foretold of the wrath of the Lord.

Amos 6

Verse 8: *The Sovereign Lord has sworn by himself—the Lord God Almighty declares: "I abhor the pride of Jacob and detest his fortresses; I will deliver up the city and everything in it."*

Amos told the people the Lord would punish the complacent and lazy people who enjoy their prosperity. He went on to tell them the Lord abhors the pride of Israel, and promised them that the wrath of God would come upon them.

Amos 7

Verse 5: *Then I cried out, "Sovereign Lord, I beg you, stop! How can Jacob survive? He is so small!"*

Amos indicated that he pleaded with the Lord to save Israel from locusts, fire, and plumb line, and the Lord relented, but eventually declared that He would no longer spare the people of Israel. While Amos was warning the people of God's wrath, Amaziah the priest went to Jeroboam to tell him that Amos was instigating a conspiracy against the king. Amaziah returned and told Amos to leave Israel and return to Judah. Amos responded that he was a shepherd, but the Lord told him to go to Israel as a prophet. He prophesied that Amaziah and his children would perish, his wife would become a prostitute, and Israel would go into exile.

Amos 8

Verse 11: *"The days are coming," declares the Sovereign Lord, "When I will send a famine through the land—not a famine of food or thirst for water, but a famine of hearing the words of the Lord."*

Amos said the Lord showed him a basket of ripe fruit and told him the time was ripe for the people of Israel to be punished. Through him, the Lord described the destruction that would occur to Israel. He promised darkness, famine, and drought.

Amos 9

Verse 15: *"I will plant Israel in their own land, never again to be uprooted from the land I have given them," says the Lord your God.*

Amos saw the Lord standing by the altar. The Lord told Amos that Israel would be destroyed, and no one would escape His wrath. Amos also described the details of the wrath of God that was to come. The Lord told him the house of Jacob would not be totally destroyed. Amos went on to describe the restoration of Israel that would follow.

OBADIAH

Verse 12: *You should not look down on your brother in the day of his misfortune, nor rejoice over the people of Judah in the day of their destruction, nor boast so much in the day of their trouble.*

Obadiah had a vision about what the LORD had to say about Edom. He declared that they will be punished for their pride and brought down; disaster awaits them. They will be defeated and cut down from their mountain strongholds. They will be held accountable for not helping their brothers in Jerusalem. They boasted during Jerusalem's destruction and profited from it. Obadiah said the day of the LORD was near for all nations—they would get what they gave out. He proclaimed that deliverers would go up on Mount Zion to govern Edom. The kingdom will be the LORD's.

JONAH

JONAH 1

Verse 9: He answered, "I am a Hebrew and I worship the LORD, the God of heaven, who made the sea and the land."

The LORD instructed Jonah to go to Nineveh and preach against its wickedness. Jonah ignored this message, ran to Joppa, and sailed for Tarshish to flee from Him. The LORD sent a violent storm, threatening the ship. The captain of the ship implored Jonah to call on his God to save them. The crew confronted him and asked what they could do to calm the sea. Jonah told them to throw him overboard, but they did not, and tried to save the ship on their own. After they failed, they did as Jonah had told them, and the sea grew calm. The men were worried that they had incited the wrath of God and made sacrifices to Him. A great fish swallowed Jonah, and he remained inside the fish for three days and three nights.

JONAH 2

Verse 2: *He said, "In my distress I called to the LORD, and he answered me. From the depths of the grave I called for help, and you listened to my cry."*

Jonah prayed to the LORD from inside the fish and praised God for answering him in his trouble. He promised he would no longer disobey God. The LORD commanded the fish to vomit him onto dry land.

JONAH 3

Verse 10: *When God saw what they did and how they turned from their evil ways, he had compassion and did not bring upon them the destruction he had threatened.*

Jonah was again instructed to go to Nineveh, and he did. He preached to the city. The people and the king listened. They fasted and put on sackcloth. They prayed to God and turned from their evil ways. The LORD had compassion on the city.

JONAH 4

Verse 2: *He prayed to the LORD, "O LORD, is this not what I said when I was still at home? That is why I was so quick to flee to Tarshish. I knew that you are a gracious and compassionate God, slow to anger and abounding in love, a God who relents from sending calamity."*

Jonah was angry that the LORD had compassion upon Nineveh. He asked that his life be taken away, but instead the LORD asked him why he thought he had the right to complain. Jonah camped outside the city and the LORD grew a vine over his head to protect him from the sun, and Jonah was pleased. The next night, the vine withered, and Jonah complained. The LORD explained to Jonah that he had no right to complain about the vine, because he did not grow it or tend it. The LORD told Jonah that he was very concerned about a vine that only lasted a day, and should understand why the LORD was concerned about a city filled with people who needed His guidance.

MICAH

MICAH 1

Verse 5: *All this is because of Jacob's transgression, because of the sins of the house of Israel. What is Jacob's transgression? Is it not Samaria? What is Judah's high place? Is it not Jerusalem?*

Micah of Moresheth in Judah lived in the waning days of Israel and Judah. The LORD spoke through him and he foretold of the impending attack on Samaria. He chastised the people for idol worship and prostitution indicating that the LORD would punish them for it. He noted that the LORD weeps and mourns for the transgressions of the Israelites.

MICAH 2

Verse 13: *One who breaks open the way will go up before them; they will break through the gate and go out. Their king will pass through before them, the LORD at their head.*

Micah indicated that the LORD was planning disaster against the people. He also warned the people not to listen to the false prophets. The LORD promised deliverance for Israel after their defeat.

MICAH 3

Verse 5: *This is what the LORD says: "As for the prophets who lead my people astray, if one feeds them, they proclaim 'peace'; if he does not, they prepare to wage war against him."*

Micah criticized the leaders of Israel for their cruel ways and noted that they would cry out to God, but He would not answer. The LORD was angered by the false prophets and would not give them any visions to share. Micah foretold of the impending defeat of Israel and the eventual collapse of Jerusalem.

MICAH 4

Verse 4: *Every man will sit under his own vine and under his own fig tree, and no one will make them afraid, for the LORD Almighty has spoken.*

Micah taught that in the last days the mountain of the LORD will be the highest point and all will come to it in peace. The LORD will rule and redemption will be made.

MICAH 5

Verses 4,5: *He will stand and shepherd his flock in the strength of the LORD, in the majesty of the name of the LORD his God. And they will live securely, for then his greatness will reach to the ends of the earth. And he will be their peace.*

Micah prophesied that a new leader would come from Bethlehem with origins from ancient times. He told of His majesty and strength. Micah foretold of the impending invasions by Assyria and Israel's future triumph over their enemies and the restoration of their faith.

MICAH 6

Verse 8: *He has shown you, O man, what is good. And what does the LORD require of you? To act justly and to love mercy and to walk humbly with your God.*

The LORD made His case against Israel. He reminded them of their exodus and the leaders He had given them. He described their guilt, including dishonesty and idolatry. The LORD would begin the destruction of Israel for their sins.

MICAH 7

Verse 7: *But as for me, I watch in hope for the LORD, I wait for God my Savior; my God will hear me.*

Micah described Israel's misery noting that there was not one godly man remaining. He told of the day of reckoning and the fall of Israel. He added Israel would rise again after her defeat and concluded that the LORD would show compassion and the nation would rise again.

Chapter 34

NAHUM

NAHUM 1

Verse 13: *Now I will break their yoke from your neck and tear your shackles away.*

The prophet Nahum shared an oracle against Nineveh (the capitol of Assyria). The LORD will take vengeance upon them. Although the LORD is good, He will take out his vengeance on Nineveh. Their allies will be useless. He will destroy them and their idols. Judah will no longer suffer from Assyrian oppression.

NAHUM 2

Verse 2: *The LORD will restore the splendor of Jacob like the splendor of Israel, though destroyers have laid them waste and have ruined their vines.*

Nineveh will be attacked and the splendor of Israel will be restored. The city will be ravaged, the people exiled, and the plunder taken away. The LORD declared that He is against Nineveh.

NAHUM 3

Verse 18: *O king of Assyria, your shepherds slumber; your nobles lie down to rest. Your people are scattered on the mountains with no one to gather them.*

The oracle continued against Nineveh. Nahum stated that their bodies would be piled in the streets. They will be punished because of their lust, witchcraft, and prostitution. They are no better than other cities the LORD had conquered. The Ninevites are told to prepare their defenses, but fire and the sword will defeat them. It is also stated that the king of Assyria will be humbled because of his cruelty, and other nations will rejoice.

Chapter 35

HABAKKUK

HABAKKUK 1

Verse 11: *Then they sweep past like the wind and go on—guilty men, whose own strength is their god.*

The prophet Habakkuk shared his oracle from the LORD. He cried out to the LORD for help because Judah was corrupt. The LORD announced that He was raising the Babylonians to conquer Judah. Habakkuk asked the LORD why He would use a nation more wicked than Judah to destroy Judah.

HABAKKUK 2

Verse 14: *For the earth will be filled with the knowledge of the glory of the LORD, as the waters cover the sea.*

The LORD answered that although Babylon would defeat Judah, in time, it would be defeated itself because of its arrogance and greed. Babylon would be punished for the plundering of other nations and for their idol worship.

HABAKKUK 3

Verse 16: *I heard and my heart pounded, my lips quivered at the sound; decay crept into my bones, and my legs trembled. Yet I will wait patiently for the day of calamity to come on the nation invading us.*

Habakkuk prayed to the LORD, and described the LORD's glory and power. He told of the LORD's deliverance of His people and the salvation of His anointed one. Habakkuk noted that he would wait patiently for the LORD's day when He would punish the other nations. The LORD gave him joy and strength.

Chapter 36

ZEPHANIAH

ZEPHANIAH 1

Verse 12: *At that time I will search Jerusalem with lamps and punish those who are complacent, who are like wine left on its dregs, who think, "The Lord will do nothing, either good or bad."*

Zephaniah, a fourth generation descendant of Hezekiah, heard the word of the Lord during Josiah's reign in Judah. He was given a warning of coming destruction. God told him that He would sweep away all living things from the earth and punish Judah. The Lord promised He would rid the land of all pagan idols and hold the people of Jerusalem accountable for their deeds. He foretold there would be much crying as He ferreted out the evildoers and the complacent. He promised that the day of the Lord was near and that His wrath would bring a sudden end to all that live on the earth.

ZEPHANIAH 2

Verse 3: *Seek the Lord, all you humble of the land, you who do what he commands. Seek righteousness, seek humility; perhaps you will be sheltered on the day of the Lord's anger.*

The Lord appealed to the people of Judah to gather together and humble themselves before the time arrived. He then detailed the destruction of each portion of the land. He foretold that Moab would become like Sodom and the Ammonites like Gomorrah, and further told that a remnant of survivors would return in conquest. The LORD also promised vengeance against Cush and Assyria by destroying them.

ZEPHANIAH 3

Verse 15: *The LORD has taken away your punishment, he has turned back your enemy. The LORD, the King of Israel, is with you; never again will you fear any harm.*

God further condemned the people of Jerusalem for their disobedience to Him. He promised utter destruction if they continued to act corruptly. He would pour out His wrath—the fire of His jealous anger—and promised redemption to those who serve Him—the meek and humble who trust in the LORD. This remnant will rejoice and never again be harmed. The LORD told them He would deal with all who oppressed them at that time and will gather these believers and bring them home.

Chapter 37

HAGGAI

HAGGAI 1

Verse 6: You have planted much, but have harvested little. You eat, but never have enough. You drink, but never have your fill. You put on clothes, but are not warm. You earn wages, only to put them in a purse with holes in it.

Haggai related a prophesy from the LORD to Zerubbabel, governor of Judah, and Joshua, the high priest. The LORD was discouraged that they took care of themselves but the LORD's house remained in ruins. Zerubbabel and Joshua obeyed and the remnant began work on the Temple.

HAGGAI 2

Verse 5: This is what I covenanted with you when you came out of Egypt. And my Spirit remains among you. Do not fear.

Haggai spoke to Zerubbabel, Joshua, and the remnant of the people. The LORD told them to be strong and He renewed His covenant. He promised to shake all the nations and that He would fill the Temple with glory. He declared that even though they were back in the Holy

Land, they still needed to obey the LORD in order to be holy. The LORD stated that He would bless them, and they would build a Temple to the LORD's specifications. Zerubbabel would be like a signet ring, the LORD's chosen leader.

Chapter 38

ZECHARIAH

ZECHARIAH 1

Verse 3: *Therefore tell the people: This is what the LORD Almighty says: "Return to me," declares the LORD Almighty, "and I will return to you," says the LORD Almighty.*

Zechariah, a prophet and a priest, told the people in Babylonian exile that the LORD was calling them to return to Him. He told them to turn from evil as their forefathers had not, and described a vision of a man riding on a red horse. An angel appeared and explained that the LORD was angry and jealous for Israel, but that after seventy years of exile, He would return them to Jerusalem, and His house would be rebuilt and Zion would prosper. He then described a vision of four horns that had scattered Judah, Israel, and Jerusalem. He explained that the horns would be defeated.

ZECHARIAH 2

Verse 5: *"And I myself will be a wall of fire around it," declares the LORD, "and I will be its glory within."*

Zechariah next saw a vision of a man with a measuring tape, prepared to take measurements of Jerusalem. The angel told Zechariah that Jerusalem would be a city without walls because the LORD would build a wall of fire around it and His glory would be inside. The LORD called His people back, promising to punish their captors and to live amongst them.

ZECHARIAH 3

Verse 9: *"See, the stone I have set in front of Joshua! There are seven eyes on that one stone, and I will engrave an inscription on it," says the LORD Almighty, "and I will remove the sin of this land in a single day."*

Zechariah saw a vision of the high priest, Joshua, standing before the Angel of the LORD and Satan. The LORD rebuked Satan. The angel told Joshua to remove his filthy clothes, taking away his sin, and put on new clothes that He gave him. The LORD told Joshua if he were faithful that he would govern His House. The LORD promised to bring His Servant, the Branch, and set a stone with seven eyes in front of Joshua. He said He would remove all the sin of the land in a single day. On that day, Israel would prosper.

ZECHARIAH 4

Verse 6: *So he said to me, "This is the word of the LORD to Zerubbabel: 'Not by might nor by power, but by my Spirit,' says the LORD Almighty."*

The angel returned to Zechariah and showed him a gold lampstand and two olive trees. The angel explained this represented a message to Zerubbabel to complete the Temple. The two olive trees represented the two (Zerubbabel and Joshua) who would be anointed by golden oil from the trees to serve the LORD and all of the earth.

ZECHARIAH 5

Verse 3: *And he said to me, "This is the curse that is going out over the whole land; for according to what it says on one side, every thief will be banished, and according to what it says on the other, everyone who swears falsely will be banished."*

Zechariah then had a vision of a flying scroll. The angel explained that it represented a curse for those who were thieves and those who gave false testimony, for they would be destroyed by the scroll. Zechariah then saw the vision of a basket with a woman inside. The basket, he was told, represented the iniquity of the people, and the woman represented wickedness. The basket was closed and two women with wind in their wings carried the basket off to Babylon.

ZECHARIAH 6

Verse 12: *Tell him this is what the LORD Almighty says: "Here is the man whose name is the Branch, and he will branch out from his place and build the temple of the LORD."*

Zechariah saw four chariots coming out from two mountains of bronze. Red, black, white, and dappled horses led the four chariots. The angel explained that these represented the four Spirits of heaven heading in different directions (black—North; white—West; Dappled—South) He sent the chariots throughout the earth. The one sent to the North gave the Spirit rest (it defeated the LORD's enemies). The LORD told Zechariah to take all the gold and silver that they brought from Babylon and make a crown for Joshua. The Branch would build the Temple and rule upon the throne. The crown would serve as a memorial in the Temple, and the Temple would be built if the people diligently obeyed the Lord.

ZECHARIAH 7

Verse 10: *Do not oppress the widow or the fatherless, the alien or the poor. In your hearts do not think evil of each other.*

The people asked the priests and prophets if they should continue to fast. The LORD asked the people if, when they fasted in the past, they were they really doing it for Him. Zechariah told the people to be righteous and compassionate. He reminded them of their stubbornness and the resulting punishment that scattered them throughout the nations. The LORD declared that since the people did not listen to Him, when they called to Him, He would not listen to them.

ZECHARIAH 8

Verse 23: *This is what the LORD Almighty says: "In those days ten men from all languages and nations will take firm hold of one Jew by the hem of his robe and say, 'Let us go with you, because we have heard that God is with you.'"*

The LORD promised Zechariah He would return to Zion and dwell in Jerusalem, the City of Truth, the Holy Mountain. It would be marvelous for the people of Jerusalem at that time. They would build the LORD's Temple in complete safety. The remnant would prosper and receive an inheritance from the LORD. The LORD promised to bless them. They would observe the customs and Laws of the LORD and be an example to nations showing that God was with them.

ZECHARIAH 9

Verse 9: Rejoice greatly, O Daughter of Zion! Shout, Daughter of Jerusalem! See, your king comes to you, righteous and having salvation, gentle and riding on a donkey, on a colt, the foal of a donkey.

Israel's enemies—Hadrach, Damascus, Hamath, Tyre, and Sidon would be destroyed. Ashkelon, Gaza, Ekron would also perish, as would Ashod and Philistia. Those left would belong to God. The LORD would defend His people. The King would come to them offering salvation, riding on a donkey. Peace will be upon all nations. Judah would grow and prosper. The Sovereign LORD would appear with the sound of trumpets. They would be victorious and the LORD would save them.

ZECHARIAH 10

Verse 9: Though I scatter them among the peoples, yet in distant lands they will remember me. They and their children will survive, and they will return.

Zechariah stated that people should depend on the LORD. He makes rain, but idols are powerless. The LORD was angry with the shepherds, the leaders of His people, and declared that He would punish them. A cornerstone would come from Judah and it will be strengthened. The LORD will redeem Israel and bring them back from foreign lands, and strengthen them and they will walk in His name.

ZECHARIAH 11

Verse 16: For I am going to raise up a shepherd over the land who will not care for the lost, or seek the young, or heal the injured, or feed the healthy, but will eat the meat of the choice sheep, tearing off their hoofs.

Zechariah prophesied that fire would destroy the cedars of Lebanon; the forests of Bashan would be cut down; lush Jordan would be ruined. The LORD (Good Shepherd) pastured the flock for slaughter and removed the bad shepherds. The flock detested the Shepherd and so he no longer cared for them. He broke his staff called *Favor* and revoked His covenant, then gave His pay to the potter. He broke his staff called *Union* and broke the brotherhood of Judah and Israel. A worthless shepherd would replace the Good Shepherd—woe to him.

ZECHARIAH 12

Verse 5: *Then the leaders of Judah will say in their hearts, "The people of Jerusalem are strong, because the LORD Almighty is their God."*

Jerusalem would be besieged but the LORD will make it an immovable Rock and it will defeat the invaders. Israel will mourn for the one they pierce—each clan will mourn amongst themselves.

ZECHARIAH 13

Verse 7: *"Awake, O sword, against my shepherd, against the man who is close to me!" declares the LORD Almighty. "Strike the shepherd, and the sheep will be scattered, and I will turn my hand against the little ones."*

On that day, a fountain will be opened to cleanse their sins. Idolatry and false prophets will be removed. The Good Shepherd will be struck and the people will suffer. Two thirds of the people will perish and one third will be left to be refined like fine silver. Those who are left will proclaim the LORD as their God.

ZECHARIAH 14

Verse 9: *The LORD will be king over the whole earth. On that day there will be one LORD, and his name the only name.*

The prophecy continued. Zechariah told the people that the day of the LORD is coming. Jerusalem will be besieged. Half of the city will go into exile and the other half will remain, then the LORD will fight against the invaders. The Mount of Olives will be split in two by an earthquake. The LORD God will come and the day will have neither darkness nor light. Living water will flow out of Jerusalem into the sea on the West and the East, and the LORD will be King over the whole earth. Jerusalem will be raised up and secured. Plague will strike all of Israel's enemies and the plunder from their defeat will go to Jerusalem. Israel's enemies who survive will worship God and celebrate the Feast of Tabernacles each year in Jerusalem. Drought and the plague will afflict those who do not come to celebrate. The horses' bells will have HOLY TO THE LORD inscribed upon them and every pot will be holy, and there will be no foreigners in the house of the LORD Almighty.

Chapter 39

MALACHI

MALACHI 1

Verse 6: *"A son honors his father, and a servant his master. If I am a father, where is the honor due me? If I am a master, where is the respect due me?" says the LORD Almighty. "It is you, O priests, who show contempt for my name." But you ask, "How have we shown contempt for your name?"*

The prophet Malachi reported an oracle from God. God loved Israel (Jacob's inheritance), but hated Edom (Jacob's brother Esau's inheritance). The LORD chided the priests for offering unfit sacrifices to Him. He declared that His name is to be great, but the priests have brought contempt upon themselves.

MALACHI 2

Verse 7: *For the lips of a priest ought to preserve knowledge and from his mouth men should seek instruction—because he is the messenger of the LORD Almighty.*

The LORD admonished the Levite priests for not obeying their covenant promises to Him, and stated they would be cursed and despised for their sins. Judah broke the covenant by marrying foreign wives. He also was angered with them for not being faithful husbands. The LORD declared that He hates divorce and a violent man, then asked where the justice was.

MALACHI 3

Verse 7: *"Ever since the time of your forefathers you have turned away from my decrees and have not kept them. Return to me, and I will return to you," says the LORD Almighty. "But you ask, 'How are we to return?'"*

The LORD will send a messenger to prepare the way for the LORD. They are seeking to come to His Temple. He will purify the Levites. He will judge the wicked and unjust. The LORD asked the sinful Israelites to return to Him. He told them they have robbed Him of tithes and offerings and admonished them to bring in the whole tithe and they would be blessed. They have said that it is futile to serve God because evildoers prosper. The LORD, however, records those who favor God and honor His name on a scroll; in compassion, they will be spared.

MALACHI 4

Verse 4: *Remember the law of my servant Moses, the decrees and laws I gave him at Horeb for all Israel.*

The day of the LORD is coming. Evildoers will stumble, but the righteous will rise. Remember the Law, the LORD says. He will send the prophet Elijah before the day of the LORD comes to turn the hearts of fathers to their children and the hearts of children to their fathers.

NEW TESTAMENT

Gospel

Chapter 40

MATTHEW

MATTHEW 1

Verse 22: All this took place to fulfill what the Lord had said through the prophet....

The genealogy of Jesus began with Abraham and continued through the generations. Abraham's son Isaac was the father of Jacob, who fathered Judah (and the other future leaders of the twelve tribes). Several generations later, Boaz (who married Ruth) was the father of Jesse, who, in turn, was the father of David. David's lineage included his son Solomon, and then a succession of kings of Judah. Several generations later, Jacob was the father of Joseph, who was married to Mary, the mother of Jesus. There were fourteen generations between Abraham and David, David and the exile of Judah (to Babylon), and the exile and the birth of Jesus Christ. Mary and Joseph were pledged to be married, but she was found to be with child through the Holy Spirit. Joseph planned a quiet divorce until an angel explained to him in a dream that Mary was to be the mother of Jesus (Immanuel) from the Holy Spirit. Joseph married Mary, but had no relations with her until after Jesus' birth.

MATTHEW 2

Verse 11: *On coming to the house, they saw the child with his mother Mary, and they bowed and worshiped him. Then they opened their treasures and presented him with gifts of gold and of incense and of myrrh.*

Magi came from the east and asked Herod, king of Jerusalem, where the baby king of the Jews was. Herod asked his advisors where Jesus was to be born and was told that prophecy told that it would be in Bethlehem. Herod told the Magi to go to Bethlehem, find the Christ child, and report back to him. They followed a star, found the Child, worshiped Him, and gave Him gifts (gold, incense, and myrrh), then returned by a different route, avoiding Herod. An angel warned Joseph in a dream to escape to Egypt, where they stayed until after Herod's death. After he learned that the Magi had outwitted him, Herod ordered all boys in Bethlehem less than two years old be put to death. After Herod died, an angel told Joseph in a dream to return with his family to his homeland. He did so, settling in Nazareth in the Galilee district.

MATTHEW 3

Verse 3: *This is he who was spoken of through the prophet Isaiah: "A voice of one calling in the desert, 'Prepare the way for the Lord, make straight paths for him.'"*

John the Baptist, who wore rough clothes and ate insects and wild honey, baptized people in the Jordan River. He admonished the Pharisees and Sadducees (Jewish leaders who strictly followed traditional customs and Old Testament Law) because they would not repent. They believed that their Jewish inheritance alone would save them. John spoke of One to come who would baptize with the Holy Spirit. Jesus came to be baptized by John, who at first objected, believing that Jesus should baptize him. Jesus was baptized and the Spirit of God came down as a dove. God announced Jesus was His Son and that He was pleased with Him.

MATTHEW 4

Verse 11: *Then the devil left him, and angels came and attended him.*

Jesus was led to the desert and tempted by the devil. After fasting for 40 days, the devil challenged Jesus to turn stones into bread, but He refused, noting that man does not live by bread alone. The devil next challenged Him to throw Himself from the highest point on the temple. Jesus again refused, saying that the Lord should not be put to the test. Finally, the devil took Jesus to a mountaintop and offered Him all of the kingdoms if He would worship him. Jesus refused, proclaiming that it is written to worship only the Lord God, then He returned to Galilee where He learned that John the Baptist was imprisoned. He then began His ministry. Jesus picked His first two disciples—Simon Peter and his brother Andrew, fishing on the shores of the Sea of Galilee. He encouraged them to join Him and become fishers of men. He then invited James and John, also brothers, to leave their boat and join Him. Jesus preached and healed the sick. News quickly spread and large crowds followed Him.

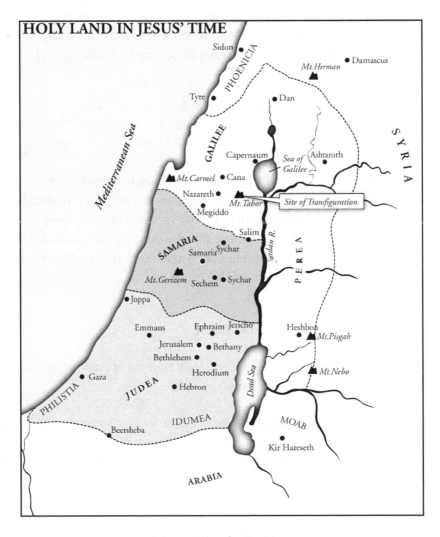

Figure 12: Israel in Jesus' time

MATTHEW 5

Verse 16: *In the same way, let your light so shine before men, that they may see your good deeds and praise your Father in heaven.*

Jesus began His Sermon on the Mount. He taught His disciples the Beatitudes. The poor in spirit, mourners, meek, righteous, merciful, pure in heart, peacemakers, and persecuted were praised. He told His followers they were the salt of the earth and the light of the world. He explained He did not come to abolish the Law but to fulfill it. He taught them they needed to be more righteous than the Pharisees. The spirit of the Law is as important as the Law itself. Therefore, anger is judged like murder and lust or divorce is considered the same as adultery. He told them not to make oaths, to turn the other cheek, and to love their enemies.

MATTHEW 6

Verse 21: *For where your treasure is, there your heart will be also.*

Jesus continued His sermon by advising His followers not to advertise when they give to the needy. He also told them to pray in solitude and taught them the Lord's Prayer. He emphasized the importance of forgiveness, instructed them to fast in secret, and to store up their treasures in heaven (not earth). He told them that the eye was the lamp of the body and that they could not serve two masters—God and money. He instructed them not to worry about tomorrow but to concern themselves first with serving His kingdom.

MATTHEW 7

Verse 21: *Not everyone who says to me, "Lord, Lord," will enter the kingdom of heaven, but only he who does the will of my Father who is in heaven.*

Jesus continued, telling His listeners that they will be judged as they judge others. He told them to teach those who are eager to learn. He assured them that if they ask they will receive, if they seek they will find, and if they knock, the doors will be opened. He told them to treat others the way they want to be treated. He also told them that the gate that leads into Life is small and few find it. He warned them about listening to false prophets; bad trees yield bad fruit. He declared that not everyone who calls the Lord by name would enter heaven; a person must do the will of the Father. Jesus concluded His sermon by saying if they believe this teaching they will have a rock for a foundation.

MATTHEW 8

Verse 10: *When Jesus heard this, he was astonished and said to those following him, "I tell you the truth, I have not found anyone in Israel with such great faith."*

A leper asked Jesus to heal him. When He did, Jesus asked the man to not tell anyone. A Roman centurion asked Jesus to heal his servant. When Jesus offered to go to his house, the centurion requested that Jesus simply heal him by saying it was so. Jesus was astounded by the centurion's faith and did what he asked. Jesus then healed Peter's mother-in-law and a person who was demon-possessed. Jesus told the people He had nowhere to rest and that to join Him they would have to give up everything. He calmed a storm from the boat that He and His disciples were in, admonishing them for their lack of faith. He removed demons from two men, driving them into a nearby herd of pigs. After this the people of the town pleaded with Him to leave.

MATTHEW 9

Verse 37: *Then he said to his disciples, "The harvest is plentiful but the workers are few."*

Jesus healed a paralytic, then rebuked a Pharisee. He asked Matthew, a tax collector, to become one of His disciples. When questioned by the Pharisees why He did this, He told them it is the sick, not the healthy, who need a doctor. When asked about fasting, Jesus replied that the guests of a bridegroom do not mourn while they are with him. He then left to heal the daughter of a ruler. En route, a woman with a bleeding problem touched His cloak and was healed. Jesus explained that it was her faith that healed her. He then healed the dead girl, two blind men, and a demon-possessed man. The Pharisees believed that the healing was the work of demons. Jesus, aware of all the needs of the people, planned to send out His disciples to help Him.

MATTHEW 10

Verse 8: *Heal the sick, raise the dead, cleanse those who have leprosy, drive out demons. Freely you have received, freely give.*

Jesus called upon His twelve disciples to drive out demons and to heal sickness. His apostles were as follows:

1. Simon (Peter)
2. Andrew (Peter's brother)
3. James (Son of Zebedee)
4. John (James' brother)
5. Phillip
6. Bartholomew
7. Thomas
8. Matthew
9. James (Alphaeus' son)
10. Thaddeus
11. Simon the Zealot
12. Judas Iscariot

Jesus sent them out with instructions and told them that the Kingdom of Heaven was near and to have courage and faith in the Lord. He explained that men would hate them and ridicule them, but to stand firm. Jesus encouraged them by stating that if they would acknowledge Him, He would acknowledge them to His Father. He proclaimed they should love the Lord above all others, and that those who receive Him will be rewarded.

Matthew 11

Verse 28: *Come to me, all you who are weary and burdened, and I will give you rest.*

John the Baptist's disciples came to Jesus with a message from John who was in prison. He wanted to be sure that Jesus was the Messiah. Jesus assured the disciples He was the Messiah by telling them to tell John of all the miracles that were being done. He told the crowd that John was the messenger who prepared the way for Him—he was His Elijah. He denounced those cities that had seen His miracles but did not repent. He praised the Father and encouraged all those who were weary to come to Him for rest.

Matthew 12

Verse 39: *He answered, "A wicked and adulterous generation asks for a miraculous sign! But none will be given it except the sign of the prophet Jonah."*

Jesus and His disciples went through the grain fields on the Sabbath and some ate grain. When criticized by the Pharisees for violating the Sabbath, Jesus answered that the Son of Man is the Lord of the Sabbath. He explained that it is lawful to do good deeds on the Sabbath. He then healed a man with a shriveled hand and the Pharisees began plotting to kill Him. Jesus then withdrew from the area, healing others on His way. He drove out demons from a man, and the Pharisees again accused Him of using the power of the devil to do so. Jesus responded by asking why Satan would drive out Satan. He proclaimed that anyone who was blasphemous against the Spirit would not be forgiven. He then foretold that just as Jonah had spent three days and nights in the belly of a large fish, He would spend three days in the heart of the earth—but that He was greater than Jonah or Solomon. Jesus exclaimed that whoever does the will of His Father in Heaven is His brother and sister.

MATTHEW 13

Verse 58: *And he did not do many miracles there because of their lack of faith.*

Jesus sat in a boat by the lake and told the parable of the sower. He explained that seeds that fell along a path, like those who did not understand the Gospel, would perish. Seeds that fell into rocky places are like those who accept the Word but quickly forget it. The seeds that fall into thorns are like those who hear the Word but have it choked out by their pursuit of wealth. Seeds that fall on good soil, however, are like those who accept and understand the Lord and yield plentiful crops. Jesus then told them the parable of the weeds, which were sown amongst the grain by the enemy (Satan). They (evil-doers) would be harvested and burned before the wheat (the righteous) was harvested. He then told them a parable of the mustard seed, explaining that the Kingdom of Heaven is like a mustard seed—it is small but yields a large plant. He also compared the Kingdom to yeast that rises, hidden treasure, and fine pearls. He compared it to a fishermen's net, where the good fish are kept and the bad discarded. Jesus then returned to Nazareth and was discouraged by their lack of faith. He noted that a prophet is without honor in his hometown.

MATTHEW 14

Verse 27: *But Jesus immediately said to them: "Take courage! It is I. Don't be afraid."*

Herod the tetrarch had arrested John the Baptist because he had denounced his marriage to his brother's wife, Herodias. Herodias' daughter danced before Herod, and he offered to grant her any wish that she had. She asked for John the Baptist's head, and it was brought to her on a platter. Jesus learned of this and was distressed. He retreated to a solitary place, but was quickly surrounded by a crowd, and healed their sick. Later that day, Jesus collected five loaves of bread and two fish, blessed it, then served the food to over 5,000 people, and there was food leftover when they were finished. Jesus' disciples returned to their boat and left the shore. After praying, He went to join them, walking on water. Peter asked to join Him, and he walked on water as well until he lost his focus on the Lord and began to sink. The disciples again recognized Jesus as the Son of God. They crossed to the other side of the water where Jesus healed more people who had gathered there.

MATTHEW 15

Verse 18: *But the things that come out of the mouth come from the heart, and these make a man "unclean."*

The Pharisees challenged Jesus again because they did not think His disciples were following the Law. He replied that the Pharisees also did not obey the Law down to the letter. A Canaanite woman asked Him to save her daughter from demon possession. Jesus said that He had come for the lost sheep of Israel (the Jews only), but He rewarded the woman for her faith. He also performed more miracles by the Sea of Galilee, then fed 4,000 with seven loaves of bread and a few small fish, and again had leftovers.

MATTHEW 16

Verse 17: *Jesus replied, "Blessed are you, Simon son of Jonah, for this was not revealed to you by man, but by my Father in heaven."*

The Pharisees and Sadducees asked Jesus for a sign from heaven. He answered that they did not recognize the signs of the time. He told His disciples that they had little faith, and to guard against the Pharisees and Sadducees. Simon Peter acknowledged Jesus as the Christ, and Jesus blessed him. Jesus then predicted His future death in Jerusalem. Peter denied this would occur, and Jesus replied, "Get behind me, Satan!" He explained that anyone who came after Him must take up his cross and follow Him, and to gain his life, he must lose it.

MATTHEW 17

Verse 12: *But I tell you, Elijah has already come, and they did not recognize him, but have done to him everything they wished. In the same way the Son of Man is going to suffer at their hands.*

Peter, James, and John went with Jesus to a mountaintop and witnessed Jesus' transfiguration (to His glorified state). Moses and Elijah appeared. God announced that Jesus was His Son and He was pleased, then urged them to listen to Him. His disciples fell to the ground and Jesus comforted them. He explained that Elijah (in the form of John the Baptist) had already come before Him as the prophets had said. After Jesus healed a boy with seizures, He told His disciples they were unable to do so because of their lack of faith. Jesus predicted His betrayal, death, and resurrection while in Galilee. When questioned about the temple tax, He told Peter to catch a fish and the coins for the tax would be in its mouth.

MATTHEW 18

Verse 3: *And he said: "I tell you the truth, unless you change and become like little children, you will never enter the kingdom of heaven."*

Jesus explained to His disciples that they had to humble themselves like a child to be the greatest in the kingdom of heaven. He taught them about the evils of sin. He told them a parable about the lost sheep that got more attention than all of the others until the lost one was found. He encouraged them to challenge fellow believers who sin against them. He also noted that when two or three come together in His name that He would be there. Jesus told Peter that he must forgive not seven, but seventy-seven times. He then told the parable of the unmerciful servant who had his debts forgiven but did not forgive the debts of others, demonstrating the importance of forgiveness.

MATTHEW 19

Verse 29: *And everyone who has left houses or brothers or sisters or father or mother or children or fields for my sake will receive a hundred times as much and will inherit eternal life.*

The Pharisees asked Jesus if divorce was legal. Jesus explained that man could not separate what God has joined together. When challenged, He explained that Moses allowed divorce in certain circumstances because their hearts were hard. Jesus then blessed the children. Jesus told a rich man that he should sell all his possessions, give to the poor, and follow Him. The man went away sad. He explained that it is difficult for a rich man to enter heaven. He promised His disciples a throne in heaven, but that the first may be the last and the last the first.

MATTHEW 20

Verse 23: *Jesus said to them, "You will indeed drink from my cup, but to sit at my right or left is not for me to grant. These places belong to those for whom they have been prepared by my Father."*

Jesus explained that heaven is like the parable of workers. They were all paid the same wage for varying amounts of work. He noted that they all worked for an agreed-upon wage and that the last were the first and the first last. Jesus approached Jerusalem and again predicted His death. The mother of James and John asked Jesus if her sons could sit on His right and left in heaven. Jesus explained that it was not His decision, but His Father's. The other ten disciples were indignant, but He explained that they should serve and not be served in order to be great in the kingdom. Jesus then healed two blind men on the outskirts of Jericho.

MATTHEW 21

Verse 32: *For John came to you to show you the way of righteousness, and you did not believe him, but the tax collectors and the prostitutes did. And even after you saw this, you did not repent and believe him.*

As they approached Jerusalem, Jesus sent two disciples into the city and they returned with a donkey. He wanted to ride it into Jerusalem to fulfill prophecy. The people praised Him and laid down palm branches in His path to honor Him as He entered. Jesus entered the temple area and drove out the merchants. He then healed the blind and lame but was criticized by local priests. He withered a fig tree because it bore no fruit, then explained it was like those without faith. The chief priests and elders challenged Jesus' authority. He told them a parable of the two sons. One was unwilling but obeyed, and the other was willing but did not obey. He explained that the priests and elders were not obedient and did not believe. Jesus then told a parable of the tenants who did not pay their rent, dishonored their master, and eventually had the land taken from them. Likewise, the Kingdom of God will be taken from those who do not believe.

MATTHEW 22

Verse 21b: *Then he said to them, "Give to Caesar what is Caesar's, and to God what is God's"*

Jesus told the listeners a parable of the wedding banquet. Those who were invited did not come, so the host invited people from the street. When the king arrived, he threw out one of the guests because, like heaven, many are invited but few are chosen. The Pharisees asked Jesus if it was right to pay taxes. He responded they should give to Caesar what was Caesar's and to give to God what is God's. The Sadducees regarding resurrection and marriage then questioned him. Jesus explained that all will be like angels in heaven. He was then questioned about the greatest commandment. Jesus answered to love the Lord God was first and to love your neighbor was second. He asked the leaders whose Son Christ was. They replied that Christ was David's Son. Then He asked them why, if that were true, did David refer to the Christ as Lord? His teaching astonished the crowds and His critics were silenced.

MATTHEW 23

Verse 37: *O Jerusalem, Jerusalem, you who kill the prophets and stone those sent to you, how often I have longed to gather your children together, as a hen gathers her chicks under her wings, but you were not willing.*

Jesus criticized the teachers of the Law. He explained that the Father was in Heaven and the Teacher was Christ. He proclaimed seven woes to the Pharisees and Sadducees, calling them blind hypocrites and snakes. He offered a lament for Jerusalem who killed the prophets and were stubborn.

MATTHEW 24

Verse 37: *No one knows about that day or hour, not even the angels in heaven, nor the Son, but only the Father.*

Jesus left with His disciples. He predicted the fall of Jerusalem and their future martyrdom for following Him. He told them that if they stood firm that they would be saved. He spoke of future disasters, the tribulation, and the second coming, and declared that heaven and earth would pass away, but His word would never pass away. He told them that only the Father knows when that day will be. Believers will suddenly disappear on that day. Keep watch and be ready,

He warned, and be ready when that day dawns. He told them He would come on a day when they least expected it.

MATTHEW 25

Verse 29: *For everyone who has will be given more, and he will have an abundance. Whoever does not have, even what he has will be taken from him.*

Jesus told a parable of ten virgins who went out to meet the bridegroom with lamps. Some were wise and brought oil, and they were invited to the wedding banquet. The foolish virgins who did not bring oil were left out in the cold. Jesus then told the parable of the talents, in which those who made wise investments were rewarded and the lazy servant was punished. He exclaimed that the Son of Man would come and separate the sheep from the goats. He noted that whatever a person does for the least of His brothers, he does for Him. He told them that those who are righteous go on to eternal life.

MATTHEW 26

Verse 39: *Going a little farther, he fell with his face to the ground and prayed, "My Father, if it is possible, may this cup be taken from me. Yet not as I will, but as you will."*

The priests and elders plotted to kill Jesus after the Passover. A woman at Bethany anointed Jesus with expensive perfume. Judas agreed to betray Jesus for 30 silver coins. Jesus celebrated Passover with His disciples and predicted that He would be betrayed, then offered the sacrament and broke bread. He then predicted that Peter would deny Him three times before the rooster crowed. Jesus went to Gethsemane to pray. As He prayed, the weak disciples could not stay awake. Judas arrived with officials and Jesus was arrested. He accosted His accusers and was led off. He stood trial before the Sanhedrin and was accused of blasphemy. Peter denied Christ three times, the rooster crowed, and Peter wept.

MATTHEW 27

Verse 51: *At that moment the curtain of the temple was torn in two from top to bottom. The earth shook and the rocks split.*

Jesus was handed over to Governor Pilate. Judas returned the coins and hanged himself, and the coins were used to buy Potter's Field that was to be used as a burial place for foreigners. Pilate questioned Jesus and found that He committed no crime. He asked the people if he should release the criminal Barabbas or Jesus. The people called for Jesus to be crucified. Pilate conceded, despite advice from his wife who shared a dream that she had advising otherwise. The soldiers put a crown of thorns on Jesus, beat Him, and mocked Him. They crucified Him and divided His clothes amongst themselves by lot. Jesus cried out to God asking why He had forsaken Him. Then He died. The curtain in the temple tore, the earth shook and holy ones were resurrected. People were amazed and finally believed that Jesus was the Son of God. He was placed in a sealed and guarded tomb.

MATTHEW 28

Verse 2: *There was a violent earthquake, for an angel of the Lord came down from heaven and, going to the tomb, rolled back the stone and sat on it.*

Jesus reappeared on the third day to Mary Magdalene and the other Mary after an angel opened the tomb. The guard was paid off by the priests to keep this quiet. The angel told the two women to tell the disciples that Jesus had risen, then Jesus Himself appeared to them and told them to have the disciples meet Him at Galilee. When He met with them, He gave them the Great Commission, telling them to go to all nations and spread the gospel.

Chapter 41

MARK

MARK 1

Verse 8: *I baptize you with water, but he will baptize you with the Holy Spirit.*

Isaiah the prophet foretold of Jesus Christ. John the Baptist, who wore rough clothes and ate locusts and wild honey, also announced the coming of Jesus. John baptized Jesus, and the Spirit descended from heaven like a dove. A voice from heaven spoke to Jesus telling everyone that He was His Son and He was pleased. Satan tempted Jesus in the desert. After John the Baptist was imprisoned, Jesus began recruiting His disciples. He asked two brothers, Simon and Andrew to be "fishers of men." He also asked two other brothers, James and John, to join Him. Jesus taught with authority in the synagogue and then healed a man possessed by an evil spirit. News of Jesus and His miracles spread. He healed Simon's mother-in-law and many sick people in Capernaum. He then traveled throughout Galilee preaching and healing. He cured a leper and told the man not to tell anyone, but he did. People came from everywhere to be healed.

MARK 2

Verse 16: *On hearing this, Jesus said to them, "It is not the healthy who need a doctor, but the sick. I have not come to call the righteous, but sinners."*

Jesus healed a paralytic whose friends lowered him from an opening in the roof. Teachers of the Law accused Him of blasphemy but Jesus rebuked them. He asked Levi (Matthew) the tax collector to become a disciple and later had dinner with him. When questioned by the teachers of the Law why He would eat with sinners, He asked them if the healthy needed a doctor. Jesus was asked about fasting and responded that it was not the proper time. He was also questioned about His disciples picking grain on the Sabbath. He reminded His accusers that David did similar things and that He was the Lord of the Sabbath.

MARK 3

Verse 25: *If a house is divided against itself, that house cannot stand.*

Jesus healed a man with a shriveled hand on the Sabbath explaining that it is permissible to do good deeds on the Sabbath. The Pharisees began plotting against Him. Jesus healed many in the crowd that surrounded Him and then preached from a boat on the lake. He appointed twelve apostles to go out to preach and heal. His apostles were Simon (Peter), James, John, Andrew, Philip, Bartholomew, Matthew, Thomas, James, Thaddeus, Simon the Zealot, and Judas Iscariot. Jesus was accused of being demon-possessed. He challenged His accusers, asking if Satan would drive out Satan. Jesus proclaimed His spiritual family as His true family.

MARK 4

Verse 41: *They were terrified and asked each other, "Who is this? Even the wind and the waves obey him!"*

Jesus taught the Parable of the Sower (only the seeds that fell on good soil produced abundant crops). He explained that a person must hear and accept the Word in order to be productive. He also told the parables concerning a lampstand, growing seeds, and a mustard seed. He and His disciples were in a boat and He calmed a storm and rebuked His disciples for not having faith.

MARK 5

Verse 34: *He said to her, "Daughter, your faith has healed you. Go in peace and be freed from your suffering."*

Jesus drove the evil spirits named Legion from a man into a herd of pigs, then the pigs ran into the lake and drowned. The man asked to join Jesus, but Jesus told him to go and spread the word instead. Jairus, a synagogue ruler, asked Jesus to help his dying daughter. On the way, a woman with a bleeding disorder touched Jesus' cloak and was healed. Jesus told her that her faith had healed her. When He arrived at Jairus' daughter's home, she was dead. Jesus told him to simply believe. He told the people who had gathered that she was asleep. He called for her to awake, and she did, then told the witnesses not to tell anyone what He had done.

MARK 6

Verse 7: *Calling the Twelve to him, he sent them out two by two and gave them authority over evil spirits.*

Jesus returned to Nazareth only to discover that a prophet is without honor in his own town and that the people there had little faith. He then sent out the twelve disciples in pairs to minister to the people and to heal the sick. Herod heard of Jesus' actions, and believed He was John the Baptist raised from the dead. Herod's men had beheaded John after Herodias' daughter asked Herod for John's head as a reward for her dancing at Herod's banquet. Jesus taught a large crowd until it was very late. He then fed 5,000 men and many others with only five loaves of bread and two fish, and there were twelve baskets of leftovers. Afterwards, Jesus sent His disciples ahead of Him by boat. After He had finished praying, He went to the boat that was well away from land by walking on the water. He healed many others on the opposite shore of the lake.

MARK 7

Verse 8: *You have let go of the commands of God and are holding on to the traditions of men.*

The Pharisees questioned Jesus about clean and unclean traditions. Jesus told them that they were hypocrites, and they should obey the commands of God and not the traditions of men. He explained that the normal understanding of clean and unclean should not be based upon tradition but what is in their heart. Jesus went to Tyre and a Greek woman asked that He heal her demon-possessed daughter. Jesus responded that He needed to feed the children (heal the Jews) before the dogs (Gentiles). She responded that even dogs eat crumbs from the children's table, and Jesus rewarded her for her faith by healing her daughter. Jesus then healed a deaf and mute man by the Sea of Galilee. People continued to spread the news about Jesus' miracles despite His instruction not to do so.

MARK 8

Verse 29: *"But what about you?" he asked. "Who do you say I am?" Peter answered, "You are the Christ."*

Jesus taught another large crowd (4,000 men), then fed them all with seven loaves and a few small fish. Again there were leftovers, this time seven baskets. Jesus warned His disciples to watch out for the Pharisees, and then criticized them for their lack of faith. In Bethsaida, Jesus healed a blind man and then told him to go the other direction so that he would not tell the villagers. When asked by Jesus who he thought He was, Peter responded that He was the Christ. Jesus then shared His fate with His disciples. Peter challenged Him, and Jesus referred to Peter as Satan and told him to get behind Him. He taught them they must deny themselves and take up their crosses to be saved when He returned.

MARK 9

Verse 42: *And if anyone causes one of these little ones who believe in me to sin, it would be better for him to be thrown into the sea with a large millstone tied around his neck.*

Peter, James, and John went with Jesus to the top of a high mountain. Jesus was transfigured before them and Elijah and Moses spoke with Him. Peter offered to put up shelters, but then a cloud appeared and a voice announced that Jesus was His Son and that they should listen to Him. He told the three disciples not to share what occurred until after His resurrection. He then explained that Elijah had already come (in the form of John the Baptist), fulfilling prophecy. Jesus joined the other disciples and healed a boy with an evil spirit. His disciples asked why they could not heal the boy. Jesus told them that this kind of spirit could only come out by prayer. He again told His disciples of His death and resurrection, but they did not understand. The disciples argued about who was the greatest, and Jesus admonished them, noting that whoever is first must be last. He praised the children and those who did good things in His name. He warned that if a person leads children to sin then he would be severely punished. He told them to avoid sin at all costs and to be at peace with one another.

MARK 10

Verse 45: *For even the Son of Man did not come to be served, but to serve, and to give his life as a ransom for many.*

The Pharisees tested Jesus about divorce. Jesus explained that divorce was not God's plan, but Moses allowed for their weakness. He encouraged His disciples to bring children to Him, noting that the kingdom of God belonged to them. A rich man asked what he needed to do to enter heaven. Jesus told him to sell everything he owned and give to the poor. The man was saddened, and left. Jesus explained that it was difficult for a rich man to enter heaven. The disciples asked who could be saved. Jesus explained that all things are possible with God. He went on to tell the disciples that they will be rewarded in heaven for their faithfulness, but that the first will be last. Jesus again predicted His death on their way to Jerusalem. James and John asked to sit on the right and left side of Jesus. Jesus explained that was not His decision, but His Father's. He admonished His disciples for arguing and told them they should serve and not be served. Jesus stopped in Jericho to heal a blind man who had faith and then resumed His journey to Jerusalem.

MARK 11

Verse 17: *And as he taught them, he said, "Is it not written: 'My house will be called a house of prayer for all nations'? But you have made it 'a den of robbers.'"*

While at the outskirts of Jerusalem, Jesus sent two of His disciples to get a colt for Him to ride into the city. He made a triumphal entry into the city and went to the Temple. He cursed a fig tree for not bearing fruit and then drove out merchants from the Temple area. The priests began planning for a way to kill Jesus. Jesus told His disciples that if they have faith in God they would receive what they asked for in prayer, and told them to forgive others so that God would forgive them. When Jesus was teaching in the Temple courts, the teachers of the Law and elders asked Him by what authority He taught. He turned the question on them and they were unable to answer.

Mark 12

Verse 29: *"The most important one," answered Jesus, "is this: 'Hear O Israel, the LORD our God, the LORD is one.'"*

Jesus told His followers the parable of the tenants that highlighted the lack of insight of those who questioned Him. The Pharisees and others questioned Him. When asked whether it was right to pay taxes, He asked for a coin with Caesar's portrait and said to give to Caesar what was Caesar's and to give to God what is God's. He was then asked about marriage in heaven and replied that it did not exist, because people would be like angels. He reminded them He was God. Then He was asked to name the greatest Commandment and responded that they should love the Lord God first and their neighbor second. Jesus taught in the temple courts pointing out that Christ did not come from David, but God. He also warned them to be careful of the Pharisees and teachers of the Law. Observing offerings, Jesus noted that a poor widow's offering of two small coins was greater than the others because she put in all that she had to live on.

Mark 13

Verse 7: *When you hear of wars and rumors of wars, do not be alarmed. Such things must happen, but the end is still to come.*

Jesus spoke to Peter, James, John, and Andrew about the end of the age (His second coming). He foretold of earthquakes, war, and famine. He told them they would be persecuted for their belief in Him. He also told them that if they stand firm and they would be saved. He added that there would be utter destruction but that He would cut the days short for the chosen. He warned them to not believe in false Christs and to be on their guard. He declared that the Son of Man would return out of darkness with His angels. He told them that no one knows when the time will come, so they need to be on guard.

Mark 14

Verse 9: *I tell you the truth, wherever the gospel is preached throughout the world, what she has done will also be told, in memory of her.*

A woman at Bethany anointed Jesus with expensive perfume. He chastised those who criticized her noting that He would not be with them much longer. Judas Iscariot made arrangements with the chief priests to betray Jesus for money. Jesus instructed His disciples to prepare for the Passover feast in the upper room of a man's house. At the meal, Jesus announced that one of them would betray Him. He offered communion and then predicted Peter's denial. He went to Gethsemane with Peter, James, and John to pray. While He was praying the disciples could not stay awake and He admonished them noting that the spirit is willing, but the body is weak. Judas appeared with priests and guards and Jesus was arrested. He was taken away to be tried by the priests and elders. He was accused of blasphemy for claiming that He was Christ. Peter denied he knew Christ three times before the rooster crowed, then recognized what he had done and wept.

MARK 15

Verse 15: *Wanting to satisfy the crowd, Pilate released Barabbas to them. He had Jesus flogged, and handed him over to be crucified.*

Jesus was brought before Pilate, the Governor. He offered to let Jesus go free, but the crowd asked that the criminal Barabbas be released instead. The soldiers mocked Jesus, beat Him, and led Him out to be crucified. He was crucified at Golgotha and the soldiers cast lots to divide His clothes. He was nailed to a cross next to two robbers with a sign noting that He was the King of the Jews. The chief priests and other people mocked him. Jesus died after asking God why He had forsaken Him. The curtain of the temple was torn. Joseph of Arimathea buried Jesus in a sealed tomb cut out of rock.

MARK 16

Verse 20: *Then the disciples went out and preached everywhere, and the LORD worked with them and confirmed his word by the signs that accompanied it.*

Three days later, Mary Magdalene, Mary (James' mother), and Salome went to the tomb and discovered that the tomb was opened. They entered and found a man (angel) dressed in white linen who told them to assemble the disciples at Galilee. Jesus appeared to them, rebuking them for not believing that He had risen. He told them to go and spread the gospel, then He was taken up into heaven.

Chapter 42

LUKE

LUKE 1

Verse 35: The angel answered, "The Holy Spirit will come upon you, and the power of the Most High will overshadow you. So the holy one to be born will be called the Son of God."

Luke introduced his gospel account by addressing it to Theophilus. Zechariah, a priest, and his wife Elizabeth, both descendants of Aaron, had no children. The angel Gabriel appeared to Zechariah while he was burning incense in the temple, and he was told that Elizabeth would bear a son and that he would be named John. The angel announced John would bring back many people to the Lord with the spirit and power of Elijah. Zechariah was unable to speak until John's birth because he did not believe what he was told. The angel Gabriel was sent to Mary in Nazareth. He told her she would bear a child from God and was to name Him Jesus. Mary went to visit Elizabeth and the baby jumped in Elizabeth's womb. Mary sang a song of rejoicing to the Lord. John was born and Zechariah was able to speak again after confirming his son's name. Zechariah praised the Lord and proclaimed that his son would be a prophet who would prepare the way for the Lord. John grew and became strong in the spirit.

LUKE 2

Verse 10: *But the angels said to them, "Do not be afraid. I bring you good news of great joy that will be for all the people."*

Caesar Augustus called for a census and everyone was required to return to their hometown. Joseph and his fiancée Mary, who was with Child, made the journey from Nazareth to Bethlehem. Mary gave birth to her Son in a manger there. An angel appeared to shepherds nearby and they came to worship Him. A week later, Mary and Joseph brought Jesus to the temple in Jerusalem where Simeon and a prophetess named Anna recognized Him as Christ. Jesus went with His parents to the Passover celebration in Jerusalem every year. When He was twelve, He remained in the city after His parents left. When they realized He was not with them, they returned and questioned Him. He told them that He had to be in His Father's house. Jesus grew in wisdom and stature.

LUKE 3

Verse 8: *Produce fruit in keeping with repentance. And do not begin to say to yourselves, "We have Abraham as our father." For I tell you that out of these stones God can raise up children for Abraham.*

John the Baptist began his ministry by baptizing believers in the River Jordan. He warned his followers that their ancestry was not enough to save them. He foretold of the One who would baptize with the Holy Spirit. Herod the tetrarch imprisoned John because he rebuked him. Before he was sent to prison, however, John baptized Jesus and the Holy Spirit announced that Jesus was His Son and He was pleased. Jesus' earthly father was from the lineage of David, Isaac, Abraham, Noah, Adam, and God Himself.

LUKE 4

Verse 21b: *Today this scripture is fulfilled in your hearing.*

Jesus was tempted by the devil for forty days in the desert. When the devil told Him to turn a rock into bread He responded that man does not live by bread alone. The devil offered Jesus authority over the entire land, but He reminded him that He served God only. The devil asked Him to jump from a high place, but Jesus told him that He would not put God to a test. Jesus began His ministry in Nazareth by first announcing that He was the fulfillment of scripture. He soon realized, however, that a prophet was without honor in his hometown. He went to Capernaum in Galilee and drove out demons and healed many, including Simon's mother-in-law.

Luke 5

Verse 35: *But the time will come when the bridegroom will be taken from them; in those days they will fast.*

Jesus met Simon (Peter) and told him to cast out his net. Simon told Jesus that they had not caught any fish all night, but he cast out the net as instructed and soon brought in so many fish that the boat almost sunk. Jesus then invited him to be a fisher of men, and he became His first disciple. Jesus healed a man with leprosy and told him not to tell anyone, but the news of His miracles spread. Next, He healed a paralytic who was lowered to Him through a hole in a roof. Jesus silenced His critics, including the Pharisees, who questioned His actions. He invited other disciples including Levi (Matthew) a tax collector, to join Him. When questioned by the Pharisees about associating with a tax collector, Jesus told them that a doctor treats the sick, not the healthy. He was then questioned about fasting but told them it was not the time, and that the old was better than the new.

Luke 6

Verse 35: *But love your enemies, do good to them, and lend to them without expecting to get anything back. Then your reward will be great, and you will be sons of the Most High, because he is kind to the ungrateful and wicked.*

The Pharisees questioned Jesus about why His disciples picked grain on the Sabbath. He reminded them that David ate consecrated bread and that He was the Lord of the Sabbath. He also told them it was ok to do good on the Sabbath after He healed a man. Jesus' apostles included Simon (Peter), his brother Andrew, James, John, Philip, Bartholomew, Matthew, Thomas, James son of Alphaeus, Simon the Zealot, Judas son of James, and Judas Iscariot. He cured many and blessed the believers, and cried woe to the rich, unbelievers, and false prophets. He told His followers to love their enemies, turn the other cheek, and to do unto others, as they would have them do to them. He instructed them not to judge others and not to be hypocritical. He told them that good trees bear good fruit, and to build their house on a strong foundation.

LUKE 7

Verse 47: *Therefore, I tell you, her many sins have been forgiven—for she loved much. But he who has been forgiven little loves little.*

A Centurion asked Jesus to heal his servant. When He offered to come to his house, the Centurion asked that Jesus just say the word and his servant would be healed. Jesus did so and was impressed with the Centurion's faith. Jesus then went to a town called Nain and raised a young boy who was in a funeral procession back to life. News of His miracles spread. John the Baptist sent messengers to ask Jesus if He were the one who was to come. Jesus answered them indirectly and went on to explain that John was the messenger who prepared the way for Him. He again rebuked the Pharisees for their lack of faith. A sinful woman anointed Jesus and the Pharisees criticized Him. He explained that those who have more sin would love Him more when He forgives them. He told the woman her faith saved her and she should go in peace.

LUKE 8

Verse 21: *He replied, "My mother and brothers are those who hear God's word and put it into practice."*

Jesus told His followers the parable of the seed, explaining that seeds that fall on fertile ground, like those who listen and apply the word, will grow and prosper. He went on to tell them that a lamp should be put on a stand so more can see the light. He then told them that His family is comprised of fellow believers, not His earthly family. Later, He calmed the storm and rebuked His disciples for their lack of faith. He then drove out the demon named Legion from a man into a herd of pigs, which ran into the water and drowned. The man who was cured asked to go with them, but Jesus told them to return home and tell everyone how much He had done for him. Jesus then went to cure Jairus' daughter who was dying. En route, a bleeding woman touched His cloak and was cured. He told her that her faith had healed her. When He arrived at Jairus' house, the girl had died but Jesus commanded her to get up, and she did. He told His followers not to tell anyone what had occurred.

LUKE 9

Verse 23: *Then he said to them all: "If anyone would come after me, he must deny himself and take up his cross daily and follow me."*

Jesus sent out His disciples without any provisions to preach and heal the sick. Herod the tetrarch heard about Jesus and was confused because he believed He was John the Baptist, who he had beheaded. Jesus then fed 5,000 men with only five loaves of bread and two fish with twelve baskets of food left over. He asked Peter who He was and Peter acknowledged that He was Christ. Jesus told Peter that He would suffer and be killed but He would rise again on the third day. He explained to them if they wanted to follow in His footsteps, they must deny themselves. Eight days later, He took Peter, John, and James up to a mountain where He was transfigured. Moses and Elijah appeared and Peter offered to build three shelters. A cloud appeared and a voice announced that Jesus was His Son whom He had chosen. Jesus returned from the mountain and healed a demon-possessed boy whom His disciples could not cure. He criticized His followers for their lack of faith and told them He would be betrayed, but they did not understand. The disciples argued amongst themselves as to who was the greatest, so He admonished them by telling them that whoever is least is the greatest, and whoever is not against them is for them. Jesus began His journey to Jerusalem, avoiding a Samaritan village that did not welcome Him. He then noted that He had no place to rest. He invited a young man to join Him on the journey. When the boy asked to bury his father first, Jesus told him that the dead will bury their own dead and not to look back.

LUKE 10

Verse 20: *However, do not rejoice that the spirits submit to you, but rejoice that your names are written in heaven.*

Jesus appointed seventy-two followers to spread out amongst the villages and spread the Word and to announce that the Kingdom of God is near. They returned noting that even demons submit to them in His name. He told them to rejoice only in their own salvation, and proclaimed that the only way to the Father is through the Son. Jesus told a teacher of the Law that if he loved the Lord and his neighbors he would inherit eternal life. He then told those around him a parable of the Good Samaritan who saved a man's life when others ignored him. He reminded His listeners to have mercy upon others. Jesus went to the home of Martha and Mary. Mary listened at Jesus' feet as Martha busily prepared food for Jesus. When Martha asked Jesus to have Mary come help her, Jesus replied that it was Mary who had chosen correctly.

LUKE 11

Verse 23: *He who is not with me is against me, and he who does not gather with me, scatters.*

Jesus taught His disciples the Lord's Prayer. He told them to be kind to others and to help those in need, then said that everyone who asks receives. Jesus healed a mute person and was accused by some onlookers as being the devil. He rebuked them, noting that Satan would not drive out demons. He proclaimed that those who hear and obey the Word of God will be blessed. Jesus noted that He was greater than Jonah and Solomon. He said that your eye is the lamp of your body and told them to shine their light. He criticized the Pharisees and teachers of the Law for valuing traditions and the letter of the Law more than the Spirit. Then they began to conspire against Him.

LUKE 12

Verse 51: *Do you think I came to bring peace on earth? No, I tell you, but division.*

Jesus warned His disciples that the Pharisees were hypocrites and were evil. He encouraged them to keep their faith and that the Holy Spirit would save them from persecution. He told a parable that discouraged those who store up things for themselves and not for God. He exhorted them to not worry about earthly concerns but to seek His kingdom. He reminded them that their treasure is where their heart is. He encouraged them to be ready because the Son of Man will come at an hour when they do not expect Him. He explained He came to bring division to the earth (between good and evil) and emphasized the urgency of making a decision to follow God.

LUKE 13

Verse 30: *Indeed there are those who are last who will be first, and first who will be last.*

Jesus warned them to repent or they will perish. He told a parable of a fig tree that did not bear fruit. The farmer dug around it and fertilized it to see if it would bear fruit. He healed a crippled woman on the Sabbath. When criticized by the synagogue ruler, He told him that it is ok to do good on the Sabbath. Jesus compared the Kingdom of God to a mustard seed and yeast. He encouraged them to make every effort to enter the narrow door to heaven. Jesus expressed His sorrow for Jerusalem's fate.

LUKE 14

Verse 11: *For everyone who exalts himself will be humbled, and he who humbles himself will be exalted.*

Jesus again healed a man on the Sabbath and explained to the Pharisees that you can do good deeds on that day. He told them if you take the least important seat at a banquet, the host may invite you to a better seat, but if you take the best seat, you may be humbled. He went on to tell them if they invited the poor, crippled, lame, and blind that they would be repaid at the resurrection of the righteous. He told them the parable of the man who hosted a banquet but his guests could not come. He invited people off the street and promised nothing for those who were invited. Jesus then explained the cost of being a disciple and carrying His cross.

LUKE 15

Verse 7: *I tell you that in the same way there will be more rejoicing in heaven over one sinner who repents than over ninety-nine righteous persons who do not need to repent.*

When criticized for associating with sinners and tax collectors, Jesus explained that if one sheep from a flock of one hundred were lost, it would command the entire attention of the shepherd. He also compared it to the joy of finding a lost coin. He told another parable of the lost son who squandered his fortune but returned to a grateful father.

LUKE 16

Verse 31: *He said to him, "If they do not listen to Moses and the Prophets, they will not be convinced even if someone rises from the dead."*

Jesus told His followers a parable of a shrewd manager who called in his master's debts at a discounted rate. The master commended the dishonest manager for his shrewdness. He noted that worldly wealth is only useful to gain friendships for the eternal dwellings. Jesus stated that one cannot serve two masters (God and money) and again rebuked the Pharisees who loved money. He taught them that the kingdom of God is more important than the Law and that divorce is a sin. He told them about the rich man who went to Hell and the beggar Lazarus who went to heaven. The rich man begged Abraham, who was at Lazarus' side, to bring him some water. Abraham refused so the rich man asked Abraham to warn his family to repent. Abraham again refused, noting that they should listen to Moses and the Prophets.

LUKE 17

Verse 10: *So you also, when you have done everything you were told to do, should say, "We are unworthy servants; we have only done our duty."*

Jesus instructed His disciples to guard against sin and to forgive those who sin against them. He also described the importance of faith. Jesus healed ten men with leprosy, but only one returned to thank Him. Asked about the kingdom of God, Jesus replied it was within them. He warned them to be careful of false Christs in the day. He said it would be like the flood in Noah's time and like the destruction of Sodom after Lot left. The righteous would be chosen and simply disappear.

LUKE 18

Verse 16: *But Jesus called the children to him and said, "Let the little children come to me, and do not hinder them, for the kingdom of God belongs to such as these."*

Jesus shared a parable about an unjust judge who brought about justice because a widow continued to bother him. Likewise, God will bring justice for His chosen ones. He told another parable about a tax collector and a Pharisee who went to the temple. The tax collector asked for mercy and the Pharisee praised himself. It was the tax collector who was justified by God. Jesus then told His followers that the kingdom of God belonged to the children. He instructed a rich ruler who said that he obeyed the Law to sell everything he owned and give it to the poor in order to gain eternal life. The man left, saddened. Jesus explained that it is difficult for the rich to enter heaven, and stated that eternal life is only possible with God. Jesus told His disciples because they left their lives for the kingdom, they would be rewarded. Jesus told His disciples again He was to die and be resurrected, but they did not understand. Jesus healed a blind man outside of Jericho because of his faith.

LUKE 19

Verse 9: *Jesus said to him, "Today salvation has come to this house, because this man, too, is a son of Abraham."*

As Jesus entered Jericho, Zacchaeus, a wealthy tax collector, climbed a tree to see Him. Jesus invited him to come down from the tree and He stayed at his house. Zacchaeus gave half of his possessions to the Lord and offered to pay back four times the amount he had cheated anyone of. Jesus then acknowledged his selflessness and said he would be saved. Jesus told a parable of three servants whom a man gave variable amounts of money to in his absence. Two of them made considerable profit with the money they invested, and they were rewarded. The third servant hid the money and made no profit. Jesus explained this man would have nothing. As He approached Jerusalem, Jesus sent two of His disciples ahead to secure a colt. Jesus made a triumphal entry into the city. He rebuked the Pharisees for not recognizing the time of God's coming. He then went to the temple where He drove out the merchants and began teaching there. His enemies could not find a way to kill Him, but they conspired to do so.

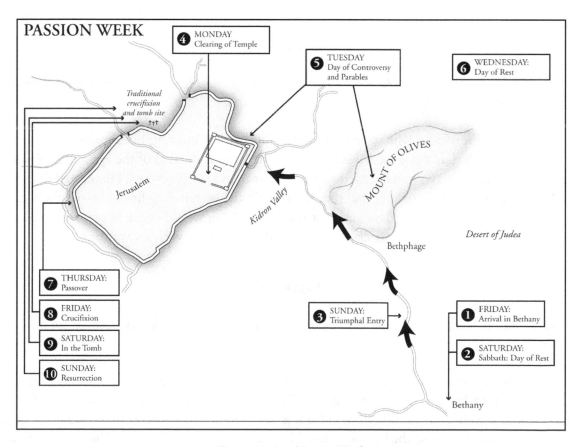

Figure 13: Jesus' Passion Week

LUKE 20

Verse 46: *Beware of the teachers of the law. They like to walk around in flowing robes and love to be greeted in the marketplaces and have the most important seats in the synagogues and the places of honor at banquets.*

The teachers of the law and elders questioned Jesus about His authority. He answered by asking whether John's baptism was from heaven or men. They were unable to answer His question and left. Jesus taught His followers the parable of the tenants. The tenants, like His followers, would eventually be accountable for their actions. When spies questioned him about taxes, He told them to give to Caesar what was Caesar's and to God what is God's. The Sadducees asked Him about marriage after the resurrection. Jesus told them that there is no marriage in heaven. He also answered that He did not come from David, because David called Him Lord. He warned His followers about the teachers of the law.

LUKE 21

Verse 28: *When these things begin to take place, stand up and lift up your heads, because your redemption is drawing near.*

Jesus praised a widow who gave two small coins for her offering noting that, unlike the others, she gave all that she owned. He was questioned about the end of the age and explained there will be false Christs, warfare, earthquakes, famine, and fearful events. He warned that His believers would be persecuted but that they would gain life by standing firm. He told them that it would be dreadful in those days and that the Son of Man would come in power and glory. He warned them to be on the watch, because the day will come without warning.

LUKE 22

Verse 46: *"Why are you sleeping?" he asked them. "Get up and pray so that you will not fall into temptation."*

Judas, with Satan's intervention, agreed to betray Jesus to the chief priests and temple guard. Jesus told His disciples to prepare the Passover feast in a large upper room. He offered communion and then admonished them for arguing over who was the greatest. He instructed that the greatest would be the best servants. He told Peter he would deny Him that evening. On the Mount of Olives, Jesus prayed, asking His Father to take His cup if He was willing.

He criticized His disciples for falling asleep and told them to pray not to fall into temptation. Men that Judas led to Him then arrested Jesus. One of the disciples used his sword to cut off an ear of one of the men, but Jesus stopped him and healed the ear. Peter followed them and later disowned Jesus three times and then wept. The guards mocked Jesus and then He was led to the chief priests and teachers of the law. They convicted Him of blasphemy for claiming that He was the Son of God.

LUKE 23

Verse 47: *The centurion, seeing what had happened, praised God and said, "Surely this was a righteous man".*

Jesus was taken to Pilate who found He committed no crime, but sent Him on to Herod who questioned Him and returned Him to Pilate. Pilate met with the chief priests and rulers and they insisted that Jesus be crucified instead of the criminal Barabbas. Two other men were crucified next to Him and Jesus asked God to forgive the people who were crucifying Him. His cross bore the inscription "King of the Jews." Jesus committed His spirit into His Father's hands and died. He was buried in a sealed tomb.

LUKE 24

Verse 39: *Look at my hands and my feet. It is I myself! Touch me and see; a ghost does not have flesh and bones, as you see I have.*

Three days later, the women came to the tomb and found it was opened. Two angels announced to them He had risen. They told the disciples who did not believe them. Peter, however, ran to the tomb to discover that He had risen indeed. Jesus appeared to two men on the road to Emmaus and then to His disciples. Jesus ascended into heaven and the disciples praised God.

Chapter 43

JOHN

JOHN 1

Verse 29: The next day John saw Jesus coming toward him and said, "Look, the Lamb of God, who takes away the sin of the world!"

John the Baptist was sent to be a witness to the Word becoming flesh in Jesus Christ. He denied being Christ but indicated that he was sent to prepare the way for Him. He baptized believers with water but foretold of the coming of Christ. John recognized Jesus as the Christ because the Spirit of the Lord came from heaven and remained on Him. Jesus chose His first disciples: John, Simon Peter, and Andrew. Jesus called Philip and Nathanael as disciples on His way to Galilee. They all believed that Jesus was the Messiah.

JOHN 2

Verse 24: But Jesus would not entrust himself to them, for he knew all men.

Jesus and His disciples attended a wedding where the host ran out of wine. His mother told Him of this, but Jesus responded that His time had not yet come. Nevertheless, He proceeded to perform His first miracle—turning water into wine. Jesus then went to Capernaum and then Jerusalem where He cleared the Temple that was being used as a marketplace. The Jews demanded a miraculous sign from Jesus, who responded that if they destroyed the Temple, He would raise it again in three days. They challenged Him, saying that it took 46 years to build the Temple (the Temple that Jesus was alluding to was His own body!). Jesus proceeded to perform a number of miracles.

JOHN 3

Verse 17: *For God did not send his Son into the world to condemn the world, but to save the world through him.*

A Pharisee named Nicodemus approached Jesus at night telling Him that He must have come from God because of the miracles He performed. Jesus replied by telling him that no one could see the kingdom of God without being born again. Jesus explained the way to God is through Him—the Son of Man. He explained His purpose on earth—to save the world. Jesus and His disciples went to the countryside and baptized new believers near where John the Baptist was also baptizing people. When John the Baptist learned this, he was pleased. He told the gatherers that whoever believes in Jesus—the Son, will have eternal life.

JOHN 4

Verse 14: *...but whoever drinks the water I give him will never thirst. Indeed, the water I give him will become in him a spring of water welling up to eternal life.*

Jesus passed through Samaria on His way back from Judea and sat down by Jacob's well. He asked a Samaritan woman for a drink, but she replied she was Samaritan, and Jews did not associate with Samaritans. He explained He could offer her living water meaning eternal life. Jesus told her that she had five husbands, and the woman thought He was a prophet because He was right. He identified Himself as the Messiah and told her to worship the Father in spirit and truth. The disciples joined Jesus and the woman left her water jug and went into town. The disciples encouraged Jesus to eat, but He explained that His food is to do the will of the Father who sent Him. The Samaritan woman returned with a crowd, and they all became believers. Later, Jesus arrived in Galilee and a royal official from Capernaum pleaded with Jesus to save his dying son. Jesus told him that his son would live, and the boy was well. This was the second miraculous sign Jesus performed.

JOHN 5

Verse 24: *I tell you the truth, whoever hears my word and believes him who sent me has eternal life and will not be condemned; he has crossed over from death to life.*

Jesus went to Jerusalem where he healed an invalid on the Sabbath. He later instructed him to stop sinning or something worse could happen to him. The man went and told the Jews Jesus had healed him. The Jewish officials criticized Jesus for working on the Sabbath and were further outraged when Jesus told them that His Father (God) also worked on the Sabbath. Jesus explained that the Father has entrusted all judgment to the Son and warned that he who does not honor the Son does not honor the Father; the way to eternal life is through the Son. He offered testimony from John the Baptist and from the Father Himself. He encouraged the people to believe in Him and told them Moses wrote about Him—but He knew they would not believe.

JOHN 6

Verse 57: *Just as the living Father sent me and I live because of the Father, so the one who feeds on me will live because of me.*

Jesus saw a large crowd gathering at the far shore of the Sea of Galilee. He asked Philip, His disciple, how He could feed such a large group of people. Philip responded that eight month's wages would not buy enough bread to even give each person one bite. Andrew told Jesus that one boy had five small loaves and two fish. Jesus gave thanks for the food and had the disciples distribute it. At the conclusion of the meal, they gathered twelve baskets of leftovers. The people were amazed by the miracle. The disciples set off in a boat and Jesus approached them walking on the water. Jesus explained to those gathered the next day that they should believe the one that God had sent rather than the miracles they had seen. He explained that He is the bread of life, and to believe in Him and not go hungry. He offered eternal life to those who believed in Him. The Jews began to grumble at this and publicly scoffed at the concept that He was the Messiah. He explained that His flesh is bread, which He would give up for the life of the world. The Jews took Him literally and did not understand or accept His explanation. Many turned away, but the twelve disciples remained. Jesus accepted them but warned that one of them (Judas Iscariot) would betray Him.

JOHN 7

Verse 15: *The Jews were amazed and asked, "How did this man get such learning without having studied?"*

Jesus' brothers tried to convince Him to go to Judea for the Feast of the Tabernacles, but He knew that many Jews were conspiring to kill Him and it was not yet His time. He did go to the Feast later and began teaching at the Temple courts. He told the people that His teaching is from the One who sent Him and to stop judging based upon appearances alone. The Pharisees attempted to have Jesus arrested, but they were unsuccessful. Many people had a hard time believing that Jesus was the Christ because He came from Galilee.

JOHN 8

Verse 58: *"I tell you the truth," Jesus answered, "before Abraham was born, I am!"*

Jesus was questioned about whether an adulterous woman should be stoned based upon the Law of Moses. He replied that if any of them were without sin that they should throw the first stone. After everyone left, He told the woman to go and leave her life of sin. The Pharisees again challenged Jesus claiming that because He appeared as His own witness His testimony was invalid. Jesus explained He could not be judged by human standards and His Father supported His testimony. He explained He will go away, but they cannot follow. The Jews were confused and did not understand Jesus' teachings. He explained to His disciples that if they believe His teachings then they would know the truth, and the truth would set them free. The Jews claimed to love the Father, but Jesus explained that if they truly loved the Father, they would love Him too. The Jews told Jesus He was demon-possessed. Jesus explained that all glory goes to the Father and He was there to glorify Him. Jesus told them He existed before even Abraham was born, referring to Himself as the "I am." At this the Jews threw stones at Him, believing Him to be speaking heresy.

JOHN 9

Verse 5: *While I am in the world, I am the light of the world.*

Jesus saw a man blind from birth and His disciples asked Him whether the man or his parents sinned. He explained that the man was blind so that the work of God could be displayed.

He spat on the ground and rubbed mud over the man's eyes and told him to wash in the Pool of Siloam. He did so and was able to see for the first time in his life. The Pharisees learned of this and were angered that Jesus again ignored the Sabbath. The man proclaimed that Jesus was a prophet. His parents were questioned, but denied any knowledge of how their son's sight was restored for fear of being put out of the synagogue. The man testified that Jesus gave him sight and that this had to have come from God Himself, but the Pharisees were too stubborn to listen. Jesus noted that He had come to this world so that the blind could see and so those who could see would become blind. He explained to some Pharisees that they claimed they could see, and therefore they were guilty of sin for not believing.

JOHN 10

Verse 27: *My sheep listen to my voice, I know them, and they follow me.*

Jesus told His followers a parable about a shepherd and his sheep in the sheep pen. When they did not understand the message, He explained He was the gate, and if they entered through the gate they would be saved. He noted He was also the good shepherd and the good shepherd lays down his life for the sheep. Unlike a hired hand, the shepherd has an interest in the life and welfare of his sheep. The Jews asked Jesus to tell them plainly if He was the Christ. Jesus answered them that He did tell them, but they did not listen. He explained that He could give His sheep eternal life because of His Father. At this, the Jews accused Jesus of blasphemy and threw stones at Him. Jesus returned to the Jordan and many others became believers.

JOHN 11

Verse 27: *"Yes, Lord," she told him, "I believe that you are the Christ, the Son of God, who was to come into the world."*

Lazarus, who was the brother of Mary and Martha, and Jesus' friend, became sick. Jesus heard about this and proclaimed that Lazarus would not die because God's Son would be glorified through the event. Despite the disciples' protest, Jesus insisted that they return to Judea to heal Lazarus, whom Jesus knew had died several days earlier. When they arrived, Lazarus had been dead and placed in a tomb for four days. Martha approached Jesus telling Him that if He had been there, Lazarus would not have died, but also indicating that she knew that Jesus could raise him. He replied that anyone who believes in Him lives even if he dies. Mary went to Jesus, who was deeply moved. Jesus asked that the stone in front of the tomb be removed.

There was some protest because they thought it would smell, but Jesus insisted. Jesus prayed to the Father and then commanded Lazarus to come out. Lazarus walked out in his grave clothes. The Jews who witnessed this miracle, but did not believe in Jesus, reported these events to the Pharisees. The Sanhedrin met and plotted to kill Jesus because they were afraid that the Romans would take away their land if they learned of Jesus. Jesus withdrew to Ephraim, a village near the desert, to remove Himself from public view.

John 12

Verse 25: *I tell you the truth, unless a kernel of wheat falls to the ground and dies, it remains only a single seed. But if it dies, it produces many seeds.*

Jesus visited Mary and Martha (Lazarus' sisters) in Bethany. Mary took expensive perfume and rubbed His feet with it and wiped His feet with her hair. Judas objected that the money for the perfume should have been used for the poor. Jesus admonished him, saying that the perfume was for His burial, and He would not be with them long. A large crowd of Jews conspired against Jesus and Lazarus, because the miracle of raising Lazarus had converted many Jews. The next day Jesus made His triumphal entry into Jerusalem, riding on a donkey (as was foretold by the Old Testament prophet Zechariah). Many people waved palm branches, celebrating His arrival. The Pharisees were distraught with this event. Jesus publicly prayed concerning His death and the Lord answered Him. He explained that the voice was for the benefit of the people present, and said He was the Light, but many continued not to believe. Jesus told the people that He did not come to judge the world, but to save it. He once again explained that His purpose was that of the Father's.

John 13

Verse 34: *A new command I give you: Love one another. As I have loved you, so you must love one another.*

Jesus knew of His fate, and of Judas' betrayal. Nevertheless, He continued to be a servant to His disciples, washing their feet at the Passover meal. He explained He did this as an example, noting that no servant is greater than his master. Jesus went on to predict His betrayal and signaled that it was Judas who would betray Him. He commanded the disciples to love one another so that all men would know they were His disciples. Jesus explained that where He was going they could not follow. Peter said that he would lay down his life for Jesus. Jesus challenged him, predicting that Peter would deny Him three times before the rooster crowed.

JOHN 14

Verse 3: *And if I go to prepare a place for you, I will come back and take you to be with me that you also may be where I am.*

Jesus comforted His disciples, telling them He is going ahead of them to prepare a place for them. He once again explained that He is the way (to eternal life), and the truth, and the life. Phillip asked to see the Father, but Jesus explained that anyone who has seen Him has seen the Father. He explained He would be with them, even after He leaves the earth. He told them if they obey His teachings that His Father would love them. He told them not to be troubled or afraid.

JOHN 15

Verse 26: *When the Counselor comes, whom I will send to you from the Father, the Spirit of truth who goes out from the Father, he will testify about me.*

While teaching His disciples, Jesus compared himself to a vine. He stated that His Father is the gardener and the people are the branches, capable of bearing much fruit if they remain attached to the vine. He told His disciples to obey His commands and to love one another. He said "…Greater love has no one than this, that he lay down his life for his friends (verse 13)." He explained that the disciples are His friends, not His servants. He warned His disciples that many people would hate them, just as they hate Him, but that the disciples need to do the work of the Father. He told them about the coming of the Holy Spirit.

JOHN 16

Verse 13: *But when the Spirit of truth comes, he will guide you into all truth. He will not speak on his own; he will speak only what he hears, and he will tell you what is yet to come.*

Jesus warned the disciples that the Jews would persecute them after He is gone. He explained that it is good that He is going away because it will allow them to have eternal life. He told them the Spirit of truth would guide them. The disciples still did not understand, so He explained they would grieve His death, but their grief will turn to joy when they see Him again. Jesus was speaking in plain language and the disciples finally understood what He was saying and acknowledged that Jesus came from God.

JOHN 17

Verse 15: *My prayer is not that you take them out of the world but that you protect them from the evil one.*

Jesus prayed to the Father, asking that His sacrifice would glorify God and lead to eternal life for all believers. Jesus then prayed for His disciples, for protection and sanctification. He then prayed for all believers, asking that they be given glory, so the world would believe that the Father had sent Him. He acknowledged to God that He had made Him known to all believers.

JOHN 18

Verse 33: *Pilate then went back inside the palace, summoned Jesus and asked him, "Are you the king of the Jews?"*

Jesus and His disciples crossed the Kidron Valley. Judas, knowing where they were, led a detachment of soldiers and Pharisees to them. Jesus told the men to leave the disciples alone, but Simon Peter attacked a servant of the high priest, cutting off his ear. Jesus told him to put his sword away, indicating that He needed to fulfill His mission. Jesus was then taken away to Annas, the father-in-law of the high priest. When questioned, Peter denied he was a disciple of Jesus. The high priest questioned Jesus and then sent Him to Caiaphas, the high priest. Peter denied that he knew Jesus a second and a third time and the rooster crowed. Jesus was then brought before the Roman governor, Pilate, who told the Jews to judge Him by their own law. The Jews persisted they did not have the right to execute anyone, so Pilate questioned Jesus himself. He returned to the Jews and indicated that he had no basis for a charge against Jesus, but offered them a choice of releasing Jesus or the criminal Barabbas, according to their custom of releasing one prisoner at Passover.

JOHN 19

Verse 28: *Later, knowing that all was now completed, and so that the Scripture would be fulfilled, Jesus said, "I am thirsty."*

Pilate had Jesus flogged and the soldiers mocked Him. Pilate attempted to release Jesus, but the Jews insisted He be crucified, threatening to report Pilate to Caesar. Jesus was taken, carrying His own cross, to Golgotha where He was crucified. Pilate fashioned a sign that read: "Jesus of Nazareth, The King of the Jews." The soldiers cast lots for Jesus' clothing. Jesus' mother and aunt, Mary the wife of Clopas, and Mary Magdalene stood by the cross. He gave the care of His mother to John, His disciple. After receiving a drink from a jar of wine vinegar, He announced, "It is finished," bowed His head, and died. One of the soldiers pierced Jesus' side with a spear, confirming that He was dead. Nicodemus and Joseph of Arimathea buried Jesus in a nearby tomb.

JOHN 20

Verse 31: *But these are written that you may believe that Jesus is the Christ, the Son of God, and that by believing you may have life in his name.*

Mary Magdalene went to the tomb on Sunday and found that the stone covering the tomb had been moved and the tomb was empty. She reported this to Peter, who ran to the tomb with another disciple and was surprised the tomb was indeed empty. The disciples returned to their homes, but Mary stayed outside the tomb weeping. Jesus appeared to her and told her to tell the others of His resurrection. He later appeared to the disciples proclaiming: "Peace be with you" (verse 21). Thomas was not with them and was not convinced until a week later when Jesus reappeared.

JOHN 21

Verse 25: *Jesus did many other things as well. If every one of them were written down, I suppose that even the whole world would not have room for the books that would be written.*

Jesus appeared to His disciples again by the Sea of Tiberias. Peter and some of the other disciples were fishing but caught no fish. Jesus instructed them to throw out the net again, and the net was filled with fish. Jesus told them to bring the fish to Him. They ate together, then Jesus reinstated Peter, asking him three times if he loved Jesus. Peter was told he would be a martyr for Christ in the future. Peter asked about John, but was told that it was not his concern. John wrote that Jesus did many other miracles while He was on earth beyond what was recorded.

Chapter 44

SYNOPTIC GOSPEL

PREAMBLE TO THE BIRTH OF JOHN THE BAPTIST (LUKE 1)

Zechariah was a priest when Herod was king of Judea. During his ceremonial duties, the angel Gabriel appeared to him and told him that he and his wife Elizabeth would have a son and they would name him John. The angel further instructed him that his son would prepare the way for the Savior who would follow. Zechariah questioned the angel because both he and his wife were very old and had been unable to have children. Because he doubted the angel, Zechariah was made mute until the birth of his son.

PREAMBLE TO THE BIRTH OF JESUS CHRIST (MATTHEW 1, LUKE 1)

Six months later, the angel Gabriel visited Mary, a virgin who was pledged to be married to a man named Joseph. The angel addressed Mary as one who was highly favored, and informed her that she would conceive a Son by the Holy Spirit. Mary was at first troubled but agreed to serve the Lord. Joseph discovered Mary was pregnant and offered to quietly divorce her. Then an angel of the Lord appeared to him and explained that the Holy Spirit conceived her Child. Joseph was instructed to name Him Jesus and, by fulfilling prophesy, He would be known as Immanuel (God with us) and Son of the Most High.

THE BIRTH OF JOHN THE BAPTIST (LUKE 1)

Mary went to visit Elizabeth, and when she greeted her, the baby leapt in Elizabeth's womb. Mary stayed with Elizabeth about three months. The baby was born, and the relatives and neighbors suggested the baby be named after his father, Zechariah. Elizabeth insisted the child be named John, and Zechariah independently named him John and was no longer mute. He praised the Lord, and prophesied that John would be the prophet of the Most High and would prepare the way for the Lord. John grew and became strong in spirit, living alone in the desert.

THE BIRTH OF JESUS CHRIST (MATTHEW 1, LUKE 2)

Caesar Augustus, the emperor of Rome at the time, mandated that all people return to their ancestral homes to be taxed. Joseph's lineage included Abraham, Judah, and King David and therefore he was required to travel to Bethlehem, the City of David. Mary was near the end of her pregnancy, and when they arrived, they were unable to find a place to stay and settled in a manger on the outskirts of town. That night, the Baby was born. An angel appeared to shepherds who were watching their flocks nearby, and announced the birth of Jesus. The shepherds, at first afraid, went to Bethlehem to witness the miracle. When Jesus was eight days old He was circumcised and given His name. After their time of purification, Mary and Joseph traveled to Jerusalem and presented Jesus in the temple. There Simeon recognized Him as the Savior.

THE EARLY DAYS OF JESUS (MATTHEW 2, LUKE 2)

Magi from the east traveled to Jerusalem, asking about the birth of the King of the Jews because they had seen His star. Herod, the king, instructed the Magi to find the child and return with news of His whereabouts. The Magi followed the star to find Jesus at His house, and presented Him with gifts. After being warned of Herod's intentions in a dream, the Magi left in a different direction and did not return to Herod.

An angel appeared to Joseph and warned him of Herod's intention to kill Jesus. Joseph and Mary escaped with the child to Egypt that night. Herod, unaware that they escaped, gave orders to kill all male children who were two years old and younger who lived in the vicinity of Bethlehem.

Years later, Herod died and an angel instructed Joseph to return with his family to Israel. They settled in the town of Nazareth, where Joseph worked as a carpenter. When Jesus was twelve years old, He went with His family to Jerusalem to celebrate the Passover. At the end of the feast, Jesus was left behind. Mary and Joseph found him sitting among the teachers in the temple, and everyone was amazed by His knowledge. He explained to Joseph and Mary that He had to be in his Father's house, indicating His recognition of His duties, even as a child.

JOHN THE BAPTIST PREPARES THE WAY (MATTHEW 3, MARK 1, LUKE 3, JOHN 1)

John lived in the Desert of Judea. He began baptizing sinners in the Jordan River. He preached to the people and warned them of the hypocrisy of the religious groups known as the Pharisees and the Sadducees. He spoke of the coming of Jesus, indicating that he was not worthy to even carry His sandals. John denied he was Christ and instructed the people to open their hearts to His coming.

Jesus came to the Jordan to be baptized by John. John told Jesus he was not worthy to baptize Him, but Jesus insisted. Following the baptism, the Spirit descended from Heaven in the form of a dove, and a voice proclaimed: "You are my Son, whom I love; with you I am well pleased." (Mark 1:11, Luke 3:22) John the Baptist was imprisoned soon after this.

JESUS' TEMPTATION (MATTHEW 4, MARK 1, LUKE 4)

The Spirit led Jesus into the desert where Satan tempted him. After fasting for forty days, the devil tempted Him by instructing Him to turn a stone into bread. Jesus replied that "Man does not live by bread alone." Satan then tempted Him to jump from a high place and trust the angels to rescue Him. Jesus replied that you should not put God to the test. Finally, the devil took Him to a high mountaintop and offered command of all that could be seen if He would bow down to him. Jesus rebuked the devil, saying you should only worship God. Satan then left, and Jesus began his ministry.

EARLY MINISTRY (MATTHEW 14, MARK 6, LUKE 4)

Jesus taught in many synagogues. When He first went to the synagogue in Nazareth, He amazed those in attendance with His knowledge. Soon, however, the people were angered with Jesus, who claimed to be the Savior, and attempted to drive Him out of town. Jesus left, recognizing that a prophet is without honor in his own country. He warned the people to repent for the Kingdom of Heaven is near.

THE TWELVE DISCIPLES (MATTHEW 4, MARK 1, 2, 3, LUKE 5, JOHN 1)

Jesus went to Galilee, and began to choose His disciples. He first called Simon (Peter) and his brother Andrew, asking them to give up their trade as fishermen to become fishers of men. He then called Zebedee's two sons, James and John, who were also fishermen, to join them. He then called Philip and Nathaniel (Bartholomew) who questioned if anything good could come from Nazareth. Nathaniel was quickly won over by Jesus after initially questioning Him. The other disciples included Levi (Matthew), who was a tax collector, Thomas, James, Simon the Zealot, Judas son of James, and Judas Iscariot (the traitor).

The Pharisees questioned Jesus regarding His selection of Levi, because tax collectors were considered to be the worst sinners in that time. Jesus replied that He did not come to call the righteous, but the sinners to repentance.

THE MIRACLES

At least thirty miracles are attributed to Jesus in the Gospels. The majority of these involved healing of the sick, crippled, demon-possessed, and blind. On several occasions He performed miracles of nature. In most of the miracles Jesus only asked that the receiver believe. Jesus' first miracle was turning water into wine (John 2). On one occasion, Jesus healed ten men with leprosy, but only one man returned to thank Him (Luke 17).

On another occasion, Jesus was with His disciples in a boat when a storm approached. The disciples panicked, but Jesus calmed the storm and then instructed His disciples to have more faith (Matthew 8, Mark 4, Luke 8). He taught the same lesson when He fed 5,000 men and at least as many women and children with only five loaves of bread and two fish (Matthew 14, Mark 6, Luke 9, John 6). He later repeated this feat for 4,000 (Matthew 15, Mark 8).

That same evening, He walked on the water and Peter followed Him until he began to sink when he lost his faith (Matthew 14, Mark 6). Jesus raised three individuals from death, not including His own resurrection (Matthew 9, Mark 5, Luke 7, 8, John 4, 11).

JESUS THE TEACHER (MATTHEW 5-7, LUKE 6, 11, JOHN 3, 8, 12 14-16)

Large crowds followed Jesus as He instructed His disciples and the people on a variety of things. Beginning with the Sermon on the Mount, in which He made several declarations of blessedness and reinforced the Commandments, Jesus wandered throughout the country teaching. He made His purpose on earth very clear and emphasized that He was the way to the Father

(John 3, 5, 8, 12). He promised to prepare a place for the Disciples in Heaven (John 14). His lessons involved loving others, unselfishness, and humility.

He emphasized that not only is the act a sin, but merely thinking of it is a sin as well. He instructed His people to "turn the other cheek," to "love their enemy," and to give to the needy in secret. He taught them how to pray and offered the Lord's Prayer:

Our Father in heaven, hallowed be your name.
Your kingdom come, your will be done.
On earth as it is in Heaven.
Give us this day our daily bread.
Forgive us our sins, as we forgive those who have sinned against us.
And lead us not into temptation, but deliver us from evil.
For thine is the kingdom and the power and the glory forever.

He further taught the concept of not collecting treasures on earth, putting faith in the Lord, and not judging others. The Golden Rule, to treat others as you would like to be treated yourself, was also taught. He visited the home of Martha and Mary where he praised Mary for staying and listening to his teachings while Martha was distracted with food preparation (Luke 10). Jesus taught many people of all ages and backgrounds.

JESUS' PARABLES

Jesus also taught extensively with the use of parables. Many of these had a hidden meaning that the disciples did not understand until Jesus explained it to them. Some of the following parables were taught:

Builders (Matthew 7, Luke 6): Jesus teaches that the person who puts His words into practice is like the builder who builds his house on rock and not sand.

New Wine in Old Wineskins (Matthew 9, Mark 2, Luke 5): Jesus compares the newness of faith to pouring new wine into old wineskins. The wineskins will burst if not expandable when new.

Sower of Seeds (Matthew 13, Mark 4, Luke 8): This parable describes seeds that are scattered: (1) on the path where the birds eat them (2) on rocky places, where they cannot take root (3) among thorns which grow up and choke the plants (4) in good soil where it produces a hundred fold. This is analogous to (1) one who hears but does not accept the message and the evil one snatches it away (2) one who accepts the message but does not practice it (3) one who listens but does not make it a priority (4) one who hears and practices it.

Parables regarding the Kingdom of Heaven (Matthew 14, 20, Mark 4, Luke 13, John 10): The kingdom of heaven is compared to the mustard seed, the smallest of all seeds, yet the largest of all garden plants. It is also compared to yeast in dough. The kingdom of heaven is also compared to hidden treasure or fine pearls. The parable of the net is used as an illustration and the good fish are kept, while the bad ones thrown away. He refers to Himself as the Good Shepherd on more than one occasion.

Jesus tells another parable about workers in a vineyard. In this story, workers are hired to work in a vineyard for a set wage. Much later in the day, the same wage is offered to other workers to work only a small portion of the day that remained. When the original workers complain, the landowner explains that he paid what he originally promised and indicates that the last will be first and the first will be last—all are treated the same in Heaven.

Lost Sheep (Matthew 18, Luke 15): Jesus compares the Lord's watch over us like the shepherd who has lost a sheep.

Unmerciful Servant (Matthew 18): This parable compares the forgiveness of sin to the king who wants to settle accounts with his servants. He forgave a large debt owed to him by one of his servants, who in turn did not forgive a much smaller debt from someone else. When the king learned of this, he imprisoned the servant and made him pay back all he originally owed.

Talents/Minas (Matthew 25, Luke 19): A man was going on a journey and left property to his servants for safekeeping while he was gone. He gave one servant five talents who invested it wisely and earned five more talents before the man returned. He gave a second servant two talents, and he also earned two more. He gave a third servant one talent and he buried it in a hole while his master was away. The man returned and praised the two servants who made profits, but scolded the one who did not make an effort with what he was given. Faith in God involves making investments.

Good Samaritan (Luke 10): A man was traveling from Jerusalem to Jericho and was robbed and left half dead. A priest passed by and walked to the other side. A Levite came by and did the same. Finally, a Samaritan took care of the man and boarded him at an Inn until he recovered. Jesus instructed His followers to be good neighbors.

Prodigal Son (Luke 15): A man divided his estate between his two sons. The younger son sold all that he had, squandered the money, and became penniless. The older son stayed and worked in the fields. The younger son finally came to his senses and returned, asking for forgiveness. The father honored the younger son, despite the protests of the older son. Jesus, in telling the parable, implied the importance of repentance of sinners and the everlasting love of the Heavenly Father.

Unjust Steward (Luke 16): An accountant for a rich man was about to be fired for mismanaging funds. He called in the rich man's debtors and offered to reduce the amount they owed so that he could receive favors from these men in the future. The rich man learned about the plan and commended the accountant for his shrewdness. People of the world are much better at worldly things than people belonging to God.

OTHER ACTIVITIES OF JESUS (MATTHEW 8, LUKE 6, 7, JOHN 2, 5, 11)

Jesus praised the work of John, who was beheaded by Herod. He continued to counter the challenges of the Pharisees and Sadducees throughout this time. They questioned some of Jesus' teachings and actions, such as when He and his disciples picked grain on the Sabbath. He explained that the Son of Man is the Lord of the Sabbath. He explained further that it is OK to do good things on the Sabbath. Nevertheless, these two groups plotted to kill Jesus.

EVENTS LEADING TO THE CAPTURE OF JESUS (MATTHEW 16-17, MARK 9, 14, LUKE 9, 22, JOHN 18)

Jesus explained to His disciples that He must return to Jerusalem and suffer many things. He predicted His death, but Peter and others pleaded with Him to no avail. He encouraged them to take up the cross after His death. He then took Peter, James, and John to a high mountain where He was transfigured (to His glorified state). Moses and the prophet Elijah talked with Jesus, and a cloud appeared and the same words uttered to Jesus during His baptism (This is my son, whom I love, and am pleased) were heard. The disciples were frightened, but were calmed by Jesus. Judas went to the priests and brokered a deal for thirty silver coins in order to betray Jesus.

TRIUMPHAL ENTRY (MATTHEW 21, MARK 11, LUKE 19, JOHN 12)

Jesus entered Jerusalem on a donkey, fulfilling scripture. Palm branches lined the way and the people rejoiced.

JESUS IS ANOINTED AT BETHANY (MATTHEW 26, MARK 14, LUKE 7, JOHN 12)

Mary, the sister of Martha and Lazarus, poured expensive perfume on Jesus' head two days prior to His capture. When questioned why she should waste the perfume that could have been sold in order to give money to the poor, Jesus defended Mary, saying she had done a beautiful thing, and helped prepare Him for his burial.

THE LAST SUPPER (MATTHEW 26, MARK 14, LUKE 22, JOHN 13)

Jesus instructed His disciples to find the upper room where they would eat together. He predicted His betrayal by one of His disciples. Jesus washed the disciples' feet, noting that He was a servant. Jesus broke bread, which He indicated symbolized His body, ate it and then poured wine, indicating that this symbolized His blood, which He would sacrifice for their sins. He then predicts Peter's denial (three times before the rooster crows).

GETHSEMANE (MATTHEW 26, MARK 14, LUKE 22, JOHN 17)

Jesus retired with His disciples to Gethsemane. He asked His disciples to stay awake while He prayed, but they quickly fell asleep. He prayed to His Father three times, and each time the disciples failed to stay awake. Judas arrived and identified Jesus to the Romans. Jesus was arrested and led away to the Sanhedrin.

THE TRIAL (MATTHEW 26-27, MARK 14, 15, LUKE 22, 23, JOHN 18)

Jesus is taken before the Sanhedrin for trial. When questioned, He confirmed that He was the Son of God, and this was enough for the nonbelievers to convict Him. Peter was questioned on three separate occasions whether he was with Jesus, and each time he denied it. A rooster then crowed, fulfilling Jesus' prophesy.

Judas saw that Jesus was condemned, was seized with remorse, and hanged himself. The money he was given was used to purchase a burial place for foreigners, the potter's field.

Jesus was brought in front of Pontius Pilate, the Roman governor, who could not find Him guilty of violating any law. He left it up to the people to decide if he should convict Jesus or a ruthless criminal named Barabbas. The people chose Jesus, and Pilate washed his hands of the matter.

THE CRUCIFIXION (MATTHEW 27, MARK 15, LUKE 23, JOHN 19)

Jesus was forced to carry His own cross to Golgotha. The authorities wrote on His cross "This is Jesus, the King of the Jews." Two robbers were crucified with Him. He was the subject of insults and struck in the head and chest. Jesus died later that night, uttering "My God, My God, why have you forsaken me?" His last words were "Father, into your hands I commit my spirit." The curtain in the temple was torn from top to bottom and the bodies of the dead were raised back to life. Jesus was buried in a tomb sealed with a stone.

THE RESURRECTION (MATTHEW 28, MARK 16, LUKE 24; JOHN 20)

Mary Magdalene and other women were the first to discover that Jesus had risen, three days after His crucifixion. An angel appeared, and calmed the frighten women. Jesus made several other appearances—to two believers on the walk to Emmaus, to the disciples on several occasions, and to others (including "doubting" Thomas). Jesus later appeared to the eleven remaining disciples, giving them the Great Commission—to spread the Word. Jesus then ascended into Heaven.

Paul's Life, Writings, and Letters

Chapter 45

ACTS

ACTS 1

Verse 8: *But you will receive power when the Holy Spirit comes on you; and you will be my witnesses in Jerusalem, and in all Judea and Samaria, and to the ends of the earth.*

Jesus appeared to the apostles and others for forty days after His resurrection. He instructed them to stay in Jerusalem until the gift of the Holy Spirit was given. The disciples asked Him when He would establish His kingdom. He would not give a date for this but said it was for God to determine. When He ascended, two angels told His followers that Jesus would return the same way He left. Peter and the other apostles chose Mathias (over Barsabbas) to replace Judas (who betrayed the Lord and took his own life in the Field of Blood).

ACTS 2

Verse 38: *Peter replied, "Repent and be baptized, every one of you, in the name of Jesus Christ for the forgiveness of your sins. And you will receive the gift of the Holy Spirit."*

The Holy Spirit filled the apostles and other believers at Pentecost, and they spoke of the wonders of God to the crowd. The people that were gathered spoke a variety of different languages, but each person understood the disciples in his own language. Some of the crowd dismissed this, saying that the believers were drunk, but Peter told the crowd that this event was foretold in Scripture. Peter also reminded them that David had foretold of the resurrection of Christ. He told the crowd that God had made Jesus, whom they crucified, both Lord and Christ. He encouraged them to believe and be baptized, and 3,000 responded. The believers lived together and shared their resources, breaking bread together and witnessing the apostles' miracles and the Lord added to their numbers daily.

ACTS 3

Verse 15: *You killed the author of life but God raised him from the dead. We are witnesses of this.*

Peter healed a crippled beggar at the Temple gates of Jerusalem. The man praised God, and the people were amazed. Peter told the onlookers that the beggar was healed by the power of Jesus Christ. He told the crowd to repent and turn from their wicked ways.

ACTS 4

Verse 32: *All the believers were one in heart and mind. No one claimed that any of his possessions was his own, but they shared everything they had.*

The priests brought Peter and John in front of the Sanhedrin, accusing them of blasphemy. Before they were able to seize them, however, the number of believers increased to 5,000. Peter told his accusers that his power comes from Jesus Christ and proclaimed Him as Lord and their only means to salvation. The leaders ordered Peter and John to cease their preaching, but the two told them that they must listen to God and not them. The priests let Peter and John go, because the people were praising God for the events that occurred. Upon their release, Peter and John praised God and the meeting place was filled with the Holy Spirit. The believers lived and thrived together, sharing all of their possessions.

ACTS 5

Verse 41: *The apostles left the Sanhedrin, rejoicing because they had been counted worthy of suffering disgrace for the Name.*

Ananias and his wife Sapphira sold a piece of property to share the proceeds with the believers. However, they kept back a portion of the money for their own use. Peter challenged them about this individually, and when they lied about their actions, both died. Great fear filled the church and everyone who heard about what happened. The apostles continued to perform miracles and they continued to meet regularly with all believers. People came from all around to be healed by the apostles and in particular, Peter. A high priest became jealous and had Peter and others jailed. That night, an angel released them and instructed them to preach the word in the temple courts. The captain of the temple guard and his officers brought the apostles before the Sanhedrin to be questioned by the high priest. The priest reminded them of the order he gave them not to preach, but Peter and the others said they must obey God. This angered the assembly, but a Pharisee named Gamaliel interceded and convinced them to let the men go. He argued that if the men were not of God, then their efforts would fail, but if they were from God, the Sanhedrin would find itself fighting against God. The believers were flogged and released, but happy to suffer for the Lord. They continued to preach the good news.

ACTS 6

Verse 6: *They presented these men to the apostles, who prayed and laid their hands on them.*

The Grecian Jews complained that their widows were being overlooked in the distribution of food, so the apostles chose seven men to take care of this task (Stephen, Philip, Procorus, Nicanor, Timon, Parmeanas, and Nicolas). Later, Stephen was brought before the Sanhedrin for blasphemy. As the group stared at Stephen, his face appeared like that of an angel.

ACTS 7

Verse 51: *You stiff-necked people, with uncircumcised hearts and ears! You are just like your fathers: You always resist the Holy Spirit.*

Stephen spoke to the crowd, recalling the story of Abraham and the covenant, his son Isaac, and Isaac's son Jacob who, in turn, became the father of the twelve patriarchs. He recounted the trials of Joseph in Egypt, concluding with the story of Moses. He then criticized his accusers for being just as stiff-necked as the Jews in the desert and resisting the Holy Spirit. He noted that they received the law but did not obey it. Stephen looked up and saw Jesus with God. When he reported this, the crowd was angered and stoned Stephen. Saul was present, and guarded the clothes of the men killing him. Before he died, Stephen asked the Lord to forgive these men.

ACTS 8

Verse 4: *Those who had been scattered preached the word wherever they went.*

Persecution of the church in Jerusalem began, with Saul initiating much of it. Believers were scattered throughout Judea and Samaria. Philip went to Samaria to preach the word and many believed and were baptized. Peter and John then went to Samaria and laid hands on the believers, and they received the Holy Spirit. An angel told Philip to go to the desert where he led an Ethiopian eunuch to the Lord. Once the eunuch was baptized, the Spirit took Philip away to Azotus, and the eunuch went on his way rejoicing.

ACTS 9

Verses 15,16: *But the LORD said to Ananias, "Go! This man is my chosen instrument to carry my name before the Gentiles and their kings and before the people of Israel. I will show him how much he must suffer for my name."*

Saul went to the high priests for permission to pursue the followers in Damascus and bring them back to Jerusalem for imprisonment. On the way to Damascus, Jesus appeared to Saul and asked him why he was persecuting Him. He temporarily blinded Saul and told him to go to the city and await further instructions. Jesus then appeared to Ananias in Damascus and told him to go to Saul to restore his sight. He had heard of Saul, and initially objected, but Jesus sternly ordered him to go. Jesus told Ananias that Saul would be expecting him. He went to the house and Saul's vision was restored. Saul was immediately filled with the Holy Spirit and began preaching with the disciples in Damascus. His behavior astounded believers and Jews alike. The Jews conspired to kill Saul, but he was rescued by his followers and escaped out of the city through an opening in the wall. Upon returning to Jerusalem, He attempted to meet with the disciples, but they were still afraid of him. Barnabas interceded and brought him to the disciples. Saul continued to openly preach the word, and the Grecian Jews conspired to kill him. With the help of the disciples, he escaped to Tarsus. Then the church throughout the region prospered and enjoyed a time of peace. Peter continued to travel and spread the word. He healed a paralytic in Lydda and raised a believer named Tabitha (Dorcas) from the dead in Joppa.

ACTS 10

Verse 45: *The circumcised believers who had come with Peter were astonished that the gift of the Holy Spirit had been poured out even on the Gentiles.*

Cornelius was a God-fearing Roman centurion who lived in Caesarea. An angel appeared to him and instructed him to send his men to Joppa and bring back Peter. Peter, who was staying with Simon the tanner, also saw a vision. Four-footed animals, reptiles, and birds were placed on a sheet and he was instructed to kill and eat them. He replied that he would not eat impure food (according to Jewish custom). The voice replied that nothing is impure that God has made clean. The Spirit then instructed him to go to meet Cornelius' messengers downstairs. The following day, Peter went to Caesarea to meet Cornelius. When he arrived he questioned Cornelius and recognized that, despite Jewish custom, the Lord intended for him to meet with a Gentile. Cornelius told Peter about his vision and Peter realized that the Lord now wished to include the Gentiles amongst believers. The Holy Spirit came on all and the new believers were baptized.

ACTS 11

Verse 17: *So if God gave them the same gift as he gave us, who believed in the LORD Jesus Christ, who was I to think that I could oppose God?*

Peter returned to Jerusalem and explained his actions to the believers who had questioned his inclusion of Gentiles. When they heard the story, they too accepted the Gentiles. Other believers, who had been scattered because of the persecution of Stephen, traveled to Phoenicia, Cyprus, and Antioch preaching the good news. Gentiles became believers there as well. Meanwhile, Barnabas visited the church in Antioch and was pleased. He then went to Tarsus to look for Saul and returned to Antioch with him, where they lived together for a year. Agabus visited Antioch and predicted a severe famine for the entire Roman world. The believers decided to send Saul and Barnabas back to Judea with their monetary gift to help the brothers there.

ACTS 12

Verse 5: *So Peter was kept in prison, but the church was earnestly praying to God for him.*

King Herod began to persecute the Christians and had James killed. When he saw this pleased the Jews, he arrested Peter. Peter was imprisoned under armed guard but was rescued by an angel and went to the house of Mary, the mother of John (Mark). Rhoda, a servant, answered the door and was surprised, as was the entire house. The next day Herod discovered what happened and executed the guards. Herod traveled to Caesarea where he accepted the praise of the people who proclaimed that he was god. The Lord struck him down on the spot, where he was eaten by worms and died. Barnabas and Saul returned from Jerusalem with John (Mark).

Acts 13

Verse 48: *When the Gentiles heard this, they were glad and honored the word of the LORD; and all who were appointed for eternal life believed.*

The Holy Spirit appeared to the leaders at Antioch including Barnabas, Simeon (Niger), Lucius, Manaen (who was with Herod), and Saul, and instructed that Barnabas and Saul be sent on a mission. They departed and began to spread the word in Cyprus. In Paphos they met a false prophet named Bar-Jesus, an attendant of the proconsul, Sergius Paulus. The proconsul sent for Saul and Barnabas over the objections of Bar-Jesus. Saul (now called Paul) accused Bar-Jesus of being the devil and blinded him, thereby converting the proconsul. Paul and Barnabas then sailed to Perga and on the Pisidian Antioch. There, Paul reminded the Jews about their ancestry and spoke of Jesus and the message of salvation. Many of the Jews were converted, and he and Barnabas were invited to return the following Sabbath. That day many more were converted, including Gentiles. However, the devout Jews were offended and expelled them from the region. They continued on to Iconium.

Acts 14

Verse 23: *Paul and Barnabas appointed elders for them in each church and, with prayer and fasting, committed them to the LORD, in whom they had put their trust.*

Paul and Barnabas preached the word at Iconium, but were opposed by the Jews. The city was divided and the two escaped before they were stoned. They traveled to Lystra, where Paul healed a cripple. The people thought that they were Zeus and Hermes, and Barnabas and Paul were distraught. Some Jews came from Antioch and Paul was stoned and left for dead. Paul recovered then went with Barnabas to Derbe where they won a large number of disciples. They appointed elders and set up churches in Lystra, Iconium, Pisidia, Pamphylia, Perga, and Attalia before returning to Antioch. In Antioch they reported their travels and their successes to the church.

ACTS 15

Verse 11: *No! We believe it is through the grace of our LORD Jesus that we are saved, just as they are.*

Some men came from Judea to Antioch and were teaching that only those who were circumcised according the custom of Moses could be saved. Paul and Barnabas strongly refuted this, and set off to Jerusalem to debate this point. In Jerusalem, Peter sided with Paul and Barnabas, as did James. They suggested that circumcision not be forced on the Gentiles, but they follow the same beliefs regarding idol worship, sexual immorality, and avoiding the meat of strangled animals. They wrote a letter to this effect and had Judas (Barsabbas) and Silas deliver the letter (along with Paul and Barnabas). The letter was well received in Antioch, and Judas and Silas returned to Jerusalem. Paul and Barnabas stayed in Antioch for a while and then decided to check on the churches they had started. They had a disagreement regarding whether to invite John (Mark) to join them. This argument resulted in them going their separate ways. Barnabas went to Cyprus with John (Mark), and Paul went to Syria and Cilicia with Silas.

ACTS 16

Verse 30: *He then brought them out and asked, "Sirs, what must I do to be saved?"*

Paul and Silas came to Lystra, where they met Timothy. Timothy's mother was Jewish and his father was Greek. He was well thought of amongst the believers, and therefore Paul invited him to join him on his journeys. To appease the Jews, Paul circumcised Timothy and became a mentor to him. They continued in their travels, preaching the Word. They came to the border of Mysia where Paul had a vision in which the Spirit of Jesus encouraged them not to go into Mysia, but instead to travel to Macedonia. They traveled to Philippi, a Roman colony and the leading city of Macedonia, and spoke to a woman named Lydia, who invited them into her home. Paul encountered a slave girl who was able to predict the future. He commanded the evil spirit to leave the girl, and it did. When the girl's owners learned what had happened, they were concerned that Paul's action would hurt them financially (as they had capitalized on this ability in the past) and had Paul and Silas arrested. They were beaten and imprisoned. Despite being carefully guarded, the two were freed by a violent earthquake. Fearing punishment for the escape of the prisoners, the jailer was about to kill himself until Paul stopped him. Paul and Silas led the jailer to salvation and they all went to the jailor's home. The next morning, the magistrates ordered that Paul and Silas be released. Paul protested that he had not even been afforded a trial (which was his right as a Roman citizen) before being imprisoned. The magistrates attempted to appease Paul and Silas and escorted them from prison.

ACTS 17

Verse 11: *Now the Bereans were of more noble character than the Thessalonians, for they received the message with great eagerness and examined the Scriptures every day to see if what Paul said was true.*

They proceeded to Thessalonica, where Paul preached in the synagogue for three Sabbaths. Some Jews were converted as well as numerous Greeks. The jealous Jews formed a lynch mob, but could not find Paul, and arrested Jason instead. Jason was later released, but Paul and Silas escaped to Berea. The Berean Jews were more receptive of the message, and many of them were converted. When the Jews at Thessalonica learned that Paul was preaching nearby, they attempted to stir up the crowd in Berea as well. Paul left for Athens where he tried to win more converts. He was disturbed by the idol worship in Athens and proposed that their altar to "an unknown god" should be for God. He converted several Greeks including Dionysius and Damaris.

ACTS 18

Verse 9: *One night the LORD spoke to Paul in a vision: "Do not be afraid; keep on speaking, do not be silent."*

Paul went to Corinth where he met a Jew named Aquila and his wife Priscilla. Silas and Timothy later joined him. The Jews persisted in their opposition, and Paul gave up on them, deciding to take the word exclusively to the Gentiles. The Lord appeared to Paul in a vision encouraging him and telling him not to worry. He worked peacefully in Corinth for a year and a half, but then was brought up on charges to the authorities by the Jews. Gallio, the proconsul of Achaia, told the Jews to settle the matter amongst themselves. The Jews then turned on Sosthenes the synagogue ruler. Paul stayed there for some time, and then left with Aquila and Priscilla for Syria. He preached the Word at Ephesus, Antioch, Galatia, and Phrygia. Meanwhile, a Jew named Apollos came to Ephesus and began to speak openly of Jesus there.

ACTS 19

Verse 15: *One day the evil spirit answered them, "Jesus I know, and I know about Paul, but who are you?"*

Paul returned to Ephesus and converted more people. He corrected some of the original teachings of Apollos who only knew to teach of John's baptism. The new believers were baptized in Jesus' name and received the Holy Spirit. God proceeded to do extraordinary miracles through Paul. Some of the Jews in Ephesus attempted to use Jesus' name to heal the demon-possessed, but were injured by the evil spirits when they did. Paul decided to return to Jerusalem. He sent Timothy and Erastus to Macedonia. Prior to his departure, a riot developed in Ephesus, largely because of a silversmith named Demetrius. He incited the riot out of concern that his business (making silver idols of Greek gods) would be affected by Paul's teachings. The city clerk quieted the crowd and encouraged the people to take up their concerns in the appropriate forum.

ACTS 20

Verse 20: *You know that I have not hesitated to preach anything that would be helpful to you but have taught you publicly and from house to house.*

After the uproar ended, Paul traveled to Macedonia and Greece. His group (which included Timothy) returned to Macedonia to avoid a Jewish plot against them, and then sailed from Philippi to Troas. Paul preached all night and actually brought a believer (Eutychus) back to life in the middle of the night. Paul and his group then sailed for Assos and Miletus, where he sent for the elders from Ephesus. When they arrived, he told them he knew that hardship and imprisonment awaited him but he intended to go on to Jerusalem. Paul gave them a farewell speech, recognizing that he would never see them again and encouraging them to go in the way of the Lord.

ACTS 21

Verse 13: *Then Paul answered, "Why are you weeping and breaking my heart? I am ready not only to be bound, but also to die in Jerusalem for the name of the LORD Jesus."*

They set sail for Cos, Rhodes, and Patara. They passed Cyprus and sailed on to Syria. After spending a week with the believers at Tyre, Paul continued on to Jerusalem (despite warnings from Spirit-filled believers). They sailed on to Ptolemais and then to Caesarea. At Caesarea,

Agabus, a prophet, warned Paul that the Jews in Jerusalem would betray him. His fellow believers attempted to dissuade Paul from continuing, but he was willing to make the sacrifice for the Lord. Paul eventually arrived at Jerusalem where he was initially welcomed. Some Jews revolted, however, and he was beaten by the Jews, and later arrested by the Roman troops. Despite a revolt by the Jews, he asked permission of the Roman commander to speak.

ACTS 22

Verse 3: *I am a Jew, born in Tarsus of Cilicia, but brought up in this city. Under Gamaliel I was thoroughly trained in the law of our fathers and was just as zealous for God as any of you are today.*

Paul proceeded to speak to the Jews in Aramaic. He told them of his own past, his conversion on the road to Damascus, his temporary blinding, and his calling. The Jews listened quietly until he told them of his ministry to the Gentiles. At that point they became riotous again. About to be flogged, Paul told the Roman commander that he was a Roman citizen, and he was therefore protected. He was released and brought before the Sanhedrin the next day.

ACTS 23

Verse 1: *Paul looked straight at the Sanhedrin and said, "My brothers, I have fulfilled my duty to God in all good conscience to this day."*

Paul told the assembly he was a Pharisee and initiated a dispute between the Sadducees and the Pharisees. The Roman commander was concerned for Paul's safety in the midst of this uproar and took him back to the barracks. The Lord appeared to him the next night and told him to be courageous and that he would testify in Rome as he had in Jerusalem. Forty Jews took an oath not to eat until they had killed Paul. They planned an ambush when he returned to address the Sanhedrin. Paul's nephew heard of the plot and warned him. He was escorted under armed guard to the Governor. The Governor kept him under guard in Herod's palace until his accusers arrived.

ACTS 24

Verse 25: *As Paul discoursed on righteousness, self-control and the judgment to come, Felix was afraid and said, "That's enough for now! You may leave. When I find it convenient, I will send for you."*

Five days later they met with the Governor and the Jews were heard. They accused Paul of being a troublemaker and inciting riots. Paul denied these charges and said he was guilty only for spreading the Good News. Felix, the governor, whose wife was a Jew, was uncomfortable with the case and deferred his decision. Festus succeeded him after two years.

Acts 25

Verse 19: *Instead, they had some points of dispute with him about their own religion and about a dead man named Jesus who Paul claimed was alive.*

When Festus succeeded Felix as governor he went to Jerusalem to hear the charges against Paul from the Jewish leaders. They wanted Paul to come to Jerusalem for a trial, because they planned to ambush him, but Festus suggested that they bring their charges to Caesarea where Paul would remain. After a week and a half, his tribunal returned to Caesarea and ordered Paul to stand before the court. He denied any wrongdoing and asked to be held accountable only to Roman law (and therefore to Caesar). Festus consulted King Agrippa, who was visiting, and he asked to hear the case himself. Festus introduced Paul, and asked that the king help to identify charges against him. Festus wanted to refer them to Caesar in Rome.

Acts 26

Verse 27: *The king is familiar with these things, and I can speak freely to him. I am convinced that none of this has escaped his notice, because it was not done in a corner. King Agrippa, do you believe the prophets? I know you do.*

Paul addressed the King. He recounted his story again of being a Pharisee, opposing the teaching of Jesus, and the miracle on the road to Damascus. He noted that he has been obedient to the Lord ever since He instructed him that day. Festus interrupted at this point and shouted to Paul that he was insane. Paul continued his defense and Agrippa asked Paul if he thought that in the short time that they spent together that he could convince him to be a Christian. The meeting ended, and Agrippa told Festus that Paul could have been set free if he had not appealed to Caesar.

Acts 27

Verse 22: *But now I urge you to keep up your courage, because not one of you will be lost; only the ship will be destroyed.*

Plans were made for Paul to go to Rome. They began their journey via ship and had a difficult time. Despite Paul's advice, Julius, the Roman centurion in charge, elected to attempt to sail on. They were caught in a storm after they left Crete, and the 276 men of the ship feared for their lives. Paul assured the men they would survive, but the ship would not, based upon a vision that he had been given. Paul urged the sailors to eat (as they had not eaten much for the previous fourteen days during the storm). Then they ran the ship aground and everyone reached land safely.

Acts 28

Verse 31: *Boldly and without hindrance he preached the kingdom of God and taught about the* Lord *Jesus Christ.*

The locals on the island of Malta welcomed them. Paul was bitten by a snake, but suffered no ill effect, which surprised the islanders. He spread the Word and put his healing hands on all the sick of the island over the next three months. Once the winter was over, they set out again for Rome in another ship. The brothers in Rome welcomed Paul. He met with them and explained the Good News to all who would listen over the next two years.

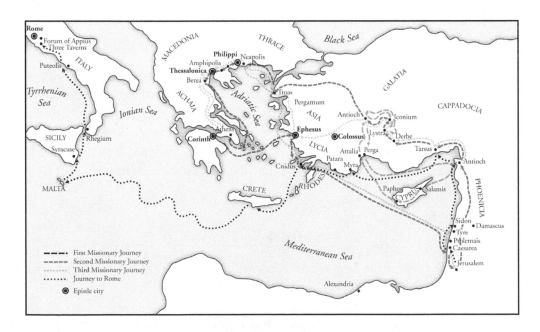

Figure 14: Paul's Missionary Journeys

Chapter 46

ROMANS

ROMANS 1

Verse 16: *I am not ashamed of the gospel, because it is the power of God for the salvation of everyone who believes, first for the Jew, then for the Gentile.*

Paul begins by introducing himself to the believers in Rome and calls himself a servant of Jesus Christ and an apostle called by Christ. He commends their faith and tells them he is not ashamed of the Gospel for it contains the power to save. He explains how men have become impure, have sinned, and also approve of others that do the same.

ROMANS 2

Verse 13: *For it is not those who hear the law who are righteous in God's sight, but it is those who obey the law who will be declared righteous.*

Paul instructs the Romans about God's judgment and warns them against judging each other. Paul stresses the importance of doing good deeds here on earth. He tells them to obey the law. He admonishes the Jews for knowing the law but not practicing it. Paul tells the Jews that circumcision alone does not fulfill the requirement to be amongst the chosen people. They must also internalize the law.

ROMANS 3

Verse 23: *...for all have sinned and fall short of the glory of God.*

Paul tells of God's faithfulness and creates a bond between Jews and Gentiles by telling them both can be believers. He teaches that righteousness from God comes through faith in Jesus Christ. Jesus' sacrifice was for all believers. God is the God of the Jews and Gentiles.

ROMANS 4

Verse 16: *Therefore, the promise comes by faith, so that it may be by grace and may be guaranteed to all Abraham's offspring—not only to those who are of the law but also to those who are of the faith of Abraham. He is the father of us all.*

Paul makes the point that Abraham was righteous before he was circumcised and that it is the acceptance grace through faith, not circumcision or being Jewish, that is important.

ROMANS 5

Verse 8: *But God demonstrates his own love for us in this: While we were still sinners, Christ died for us.*

Paul points out that we should rejoice in the hope of the glory of God. He also notes that we should rejoice in our suffering because it brings us closer to God. Paul instructs that Christ died for the ungodly and for all sinners. He tells the Romans death came through Adam and his sin but life comes through Christ.

ROMANS 6

Verse 16: *Don't you know that when you offer yourselves to someone to obey him as slaves, you are slaves to the one whom you obey—whether you are slaves to sin, which leads to death, or to obedience, which leads to righteousness?*

Paul goes on to explain that because Christ died and rose again, believers may live a new life. He noted that they must no longer be slaves to sin but instead be slaves to righteousness. He states that the wages of sin is death, but the gift of God is eternal life in Jesus Christ.

ROMANS 7

Verse 18: *I know that nothing good lives in me, that is, in my sinful nature. For I have the desire to do what is good, but I cannot carry it out.*

Paul uses an analogy: just as a woman whose husband dies is freed from the bonds of marriage and may remarry, accepting Jesus Christ may also free us from sin. Paul goes on to discuss the constant conflict we have with sin, and that Jesus is the only answer to the dilemma.

ROMANS 8

Verses 1,2: *Therefore, there is now no condemnation for those who are in Christ Jesus, because through Christ Jesus the law of the Spirit of life set me free from the law of sin and death.*

Paul instructs the followers not to live by a sinful nature, but according to the Spirit. He notes that believers are heirs to the Kingdom and should share in the sufferings in order to also share in the glory. He notes that nothing can separate a believer from the love of Jesus Christ.

ROMANS 9

Verse 6: *It is not as though God's word had failed. For not all who are descended from Israel are Israel.*

Paul instructs the people that acceptance by God is not based on man's desire or effort, but on God's mercy. He uses the examples of Abraham's offspring and Moses' dealings with Pharaoh to make the point. He again uses scripture references to point out that God calls the Gentiles as well as the Jews. He criticizes the Jews for not accepting Jesus Christ.

ROMANS 10

Verse 9: *That if you confess with your mouth, "Jesus is LORD," and believe in your heart that God raised him from the dead, you will be saved.*

Paul instructs that a person must believe with his heart as well as his mouth. He again states that in the Lord's eyes there is no difference between Jew and Gentile. He sites other scriptural references to try to convince the stubborn non-believing Jews that Jesus is the Christ.

ROMANS 11

Verse 25: *I do not want you to be ignorant of this mystery, brothers, so that you may not be conceited: Israel has experienced a hardening in part until the full number of the Gentiles has come in.*

Paul assures the people that God did not reject Israel, but He has followers who are chosen by grace. Using an analogy of an olive tree, Paul explains that the natural branches (the Jews) of the tree were removed because of their faithlessness and replaced with those who are faithful, regardless of their heritage. The shared root is God. He suggests that by giving salvation to the Gentiles, the Jews should be envious and seek it themselves. Paul praises God.

ROMANS 12

Verse 18: *If it is possible, as far as it depends on you, live at peace with everyone.*

Paul tells the people to offer themselves as a living sacrifice. He encourages the believers in Rome to use their individual gifts in the service of others and gives a series of instructions to them about being kind, humble, and righteous. He tells them to overcome evil with good.

ROMANS 13

Verse 10: *Love does no harm to its neighbor. Therefore love is the fulfillment of the law.*

Paul tells the people to submit to authority, pay taxes, and love one another. He also reminds them to obey the Ten Commandments, indicating that the day of salvation is near.

ROMANS 14

Verse 17: *For the kingdom of God is not a matter of eating and drinking, but of righteousness, peace and joy in the Holy Spirit….*

Paul encourages the people to stop passing judgment on each other, and each person should serve in his or her own way. He discusses that all food is clean to eat and suggests that the larger issue is one's relationship with God, and doing everything through faith.

ROMANS 15

Verse 7: *Accept one another, then, just as Christ accepted you, in order to bring praise to God.*

Paul tells the people to encourage their neighbors. He ministers to the Jews and Gentiles. He also outlines his plans to visit the Romans on his way to Spain and notes that he is en route to Jerusalem.

ROMANS 16

Verse 19: *Everyone has heard about your obedience, so I am full of joy over you; but I want you to be wise about what is good, and innocent about what is evil.*

Paul concludes by commending and acknowledging many people who have served the cause of Christ. He gives some final advice and final greetings in the name of God.

Chapter 47

1 CORINTHIANS

1 CORINTHIANS 1

Verse 26: *Brothers, think of what you were when you were called. Not many of you were wise by human standards; not many were influential; not many were of noble birth.*

Paul begins this letter with a greeting to the believers in Corinth. He gives thanks for their faith and testimony. He encourages them not to be divided in who they follow; that they should all follow Jesus Christ. He reminds them that the message of the cross is the power of God for those who believe; Jesus Christ is the power and wisdom of God. He tells them that God chose the foolish to shame the wise, the weak to shame the strong, and the lowly to counter the high. Paul says "Let him who boasts boast to the Lord."

1 CORINTHIANS 2

Verse 7: *No, we speak of God's secret wisdom, a wisdom that has been hidden and that God destined for our glory before time began.*

Paul reminds the Corinthians that he came to them weak, and his message was a result of God's power. He notes that he speaks a message of wisdom revealed by God's Spirit and that words taught by the Spirit express spiritual truths in spiritual words. Paul tells them a man without the Spirit does not understand.

1 CORINTHIANS 3

Verse 5: *What, after all, is Apollos? And what is Paul? Only servants, through whom you came to believe—as the LORD has assigned to each his task.*

Paul then admonishes the Corinthians, telling them that their quarreling and jealousy show spiritual immaturity. He tells them it is not Apollos (who carried on Paul's original ministry) or Paul who are important, but God. The foundation of what they are building is based upon Jesus Christ. Paul instructs them that they are God's temple, and the temple is sacred. He teaches them that worldly wisdom is foolishness.

1 CORINTHIANS 4

Verse 7: *For who makes you different from anyone else? What do you have that you did not receive? And if you did receive it, why do you boast as though you did not?*

Paul then tells the Corinthians the apostles are servants of Christ, entrusted with the secret things of God. He teaches them not to judge others, because the Lord will judge at the appointed time. He tells them that the apostles have born the brunt of the journey for them, and that the apostles are weak, but the followers are strong. He indicates that he is their father in Christ through the gospel and urges them to imitate him. He informs them he will send Timothy to them to serve as a role model. He tells them not to be arrogant, and he will come soon to find out how much power the arrogant really have. He wants to be able to come to them with a gentle spirit.

1 CORINTHIANS 5

Verse 5: *…hand this man over to Satan, so that the sinful nature may be destroyed and his spirit saved on the day of the LORD.*

Paul relates that he heard that an immoral man was having sexual relations with his mother. He tells the Corinthians that they should expel this man, and hand him over to Satan so that the whole church is not hurt. He again tells them not to be boastful about the sin among them, and not to associate with immoral people who claim to be believers. One should not judge the behavior of those outside the church, but only those inside the church.

1 CORINTHIANS 6

Verse 12: *Everything is permissible for me—but not everything is beneficial. Everything is permissible for me—but I will not be mastered by anything.*

Paul asks the Corinthians to take their disputes before a judge whom they appoint from the church. He reminds them that the wicked will not inherit the earth, but that the believers are justified in Christ. Again, he discusses sexual immorality, telling them that the body is not meant for that, but for the Lord. He tells them that all other sins are committed outside the body, but sexual sins are against the body (a temple of the Holy Spirit). He tells them to honor God with their bodies.

1 CORINTHIANS 7

Verse 24: *Brothers, each man, as responsible to God, should remain in the situation God called him to.*

Paul instructs the Corinthians regarding husband and wife duties, including belonging to each other. He encourages the widowers and others to marry if they cannot control themselves. He reminds them of their vows and tells them how to deal with non-believing spouses. He exhorts all believers that keeping God's commands are what counts. He tells them that time is short, and they should spend less time on worldly matters. He implies that being unmarried may actually be better because one can devote more time to the Lord.

1 CORINTHIANS 8

Verse 8: *But food does not bring us near to God; we are no worse if we do not eat, and no better if we do.*

Paul addresses the issue of eating food sacrificed to idols, indicating that the food in-and-of-itself is not forbidden. Idols mean nothing to Christians, and therefore the fact that it was sacrificed for idols means nothing. The only issue is if others see them and feel that they are doing this to honor or worship the idols. If this is the case, the believer should abstain from eating this meat.

1 Corinthians 9

Verse 22: *To the weak I became weak, to win the weak. I have become all things to all men so that by all possible means I might save some.*

Paul justifies his apostleship and explains that apostles have rights and should share in any material harvest. He tells the Corinthians that he tries to reach his audience by understanding them and approaching them from their perspective. He states that he does this for the sake of the gospel, so that he may share in its blessings. Unlike the competitive runner, a believer runs a race to get a crown that will last forever and Paul says he runs the race to win the prize.

1 Corinthians 10

Verse 13: *No temptation has seized you except what is common to man. And God is faithful; he will not let you be tempted beyond what you can bear. But when you are tempted, he will also provide a way out so that you can stand up under it.*

Paul explains that even though their forefathers were with Moses and experienced many of the miracles of God, the Lord was not pleased with most of the Israelites. He states that the Corinthians should not commit the sins of their fathers. Their forefathers' sins should be examples to them to keep them from giving in to temptation. Paul implores them again to flee from idolatry. He clarifies his instructions regarding eating meat sacrificed to idols and makes it clear that they should not eat in the temple of idols or in any way participate in pagan rituals.

1 Corinthians 11

Verse 27: *Therefore, whoever eats the bread or drinks the cup of the Lord in an unworthy manner will be guilty of sinning against the body and blood of the Lord.*

Paul encourages the Corinthians to follow his example. He explains the proper relationships between men and women, an example of this being that a woman should have her head covered as a sign of authority to her husband. He also states, however, that in the Lord men and women are not independent. Paul gives them instructions for celebrating the Lord's Supper. He tells them to do so in a worthy manner, and that each person should examine himself prior to participating in it.

1 CORINTHIANS 12

Verse 31: *But eagerly desire the greater gifts.*

Paul explains that each believer has been given a special gift. These may include wisdom, knowledge, faith, healing, prophecy, tongues, or other gifts, but they are all from the same Spirit and should be used for the common good. He explains that there are many parts, but one body—the body of Christ. He tells the Corinthians that if one part suffers, they all should suffer and if one part is honored, they should all rejoice.

1 CORINTHIANS 13

Verse 11: *When I was a child, I talked like a child, I thought like a child, I reasoned like a child. When I became a man, I put childish ways behind me.*

Paul notes that without love, a person has nothing. He tells the Corinthians that love is patient, kind, and not envious, boastful, or proud; it is not selfish or easily angered and keeps no record of wrongs; it rejoices in the truth, protects, trusts, and perseveres. Love never fails. He explains that where other gifts will disappear, faith, hope, and love will remain, and the greatest of them all is love.

1 CORINTHIANS 14

Verse 33: *For God is not a God of disorder but of peace.*

Paul states that he values the gift of prophecy more than tongues because those who prophesy edify the church, but those who prophesy edify unbelievers as well. He encourages the Corinthians to try to excel in gifts that would build up the church. He writes that if someone speaks in tongues, then someone else should interpret so that the whole Church may benefit. He lays out guidelines for orderly worship.

1 Corinthians 15

Verse 22: *For as in Adam all die, so in Christ all will be made alive.*

Paul encourages the Corinthians to follow the gospel. He tells them he is the least of the apostles and reminds them that he persecuted the church before he was called. He also reminds them that Christ was resurrected, which is the basis of their faith—the resurrection of the dead comes through the man Jesus Christ. He writes that Jesus will reign until He has put all His enemies under His feet. Paul explains that resurrection is of the spirit. He tells them that their labor in the Lord is not in vain.

1 Corinthians 16

Verse 13: *Be on your guard; stand firm in the faith; be men of courage; be strong.*

Paul instructs the Corinthians to take collections from their church to be sent to Jerusalem. He indicates to them that he will stop and see them after he goes through Macedonia. He encourages them to welcome Timothy. He gives them further instructions regarding various people and then gives his final greetings as he closes the letter.

Chapter 48

2 Corinthians

2 Corinthians 1

Verse 6: *If we are distressed, it is for your comfort and salvation; if we are comforted, it is for your comfort, which produces in you patient endurance of the same sufferings we suffer.*

Paul, along with Timothy, addresses the Corinthians, wishing them grace and peace. He praises the God of all comfort and recalls the hardships they suffered in Asia. He relates that they were worried for their lives, but God delivered them from peril. Paul announces a change in his original plans. He was going to visit Corinth on the way to and the way back from his latest mission trip, but tells them that he will only see them on the way back. He praises God and encourages them to stand firm in Christ. He indicates that he did not visit them as planned in order to spare them.

2 Corinthians 2

Verse 4: *For I wrote you out of great distress and anguish of heart and with many tears, not to grieve you but to let you know the depth of my love for you.*

Paul had decided not to make another painful visit to Corinth because the instructions in his last letter had grieved them. He tells the people to forgive the individual in their church who had sinned and to reaffirm their love for him. He tells them of his successful ministry in

Troas, and of his disappointment in not finding Titus there. Paul praises Christ and His leading of believers in triumphal procession and states that, unlike some others, he does not preach for money.

2 CORINTHIANS 3

Verse 6: *He has made us competent as ministers of a new covenant—not of the letter but of the Spirit; for the letter kills, but the Spirit gives life.*

Paul indicates that the Corinthian believers are his letter of recommendation. He declares that a believer's confidence comes from Christ. Paul also compares the ministries of death and life. He reminds the church about Moses, who had to put a veil over his face so that people could not see the glory of God fading, and compares it to the surpassing glory, shared by all believers, that comes through Jesus Christ. Believers reflect the ever-increasing glory of Christ.

2 CORINTHIANS 4

Verse 16: *Therefore we do not lose heart. Though outwardly we are wasting away, yet inwardly we are being renewed day by day.*

Paul notes that he does not distort the word of God, but that his message is veiled to those who do not believe. He declares that God's light shines in their hearts. He tells them to fix their eyes on what is unseen, for what is seen is temporary, but what is unseen in eternal.

2 CORINTHIANS 5

Verse 21: *God made him who had no sin to be sin for us, so that in him we might become the righteousness of God.*

Paul states that all believers have an eternal house in heaven and should make it their goal to please Christ. He tells the Corinthians that their bodies must reflect this. Paul declares that Christ died for all, therefore everyone should live their lives for Him. He states that anyone who is in Christ is a new creation and that Jesus gave His followers the ministry of reconciliation—believers are His ambassadors.

2 CORINTHIANS 6

Verse 17: *Therefore come out from them and be separate," says the LORD. "Touch no unclean thing, and I will receive you."*

Paul urges the Corinthians not to receive God's grace in vain; the day of salvation is now. He describes his hardships, in order to convince the people that the life for Christ is worth the journey. He encourages them not to be yoked with unbelievers and to remain clean.

2 CORINTHIANS 7

Verse 3: *I do not say this to condemn you; I have said before that you have such a place in our hearts that we would live or die with you.*

Paul encourages the Corinthians to purify themselves. He is joyful and tells of how Titus comforted him because of his news of the Corinthians. Paul expresses his happiness that their sorrow led them to repentance. He states that repentance leads to salvation, but worldly sorrow brings death. The Corinthians have encouraged him, and he is pleased that they refreshed Titus' spirit.

2 CORINTHIANS 8

Verse 7: *But just as you excel in everything—in faith, in speech, in knowledge, in complete earnestness and in your love for us—see that you also excel in this grace of giving.*

Paul shares the encouragement he felt through the generosity of the Macedonian church. He urges the Corinthians to be generous also. He reminds them of the poverty that Jesus experienced for their sakes and tells them he will be sending Titus and another brother to encourage them and to organize the collection.

2 Corinthians 9

Verse 7: *Each man should give what he has decided in his heart to give, not reluctantly or under compulsion, for God loves a cheerful giver.*

Paul reiterates his plans to send some brothers to collect the Corinthians' gift. He encourages them to be generous.

2 Corinthians 10

Verse 3: *For though we live in the world, we do not wage war as the world does.*

Paul defends his ministry to the Corinthians. He tells them that they should fight their battles spiritually, not as the world fights. Paul wishes to use his authority to build up the church. He hopes that as their faith grows, he will be able to preach the gospel beyond their territory. Paul states that his commendation comes from God.

2 Corinthians 11

Verse 30: *If I must boast, I will boast of the things that show my weakness.*

Paul warns the Corinthians of false apostles. He excuses himself for boasting about what he has done for the Corinthians in an effort to lead them to Christ. He warns them that false apostles are from Satan. Paul reminds them of his sufferings and boasts in his weaknesses to show them the power and glory of Christ.

2 Corinthians 12

Verse 9: *But he said to me, "My grace is sufficient for you, for my power is made perfect in weakness." Therefore I will boast all the more gladly about my weaknesses, so that Christ's power may rest on me.*

Paul describes an experience of being caught up in the third heaven. In this experience, he learned of the glory of Heaven. He states that to keep him from being conceited by the revelations he saw, he was given a thorn in his flesh. He delights in his persecutions because when he is weak, God is strong in him. Paul concludes by reaffirming his concern for the Corinthians. He tells them of his upcoming visit and is concerned that there may be infighting in the church when he arrives.

2 CORINTHIANS 13

Verse 9: *We are glad whenever we are weak but you are strong; and our prayer is for your perfection.*

By way of final warning, Paul states that in his third visit he will not spare the sinners. He reminds the Corinthians of God's power and encourages them to examine themselves to ensure that Christ is in them. He prays for their perfection and for the grace, love, and fellowship of the Spirit to be with them.

Chapter 49

GALATIANS

GALATIANS 1

Verse 9: *As we have already said, so now I say again: If anybody is preaching to you a gospel other than what you accepted, let him be eternally condemned!*

Paul begins this letter by greeting the churches in Galatia. He admonishes them for turning to a different gospel—something made up by man, rather than the one true gospel. He reminds them of his past faith in Judaism and his persecution of Christians, and then his new role after he was called. He writes of God's revelation to him that made it possible for him to preach the gospel without consulting other men. He states that he met with Peter and James in Jerusalem only after three years of ministry.

GALATIANS 2

Verse 20: *I have been crucified with Christ and I no longer live, but Christ lives in me. The life I live in the body, I live by faith in the Son of God, who loved me and gave himself for me.*

Paul recalls how he went to Jerusalem again fourteen years later with Barnabas and Titus. At this time the idea that all believers needed to be circumcised was discussed and refuted. He and his party met with James, Peter, and John and agreed that those apostles would concentrate on the Jews and Paul and his associates, the Gentiles. The other apostles asked that Paul and his group remember the poor, which they agreed to do. Paul continues by stating that when Peter came to Antioch, he tried to separate himself from the Gentiles, so Paul opposed him. Some believers were forcing the Gentiles to follow Jewish traditions before they would accept them as Christians. At that time, Paul emphasized the importance of being justified by faith in Jesus Christ and not the law.

GALATIANS 3

Verse 13: *Christ redeemed us from the curse of the law by becoming a curse for us, for it is written: "Cursed is everyone who is hung on a tree."*

Paul asks the Galatians whether they received the Spirit by observing the law or by believing in Christ. He tells them that the Scriptures foresaw that the Gentiles would be justified by faith even at the time of Abraham. He asserts that salvation is through faith and not the law; that no one is completely innocent based on the law, therefore the righteous will live by faith. Paul tells them that the promise of the Spirit is received by faith. He points out that Abraham was righteous even before the law existed because of his faith. He goes on to state that if the inheritance depends on the law, it no longer depends on a promise (of grace). He tells them that the purpose of the law was to address transgressions until Christ came. Before faith in Jesus Christ came, everyone was a prisoner of the law, but now believers are no longer under the supervision of the law. Paul tells the Galatians that through baptism, they are all sons of God through Jesus Christ.

GALATIANS 4

Verse 8: *Formerly, when you did not know God, you were slaves to those who by nature are not gods.*

Paul tells the Galatians that God sent His Son to redeem those under law so that they might receive the full rights of sons and heirs. He asks them why they are turning back to their old ways and encourages them to regain their initial zeal for Christ. He reminds the people of Abraham's two sons—Ishmael and Isaac. Ishmael, born of a slave woman, represents the slaves in Arabia. Isaac, born of a free woman and as the result of a promise from God, represents believers who are free.

GALATIANS 5

Verse 13: *You, my brothers, were called to be free. But do not use your freedom to indulge the sinful nature; rather, serve one another in love.*

Paul reminds the Galatians they are free. He implores them not to be circumcised, because this represents the law and not justification through Christ. He tells them that circumcision is not important, only faith in Christ and the expression of that faith through love for Christ and one another. He tells them to live by the Spirit; if the Spirit leads them, they are not under the law. He warns them that the acts of sinful nature will keep them from inheriting the kingdom of God but that the fruit of the Spirit in their lives frees them from the law.

GALATIANS 6

Verse 7: *Do not be deceived: God cannot be mocked. A man reaps what he sows.*

Paul encourages the Galatians to help their brothers, especially when they fall into sin. He instructs them not to please their sinful nature, but to please the Spirit and reap eternal life. He emphasizes, once again, that not even the men who are encouraging them to be circumcised obey the law. Circumcision does not matter, only belief in the new creation. He offers peace and mercy to all who follow this rule.

Chapter 50

EPHESIANS

EPHESIANS 1

Verse 13: *And you were also included in Christ when you heard the word of truth, the gospel of your salvation. Having believed, you were marked in him with a seal, the promised Holy Spirit....*

Paul addresses the Ephesians by first offering spiritual blessings in Christ. In Him we have redemption through His blood. In Him, heaven and earth will come together. We are chosen to praise His glory. Believers are marked with a seal, guaranteeing our inheritance. Paul prays for them to know the Lord and His power better. His power is awesome in the present age and the one to come. The church is His body and God is the head of the church.

EPHESIANS 2

Verse 8: *For it is by grace you have been saved, through faith—and this not from yourselves, it is the gift of God....*

We were dead in sin, but Christ made us alive—we were saved by His grace. We are saved by a gift from God and not our works. The Gentiles also became alive to Christ through His blood. He destroyed the wall dividing Jews from Gentiles. He preached peace to all, and through Him we can reach the Father. We are all fellow citizens of God. The apostles and prophets and Jesus are the foundation of our household.

EPHESIANS 3

Verses 20, 21: *Now to him who is able to do immeasurably more than all we ask or imagine, according to his power that is at work within us, to him be glory in the church and in Christ Jesus throughout all generations, for ever and ever! Amen.*

Paul states that, through the mystery of the Gospel, the Gentiles are also heirs to the promise of Jesus Christ. Paul notes that his imprisonment and suffering were for their glory. He offers a prayer in behalf of the Ephesians asking Christ to dwell in their hearts. He asks for glory for Christ and the church.

EPHESIANS 4

Verse 29: *Do not let any unwholesome talk come out of your mouths, but only what is helpful for building others up according to their needs, that it may benefit those who listen.*

Paul urges the Ephesians to live a life worthy of their calling. He calls them to be humble, gentle, patient, and peaceful. Grace comes from Christ and He encourages us to build up the body of Christ. They should know Christ and put on their new self with righteousness and holiness. Be truthful, not angry, and be honest. Be wholesome, build others up, and do not be bitter and full of malice. Be kind to one another and forgive others as Christ did for us.

EPHESIANS 5

Verse 31: *For this reason a man will leave his father and mother and be united to his wife, and the two will become one flesh.*

Paul goes on to tell them to imitate God and to live a life of love. They should be pure and thankful, and live as children of light, pleasing God. Do not get drunk, but live wisely and be filled with the Holy Spirit. Sings songs to the Lord. Submit to one another out of reverence for Christ. He encourages wives to submit to their husbands and husbands to love their wives.

EPHESIANS 6

Verse 13: *Therefore put on the full armor of God, so that when the day of evil comes, you may be able to stand your ground, and after you have done everything, to stand.*

Paul tells the Ephesian children to obey their parents and for fathers to bring their children up in the ways of the Lord. He encourages slaves to obey their masters and masters to treat their slaves well. He tells them to be strong in the Lord and to put on the armor of God with truth, righteousness, readiness, faith, and salvation. He asks for their prayers before giving his final greetings.

PHILIPPIANS

PHILIPPIANS 1

Verse 18: *But what does it matter? The important thing is that in every way, whether from false motives or true, Christ is preached. And because of this I rejoice. Yes, and I will continue to rejoice.*

Paul offers greetings and thanksgiving for the Philippian partnership in spreading the gospel. He prays they would be filled with the fruit of righteousness through Jesus Christ. Paul notes that his imprisonment served to glorify God. He rejoices in the teaching of Christ. He notes that to live is Christ and to die is gain. He tells the Philippians to conduct themselves in a manner worthy of the gospel, and to be strong, believe in Christ, and suffer for Him.

PHILIPPIANS 2

Verse 4: *Each of you should look not only to your own interests, but also to the interest of others.*

Paul encourages the Philippians to be humble and to look out for the interests of others. He also exhorts them to keep working on their salvation and to work without complaint or arguing. He notes that he hoped to send Timothy to them soon because he takes a genuine interest in their welfare. He also announced that he was sending back Epaphroditus, who almost died, but was saved by God's mercy.

PHILIPPIANS 3

Verse 7: *But whatever was to my profit I now consider loss for the sake of Christ.*

Paul tells the Philippians to rejoice in the Lord and to watch out for evildoers. Paul recounts his background and notes that whatever was for his profit before, now was a loss to him. He writes that he is grateful that his righteousness is from Christ. Paul notes that he looks forward to the prize of meeting Christ in heaven. He also encourages the Philippians to remember that their citizenship is in heaven, not the world.

PHILIPPIANS 4

Verse 8: *Finally, brothers, whatever is true, whatever is noble, whatever is right, whatever is pure, whatever is lovely, whatever is admirable—if anything is excellent or praiseworthy—think about such things.*

Paul pleads with the Philippians to help two women get along. He encourages the church in Philippi to rejoice in the Lord and to remain righteous. He thanks them for their gifts and encouragement and states that God will meet all of their needs according to His glorious riches in Christ Jesus. Paul offers his final greetings and asks that the grace of Jesus Christ to be with their spirits.

Chapter 52

COLOSSIANS

COLOSSIANS 1

Verse 27: *To them God has chosen to make known among the Gentiles the glorious riches of this mystery, which is Christ in you, the hope of glory.*

Paul begins his letter by greeting his brothers in Colossae and thanking them for their faith. He notes that the gospel is growing and bearing fruit all over the world. The Colossians had learned the gospel from Epaphras, their faithful minister, who told Paul of their love in the spirit. Paul states that he and others are praying for the Colossians to live a life worthy of the Lord and to be strengthened in His power. Paul stated that the Son lives and gives redemption and forgiveness of sins. He continues to write that all things were created for Christ and He is the head of the church. He explains that Jesus made peace through His blood shed on the cross. He tells them that it is this gospel that he is a servant to. Paul also rejoices in his suffering on their behalf, and for his labor for the ministry of Christ.

COLOSSIANS 2

Verse 23: *Such regulations indeed have an appearance of wisdom, with their self-imposed worship, their false humility and their harsh treatment of the body, but they lack any value in restraining sensual indulgence.*

Paul encourages the Colossians, noting that he is with them in spirit. He writes that his goal is to spread the news of Christ. He pleads with them to continue to live in Him and to avoid the temptations of the world. He writes that Christ, who has authority over everything, empowers believers to cast off their sinful natures. Paul states that Jesus forgave all sins on the cross. He warned of those who emphasize ceremonials, angel worship, and false humility, saying that this type of activity shows a loss of connection with the Head, who is Christ.

COLOSSIANS 3

Verse 12: *Therefore, as God's chosen people, holy and dearly loved, clothe yourselves with compassion, kindness, humility, gentleness and patience.*

Paul encourages the Colossians to set their minds on Christ and not earthly things. He exhorts them to put sin to death and put on a new self in the image of Christ. Paul states that Christ is all and is in all. He tells the Colossians to be kind and righteous, forgive others, and let the peace of Christ rule in their hearts. He reminds them of the rules for Christian households (wives submit to your husbands, husbands love your wives, children obey your parents, fathers encourage your children, slaves obey your masters). Paul also tells them that if they serve the Lord they would receive an inheritance from Him as a reward.

COLOSSIANS 4

Verse 6: *Let your conversation be always full of grace, seasoned with salt, so that you may know how to answer everyone.*

Paul continues with his advice, concluding that masters must be fair because everyone has a Master in heaven. He instructs the Colossians to pray, to be wise, and keep their conversations full of grace. Paul indicates that Tychicus and Onesimus would join them and share further news. He sends greetings from his fellow prisoners and associates Aristarchus, Mark, Justus, Epaphras, Luke, and Demas. He concludes with a charge to Archippus and a blessing of grace to the Colossians.

1 THESSALONIANS

1 THESSALONIANS 1

Verse 6: *You became imitators of us and of the LORD; in spite of severe suffering, you welcomed the message with the joy given by the Holy Spirit.*

Paul begins his letter to the Thessalonians with greetings of grace and peace. He encourages them, noting that everyone with him was thankful for them. He states that the gospel came to them with power and deep conviction and is a model for others. He also writes that their faith in God has become known everywhere; they trusted in Jesus who will rescue them from the coming wrath.

1 THESSALONIANS 2

Verse 4: *On the contrary, we speak as men approved by God to be entrusted with the gospel. We are not trying to please men but God, who tests our hearts.*

Paul writes that their visit to Thessalonica was not a failure, because they had shared the gospel in Philippi in spite of strong opposition. They spoke to please God, not men. They were gentle and loving in their actions, and worked so as not to be a burden to the people. Paul encourages the Thessalonians and asks them to live a life worthy of God who called them into His kingdom and glory. Paul thanks God that they have received the Word and helped to spread it amongst the Gentiles despite persecution. He states that the wrath of God would come to the persecutors. Paul writes of his longing to return to them, but that Satan had prevented it. He encourages them by writing that the Lord Jesus would be their glory and joy when He returns.

1 Thessalonians 3

Verse 13: *May he strengthen your hearts so that you will be blameless and holy in the presence of our God and Father when our LORD Jesus comes with all his holy ones.*

Paul writes that they had stayed in Athens and sent Timothy to encourage the Thessalonians. Paul acknowledges their faith in the face of persecution. He tells them that Timothy had returned with an encouraging report of their faith and love. Paul praises them because they stood firm in their faith. He prays that God would help them prepare the way for Jesus to return and increase their love for each other and for Christ.

1 Thessalonians 4

Verse 13: *Brothers, we do not want you to be ignorant about those who fall asleep, or to grieve like the rest of men, who have not hope.*

Paul tells them how to live in order to please God. He states that the Thessalonians should avoid sexual immorality and show self-control with their bodies. He writes that they should love one another and be respectful, living a quiet life and working hard so that they were not dependent on anybody. He states that the coming of the Lord will be announced with a loud command and trumpets and that the dead in Christ, then those living in Christ, will be called to meet Him in the air.

1 Thessalonians 5

Verse 9: *For God did not appoint us to suffer wrath but to receive salvation through our LORD Jesus Christ.*

Paul tells the Thessalonians that the day of the Lord is not known, but will come like a thief in the night. He assures them that because they are not in darkness, the day should not surprise them; they are sons of the light and should put on faith and love as the armor of God.

He states that Jesus Christ is their salvation and they should encourage one another. He instructs them to encourage those who work hard, to live in peace, help the weak, and be kind to one another. He further tells them to be joyful, pray continually, and give thanks to God—doing good and avoiding evil.

2 THESSALONIANS

2 THESSALONIANS 1

Verse 3: *We ought always to thank God for you, brothers, and rightly so, because your faith is growing more and more, and the love every one of you has for each other is increasing.*

Paul, along with Silas and Timothy, begins his second letter to the Thessalonians with a greeting and thanksgiving for their faith and love. He boasts about their perseverance. He writes that they were worthy because they have spread the Word even when they were suffering. He assures them that the Lord Jesus will punish those who do not know God when He comes to be glorified. Paul tells them that he, Silas, and Timothy continue to pray that the Lord Jesus will be glorified in them.

2 THESSALONIANS 2

Verse 9: *The coming of the lawless one will be in accordance with the work of Satan displayed in all kinds of counterfeit miracles, signs and wonders....*

Paul writes of the coming of the Lord. He tells the Thessalonians not to be afraid, and that a man will set himself up as God. He states that the day would come, after the rebellion occurred, when the lawless one would be doomed to destruction. He writes that the Lord Jesus will destroy lawlessness and those that follow Satan's counterfeit miracles and signs. Paul encourages them to stand firm in their belief of the gospel and the glory of Jesus Christ. He offers them encouragement and reminds them to encourage others.

2 THESSALONIANS 3

Verses 14,15: *If anyone does not obey our instruction in this letter, take special note of him. Do not associate with him, in order that he may feel ashamed. Yet do not regard him as an enemy, but warn him as a brother.*

Paul asks the Thessalonians to pray for him and his followers so that they might be delivered from their persecution by the wicked. He notes that they have confidence in the Lord's love and exhorts them to direct their hearts to God's love and Christ's perseverance. He cautions them not to be idle and to follow his example. He concludes with a word of grace from the Lord Jesus Christ.

Chapter 55

1 TIMOTHY

1 TIMOTHY 1

Verse 13: Even though I was once a blasphemer and a persecutor and a violent man, I was shown mercy because I acted in ignorance and unbelief.

The apostle Paul writes this letter to Timothy, telling him to stay in Ephesus and oppose those who teach false doctrines. They want to be teachers of the Law, but do not know what they are talking about. The Law is not made for the righteous, but for sinners. Paul acknowledges the Lord's grace in his own life. He was the worst sinner and Christ used him as an example. He tells Timothy to hold onto faith and to have a good conscience. Those who rejected this advice (such as Hymenaeus and Alexander) have been handed over to Satan.

1 TIMOTHY 2

Verse 15: But women will be saved through childbearing—if they continue in faith, love and holiness with propriety.

Paul urges Timothy to pray for everyone, including those in authority, so all believers may live quiet lives in godliness. He states that God wants all people to be saved through His mediator, Jesus Christ. He encourages everyone to lift up holy hands in prayer. He tells Timothy that women should dress appropriately and should learn in silence and submission.

1 TIMOTHY 3

Verse 16: Beyond all question, the mystery of godliness is great: He appeared in body, was vindicated by the Spirit, was seen by angels, was preached among the nations, was believed on in the world, was taken up in glory.

Paul outlines for Timothy the qualifications for overseers (elders) and deacons of the church. He notes that overseers need to be above reproach, good teachers and fathers, and not recent converts to Christianity. Deacons also must be worthy of respect, be faithful and honest, and be tested before serving. Paul notes that the church is the pillar and foundation of the truth. He reminds Timothy of the mystery of godliness, which is the gospel of Jesus Christ.

TIMOTHY 4

Verse 16: Watch your life and doctrine closely. Persevere in them, because if you do, you will save both yourself and your hearers.

Paul warns of deceiving spirits who teach that marriage and eating certain foods is forbidden. Paul encourages Timothy to train himself to be godly. Paul also tells Timothy to teach the word and to not let others look down on him because of his youth. Paul instructs him to read Scripture publicly and to preach, using his gift. He also tells Timothy to watch his life carefully.

1 TIMOTHY 5

Verse 17: The elders who direct the affairs of the church well are worthy of double honor, especially those whose work is preaching and teaching.

Paul tells Timothy to treat others with kindness. He instructs him to teach that the care of widows should first fall to the families of the widow. The church is to support widows without families who were over sixty years old and had lived a righteous life. Paul encourages young widows to remarry and to avoid slander. He writes that elders were worthy of a double honor and should not be accused of sinning unless there were two or three witnesses who would testify against them. Paul also writes that Timothy should choose elders carefully and to look for hidden sins.

1 Timothy 6

Verse 9: *People who want to get rich fall into temptation and a trap and into many foolish and harmful desires that plunge men into ruin and destruction.*

Paul continues in his letter that slaves should respect their masters, especially if their masters are believers. He writes to Timothy about false doctrines that use godliness for financial gain. He declares that godliness and contentment result in real gain and that the love of money was the root of all kinds of evil. Paul encourages Timothy to pursue righteousness, faith, love, and endurance. He tells him to fight the good fight. Paul tells Timothy to instruct the rich to put their faith in God and not wealth; they should lay up their treasures in heaven. Paul concludes with instructions for Timothy to guard what was entrusted into his care and to turn away from evil.

Chapter 56

2 TIMOTHY

2 TIMOTHY 1

Verse 12: That is why I am suffering as I am. Yet I am not ashamed, because I know whom I have believed, and am convinced that he is able to guard what I have entrusted to him for that day.

Paul greets Timothy in a letter, noting that he longs to see him. Paul encourages Timothy to remain faithful and to "fan into flame" the gift of God within him. Paul, imprisoned, asks Timothy to join him in suffering for the gospel. He reminds Timothy that grace was revealed through Jesus Christ and declares that he is not ashamed. Paul encourages Timothy to guard this grace given to him and to pursue sound teaching. Paul notes that Phygelus and Hermogenes had deserted him, but Onesiphorus still accompanied him.

2 TIMOTHY 2

Verse 15: Do your best to present yourself to God as one approved, a workman who does not need to be ashamed and who correctly handles the word of truth.

Paul tells Timothy to be strong in the grace of Jesus Christ. He instructs Timothy to endure hardships as a good soldier and a hard worker. He writes that he suffers because of his work for the gospel; he is in chains, but God's word is not chained. Paul encourages Timothy to present himself as a workman approved by God. He should avoid godless chatter and the ungodly teaching that comes from it. Paul states that God's foundation was inscribed with two points—the Lord knows those who are His, and those who confess the name of the Lord must turn away from wickedness. Paul tells Timothy to do noble things, be righteous, avoid arguments, and to instruct gently.

2 TIMOTHY 3

Verse 16: *All Scripture is God-breathed and is useful for teaching, rebuking, correcting and training in righteousness....*

Paul warns Timothy of the last days and to avoid godless people during this time. He writes that men will oppose the truth but they will become transparent. Paul instructs Timothy to see Paul as an example and to realize that everyone who wants to live a godly life will be persecuted. He also tells him to continue what he learned and to learn more from God-breathed Scripture, which is useful for godly living.

2 TIMOTHY 4

Verse 7: *I have fought the good fight, I have finished the race, I have kept the faith.*

Paul charges Timothy to preach the word and tells him that false teachers would challenge him, but to keep his head and discharge his duties of the ministry. He notes that his own days were limited and he will be awarded the crown of righteousness for fighting the good fight. Paul tells Timothy that only Luke was with him and to come quickly to visit. Paul recalls that, although many deserted him at his Roman trial, the Lord was with him and he proclaimed His message to the Gentiles.

TITUS

TITUS 1

Verse 16: *They claim to know God, but by their actions they deny him. They are detestable, disobedient and unfit for anything good.*

Paul writes this letter to Titus, whom he left in Crete to appoint elders for the church there. Paul describes the requirements for becoming an elder including that they must be blameless, have only one wife, and have obedient children. He notes that they must also be honest, self-controlled, holy, and disciplined. Paul tells Titus to rebuke the rebellious Cretans and calls them detestable.

TITUS 2

Verse 11: *For the grace of God that brings salvation has appeared to all men.*

Paul tells Titus to teach sound doctrine. He instructs him to teach the older men to be temperate and to be sound in faith. He writes that the older women should be taught to be reverent and to teach the younger women what is good. He encourages Titus to teach the young men to be self-controlled. He told Titus to set a good example. He notes that slaves should be subject to their masters. He declares that the grace of God teaches to live self-controlled, upright, and godly lives in anticipation of Christ's glorious appearance.

Titus 3

Verse 10: *Warn a divisive person once, and then warn him a second time. After that, have nothing to do with him.*

Paul instructs Titus to teach the people to be subject to authorities, obedient, and to do what is good. He writes that everyone has been foolish at one time, but the kindness and love of the Savior shows His followers how to act. Paul continues that Jesus saved them so they may become heirs with the hope of eternal life. He offers final instructions to avoid arguments. He asks that Titus join him in helping other church leaders.

Chapter 58

PHILEMON

Verse 11: *Formerly he was useless to you, but now he has become useful both to you and to me.*

Paul writes this letter to Philemon and greets others who attended the church in his home. Paul gives thanks for Philemon and his love for the saints. Philemon lives in Colossac and is the master of the slave named Onesimus. Onesimus had escaped from slavery and had become a Christian under Paul's ministry. Paul appeals to Philemon in the letter to accept Onesimus back, not as a slave, but as a brother in the Lord. He tells Philemon he will pay any debt that Onesimus owed Philemon. Paul encourages and blesses Philemon.

Other Letters

HEBREWS

HEBREWS 1

Verse 4: *So he became as much superior to the angels as the name he has inherited is superior to theirs.*

The author gives proof that Jesus is superior to the angels. He writes that in the past God spoke through the prophets, but since Jesus, He has spoken through His Son—the radiance of God's glory. After He purified the believer's sins, He sat down at the right hand of the Father, making Jesus superior to angels who are only ministering spirits.

HEBREWS 2

Verse 18: *Because he himself suffered when he was tempted, he is able to help those who are being tempted.*

The author writes that the readers must pay careful attention to the lessons of the great salvation. He states that Jesus suffered death so that He might taste death for His brothers. He suffered in humanity in order to defeat the devil and to atone for the sins of the people. Because He suffered when tempted, He can help others who are tempted.

HEBREWS 3

Verse 13: *But encourage one another daily, as long as it is called Today, so that none of you may be hardened by sin's deceitfulness.*

The author states that Jesus is the faithful High Priest and worthy of greater honor than Moses. Christ is faithful as a Son over God's house (believers). The author encourages the reader not to have a sinful unbelieving heart, but to encourage one another daily. He writes that just as Moses' people could not enter into the Promised Land because of their unbelief, those who do not believe in Christ will not have eternal rest.

HEBREWS 4

Verse 12: *For the word of God is living and active. Sharper than any double-edged sword, it penetrates even to dividing soul and spirit, joints and marrow; it judges the thoughts and attitudes of the heart.*

The author writes of the Sabbath-rest for God's people. Acceptance of the gospel, faith, and obedience are required to enter the Sabbath-rest. The reader is told that every effort should be made to enter that rest. It is stated that the Word of God is living and sharp, and that nothing is hidden from God. Everyone will one day have to give an account to God. Jesus is the great High Priest and believers must hold firmly to the faith. Believers can approach the throne with confidence, seeking mercy, and grace.

HEBREWS 5

Verse 12: *In fact, though by this time you ought to be teachers, you need someone to teach you the elementary truths of God's word all over again. You need milk, not solid food!*

The duties of the high priest were reviewed. The high priest is required to offer sacrifices for his own sins as well as the sins of others. Every priest is called by God, like Aaron was. God named Christ as the High Priest forever, in the order of the high priest Melchizedek. Jesus was made perfect by His suffering, and became the source of eternal salvation for all who obey Him. The author notes that the readers have a hard time understanding these things because they are not mature in understanding the truths of God's Word.

HEBREWS 6

Verse 10: *God is not unjust; he will not forget your work and the love you have shown him as you have helped his people and continue to help them.*

The author urges believers to move beyond elementary teachings about the faith. He tells them that it is impossible for the enlightened to be brought back to repentance if they fall away because they would be crucifying the Son of God a second time. Land that accepts rain and produces crops is blessed, whereas unfruitful land is in danger of being cursed and its produce burned. The author is confident of better things for his readers. He encourages the Hebrews to remain diligent until the end. He writes that God kept His oath with Abraham and that God's promise is sure. Believers all have the hope, which is an anchor for the soul, of entering the inner sanctuary to join Jesus who has become a High Priest in the order of Melchizedek.

HEBREWS 7

Verse 27: *Unlike the other high priests, he does not need to offer sacrifices day after day, first for his own sins, and then for the sins of the people. He sacrificed for their sins once for all when he offered himself.*

The author writes about Melchizedek who was a king and a priest that Abraham tithed to. Melchizedek was a priest without lineage and so he is a priest forever. He collected a tithe from Abraham and blessed him, making Melchizedek greater than Abraham. The author writes that if perfection could have been attained through the traditional Levitical line, it would not have been necessary for another priest to come who was like Melchizedek; not a Levite. Because it was necessary to make a change in the Law, Jesus came from the tribe of Judah and became a priest that was not based on ancestry, but on the power of an indestructible life. The Lord gave an oath making Jesus a priest forever, offering a new and better Covenant. Jesus is a permanent priest and is able to save those who come to God. Jesus, as the High Priest, is holy, blameless, and exalted. He does not require sacrifices because He offered himself as the perfect sacrifice.

HEBREWS 8

Verse 13: *By calling this covenant "new," he has made the first one obsolete; and what is obsolete and aging will soon disappear.*

The author writes that the High Priest of the new covenant sits at the right hand of God. He serves in the true tabernacle set up by God. The new covenant is superior to the old one and is founded on better promises. If there had been nothing wrong with the old covenant, there would have been no need for a new one. The new covenant replaces the old, which is obsolete and will disappear.

HEBREWS 9

Verse 15: *For this reason Christ is the mediator of a new covenant, that those who are called may receive the promised eternal inheritance—now that he has died as a ransom to set them free from the sins committed under the first covenant.*

The author describes the earthly Tabernacle and its regulations. The first covenant had the Tabernacle and the Ark. The high priest entered into the Most Holy Place only once a year after a blood offering was made. Christ entered the Most Holy Place with His own blood. The blood of Christ cleansed the consciousness of the believer so that he may serve God. Christ is the mediator of the New Covenant. Those who are called may receive eternal inheritance to set them free from the first covenant. Christ suffered for all, taking away the sins of many people. He will appear a second time to bring salvation for those waiting for Him.

HEBREWS 10

Verse 16: *This is the covenant I will make with them after that time, says the LORD. I will put my laws in their hearts, and I will write them on their minds.*

The author writes that the Law was never complete—sacrifices were always necessary, year after year, but still did not cleanse worshippers of their sins. Christ's sacrifice was once and for all. His sacrifice was perfect, then He sat down at the right hand of God. Therefore, the author declares that believers should draw near to God with a sincere heart and in assurance of faith and encourage each other as the Day approaches. He states that not accepting the New Covenant would result in dreadful consequences when the Lord judges His people. He tells the Hebrew readers to remain confident and persevere because the Day is near.

HEBREWS 11

Verse 6: *And without faith it is impossible to please God, because anyone who comes to him must believe that he exists and that he rewards those who earnestly seek him.*

The author gives a definition of faith and lists heroes from the past that lived by faith. By faith:

Believers understand how the universe was created.
Abel offered a better sacrifice than Cain.
Enoch did not have to experience death.
Noah built the ark.
Abraham obeyed instructions to leave his home, fathered Isaac, and was willing to sacrifice him.
Isaac blessed Jacob and Esau.
Jacob blessed Joseph's sons.
Joseph promised the Exodus from Egypt.
Moses was hidden by his mother, chose to be with his people rather than a nobleman, and led them out of captivity.
Jericho fell.
Rahab helped the Israelites.

The author continues that the Lord has prepared a place for these heroes of faith, and many more who have been good examples of faith in the face of defeat, death, persecution, punishment, and imprisonment. God has planned something even better for those who have heard the gospel of Christ, so that together with the forefathers, believers can be made perfect.

HEBREWS 12

Verse 2: *Let us fix our eyes on Jesus, the author and perfecter of our faith, who for the joy set before him endured the cross, scorning its shame, and sat down at the right hand of the throne of God.*

The author writes that since the Hebrew believers had such a great group of witness surrounding them, they should run the race with perseverance with their eyes fixed on Jesus. He tells them to consider Him so they do not grow weary and lose heart. They are to endure hardship as discipline, because God disciplines those He loves. God disciplines for the good of the believers, so they may share in His holiness. Believers are encouraged to make every effort to live in peace, to be holy, and to help keep others from sinning. The new Covenant does not require believers to ascend a mountain burning with fire as Moses did to obtain the Law. Instead all believers have come to Mount Zion, along with the angels, to be with God, and with Jesus Christ as the mediator. Those who refuse Him were warned of the dire consequences. The Hebrew readers are told they are receiving a kingdom that cannot be shaken. They should be thankful and should worship God, a consuming fire.

HEBREWS 13

Verse 8: *Jesus Christ is the same yesterday and today and forever.*

The author encourages the Hebrew believers to continue loving each other and to be kind to others. He reminds them to remember those in prison, to honor marriage, to avoid the love of money, and to obey their leaders. He also warns them not to be carried away by false teachings, and to refrain from following the old order. He tells them to look to Jesus and the city to come, and encourages them to offer a sacrifice of praise. He asks them to pray for those writing the letter and for a reunion with them. He offers a blessing for the Hebrews that God would equip them to do His will.

Chapter 60

JAMES

JAMES 1

Verse 5: If any of you lacks wisdom, he should ask God, who gives generously to all without finding fault, and it will be given to him.

James begins with a greeting to the twelve tribes. He notes that testing of faith develops perseverance, which brings the crown of life. He encourages them to ask God for help, but not to doubt His answer. He advises them to be humble and notes that the rich man will fade away. Every perfect and good deed is from God. Listen before you speak; don't get angry; get rid of evil. Don't just listen to the word—apply it. Look after orphans and widows, and keep yourself pure.

JAMES 2

Verse 18: But someone will say, "You have faith; I have deeds." Show me your faith without deeds, and I will show you my faith by what I do.

James continues to advise the believers not to show favoritism. The poor can be rich in faith and the rich can exploit you. Love your neighbor, and follow the law. Mercy triumphs over judgment. Faith is no good without deeds.

JAMES 3

Verse 9: *With the tongue we praise our LORD and Father, and with it we curse men, who have been made in God's likeness.*

Teachers are judged more strictly than others. The tongue, a small part of the body, can corrupt the whole person. You cannot praise the Lord and curse men out of the same mouth. A good life with deeds done out of mercy and in humility comes from wisdom. Envy and self-ambition lead to evil. The wisdom that comes from heaven is pure, impartial, and sincere. Sow in peace and reap righteousness.

JAMES 4

Verse 7: *Submit yourselves, then, to God. Resist the devil, and he will flee from you.*

Fights and quarrels come from not having what you want, and you do not have what you want because you did not ask God. Being a friend to the world makes you an enemy of God. Submit yourselves to God—resist the devil. Purify your heart and humble yourself before the Lord. Do not slander or judge one another. Do not plan out the details of your life—allow God's will to act. Boasting is evil. Do what God tells you to do.

JAMES 5

Verse 16: *Therefore confess your sins to each other and pray for each other so that you may be healed. The prayer of a righteous man is powerful and effective.*

Misery is coming to the rich. Be patient until the Lord's coming. Like Job, persevere. Above all, do not swear. Encourage prayer for all moods and circumstances—confess your sins. Turn sinners from the errors of their ways and you will be rewarded.

Chapter 61

1 PETER

1 PETER 1

Verse 7: *These have come so that your faith—of greater worth than gold, which perishes even though refined by fire—may be proved genuine and may result in praise, glory and honor when Jesus Christ is revealed.*

The Apostle Peter addresses God's chosen who are scattered amongst many nations. He encourages them to give praise to God for giving us a new birth, a living home, and an inheritance through the resurrection of Jesus Christ. We may have to suffer some, but salvation will come in the last time. Faith is greater than gold, and believing without actually seeing Jesus brings joy. Salvation was promised by the prophets and is desired even by angels. Therefore, be obedient and holy. Redemption is from the precious blood of Christ. Love your brothers. We have been born again through the enduring word of the Lord.

1 PETER 2

Verse 9: *But you are a chosen people, a royal priesthood, a holy nation, a people belonging to God, that you may declare the praises of him who called you out of darkness into his wonderful light.*

Peter writes that believers should rid themselves of evil and grow in Christ. As Christ was a perfect Living Stone, so should believers be as a chosen people. We are called out of darkness to

His wonderful light and should live a good life avoiding evil. Submit to authority for the Lord's sake to silence the ignorant talk of foolish men. Live as servants of God. Be obedient even in the face of suffering, as did Christ. The sheep will return to the Shepherd.

1 Peter 3

Verse 15: *But in your hearts set apart Christ as Lord. Always be prepared to give an answer to everyone who asks you to give the reason for the hope that you have. But do this with gentleness and respect....*

Peter instructs wives to be submissive to their husbands. He notes that beauty is from the inner self. He tells husbands to respect their wives. Live in harmony with one another—be compassionate and humble. Do not fear. Do what is right, and share your spirit. Christ died for our sins and His Spirit lives. Noah's ark only saved eight people through water. The same water can save numerous people through baptism and the resurrection of Jesus Christ.

1 Peter 4

Verse 8: *Above all, love each other deeply because love covers over a multitude of sins.*

Peter states that as Christ suffered, so must we as well. We should live our lives for the will of God. The end of things is near. Love each other deeply. Give, speak, and serve with the strength of God. Rejoice in suffering for Jesus Christ and God will judge you favorably.

1 Peter 5

Verse 8: *Be self-controlled and alert. Your enemy the devil prowls around like a roaring lion looking for someone to devour.*

Peter appeals to the elders to be shepherds of the flock and they will receive the crown of glory. He appeals to the youth to be humble and submissive to their elders and to resist evil. He states that God will restore them. Peter offers final greetings and makes an acknowledgement of Silas' help in composing this letter. Peace to all in Christ.

Chapter 62

2 PETER

2 PETER 1

Verse 3: *His divine power has given us everything we need for life and godliness through our knowledge of him who called us by his own glory and goodness.*

Peter addresses the believers reminding them that Jesus gave us great promises, therefore, we must be good, faithful, knowledgeable, and practice self-control, perseverance, love, and kindness. Make your calling and election sure. Peter promises to remind them of this. He recalls his personal experience with Jesus Christ at the transfiguration. He advises them to pay attention to prophesy which comes from God.

2 PETER 2

Verse 21: *It would have been better for them not to have known the way of righteousness, than to have known it and then to turn their backs on the sacred command that was passed on to them.*

Peter gives the believers warnings about false prophets. God punished angels that sinned, evildoers of Noah's time, and Sodom and Gomorrah; but he rescued the righteous (Noah, Lot, and others). Therefore, God knows how to judge the righteous from the sinners. The false prophets will be punished for their blasphemy. They will be rebuked like Balaam was by a donkey. It is worse to stray from righteousness than to never have known it.

2 Peter 3

Verse 9: *The Lord is not slow in keeping his promise, as some understand slowness. He is patient with you, not wanting anyone to perish, but everyone to come to repentance.*

Peter writes that in the last days, there will be scoffers, but they do not understand that on the Day of Judgment there will be fire and destruction for ungodly men. The day of the Lord, which may be like a thousand years, will come like a thief. Therefore, we should live holy and godly lives and look forward to a new heaven and earth. Remain spotless and blameless and beware of those who misinterpret the scripture and lawless men. Grow in grace and knowledge of our Lord and Savior.

Chapter 63

1 JOHN

1 JOHN 1

Verse 7: But if we walk in the light, as he is in the light, we have fellowship with one another, and the blood of Jesus, his Son, purifies us from all sin.

John begins with a proclamation concerning the Word of life and his personal witness of Jesus Christ who makes our joy complete. He encourages us to walk in the light, because God is light. The blood of his Son purifies us from sin. If we confess our sins, He will forgive us and purify us from unrighteousness. If we deny our sins, His word has no place in our lives.

1 JOHN 2

Verse 6: Whoever claims to live in him must walk as Jesus did.

Jesus Christ is the atoning sacrifice for our sins and the sins of the world. We must not only know Him, but also obey His commands. John instructs us to revive the old command to love your brother in order to live in the light. He exhorts us not to love the world, which is sinful, but to love the Father. The world and its desires pass away, but the man who does the will of God lives forever. John notes that this is the last hour and warns of the antichrist. He encourages his brothers, reminding them that they are anointed, and should remember the truth and the promise of eternal life. The anointing is real and they should remain in Him. We should not be ashamed at His coming. Everyone who does what is right has been born of Him.

1 John 3

Verse 1: *How great is the love the Father has lavished on us, that we should be called children of God! And that is what we are! The reason the world does not know us is that it did not know him.*

We are children of God. The world does not know Him. When He appears we will be like Him and our hope in Him will purify us. He takes away our sins and keeps us from further sin. Do what is right and be righteous; sinfulness is from the devil. The Son of God appeared in order to destroy the devil's work. Do what is right and love your brother, as a child of God. Love one another, not like Cain. The world may hate us, but if we love our brothers, we will pass from death to life. Jesus Christ laid down His life in love for us; we should do the same for our brothers and be merciful to them. We should demonstrate our love with action and truth. We must obey the commands that Jesus Christ puts on our hearts.

1 John 4

Verse 6: *We are from God, and whoever knows God listens to us; but whoever is not from God does not listen to us. This is how we recognize the Spirit of truth and the spirit of falsehood.*

Test the spirits to see if they truly are from God. Only spirits that testify that Jesus Christ came in the flesh are from Him. He will help you to overcome spirits from the antichrist and the world. Listen only to those who are from God. Love one another because love comes from God. He showed His love through the sacrifice of His Son. We know God's love through His Son, and He lives in those who acknowledge Jesus as the Son of God. Our love in Him will give us confidence on the Day of Judgment. In order to love God, we must also love our brother.

1 John 5

Verse 14: *I write these things to you who believe in the name of the Son of God so that you may know that you have eternal life.*

Love God and obey His commands. Only those who believe that Jesus is the Son of God will overcome the world. Jesus Christ came by water and blood. The Spirit is the truth. The

Spirit, the water, and the blood are in agreement. If you have the Son, you have life. We should have confidence in approaching God. We should pray for our brothers who sin. God keeps us from sin. John concludes with a warning to keep ourselves from idols.

Chapter 64

2 John

Verse 5: *And now, dear lady, I am not writing you a new command but one we have had from the beginning. I ask that we love one another.*

John, an elder in the church, addresses a chosen lady (or the church). He is encouraged that many children are walking in the truth. He instructs them to love one another and to walk in obedience with God's commands. He warns of deceivers and the antichrist. He encourages them to continue in the teaching of Christ. He instructs them to not welcome those who do not bring this teaching or they will share in their wickedness.

Chapter 65

3 JOHN

Verse 4: *I have no greater joy than to hear that my children are walking in the truth.*

John, an elder, addresses this letter to Gaius, a Roman Christian. He notes that he was encouraged with news of Gaius' faithfulness to the truth. Gaius shared his love with brothers who were strangers so that they could spread the Word. He admonished Diotrephes, who put himself above the church and did not welcome fellow believers. He encouraged Gaius to continue to do what is good, as that is from God. John recognized Demetrius for doing good deeds as well.

JUDE

Verse 11: *Woe to them! They have taken the way of Cain....*

Jude, likely the brother of Jesus and James, begins with blessings of peace and love. He then warns Christians of godless men who have infiltrated their ranks. Jude notes that these evil men will be punished, but encourages them to guard against them. He describes the evilness of these men who boast about themselves and flatter others for their own advantage. Jude calls upon the believers to remember what Christ's apostles foretold about scoffers in the last times. He encourages them not to be divided, but to build themselves up with faith and prayer. He tells them to keep themselves in God's love and wait for the mercy of Jesus Christ to give them eternal life. He asks them to be merciful to others and to save them. He encourages them not to fall and to be presented to the Savior before all ages.

Prophecy

REVELATION

REVELATION 1

Verse 8: *"I am the Alpha and the Omega," says the* LORD *God, "Who is, and who was, and who is to come, the Almighty."*

John introduces Revelation, indicating that he witnessed the events in the book as shown to him by an angel of God. The book is a letter to the seven churches founded by the apostles in Asia. He begins with greetings in the name of Jesus Christ, whom as he reminds the reader, is the Savior who has promised to come again. John states that he was asked to record the events in the book while he was on the island of Patmos. An angel instructed him to write down his experiences. John turned and saw seven lampstands and the Son of Man dressed in a robe and a golden sash. His hair was white, His face brilliant, His eyes like fire, His feet bronze, and His voice was like rushing waters. He held seven stars in His right hand, and His voice was like a sharp sword. John was terrified and fell at His feet, but the Lord told him not to be afraid. He explained that the seven stars represented the angels of the seven churches, and the lampstands were the churches themselves.

REVELATION 2

Verse 7: *He who has an ear, let him hear what the Spirit says to the churches. To him who overcomes, I will give the right to eat from the tree of life, which is in the paradise of God.*

John addresses each of the seven churches of central Asia individually with what God had told him. He begins with the eastern-most churches and proceeds clockwise. Through John, the Lord commends the church in Ephesus for its hard work and intolerance of false prophets and wicked men like the pagan-worshiping Nicolaitans. He criticizes the church, however, for forgetting its first love. To the Church in Smyrna, He offers words of encouragement, assuring the people that they are rich despite their poverty, and telling them to be strong if the Jews imprison them for their beliefs. John addresses Pergamum, noting that it was previously Satan's throne. He warns the people that Nicolaitans and other pagans are still worshiping there, and tells them to repent. He next addresses the Church in Thyatira, first recognizing the good deeds of the people, and then criticizing them for tolerating the pagan woman Jezebel. He promises great rewards for those who obey, and severe punishment for Jezebel and her followers.

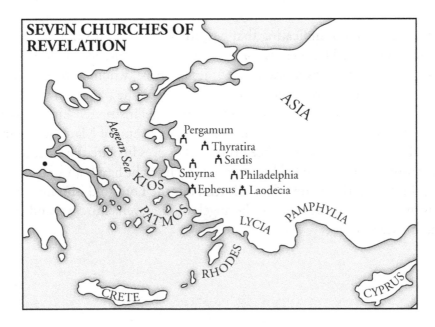

Figure 15: Churches in Revelation

REVELATION 3

Verse 20: *Here I am! I stand at the door and knock. If anyone hears my voice and opens the door, I will come in and eat with him, and he with me.*

The Lord tells the church in Sardis that it is dead (in spirit) and its deeds are incomplete. He warns the people of the consequences of not changing their ways immediately. He promises to reward the few true believers in Sardis. He commends the church in Philadelphia for its martyrdom and tells the people to hold on because He is coming soon. He admonishes the church in Laodicea for its mediocrity. He instructs the people to find riches in their faith and not in material possessions. To each church He promises a seat near His throne for its loyalty and asks the people to respond to His knock at the door.

REVELATION 4

Verse 11: *You are worthy, our LORD and God, to receive glory and honor and power, for you created all things, and by your will they were created and have their being.*

John was instructed to enter the doors of heaven where he witnessed an ornate throne with God seated there. There were twenty-four other thrones occupied by elders in white robes surrounding God's throne. A sea of glass with seven lamps was in front of the throne. Four living creatures with six wings and covered with eyes (a lion, an ox, a creature with the face of man, and an eagle) guarded the throne. The creatures and the elders exalted the occupant of the throne.

REVELATION 5

Verse 11: *Then I looked and heard the voice of many angels, numbering thousands upon thousands, and then thousand times ten thousand. They encircled the throne and the living creatures and the elders.*

The one sitting on the throne held a scroll with seven seals. An angel asked who was worthy to break the seals, but no one answered. The Lamb approached and took the scroll, and the four creatures and twenty-four elders bowed before Him. They proclaimed that He was worthy because of the blood that He shed for men. Thousands of angels, and then every creature in Heaven and on earth echoed His worthiness.

REVELATION 6

Verse 17: *For the great day of their wrath has come, and who can stand?*

The first seal was opened, and a rider on a white horse rode away, bent on conquest. The second seal was opened, and a rider with a large sword on a fiery red horse rode off. When the third seal was opened, a black horse carried a rider who held a pair of scales, suggesting that a famine would occur and food would be so scarce that it would have to be weighed—a day's wages would only provide enough food for one person. Removal of the fourth seal produced a horse that carried a pale rider, given power to kill a fourth of the earth by sword, famine, plague, and wild beasts. The fifth seal was opened, and all the Christian martyrs asked that their deaths be avenged. Each was given a white robe and told to wait a little longer. Opening of the sixth seal resulted in an earthquake, an eclipse with a red moon, and the stars falling from the heavens. All of the people, including the leaders of the earth, cowered in fear.

REVELATION 7

Verse 17: *For the Lamb at the center of the throne will be their shepherd; he will lead them to springs of living water. And God will wipe away every tear from their eyes.*

Before the seventh seal was opened, an angel commanded that the believers receive a seal on their forehead to protect them from the final judgment. 144,000 were sealed, 12,000 from each tribe of Israel. Multitudes of people in white robes surrounded the throne and praised God. John was told that these were the believers who had survived the great tribulation, and that they would be rewarded in heaven; and that the Lamb would be their shepherd.

REVELATION 8 - 9

Verse 9:4: *They were told not to harm the grass of the earth or any plant or tree, but only those people who did not have the seal of God on their foreheads.*

The seventh seal was opened and there was silence. An angel offered incense from a golden censer, along with the prayers of all the saints to the throne. Then the censer was used to hurl fire upon the earth. Then the seven trumpets sounded with the following results:

Trumpet	Action	Result
1	Hail, Fire, and Blood	1/3 of the earth was burned
2	Volcano spewed into the sea	1/3 of the sea creatures and ships perished
3	Comet—Wormwood	1/3 of the fresh water was poisoned
4	Partial Darkness	1/3 of brightness of sun, moon, stars lost
5	Comet to Abyss	Smoke-Locusts escaped, attacking unsaved
6	Released 4 Angels	1/3 of mankind killed by demonic horsemen

An eagle cried out "Woe! Woe! Woe to the inhabitants of the earth" between the fourth and fifth trumpets. The locusts (which looked like horses with human faces adorned with crowns, armor, and scorpion tails) resulting from the fifth trumpet, tortured those attacked for five months, but did not kill them. Abaddon, the angel of the Abyss was their leader. The sixth trumpet resulted in the release of the four angels who were bound at the River Euphrates. Two hundred million armed horsemen, breathing fire from their lion heads and their horses with tails comprised of snakes attacked mankind. Still the people did not repent and continued to worship idols and demons.

REVELATION 10

Verse 8: *Then a voice that I had heard from heaven spoke to me once more: "Go, take the scroll that lies open in the hand of the angel who is standing on the sea and on the land."*

A mighty angel came down from heaven and stood with one foot on land and the other in the sea. He held a small scroll. He let out a shout and the seven thunders rumbled. John was instructed not to record what the seven thunders said. The angel announced that the seventh trumpet would reveal the mystery of God. A voice from heaven instructed John to take the scroll and eat it. It tasted like honey but it soured his stomach. He was told to prophesy again.

REVELATION 11

Verse 12: *Then they heard a loud voice from heaven saying to them, "Come up here." And they went up to heaven in a cloud, while their enemies looked on.*

John was told to measure the temple of God with a rod he was given and to count the worshipers. He was instructed not to measure the outer court that was given to the Gentiles for forty-two months. Two witnesses, clothed in sackcloth, would prophesy there for the same time period. Anyone who tried to harm them would be killed. They were given power to cause a drought and cause plagues for the entire time period. After that time, the beast from the Abyss would kill them and their bodies would remain for three and a half days until they are resurrected and returned to heaven. Then there would be a great earthquake destroying one tenth of the city. The survivors would be terrified and give glory to the Lord. Next, the seventh trumpet sounded. Voices in heaven praised God, as did the twenty-four elders. God's temple in heaven opened with flashes of lightning, an earthquake, and a great hailstorm. In the temple was the Ark of the Covenant.

REVELATION 12

Verse 10: *Then I heard a loud voice in heaven say: "Now have come the salvation and the power and the kingdom of our God, and the authority of his Christ. For the accuser of our brothers, who accuses them before our God day and night, has been hurled down."*

A pregnant woman, about to give birth, appeared in heaven. She wore a crown with twelve stars. An enormous red dragon with seven crowned heads and ten horns swept a third of the stars from heaven with its tail. It stood, ready to devour the child after it was born. The male child was snatched up to heaven as soon as it was born and the woman escaped to the desert. Michael and his angels defeated the dragon and hurled him down to earth where he pursued the woman. The dragon tried to capture her with a flood of water from his mouth, but the water was diverted by a chasm that suddenly appeared. The dragon was enraged and set out to make war on all other believers.

REVELATION 13

Verse 10: *If anyone is to go into captivity, into captivity he will go. If anyone is to be killed with the sword, with the sword he will be killed. This calls for patient endurance and faithfulness on the part of the saints.*

A beast resembling a leopard with the feet of a bear and the mouth of a lion, ten horns with ten crowns, and seven heads with blasphemous names, came out of the sea. The dragon gave the beast his power and throne. One of the heads of the beast had a fatal wound that was healed. This amazed the whole world and they followed and worshiped the beast. The beast boasted and blasphemed God for forty-two months. He waged war against the saints who did not worship him. Another beast with two horns and who spoke like a dragon came out of the earth. He made the earth and its inhabitants worship the first beast with the fatal wound.

He performed great and miraculous signs and deceived the inhabitants of the earth. He made them worship an image of the beast that spoke. All who refused to worship the image were to be killed. All people were required to receive a mark of the beast (666) on their right hand or forehead in order to buy or sell anything.

REVELATION 14

Verses 9b, 10a: ...*If anyone worships the beast and his image and receives his mark on the forehead or on the hand, he, too, will drink of the wine of God's fury, which has been poured full strength into the cup of his wrath....*

The Lamb stood on Mount Zion with 144,000 who had the mark of the Father on their foreheads. Harps played in heaven and a new song was song before the throne and the four living creatures and elders. Only the righteous and pure could sing. An angel urged all on earth to worship God. A second angel announced that Babylon had fallen. A third angel warned that anyone who received the mark of the beast would suffer and be tormented forever. Blessed are the saints who patiently endure and those who die in the Lord's name. The Son of Man, seated on a cloud, swung a sickle to reap the harvest of the earth. He swung his sickle again and gathered the grapes (nonbelievers) to be trampled in the winepress. Blood from the winepress covered hundreds of miles and was several feet deep.

REVELATION 15

Verse 8: *And the temple was filled with smoke form the glory of God and from his power, and no one could enter the temple until the seven plagues of the seven angels were completed.*

Seven angels with seven last plagues appeared. All the believers who had been victorious over the beast gathered at the sea of glass mixed with fire. They played harps and sang praises to God. The Tabernacle of the Testimony was opened. The seven angels, dressed in shinning linen and gold sashes, were given golden bowls by one of the four living creatures. The bowls were filled with the wrath of God. The glory of God filled the Temple with smoke. No one could enter the Temple until the seven plagues of the seven angels were completed.

REVELATION 16

Verse 15: *Behold, I come like a thief! Blessed is he who stays awake and keeps his clothes with him, so that he may not go naked and be shamefully exposed.*

A voice from the Temple told the seven angels to go pour out the seven bowls of God's wrath on the earth. The first six bowls had the following effect on those with the mark of the beast who worshiped his image:

First Bowl	Ugly and painful sores
Second Bowl	Seas turned into blood
Third Bowl	Rivers turned into blood
Fourth Bowl	Sun scorched people with fire
Fifth Bowl	Darkness
Sixth Bowl	Euphrates River dried up

Despite the Lord's wrath, the people refused to repent. The Euphrates riverbed prepared the way for kings from the East. Three evil spirits that looked like frogs came out of the mouth of the dragon, the beast, and the false prophet. These demon spirits gathered kings for the battle at Armageddon. A voice announced that He had come like a thief and that He blessed those who had stayed awake. The seventh bowl was poured out and a severe earthquake split the great city into three parts. The quake leveled the earth and one hundred-pound hailstones rained from heaven.

REVELATION 17

Verse 8: *The beast, which you saw, once was, now is not, and will come up out of the Abyss and go to his destruction. The inhabitants of the earth whose names have not been written in the book of life from the creation of the world will be astonished when they see the beast, because he once was, now is not, and yet will come.*

One of the seven angels showed John the great prostitute whose punishment was to sit on many waters dressed in purple and scarlet atop the beast. She held a cup filled with abominable things. *Babylon the Great—The Mother of Prostitutes—The Abomination of the Earth* was written on her forehead. She was drunk with the blood of saints. The angel explained that the beast once was, now is not, and yet will come. He told John that the seven heads represented the seven hills of Rome and seven kings—five who have fallen, one who is a current king, and one king who is yet to come. The beast represents an eighth king, going to his destruction. The ten horns are the ten kings who will reign for only one hour until the Lamb overcomes them in battle. The waters that the prostitute sat on represent people, nations, and languages. The beast and ten horns will try to destroy the prostitute who represents the city of Babylon that rules over the kings of the earth.

REVELATION 18

Verse 10b: *Woe! Woe, O great city, O Babylon city of power! In one hour your doom has come!*

A great angel descended from heaven and announced that Babylon the Great had fallen. He appealed to the people to come out of her and to repay her with a double portion of torture and grief that she had administered. Kings, merchants, and seamen lamented the death of the great city. A mighty angel threw a giant millstone into the sea, signifying the destruction of the great city of Babylon.

REVELATION 19

Verse 7: *Let us rejoice and be glad and give him glory! For the wedding day of the Lamb has come, and his bride has made herself ready.*

A great multitude in heaven shouted Hallelujah and praised God for condemning the great prostitute. The twenty-four elders and four creatures fell down and worshiped God who sat on the throne. The wedding day of the Lamb had arrived and there was much rejoicing. The angel told John to record, "Blessed are those who are invited to the wedding supper of the Lamb." John fell at the feet of the angel who told him not to worship him, but God. Heaven was opened and a rider of a white horse who was called *Faithful and True, The Word of God,* and KING OF KINGS AND LORD OF LORDS, prepared for battle. The armies of heaven were assembled behind Him. He wore many crowns, had on a robe dipped in blood, and wielded an iron scepter and a sword coming from His mouth. The armies of the earth were soundly defeated. The beast and false prophet were captured and thrown into the fiery lake of burning sulfur. The birds of the earth gorged themselves on the corpses that were strewn across the battlefield.

REVELATION 20

Verse 10: *And the devil, who deceived them, was thrown into the lake of burning sulfur, where the beast and the false prophet had been thrown. They will be tormented day and night for ever and ever.*

An angel with the key to the Abyss came down from heaven. He bound the dragon (Satan) and threw him into the Abyss and locked it for a thousand years. Judgment of the martyrs was carried out and those found worthy reigned with Christ for a thousand years. After the thousand years, a second resurrection will occur and Satan will be released from prison. He will gather an army but will be defeated and thrown into the lake of burning sulfur to join the beast and false prophet to be tormented forever. The dead will be judged before the throne. Anyone whose name is not in the Book of Life will be thrown into the lake of fire.

REVELATION 21

Verse 6: *He said to me: "It is done. I am the Alpha and the Omega, the Beginning and the End. To him who is thirsty I will give to drink without cost from the spring of the water of life."*

A new heaven and a new earth appeared and a New Jerusalem came down from heaven prepared as a bride. God announced that He would live with men in the city and that He would be their God. There will be no sadness or death. He will make everything new. He told John that He was the Alpha and the Omega and that anyone who was thirsty could drink from the spring of the water of life. He who overcomes will inherit His kingdom. Those who are unbelievers or sinners will be thrown into the fiery lake. An angel showed John the bride. The holy city of Jerusalem, made from Jasper and pure gold, shined with glory. It had twelve pearl gates named for the twelve tribes of Israel and twelve foundations made from precious gems named after the twelve Apostles. The city was measured with a golden rod and its dimensions recorded. There was no temple in the city because the Lord and the Lamb were the Temple. There was no darkness because the Glory of God gives the city light and the Lamb is its lamp. There will be no night and the gates of the city will always be open, but only to the pure.

REVELATION 22

Verse 7: *Behold, I am coming soon! Blessed is he who keeps the words of the prophecy in this book.*

A river of the water of life flowed from the throne and through the city. The tree of life stood on each side of the river with twelve crops of fruit and leaves that allowed healing of the nations. The Lord and Lamb will rule the city forever. John again worshiped the angel, and he told him to worship the Lord. He instructed him to record that the time is near and that the righteous should continue to be holy and right. Jesus announced that His reward is with Him and invited believers to drink the water of life. He is coming soon!

CHARACTER INDEX

MAJOR BIBLE CHARACTERS: ALPHABETICAL
(CITED BASED ON FIRST INTRODUCTION)

A

Aaron—Moses' brother; spokesman for Moses; and later high priest *Exodus 4*

Abednego (Azariah)—One of Daniel's friends; would not bow down to idol *Daniel 1*

Abel—Second son of Adam and Eve; killed by his brother Cain *Genesis 4*

Abiathar—Priest for David; supported Adonijah as king after David's death *1 Samuel 22*

Abigail—Wife of Nabal; helps David; married David after Nabal's death *1 Samuel 25*

Abihu—Aaron's second son; killed by God for violating His instructions *Exodus 28*

Abijah—Rehoboam's son; succeeded him as king of Judah; evil *1 Kings 14*

Abimelech—Gideon's son by a concubine, named himself leader *Judges 8*

Abimelech—King of Gerar; called for Sarah but the LORD intervened *Genesis 20*

Abinadab—Kept the Ark at his house *1 Samuel 7*

Abiram—A Reubenite; challenged Moses and Aaron; punished by God *Numbers 16*

Abishag—Young virgin brought to take care of aging David *1 Kings 1*

Abishai—Joab's brother; one of David's mighty men; saved David's life *2 Samuel 20*

Abner—Commander of Saul's army; made Ish-Bosheth king of Israel *1 Samuel 26*

Abram/Abraham—Heirs promised to inherit the Holy Land *Genesis 11*

Absalom—David's estranged son; killed Ammon; tried to take crown *2 Samuel 13*

Achan—Kept some of the bounty supposed to be given to the LORD *Joshua 7*

Achish—King of Philistia during Saul's reign; befriended David *1 Samuel 21*

Adam—first man *Genesis 1*

Adonijah—David's fourth son; proclaimed himself king after David's death *2 Samuel 3*

Adoni-Zedek—King of Jerusalem defeated by Joshua when the sun stood still *Joshua 10*

Agabus—Predicted severe famine for Roman world *Acts 11*

Agrippa—King of Israel who heard Paul's testimony in Caesarea *Acts 25*

Agur—Quoted in Proverbs 30 *Proverbs 30*

Ahab—Omri's son, became king of Israel; married Jezebel; very evil *1 King 16*

Ahaziah—Ahab's son; succeeded him as king of Israel; consulted pagan god *1 Kings 22*

Ahaziah—Jehoram's son; succeeded him as king of Judah; killed by Jehu *2 Kings 8*

Ahaz—Jotham's son; king of Judah; given sign of Immanuel by Isaiah; *2 Kings 16*

Ahijah—Prophet; told Jeroboam that he would rule 10 tribes *1 Kings 11*

Ahimelech—Priest who helped David in his flight from Saul; killed by Saul *1 Samuel 21*

Ahinoam—Wife of David *1 Samuel 25*

Ahithophel—Advisor to Absalom; killed himself when advice not followed *2 Samuel 15*

Amasa—Commander for David and his nephew *2 Samuel 17*

Amasai—Chief of the thirty mighty men *1 Chronicles 12*

Amaziah—Joash's son; succeeded him as king of Judah; righteous *2 Kings 12*

Amaziah—Joash's son; succeeded him as king of Judah; righteous *2 Kings 12*

Amnon—David's first son; raped Tamar; killed by Absalom *2 Samuel 3*

Amon—Son of Manasseh; succeeded him as king of Judah; evil; assassinated *2 Kings 21*

Amos—A shepherd from Tekoa; prophesied before a major earthquake *Amos 1*

Ananias—Believer in Damascus; restored Saul's sight *Acts 9*

Ananias—Husband of Sapphira; held back money from apostles *Acts 5*

Andrew—Apostle of Jesus; Simon Peter's brother *Matthew 4*

Anna—Prophetess; spoke to Joseph and Mary about Jesus at 8 days old *Luke 2*

Annas—Caiaphas' father-in-law; Jesus was brought to him *John 18*

Apollos—Jewish believer who traveled to Ephesus and Corinth *Acts 18*

Aquila—Jewish believer in Corinth; husband of Priscilla; friend to Paul *Acts 18*

Araunah—Provided his threshing floor for David to sacrifice on *2 Samuel 24*

Artaxerxes—King of Babylon; supported rebuilding of wall *Nehemiah 2*

Asa—King of Judah after Abijah; good *1 Kings 15*

Asaph—One of David's chief musicians; one author of the psalms *Psalm 50*

Asher—Eighth son of Jacob (second with Zilpah) *Genesis 30*

Athaliah—Ahaziah's mother; killed royal family so she could rule; killed *2 Kings 11*

Azariah—High Priest for Solomon; reform in Judah; confronted Uzziah's pride *1 Kings 4*

Azariah—King of Judah; afflicted with leprosy *2 Kings 14*

B

Baalis—King of Ammon; sent Ishmael to kill Gedaliah *Jeremiah 40*

Baasha—Assassinated Nadab; became king of Israel *1 Kings 15*

Balaam—Hired by Balak to curse the Israelites; spoken to by a donkey *Numbers 26*

Balak—Moabite king; hired Balak to curse the Israelites *Numbers 26*

Barabbas—The prisoner who was released instead of Jesus *Matthew 27*

Barnabas—Son of Encouragement; partnered with Saul in missions *Acts 9*

Bartholomew—Apostle of Jesus *Matthew 10*

Baruch—Scribe for Jeremiah; read the scroll to the people at the temple *Jeremiah 36*

Bathsheba—Uriah's wife; David's wife after affair; Solomon's mother *2 Samuel 11*

Belshazzar—Nebuchadnezzar's son; saw handwriting on the wall *Daniel 5*

Benaiah—Officer of David; commander-in-chief under Solomon *2 Samuel 8*

Benaiah—One of David's mighty men *2 Samuel 23*

Ben-Ammi—Son of Lot and his younger daughter; father of the Ammonites *Genesis 19*

Ben-Hadad—King of Aram; made a treaty with Asa *1 Kings 15*

Benjamin—Twelfth son of Jacob (second with Rachel, who died in childbirth) *Genesis 30*

Bezalel—Craftsman from the tribe of Judah who built tabernacle *Exodus 31*

Bildad—One of Job's friends; a Shuhite *Job 2*

Bilhah—Servant given to Jacob with Rachel; mother of Dan and Naphtali *Genesis 30*

Boaz—Wealthy landowner; Naomi's kinsman-redeemer; married Ruth *Ruth 2*

C

Caesar Augustus—Called for census bringing Joseph and Mary to Bethlehem *Luke 2*

Caiaphas—High Priest who questioned Jesus *John 18*

Cain—First son of Adam and Eve; killed his brother Abel *Genesis 4*

Caleb—Sent with ten others to spy the land; given an inheritance by God *Numbers 13*

Canaan—Noah's grandson, son of Ham; sentenced to slavery *Genesis 9*

Cornelius—God-fearing Roman; sent for Peter and became a believer *Acts 10*

Cyrus—King of Persia; authorized rebuilding of Temple *2 Chronicles 36*

D

Dan—Fifth son of Jacob (first with Bilhah) *Genesis 30*

Daniel—Young exile taken to Babylon; served the kings 70 years *Daniel 1*

Darius—A Mede; took over Babylon; confirmed Cyrus' decree to rebuild Temple *Ezra 5*

Dathan—A Reubenite; challenged Moses and Aaron; punished by God *Numbers 16*

David—Played harp for Saul, killed Goliath, second king of Israel *1 Samuel 16*

Deborah—Judge of Israel; defeated Canaan *Judges 4*

Delilah—Philistine woman who betrayed Samson, leading to his capture *Judges 15*

Dinah—Daughter of Jacob and Leah; raped by Shechem *Genesis 30*

Doeg—Saul's servant; killed priests for Saul *1 Samuel 22*

E

Ehud—Judge of Israel; killed king of Moab *Judges 3*

Elah—Succeeded Baasha as king of Israel; evil *1 Kings 16*

Eldad—Israelite missing from the leaders' assembly *Numbers 11*

Eleazar—Aaron's third son *Exodus 28*

Eleazar—Abinadab's son; guarded the Ark at his house *1 Samuel 7*

Eleazar—One of David's mighty men *1 Chronicles 11*

Eliakim (Jehoiakim)—Jehoahaz' brother made king of Judah by Neco; evil *2 Kings 23*

Eliezer—Moses' second son *Exodus 18*

Eli—High Priest at Shiloh; raised Samuel *1 Samuel 1*

Elihu—The youngest of Job's friends; a Buzite *Job 32*

Elijah—Prophet in Israel; taken up by chariots of fire *1 Kings 17*

Elimelech—Naomi's wife; died in Moab *Ruth 1*

Eliphaz—One of Job's friends; a Temanite *Job 2*

Elisha—Apprentice to Elijah; receives double portion of his spirit *1 Kings 19*

Elizabeth—Mother of John the Baptist; Mary's cousin *Luke 1*

Elkanah—Hannah's husband *1 Samuel 1*

Enoch—Son of Cain *Genesis 4*

Enoch—Walked with God; did not experience death *Genesis 5*

Enosh—Son of Seth *Genesis 4*

Ephraim—Joseph's second son; Jacob blessed him ahead of Manasseh *Genesis 41*

Er—Judah's first son; killed by God for his wickedness *Genesis 38*

Esau—Older twin of Isaac; his descendants were the Edomites *Genesis 25*

Esther—Jewish woman selected to be Queen of Persia; saved the Jews *Esther 2*

Ethan—A Levite leader; one of the writers in Psalms *Psalm 89*

Eve—First woman *Genesis 2*

Ezekiel—Prophet exiled in Babylon *Ezekiel 1*

Ezra—Chief Priest came from Babylon after Temple completed; read the Law *Ezra 7*

F

Felix—Governor of Judea; heard charges against Paul *Acts 24*

Festus—Governor of Judea; succeeded Felix *Acts 25*

G

Gabriel—Angel of the Lord; appeared to Daniel, Zechariah, Mary, Joseph *Daniel 8*

Gad—Seventh son of Jacob (first with Zilpah) *Genesis 30*

Gaius—Roman Christian; recipient of one of John's letters *3 John*

Gamaliel—Pharisee; mentor of Saul (Paul) *Acts 5*

Gedaliah—Appointed by Nebuchadnezzar to govern remains of Judah *2 Kings 25*

Gehazi—Elisha's servant; accepted payment that Elisha refused *2 Kings 5*

Gershom—Moses and Zipporah's first son *Exodus 2*

Gideon—Led Israel against the Midianites *Judges 6*

Goliath—Giant Philistine; defeated by David *Samuel 17*

Gomer—Hosea's unfaithful wife *Hosea 1*

H

Habakkuk—Prophet in Judah before exile *Habakkuk 1*

Hagar—Sarai's servant who bore Abram's first child, Ishmael *Genesis 16*

Haggai—Prophet to Judah; told Zerubbabel and Joshua about the Temple *Ezra 5*

Haman—Chief of all nobles in Persia; plotted to kill all Jews *Esther 3*

Ham—Noah's second son; father of Canaan *Genesis 5*

Hananiah—Appointed commander of Jerusalem *Nehemiah 7*

Hananiah—False prophet for King Zedekiah; died for false prophecies *Jeremiah 28*

Hanani—Nehemiah's brother; put in charge of Jerusalem *Nehemiah 7*

Hannah—Prayed for a son; mother of Samuel; dedicated him to the Lord *1 Samuel 1*

Hazel—King of Aram; appointed by Elijah *1 Kings 19*

Heman—One of the writers of Psalms *Psalm 88*

Herod (the Tetrarch)—Arrested and beheaded John the Baptist *Matthew 14*

Herodias—Herod's wife; schemed to have John the Baptist beheaded *Matthew 14*

Herod—King of Jerusalem; spoke with Magi; had babies in Bethlehem killed *Matthew 2*

Herod—King; persecuted Christians; killed James; struck down by God *Acts 12*

Hezekiah—Son of Ahaz; succeeded him as king of Judah; good *2 Kings 16*

Hiel—Rebuilt Jericho against God's wishes *1 Kings 16*

Hilkiah—High priest under Josiah; found Book of the Law *2 Kings 22*

Hiram—King of Tyre; helps build the palace and Temple in Israel *2 Samuel 5*

Hobab—Jethro's son; a Midianite *Numbers 10*

Hosea—Prophet in last days of Israel; married Gomer *Hosea 1*

Hoshea—Assassinated Pekah and became king of Israel; evil *2 Kings 15*

Huldah—Prophetess; told Josiah about Judah's future punishment *2 Kings 22*

Huram—Did all the bronze work for the Temple *1 Kings 7*

Hur—Helps Aaron hold up Moses' arms during battle with Amalekites *Exodus 17*

Hushai—Loyal to David; gave bad advice to Absalom *2 Samuel 15*

I

Icabod—Eli's grandson; born on the day the Philistines captured the Ark *1 Samuel 4*

Immanuel—God with us; prophesied by Isaiah *Isaiah 7*

Isaac—Abraham and Sarah's son *Genesis 21*

Isaiah—Prophet in Judah; foretold of fall of Jerusalem; foretold of Messiah *2 Kings 20*

Ish-Bosheth—King of Israel after Saul's death; killed by raiders *2 Samuel 2*

Ishmael—Assassinated Gedaliah during exile *Jeremiah 41*

Ishmael—Son of Hagar and Abram *Genesis 16*

Issachar—ninth son of Jacob (fifth with Leah) *Genesis 30*

Ithamar—Aaron's fourth son *Exodus 28*

J

Jabez—A descendant of Judah who asked God to bless him *1 Chronicles 4*

Jabin—King of Hazor; attacked Israel under Joshua and lost *Joshua 11*

Jacob—Younger twin of Isaac; his descendants are the Israelites *Genesis 25*

Jael—Killed Sisera, commander of Canaan army *Judges 4*

Jahaziel—Prophet for Jehoshaphat *2 Chronicles 20*

Jairus—A synagogue leader; asked Jesus to heal his dying son *Mark 5*

James—Apostle of Jesus; Alphaeus' son *Matthew 10*

James—Apostle of Jesus; brother of John; killed by King Herod *Matthew 4*

James—Jesus' brother; wrote letter to the twelve tribes of Israel *James 1*

Japheth—Noah's third son *Genesis 5*

Jashobeam—One of David's mighty men *1 Chronicles 11*

Jehoahaz—Josiah's son; succeeded him as king of Judah; evil *2 Kings 23*

Jehoahaz—Son of Jehu; king of Israel; evil *2 Kings 10*

Jehoash—Son of Jehoahaz; king of Israel; evil *2 Kings 13*

Jehoiachin—Jehoiakim's son; succeeded him as king of Judah *2 Kings 24*

Jehoiada—High Priest for Joash *2 Kings 11*

Jehoram—Jehoshaphat's son; succeeded him as king of Judah; evil *2 Kings 8*

Jehoshaphat—King of Judah; allied himself with Ahab *1 Kings 15*

Jehu—Killed Ahab's descendants; became king of Israel *1 Kings 19*

Jehu—Prophet in Israel *1 Kings 16*

Jephthah—Beat the Ammonites; sacrificed his daughter for a vow *Judges 11*

Jeremiah—Priest for Josiah; Weeping Prophet; told of Judah's fate *2 Chronicles 35*

Jeroboam—Rebelled against Solomon; king of Israel; evil *1 Kings 11*

Jeroboam—Son of Jehoash; king of Israel; evil *2 Kings 13*

Jeshua—Priest that helped rebuild the Temple *Ezra 3*

Jesse—Father of David; branch of the Messiah *1 Samuel 16*

Jethro—Moses' father-in-law; father of Zipporah; also known as Reuel *Exodus 2*

Jezebel—Ahab's wife; hated Elijah *1 Kings 19*

Jezreel—Gomer's first son *Hosea 1*

Joab—Commander of David's army; killed Abner; took David's census *2 Samuel 2*

Joash—Ahaziah's son; rescued from Athaliah; crowned by Jehoiada; good *2 Kings 11*

Job—Righteous man of Uz tested by God *Job 1*

Joel—A prophet to Judah *Joel 1*

Johanan—Army officer for Gedaliah; took survivors of exile to Egypt *Jeremiah 40*

John—Apostle of Jesus; brother of James; author of fourth gospel and Revelation *Matthew 4*

John—The Baptizer; prepared the way for Jesus; baptized Jesus *Matthew 3*

Jonah—Tried to avoid preaching in Nineveh; swallowed by big fish *Jonah 1*

Jonathan—Son of Saul; David's best friend *1 Samuel 13*

Joram—Succeeded Ahaziah as king of Israel; bad *2 Kings 1*

Joseph—Eleventh son of Jacob (first with Rachel); sold into slavery by brothers *Genesis 30*

Joseph—From the line of David; married Mary, mother of Jesus *Matthew 1*

Joseph—Of Arimathea; buried Jesus after the crucifixion *Mark 15*

Joshua—High priest after exile; started work to rebuild temple *Haggai 1*

Joshua—Moses' assistant and successor; sent to spy out the land *Exodus 17*

Josiah—Son of Amon; appointed king of Judah at eight years old; good *1 Kings 13*

Jotham—Son of Azariah (Uzziah); succeeded him as king; righteous *2 Kings 15*

Judah—Fourth son of Jacob (and Leah) *Genesis 29*

Judas Iscariot—Apostle of Jesus; betrayed Him *Matthew 10*

K

Keturah—Abraham's wife after Sarah's death *Genesis 25*

Kilion—Naomi's son; died in Moab *Ruth 1*

Korah—A Levite; challenged Moses and Aaron; punished by God *Numbers 16*

Korah—Father of writers of the Psalms *1 Chronicles 6*

L

Laban—Rebekah's brother; father of Rachel and Leah *Genesis 24*

Lamech—Offspring of Cain *Genesis 4*

Lamech—Offspring of Seth; father of Noah *Genesis 5*

Lazarus—Brother of Martha and Mary; raised from the dead by Jesus *John 11*

Leah—Older daughter of Laban; Jacob's 1st wife (by deceit) *Genesis 29*

Lemuel—A king whose mother wrote the qualities of a noble woman *Proverbs 31*

Levi—Third son of Jacob (and Leah) *Genesis 29*

Lo-Ammi—Gomer's third son *Hosea 1*

Lo-Ruhamah—Gomer's second son *Hosea 1*

Lot—Abram's cousin; rescued by Abram; escaped from Sodom *Genesis 11*

Luke—Author of the third gospel; companion of Paul; author of Acts *Luke 1*

Lydia—A Philippian woman who believed Paul's preaching *Acts 16*

M

Maacah—Rehoboam's favorite wife *2 Chronicles 11*

Maher-Shalal-Hash-Baz—Son of a prophetess, foretold Judah's suffering *Isaiah 8*

Mahlon—Naomi's son; died in Moab *Ruth 1*

Malachi—A prophet; told of coming of Elijah to prepare for the Lord *Malachi 1*

Manasseh—Joseph's first son; Jacob blessed him *Genesis 41*

Manasseh—Son of Hezekiah; succeeded him as king of Judah; evil *2 Kings 20*

Mark—Author of second gospel; companion of Barnabas and Paul *Mark 1*

Martha—Prepared meals for Jesus; sister of Lazarus and Mary *Luke 10*

Mary Magdalene—Jesus appeared to her at the tomb *Matthew 28*

Mary—Mother of James and Joses; at the cross when Jesus died *Matthew 27*

Mary—Mother of John Mark; believers at her house when Peter escaped *Acts 12*

Mary—Sat at Jesus' feet; sister of Lazarus and Martha; anointed Jesus *Luke 10*

Mary—Wife of Clopas; stood at the cross with other women *John 20*

Mary—Young virgin chosen to bear Jesus; married to Joseph *Matthew 1*

Mattaniah (Zedekiah)—Jehoiachin's uncle; made king of Judah; evil *2 Kings 24*

Matthew—Apostle of Jesus; former tax collector; author of first gospel *Matthew 9*

Matthias—Chosen by the Apostles to replace Judas *Acts 1*

Medad—Israelite missing from leaders' assembly *Numbers 11*

Melchizedek—King of Salem; priest of God Most High; Abram tithed to him *Genesis 14*

Menahem—Assassinated Shallum and became king of Israel; evil *2 Kings 15*

Mephibosheth—Jonathan's son; David showed him kindness *2 Samuel 4*

Meshach (Mishael)—One of Daniel's friends; would not bow down to idol *Daniel 1*

Methuselah—Oldest Bible character (969 yrs) *Genesis 5*

Micah—Prophet in last days of Israel and Judah *Micah 1*

Micaiah—Prophet in Israel; Ahab did not like him *1 Kings 22*

Mica—Mephibosheth's son; David took care of him *2 Samuel 9*

Michael—Archangel over Israel *Daniel 10*

Michal—David's first wife; Saul's daughter *1 Samuel 19*

Miriam—The sister of Moses and Aaron *Exodus 15*

Moab—Son of Lot and his older daughter; father of the Moabites *Genesis 19*

Mordecai—Esther's uncle, refused to bow to Haman *Esther 2*

Moses—Leader of Israelites during exodus from Egypt and in Desert *Exodus 1*

N

Naaman—Army commander of Aram with leprosy; cured by Elisha *2 Kings 5*

Nabad—Aaron's first son; killed by God for violating His instructions *Exodus 28*

Nabal—Wealthy man from Maon; would not help David; died ten days later *1 Samuel 25*

Naboth—Owned a vineyard that Ahab wanted; Jezebel killed him for it *1 Kings 21*

Nadab—Aaron's first son; killed by God for violating His instructions *Exodus 28*

Nadab—King of Israel after Jeroboam; evil *1 Kings 14*

Nahor—Abraham's brother and Rebekah's grandfather *Genesis 24*

Nahum—Prophesied against Nineveh *Nahum 1*

Naomi—Jewish widow in Moab; returned to Judah with Ruth *Ruth 1*

Naphtali—Sixth son of Jacob (second with Bilhah) *Genesis 30*

Nathanael—A disciple of Jesus; met Him on His way to Galilee *John 1*

Nathan—Prophet during David's reign; confronted David's adultery *2 Samuel 7*

Nebuchadnezzar—King of Babylon; invaded and defeated Judah *2 Kings 24*

Nebuzaradan—Babylonian commander of imperial guard *Jeremiah 40*

Neco—Pharaoh in Egypt; killed Josiah in battle; imprisoned Jehoahaz *2 Kings 23*

Nehemiah—Cupbearer to Artaxerxes; asked to rebuild Jerusalem walls *Nehemiah 1*

Nicanor—One of the Seven *Acts 6*

Nicodemus—A Pharisee who came to Jesus at night; helped bury Jesus *John 3*

Nicolas—One of the Seven *Acts 6*

Noah—From Seth's lineage; built the ark *Genesis 5*

O

Obadiah—Prophet and contemporary of Elijah; prophesied about Edom *1 Kings 17*

Obed-Edom—The man who kept the Ark for three months *2 Samuel 6*

Obed—The son of Boaz and Ruth; grandfather of David *Ruth 4*

Og—King of Bashan; defeated by the Israelites *Deuteronomy 3*

Oholiab—Craftsman from tribe of Dan who helped Bezalel with tabernacle *Exodus 31*

Omri—Overthrew Zimri and became king of Israel; evil *1 Kings 16*

Onan—Judah's second son; killed by God for disobedience *Genesis 38*

Onesimus—Philemon's slave who ran away and became a believer *Philemon*

Orpah—Naomi's daughter-in-law; did not stay with Naomi *Ruth 1*

Othniel—Captured Kiriath Sepher for Caleb; married Caleb's daughter; Judge *Joshua 15*

P

Parmeanas—One of the Seven *Acts 6*

Pashhur—Chief priest had Jeremiah beaten for his prophecies *Jeremiah 20*

Pekah—Assassinated Pekahiah and became king of Israel; evil *2 Kings 15*

Pekahiah—Menahem's son; succeeded him as king of Israel *2 Kings 15*

Perez—Second son of Tamar and Judah *Genesis 38*

Philemon—Believer in Colossae whose slave, Onesimus, ran away *Philemon*

Philip—Apostle of Jesus; asked Jesus to see the Father *Matthew 10*

Philip—One of the Seven; converted Ethiopian eunuch; *Acts 6*

Phinehas—Grandson of Aaron; rewarded by God for punishing sexual sin *Numbers 25*

Pilate—Governor of Jerusalem; turned Jesus over to be crucified *Matthew 27*

Potiphar—Pharaoh's official; bought Joseph as a slave in Egypt *Genesis 37*

Priscilla—Jewish believer in Corinth; wife of Aquila; friend to Paul *Acts 18*

Procorus—One of the Seven *Acts 6*

Q

Queen of Sheba—Visited Solomon; impressed by his wisdom *1 Kings 10*

R

Rachel—Younger daughter of Laban; Jacob's love and wife *Genesis 29*

Rahab—Prostitute who helped the Israelite spies in Jericho *Joshua 2*

Rebekah—Abraham's brother's granddaughter; Isaac's wife *Genesis 24*

Rehoboam—Solomon's son; fourth king of Israel before split; king of Judah; evil *1 Kings 11*

Reuben—Oldest son of Jacob (and Leah) *Genesis 29*

Reuel—Moses' father-in-law; father of Zipporah; also known as Jethro *Exodus 2*

Rezin—King of Aram; allied with Pekah of Israel against Judah *Isaiah 7*

Ruth—Naomi's daughter-in-law; returned to Judah with Naomi; married Boaz *Ruth 1*

S

Salome—Went with other women to tomb on the third day *Mark 16*

Samson—Nazirite from birth; betrayed by Delilah; defeated the Philistines *Judges 13*

Samuel—Prophet and judge of Israel; anointed Saul and David *1 Samuel 1*

Sanballat—Tried to stop the rebuilding of Jerusalem *Nehemiah 4*

Sapphira—Wife of Ananias; held back money from apostles *Acts 5*

Sarai/Sarah—Abram/Abraham's wife; was barren *Genesis 11*

Saul (Paul)—Pharisee; persecuted believers; Apostle; wrote many letters *Acts 7*

Saul—First king of Israel; anointed by Samuel; disobedient *1 Samuel 9*

Sennacherib—King of Assyria; invaded Judah; destroyed by and angel *2 Chronicles 32*

Seth—Third son of Adam and Eve; lineage to Noah *Genesis 4*

Shadrach (Hananiah)—One of Daniel's friends; would not bow down to idol *Daniel 1*

Shallum—Assassinated Zechariah and became king of Israel; assassinated *2 Kings 15*

Shamgar—Judge of Israel; defeated the Philistines *Judges 4*

Sheba—A Benjamite; rebelled against David unsuccessfully *2 Samuel 20*

Shechem—Son of Hamor, a Canaan ruler, who raped Dinah *Genesis 30*

Shelah—Third son of Judah *Genesis 38*

Shemaiah—False prophet during Jeremiah's time *Jeremiah 29*

Shemaiah—False prophet to Rehoboam *2 Chronicles 11*

Shem—Noah's first son *Genesis 5*

Shimei—Loyal to Saul; threw stones and cursed David *2 Samuel 16*

Shishak—King of Egypt; ransacked Temple and palace *1 Kings 14*

Sihon—King of Heshbon; defeated and plundered by Israelites *Deuteronomy 2*

Silas—Teamed with Paul on missions; imprisoned Philipi *Acts 15*

Simeon—Second son of Jacob (and Leah) *Genesis 29*

Simeon—In the temple for Jesus' circumcision; God's promise to him fulfilled *Luke 2*

Simon Peter—Apostle of Jesus; brother of Andrew *Matthew 4*

Simon—Apostle of Jesus; the Zealot *Matthew 10*

Solomon—David's son and successor *2 Samuel 5*

Stephen—One of the Seven; first Christian martyr *Acts 6*

T

Tabitha—(Dorcas); raised from the dead by Peter *Acts 9*

Tamar—David's daughter; raped by David's son Amnon *2 Samuel 8*

Tamar—Judah's daughter-in-law who had his twin sons *Genesis 38*

Terah—Abraham's father *Genesis 11*

Thaddeus—Apostle of Jesus *Matthew 10*

Theophilus—Received Luke's letter concerning Jesus *Luke 1*

Thomas—Apostle of Jesus; doubted the resurrection *Matthew 10*

Timon—One of the Seven *Acts 6*

Timothy—Paul's son in the faith; helped Thessalonians; church in Ephesus *Acts 16*

Titus—Companion of Paul; helped church in Crete *Galatians 2*

Tobiah—Tried to stop the rebuilding of Jerusalem *Nehemiah 4*

U

Uriah—Officer in David's army; Bathsheba's wife; David had him killed *2 Samuel 11*

Uzzah—Struck down by God when he touched the Ark *2 Samuel 6*

Uzziah—Son of Amaziah, king of Judah; burned incense; leprosy; good *2 Chronicles 26*

V

Vashti—Queen of Persia; refused to come to Xerxes; expelled *Esther 1*

X

Xerxes—King of Persia; married Esther *Esther 1*

Z

Zacchaeus—A tax collector who climbed a tree to see Jesus *Luke 19*

Zadok—Priest; ordained Solomon king *1 Kings 1*

Zebulun—Tenth son of Jacob (sixth with Leah) *Genesis 30*

Zechariah—A priest; Elizabeth's husband; John the Baptist's father *Luke 1*

Zechariah—Prophet and priest for the Jews during rebuilding the Temple *Ezra 5*

Zechariah—Son of Jeroboam; king of Israel; assassinated after six months *2 Kings 14*

Zelophehad—Died with no sons; his daughters were granted his inheritance *Numbers 27*

Zephaniah—descendant of Hezekiah; prophet for Josiah *Zephaniah 1*

Zerah—First born son of Tamar and Judah *Genesis 38*

Zerubbabel—Governor of Judah that helped rebuild the Temple *Ezra 3*

Ziba—Saul's servant; betrayed Mephibosheth *2 Samuel 16*

Zilpah—Servant given to Jacob with Leah; mother of Gad and Asher *Genesis 30*

Zimri—Killed Elah and became king of Israel for 7 days *1 Kings 16*

Zipporah—Jethro's daughter; Moses' wife *Exodus 2*

Zophar—One of Job's friends; a Naamathite *Job 2*

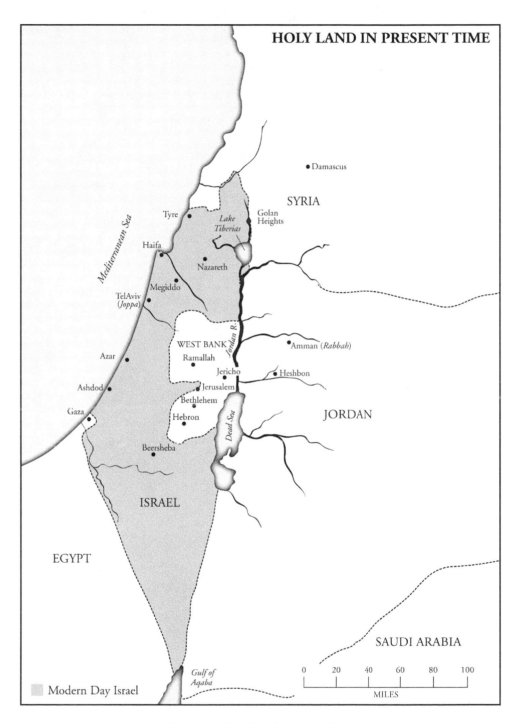

Figure 16: Holy Land in Present Time

CPSIA information can be obtained
at www.ICGtesting.com
Printed in the USA
BVHW011916150821
614472BV00012B/343